Public Health in the 21st Century

Public Health in the 21st Century

Volume 3: Current Issues in Public Health Policy

Madelon L. Finkel, Editor
Foreword by David J. Skorton, MD

PRAEGER

AN IMPRINT OF ABC-CLIO, LLC
Santa Barbara, California • Denver, Colorado • Oxford, England

Copyright 2011 by Madelon L. Finkel

All rights reserved. No part of this publication may be reproduced, stored in a retrieval system, or transmitted, in any form or by any means, electronic, mechanical, photocopying, recording, or otherwise, except for the inclusion of brief quotations in a review, without prior permission in writing from the publisher.

Library of Congress Cataloging-in-Publication Data

Public health in the 21st century / Madelon L. Finkel, editor ; foreword by David J. Skorton.
  p. ; cm.
  Public health in the twenty-first century
  Includes bibliographical references and index.
  ISBN 978-0-313-37546-0 (hard copy : set : alk. paper) — ISBN 978-0-313-37548-4 (hard copy : vol. 1 : alk. paper) — ISBN 978-0-313-37550-7 (hard copy : vol. 2 : alk. paper) — ISBN 978-0-313-37552-1 (hard copy : vol. 3 : alk. paper) — ISBN 978-0-313-37547-7 (ebook : set) — ISBN 978-0-313-37549-1 (ebook : vol. 1) — ISBN 978-0-313-37551-4 (ebook : vol. 2) — ISBN 978-0-313-37553-8 (ebook : vol. 3)
  1. Public health. 2. World health. 3. Health policy.
I. Finkel, Madelon Lubin, 1949– II. Title: Public health in the twenty-first century.
  [DNLM: 1. Public Health. 2. Disease Management. 3. Health Policy. 4. World Health. WA 100]
  RA424.8.P83 2011
  362.1—dc22   2010039064

ISBN: 978-0-313-37546-0
EISBN: 978-0-313-37547-7

15 14 13 12 11   2 3 4 5

This book is also available on the World Wide Web as an eBook.
Visit www.abc-clio.com for details.

Praeger
An Imprint of ABC-CLIO, LLC

ABC-CLIO, LLC
130 Cremona Drive, P.O. Box 1911
Santa Barbara, California 93116-1911

This book is printed on acid-free paper ∞

Manufactured in the United States of America

*To my husband Arnold,
whose ideas, insight, and, most of all,
support and love are so important to me.*

Contents

Foreword
David J. Skorton, MD ix

Acknowledgments xi

Introduction
Madelon L. Finkel, PhD 1

SECTION 1   HEALTH CARE POLICY 27

  Chapter 1 Comparative Health Care Systems: How Does the United States Stack Up?
Madelon L. Finkel, PhD 29

  Chapter 2 Clinical Quality and Patient Safety
Eliot J. Lazar, MD, MBA, Anthony Dawson, RN, Dan Hyman, MD, MMM, Karen Scott Collins, MD, MPH, Brian K. Regan, PhD, Steven Kaplan, MD, Robert A. Green, MD, MPH, Joseph T. Cooke, MD, and Phillip L. Graham III, MD, MPH 43

  Chapter 3 Consumer-Directed Health Plans, Managed Care, and Future Directions in the Organization of Health Care Payment Systems
William D. White, PhD 55

  Chapter 4 Health Information Technology and Public Health
Jessica S. Ancker, MPH, PhD, Lisa M. Kern, MD, MPH, Vaishali Patel, PhD, MPH, Erika Abramson, MD, and Rainu Kaushal, MD, MPH 73

SECTION 2   HEALTH CARE DISPARITIES 89

  Chapter 5 Racial and Ethnic Diversity in Academic Medicine
Carla Boutin-Foster, MD, MS 91

SECTION 3   ETHICS AND HUMAN RIGHTS   107

Chapter 6   Human Rights: A Necessary Framework for Public Health
Holly G. Atkinson, MD   109

Chapter 7   Genetic Testing and Public Health: Ethical Issues
Inmaculada de Melo-Martín, PhD, MS   123

Chapter 8   Palliative Care
Roma Tickoo, MD, MPH, and Paul Glare, MD   139

SECTION 4   PUBLIC HEALTH PRACTICE AND EDUCATION   159

Chapter 9   The Role of Epidemiology and Biostatistics in Health News Reporting
Paula Trushin and Heejung Bang, PhD   161

Chapter 10   Evidence-Based Public Health: A Fundamental Concept for Public Health Practice
Christopher M. Maylahn, MPH, Ross C. Brownson, PhD, and Jonathan E. Fielding, MD, MPH, MA, MBA   191

Chapter 11   Public Health and Medical Education in the United States
Rika Maeshiro, MD, MPH   215

SECTION 5   ASSURING THE HEALTH OF THE PUBLIC: PUBLIC HEALTH CHALLENGES IN THE 21ST CENTURY   233

Chapter 12   The Stem Cell Controversy: Navigating a Sea of Ethics, Politics, and Science
Ryan Cauley, MD   235

Chapter 13   Application of Novel Analytical Tools in Global Disease Monitoring: Remote Sensing in Public Health Research and Practice
Jesse C. McEntee, MA, Denise Castronovo, MS, Jyotsna S. Jagai, MS, MPH, PhD, Kenneth K. H. Chui, MS, MPH, PhD, and Elena N. Naumova, PhD   253

Chapter 14   Thinking Creatively about Public Health for the 21st Century
Barry H. Smith, MD, PhD   267

About the Editor   283

About the Contributors   285

Index   289

Foreword

As we enter the second decade of the 21st century, myriad issues compete for the world's attention, from the continuing stresses of the deep and widespread recession, to personal and national security, to climate change. But no issue looms larger than that of public health. Within this general rubric fall multiple issues critical to the individual, the country, and the world. Infectious diseases, including malaria, multiple drug–resistant tuberculosis, pandemic influenza, and HIV/AIDS pose even greater threats because of enormously increased international travel. In the developing world, the traditional diseases of poverty—communicable disease, especially infectious diarrhea and other waterborne diseases, malnutrition, and inadequate maternal and child health care—and displacement and violence, which are the sequelae of political instability, increasingly are being joined by the ailments of excess such as obesity, diabetes, and atherosclerotic cardiovascular disease, making the burden infinitely greater. Long overdue recognition of the worsening plight of women, particularly but not only in resource-poor environments, compounds the ongoing dilemmas of maternal-child health. Even within rich societies, such as the United States, shocking health disparities stubbornly continue.

Despite these daunting challenges, the tools of public health are more robust than ever. In addition to the traditional tools of medicine and the social sciences, the use of molecular genetics techniques and advanced statistical analysis presents new opportunities for the student and practitioner of public health. This comprehensive work on public health thus appears at a most opportune time.

Including a carefully assembled combination of original work and important recent literature and covering a huge sweep of relevant problems, *Public Health in the 21st Century* succeeds admirably in bringing together much of the broad field into one work that should find its place as a reference for public health workers and academics as well as policy makers and those in the private sector, whether health care providers, insurers, or drug or device manufacturers. Dr. Madelon Finkel, an experienced and recognized expert in several aspects of public health and, importantly, in the pedagogy of public health, has assembled a most impressive group of writers on a huge variety of public health topics, covering everything from global population health, to special needs cohorts, to health care policy, to the often-ignored topic of public health teaching strategies and tactics. Readers from across the spectrum of public health concerns will find thought-provoking material of great value.

I commend Professor Finkel and her many colleagues on bringing to fruition a work that undoubtedly will receive wide use.

David J. Skorton, MD
President, Cornell University

Acknowledgments

This three-volume set could not have been produced without the contributions of the authors who so generously took the time to research and write their respective chapter. Most of the authors are my friends and colleagues who gladly agreed to accept my invitation to be included in the effort. I thank each of the authors for their time, effort, and especially their friendship.

My editorial assistant, Sophia Day, was tremendously helpful in organizing the huge volume of material and keeping track of missing information. Editorial reviews of many of the chapters were graciously and professionally done by Dr. Rebecca Finkel, an author and former editor who also happens to be my accomplished daughter. Technical computer work and support was provided by Jean Policard of the Department of Public Health at Weill Cornell Medical College. His assistance was invaluable to me.

Many thanks to my editor, Debbie Carvalko of Praeger, who invited me to write this multivolume text. Her support and faith in my being able to deliver the goods on time was reassuring.

Introduction
Madelon L. Finkel, PhD

Compiling topics for inclusion in a multivolume text on public health at first seemed like a simple task. Because so many significant advances have been made in disease prevention and health promotion, and so many public health initiatives have been put in place over the years to improve health and well-being, deciding which topics to select proved more difficult than anticipated. Which ones should be included? Which ones are the most relevant, the most important to highlight? Narrowing the focus, but being as comprehensive and inclusive as possible, seemed the most prudent way to proceed. And, therein lay the problem. How was I to select from such a wide array of public health issues to produce a comprehensive text on current public health topics? In an effort to be both comprehensive and inclusive, I endeavored to select as many important and timely subjects as possible for these three volumes. For fear of overwhelming the readers with chapters on every conceivable public health issue, a careful selection was made to highlight topics that represent and reflect the field of public health's breadth and scope. As such, the three volumes include chapters on topics reflecting advances and progress in knowledge and practice as well as challenges that remain. Naturally, many more topics could have been included. The essays selected for inclusion, many written specifically for this multivolume set and others reprinted from the published literature, represent a broad overview of important public health issues in the 21st century.

Charles-Edward A. Winslow, a bacteriologist and professor of public health at the Yale School of Medicine from 1915 to 1945, proposed a definition of public health as

> the science and art of preventing disease, prolonging life, and promoting physical health and efficiency through organized community efforts for the sanitation of the environment, the control of community infections, the education of the individual in principles of personal hygiene, [and] the organization of medical and nursing service for the early diagnosis and preventive treatment of disease.[1]

To a large extent, his definition has not been changed or amended over the ensuing decades. Public health's focus, then and now, is to safeguard the public's health and to handle threats to public health.

Public health has its roots in antiquity. It has long been recognized that polluted water and air, inadequate waste disposal, overcrowding and a concomitant lack of hygiene, and lifestyle behavior contributed to the spread of disease. Moving away from the miasma theory of disease, which argues that most diseases are caused by miasma (Greek for "pollution," that is, a noxious form of "bad air"), to the germ theory of disease was an important step in disease prevention. The 19th century witnessed so many discoveries and advances in the fields of medicine and public health. Essentially, pre-20th-century efforts focused on the eradication of infectious diseases and improvements in hygiene and sanitation, which led to a dramatic increase in average life expectancy. For example, the science of epidemiology probably dates from Dr. John Snow's identification of polluted public water wells as the source of the 1854 cholera outbreak in London. Hungarian physician Ignaz Semmelweis, for example, successfully reduced infant mortality at a Vienna hospital by instituting a disinfection procedure. His findings were published in 1850, but his work was ill received by his colleagues, who unwisely discontinued the procedure. Disinfection did not become widely practiced until British surgeon Joseph Lister "discovered" antiseptics in 1865, helped significantly by the work of the French chemist and microbiologist Louis Pasteur and German physician and bacteriologist Robert Koch.

The early 20th century expanded the scope and complexity of public health concerns. High rates of infant mortality led to the establishment of maternal and child health programs that emphasized nutrition. The disgraceful state of the food processing industry was notably depicted in Upton Sinclair's book, *The Jungle*. The book dealt with conditions in the U.S. meat-packing industry, causing a public uproar that partly contributed to the passage of the Pure Food and Drug Act and the Meat Inspection Act in 1906. High rates of occupational injuries and occupational-related diseases led to programs for industrial hygiene and occupational health, but it was not until 1970 that the U.S. Occupational Safety and Health Administration (OSHA) was created by Congress under the Occupational Safety and Health Act. Its mission is to prevent work-related injuries, illnesses, and occupational fatality by issuing and enforcing rules called standards for workplace safety and health.

These and other public health efforts contributed substantially to a dramatic decrease in mortality. From 1900 to 1940, for example, mortality rates in the U.S. fell by 40 percent, and life expectancy at birth increased from 47 years to 63 years.[2] No other period in American history showed such a dramatic decline in overall death rates. Nearly all of this decrease can be accounted for by reductions in infectious diseases, which in 1900 accounted for 44 percent of deaths. Contributing to the decrease in infectious diseases was the implementation of clean water technologies, one of the most important public health interventions of the early 20th century. At the turn of the century, waterborne diseases accounted for one-quarter of reported infectious disease deaths in urban areas. By 1936, less than 20 percent of deaths were due to infectious diseases. Perhaps the greatest public health feat was the worldwide eradication of smallpox, a highly contagious, serious viral disease that was a worldwide scourge. The last case was recorded in 1977 in Somalia, and the eradication was certified by the World Health Organization (WHO) in 1979.

By the mid- to late-20th century, achievements saw a shift in focus from acute infectious diseases to the treatment and prevention of the growing burden of noninfectious, chronic diseases. English physician-researcher Sir Richard Doll and English epidemiologist and statistician Sir A. Bradford Hill pioneered the randomized clinical trial, and together were the first to demonstrate the connection between cigarette smoking and lung cancer. The focus on individual behaviors and risk factors (for example, antismoking campaigns) was an important step in addressing the *social determinants of disease*. The *new* public health sought to address the burden of chronic disease in a more comprehensive way by focusing on the effects of disease on vulnerable populations (for example, the elderly, the young, and the disabled), how health status differs among population groups (health inequalities), and how health care systems are organized and financed. Indeed, the challenges facing modern public health in the 21st century must be broad and inclusive, and focus on improvement in population health through the reduction of preventable diseases, both communicable and noncommunicable.

Looking back over the last century, public health is credited with adding 30 years to the life expectancy of people in the United States over the course of the 20th century; 25 years of this gain are attributable to advances in public health.[3] The Centers for Disease Control and Prevention (CDC) cataloged 10 of what it considered to be the most notable public health achievements based on the opportunity for prevention and the impact on death, illness, and disability.[4] These include (not ranked by order of importance) the following:

- Vaccination programs (as a result of widespread vaccine use, many of the infectious diseases that once killed so many have been almost eliminated);
- Fluoridation of drinking water (fluoride was first added to the public water system in 1945; tooth decay and tooth loss has declined substantially as a result);
- Occupational safety policies (since 1980, the rate of fatal occupational injuries has decreased by 40 percent);
- Access to safe, improved family planning and contraceptive services;
- Control of infectious diseases as a result of antibiotics, clean water, and improved sanitation;
- Food safety (safer and more healthful foods can be attributed to decreased microbial contamination and increased nutritional;
- Recognition of tobacco use as a health hazard;
- Motor vehicle safety (safety belts, child safety seats, motorcycle helmets, and engineering improvements in both vehicles and highways have helped reduce fatal motor vehicle accidents);
- Decline in deaths from coronary heart disease and stroke (lifestyle modifications and pharmaceuticals have led to a decline in deaths for these diseases); and
- Healthier mothers and babies as a result of better hygiene, prenatal health care and nutrition.

The 21st century presents new challenges. Largely preventable infectious diseases, such as tuberculosis (TB), polio, measles, and cholera continue to plague millions of people around the globe, especially children. HIV/AIDS, which appeared on the scene in the mid-1980s, continues to be a major public health problem, although antiretroviral medications have done wonders in terms of extending life. Malaria, multidrug-resistant TB, and global outbreaks of viral diseases, most recently the H1N1 swine flu pandemic of 2009, continue to challenge public health efforts. That being said, chronic diseases such as diabetes and heart disease are now prevalent around the world. Obesity is not just a problem of the wealthy nations, as the increase in adult and childhood obesity in the developing world threatens to jeopardize progress. Statistics compiled by WHO show that chronic diseases are the largest cause of death in the world today and that global prevalence of all the leading chronic diseases is increasing, with the majority occurring in developing countries. Cardiovascular disease is already the leading cause of mortality in the developing world.[5] The increased burden of chronic diseases in countries that also have a high burden of infectious diseases is creating both a tremendous economic and public health strain. Furthermore, the recognition that health is affected by many factors, including genetics, economics, ethnicity and race, and geography, has necessitated a shift in focus in thinking. Public health in the 21st century must address these health inequalities to reduce the incidence of disease and improve health and well-being. Malnutrition, poverty, lack of access to health care, and so forth threaten to undermine the progress made in disease control and prevention.

In summary, over the past 150 years, much of the focus has been on disease control, understanding sources of contagion, and implementing programs to prevent the spread of disease. As scientific knowledge grew, public health's purview expanded to include maternal and child health care, health education, nutrition, aging of the population, the recognition of the role of behavioral factors in determining health, the impact of violence (domestic, civil, and international), health care disparities, and globalization. Indeed, increased globalization and technological advances have contributed to a worldwide economic, political, and social interdependence. In 1945, the United Nations Conference in San Francisco unanimously approved the establishment of a new, autonomous international health organization, the WHO, which came into being on April 7, 1948. The WHO was established as a specialized agency of the United Nations to serve as a coordinating authority on international public health issues.

Despite the progress made in improving the health, so much still remains to be done, not just in the United States, but also globally. In 2000, for example, 11.1 million children under the age of 5 died from preventable diseases such as diarrhea and acute respiratory infection.[6] These and other primarily preventable diseases kill more people each year than conflicts alone. Worldwide, poverty is one of the most significant causes of preventable mortality. Gender inequality persists and perhaps in some areas of the world actually has increased. Population growth remains a serious concern as the world's population has surged to 6.7 billion, most of the increase occurring within the last century. Environmental degradation and climate concerns have significant health implications. Each has a dimension that necessarily involves public health. As such, public health must be looked at in a global context if it is to be successful in fulfilling its mandate. Microbes have no boundaries, and we have seen over and over again, localized outbreaks can quickly spread to national epidemics, and even worldwide pandemics.

Global health refers to health problems that transcend national borders and are of such magnitude that they have a global political, social, and economic impact. Assessing and measuring the impact of globalization on population health status should not be done in a vacuum; a global public health perspective needs to be integrated into health, social, and economic policies and programs to be effective. Reducing social and economic deprivation, reducing health inequalities, and improving health status go hand-in-hand. Domestic and international entities whose function and purpose is promulgating public health policy need to work together to achieve common goals. Collectively, progress can be made; individually, the effect is more muted. At their summit in 2000, heads of state of the G8 countries went on record as recognizing health as a global challenge and acknowledging that health is the "key to prosperity" and that "poor health drives poverty."[7] Following up on this challenge, G77 heads of state from 130 developing countries also expressed support for working toward the reduction of disease worldwide.[8] The motives and intent are laudable, but a decade later, the world still finds itself grappling with disease control and health prevention issues. Indeed, a WHO assessment of the capacity of 185 countries to prevent, conduct surveillance, and control disease showed that while health ministries had a high level of awareness of the issues, they had little or no allocation of significant resources to address the problems.[9]

Global nongovernmental organizations (NGOs) have played and continue to play a critical role in building capacity and sustainable development in specific areas of the world, although often the focus is narrow (for example, tobacco, TB, malaria, diet and nutrition, and so forth). Foundations, such as the Bill and Melinda Gates Foundation, have provided extraordinary sums of money and manpower to address pressing global health issues. Their importance and impact cannot be denied or ignored. These private investments in global health far exceed government assistance. The pharmaceutical industry also has the potential for being an effective player in the global health arena, but the industry is constantly criticized for not taking a greater role in the access to life-saving drugs, particularly in developing nations. The arguments are plentiful, ranging from focusing research and development efforts on health issues for rich countries to pricing drugs at unaffordable levels. That being said, despite the challenges that the pharmaceutical industry faces, it has been involved in a number of global health initiatives. Often, this means that companies are donating drugs, cutting prices, and developing partnerships with local governments and NGOs.

The World Bank and the United Nations play a major role in setting priorities for global health. The World Bank recognizes the negative effect of the increasing burden of disease, especially on the poor. Billions of dollars have been provided to countries for disease prevention. These efforts are crucially important as most developing countries have inadequate financing, lack of manpower, and poor infrastructure. Numerous UN organizations are specifically designed to focus on the global burden of disease. For example, the United Nations Population Fund, the United Nations Children's Fund, and many other UN agencies and organizations focus on providing assistance to the poorest countries in an effort to "make a difference." The Millennium Development Goals (MDGs), also, are an agreed-upon set of goals that were developed in response to the world's main development challenges. They were drawn from the actions and targets contained in the Millennium Declaration that was adopted by 189 nations and signed by 147 heads of state and governments during the UN Millennium Summit held in September 2000. The MDGs are targeted to promote poverty reduction, education, maternal health, and gender equality, and to combat child mortality, AIDS, and other diseases. Poor countries pledged to govern better and invest in their people through health care and education. Rich countries pledged to support them, through aid, debt relief, and fairer trade. The MDGs represent a global partnership that has grown from the commitments and targets established at the world summits of the 1990s. The eight goals are to be achieved by 2015.[10]

Many stakeholders, public and private, are working toward similar goals, but it seems at times as if progress has taken one step forward and two steps back. While tremendous progress has been made over the past century, substantial challenges remain. Capacity development for prevention, treatment, and research remains weak; global economic factors impede progress; and the need for health systems change (delivery, financing, organization, and insurance coverage) remains unmet. The three volumes in this text were formulated to address public health issues from a national and global perspective. Volume 1 focuses on global population health issues, while volume 2 presents chapters on various aspects of determinants of health and disease, and volume 3 examines current public health policy issues, including ethics and human rights, public health education, and challenges we face as we enter the second decade of the 21st century. I made a concerted effort to include authors from around the world. Colleagues from Africa, Australia, Canada, China, Europe, India, Latin America, and New Zealand are well represented in this multivolume text. Their perspective and insight add a global dimension to the set.

VOLUME 1

Section 1 of volume 1 focuses on global population health issues. In their chapter on the global burden of disease, Kishore and Michelow carefully review the salient features of the global burden of disease, including its distribution and changing patterns over time. If current trends continue, diseases such as diarrhea, AIDS, TB, and malaria will become less important causes of morbidity and mortality as heart disease, cancer, diabetes, and traffic accidents increase in prevalence. Although the "burden" of a disease can be defined in a variety of senses, the consensus definition, particularly from the WHO, is a fairly specific one. The global burden of disease (GBD) as defined by the WHO is a comprehensive regional and global assessment of mortality and disability from 136 diseases and injuries and 19 risk factors. While useful, the thinking was that a better measurement of the GBD was needed, one that integrated morbidity, mortality, incidence, and prevalence into a single common metric that can be compared across time, space, and interventions. A new metric, the Disability-Adjusted Life Year (DALY), is a summary measure of population health, measured in units of time (years), combining estimations of both fatal and nonfatal health outcomes (morbidity and mortality) to provide an estimate of the number of years of fully healthy life lost by an individual with a particular illness or condition. When DALYs are used to estimate the GBD, communicable diseases displace noncommunicable diseases as leading drivers of illness. The authors discuss the explosion of noncommunicable chronic diseases worldwide and the existing burden of communicable diseases, the combination of which poses a significant threat to the public's health. The challenge we face is how to best deal with the double burden of disease.

China and India together account for 37 percent of the world's population, about 6.8 billion. In 2025, India will surpass China in total population. India thus will have the distinction of being the world's most populous country. China's fertility rate is decreasing, whereas India's continues to increase. The United States is the third most populous country. Bongaarts focuses on population projections to the year 2050 for the world and major regions, and then identifies the demographic factors responsible for continued expansion of human numbers. Discussion focuses on policy options for slowing population growth in the developing world, where the growth continues to surpass that in the industrial world. Four main demographic factors contribute to future population growth: continued high fertility, declining mortality, young age structure, and migration. Bongaarts concludes by noting that the unprecedented pace at which the world's population has grown over recent decades has had an adverse impact on social and economic development, on health care, and on the environment. Despite substantial and partially successful efforts to reduce growth in the less developed countries, this expansion of human members is expected to continue at a rapid pace over the next decades with nearly all of this growth occurring in Africa, Asia, and Latin America. He advocates for three key strategies to reduce this growth rate: strengthen family planning programs to provide women with the knowledge and means to regulate their fertility; emphasize "human development," in particular education, gender equality, and child health; and encourage delays in subsequent childbearing.

The effect of urbanization on the public's health is discussed by Galea and Vlahov. The authors focus on the substantial change from how most of the world's population lives, reflecting on how the characteristics of the urban environment affect population health. The key factors affecting health in cities are considered within three broad themes: the physical environment, the social environment, and access to health and social services.

Continuing the theme of adverse effects of rapid population growth and urbanization, Brown and DeGaetano present a scholarly piece on the consequences of climate change on health. Concerns about recent changes in global climates and possible future trends on the health of the world's population are now considered important policy topics. With the election of Barack Obama, who has pledged a new era of leadership and responsibility to reduce the serious negative effects of climate degradation, the United States resumed its leading role in combating climate change and the adverse effects thereof. The United States is the world's largest source of cumulative emissions in the atmosphere, and as such, needs to lead the way for other nations to make a serious effort on climate change. Brown and DeGaetano make the case that climatic changes have, and will continue to have, direct negative health effects from altered weather patterns, but state also that the indirect effects on agriculture and wider population systems are important factors for the GBD. Global warming (that is, melting of Arctic ice), extreme weather (for example, heat waves, cold spells), flooding (for example, Hurricane Katrina), erosion of ocean coastlines (that is, a result of extreme and heavy precipitation), and drought (for example, dust bowls) are leading to a disruption of food production and to disease. The authors note that exposure to infectious diseases has altered because of changes in temperature, humidity, rainfall, and sea-level rise. Specifically, some evidence of changes in the distribution of mosquito, tick, and bird vectors has been attributed to climate change. Mosquitoes, for example, can transmit diseases, such as malaria, dengue, yellow fever, and Japanese encephalitis, but their sensitivity to weather conditions can inhibit or enhance their efficacy as a vector. Malaria is spread by mosquitoes, which are inhibited from transmitting the parasite in cooler temperatures. Air quality and pollutants are affected by the weather and climate, and can cause negative health effects; the incidence of asthma has soared over the past decades. The authors caution that vulnerability to climate change will depend on responses to prevention, adaptation, adaptive capacity, mitigation, and future advances in disease control. It is clear that doing nothing will only make the situation worse than it already is.

The issue of global health and nutrition is a complex interplay of many factors ranging from politics to economics to food production policies to environmental degradation. Food is a basic human need. With roughly 1 billion humans suffering from overnutrition and a similar number unable to find enough food to subsist, no one seriously disagrees about the urgency of world hunger. One in six individuals does not get enough food to be healthy and to lead an active life. Hunger and malnutrition adversely affect physical and mental development; indeed, one might argue that hunger and malnutrition are leading risks to the health and well-being of individuals worldwide. Davison presents a comprehensive overview of the salient issues and focuses in particular on the interdependence of nutrition, economic development, and health. His discussion of the topic includes an assessment of the MDGs drafted to address the issue of alleviating hunger and malnutrition and a brief overview of some of the programs designed to eliminate global nutrition disparities, including the Millennium Village Projects, the Grameen enterprises and "microcredit" initiatives in resource-poor countries, and the role that foundations play in providing the financial means to reduce poverty and, in turn, to alleviate hunger and malnutrition.

No matter how one defines "health," prevention and treatment of disease is an essential prerequisite for achieving health and well-being. Implicit in this is that the right medicine be available at the time and place of need. Reidenberg presents an overview of the WHO Essential Medicines Program. By definition, an "essential drug" is a drug needed to satisfy the health needs of the majority of the population. The essential drugs concept of purchasing a limited list of essential drugs for a health service and making them generally available has been accepted by 156 countries and most, if not all, donor organizations. The essential medicines idea was developed to help limited resource countries make choices to use their medical resources for the greatest good for the greatest number. Thirty years after the WHO initiated the Essential Medicines Model List, four out of five countries have adopted a national essential medicines list. More than 100 countries have a national drug policy in place or under development. Furthermore, a network of 83 countries provides global monitoring for adverse drug reactions and as well as for potential safety problems. Regarding pricing, 30 years ago, virtually no publicly available price information was available, and few countries actively encouraged generic substitutions. In the 21st century, at least 33 countries provide such information.

Prevention and safety have long been an integral component of public health. Section 2 of volume 1 presents several essays on the topic. By focusing on ways to control risks, public health works toward making the environment a safer and healthier place in which to live. Silverstein presents an historical account of occupational health and safety in the United States. The Occupational Safety and Health Act of 1970 (OSHAct) declared that every worker in America is entitled to a safe and healthful workplace, and that employers are responsible for work being free from recognized hazards. Now, forty years later, many of the promises of the OSHAct have yet to be met. Silverstein reviews the history of occupational health and safety in the United States and exposes the barriers to OSHA's success (predominantly linked to the statutory design of regulation, inspection, and education) and the challenges that remain in preventing injury and illness at the workplace.

Hupert, Wattson, and Xiong present a sophisticated analysis of the complexity of planning for and responding to public health emergencies. Using the example of a large-scale aerosol anthrax exposure over an urban locale, they explore key determinants of health outcomes and health system surge capacity using several modeling techniques (state transition, queuing network). They suggest that such models can provide valuable insights for forecasting the logistical and staffing needs of large-scale prophylaxis campaigns for a range of intentional and natural disease outbreaks, such as the 2009 influenza A (H1N1) pandemic. While all model-based studies have their potential limitations, they may serve many functions in emergency preparedness and planning that cannot be provided through other means.

Food safety has periodically seeped into the consciousness of the lay public, almost always after a public tragedy involving tainted food. In 2006, there were 1,270 reported U.S. foodborne disease outbreaks, resulting in 27,634 illnesses and 11 deaths. Since then, many other well-publicized incidents have involved the safety of food products, including food recalls (berries from California, grapes from Chile, and so forth), contaminated beef or poultry, and recalls due to contamination (peanuts, almonds, and pistachio salmonella outbreaks occurred in 2009). Furthermore, public concerns over the use of food additives as well as use of pesticides have spurred interest in organically grown food products. Perhaps in response to the recent food outbreaks in the United States, the Food and Drug Administration (FDA) recently named a highly qualified food safety expert to be deputy commissioner for foods at the FDA. The newly created position is the first to oversee all the agency's numerous food and nutrition programs, and setting safety standards for produce is a top priority.

The article on foodborne illnesses by Tauxe, Doyle, Kuchenmuller, Schlundt, and Stein focuses on this important topic. Foodborne diseases are caused by a broad variety of pathogens and toxins. In their comprehensive and scholarly article, the authors review the epidemiological, microbiological, and public health aspects of foodborne diseases resulting from the ingestion of contaminated foods and food products, and discuss the evolving public health approaches to the global challenges of foodborne infections. The global challenge of safeguarding the world's food supply is complicated by growing international trade, migration, and travel. Through the globalization of food marketing and distribution, contaminated food products can and do affect the health of people in numerous countries at the same time.

Pharmaceutical safety in the United States is under the purview of the FDA. Haas presents an overview of how the benefits and risks of pharmaceuticals are managed and discusses the implications for global drug safety. As more pharmaceutical products are manufactured in countries around the world (including Canada, China, and India), concerns about safety of the products are quite valid. The FDA does not have the money or the manpower to inspect each plant overseas; yet, the final product is distributed and marketed in the United States. Haas provides an excellent historical overview of key issues in drug safety, which led to regulation of the marketing of approved drug products, most notably the Food and Drug Amendment Act of 2007. The act mandated that product label changes for safety were to be imposed and executed promptly. To ensure an acceptable benefit-risk balance, the FDA was empowered to require additional studies or trials, and it could stipulate specific conditions limiting the market availability of a product to ensure its safe use. The FDA was instructed to promptly communicate evolving product safety concerns even if the available information was limited. In addition, the act mandated that virtually all clinical trials, regardless of sponsorship, be registered and that efficacy and safety results be publicly posted in a timely manner. The act created a major new safety information system (the Sentinel System) that would complement spontaneous adverse event reporting. Despite efforts to tighten the mechanisms to ensure drug safety, the system is not fail-safe. The goal for drug safety is to have a flexible and responsive system able to recognize potential risks early, collect information efficiently, and take action that is appropriate in the context of both benefits and risks.

Focusing on the needs of vulnerable populations is an important component of public health. Section 3 of volume 1 highlights health care issues of special population groups. Karpur, Bjelland, and Bruyère from the Employment and Disability Institute of Cornell University highlight the role of public health in improving the health, well-being, and overall quality of life for people with disabilities through the consideration of epidemiological trends in disability prevalence, issues related to health disparities, the legal and regulatory environment affecting access to preventive and curative health services, methods of measuring and tracking the population of people with disabilities, and specific priorities in public health. The Institute of Medicine (IOM) refers to disability as "the nation's largest public health problem," one that affects not only the health of people with disabilities, but also their immediate families and the population at large. Key issues for people with disabilities requiring attention in the U.S. public health system need to be addressed at the global level. It is estimated that there are approximately 650 million people with disabilities in the world with about 80 percent living in developing countries. The authors discuss various models and strategies to improve health and well-being for people with disabilities, focusing on health disparities for people with disabilities; addressing the unique considerations for youth, women, and the aging with disabilities; and working toward an equitable access to health care, health care insurance coverage, health promotion, and prevention of secondary conditions—universal concerns that public health systems in all countries should be taking into account in the development of their national strategy.

Immigrant health care traditionally has largely been ignored by health policy makers. Yet, in 2009, an estimated 16 million children lived in immigrant families in the United States, representing one of the fastest-growing segments of the population. Clearly, policies and programs are needed to support immigrant parents and children, but the reality is haphazard at best. Mohanty, Woolhandler, Himmelstein, Pati, Carrasquillo, and Bor present compelling data based on the 1998 Medical Expenditure Panel Survey (MEPS) and found that immigrants have less access to health care and less health care use than do U.S.-born individuals. They also found that per capita health care expenditures for immigrants were far lower than expenditures for the U.S.-born. The study convincingly showed that the widely held assumption that immigrants consume large amounts of scarce health care resources is not supported by the data. The authors conclude that the low expenditures of publicly insured immigrants also suggest that policy efforts to terminate immigrants' coverage would result in little savings.

The provision of health care (or lack thereof) to those incarcerated has a long, sordid history. Finkel presents statistical evidence to illustrate the spectrum of health problems in correctional facilities. Inmate health and medical conditions range the gamut from minor (colds or viruses) to the significant (HIV/AIDS, TB). In addition to the communicable diseases, the prevalence of mental health and psychiatric diseases and substance abuse is higher among the prison population than the general population. The public health consequences of not paying attention to the health of prisoners can be quite significant; infectious diseases transmitted or exacerbated in prisons have the potential to become full-blown public health problems when prisoners return to their communities. The scope of this chapter provides an overview of the state of health among prisoners, assesses the provision of health care to those incarcerated, examines the policies regulating care of prisoners, including the challenges governments face in their ability to provide health and medical care to inmates, and discusses the pros and cons of having the private sector (privatization) involved in prison health care delivery.

Lesbian, gay, bisexual, and transgender (LGBT) health care also has received marginal interest and attention among policy makers and in the medical school curriculum. Medical education in the United States, both during medical school and in residency, is often unlikely to include adequate cultural competency related to the care of sexual orientation and gender identity minorities. A survey conducted to assess curricula in U.S. medical schools found that less than 3.5 hours were dedicated to teaching about health issues related to homosexuality. Part of the problem is the paucity of data on population demographics and health status for this population. For public health departments and providers to plan appropriate services for this vulnerable population, it is essential to have reliable data. Until recently, many of the research studies conducted in the LGBT community were community-based studies using nonprobability sampling techniques. Radix and Mayer discuss the barriers to access to care as well as the health issues prevalent among the LGBT community. Of course, each group has its own set of health care needs, as lesbian health care is necessarily different from gay health care. The authors make the point that LGBT individuals have specific health needs that require targeted and culturally appropriate interventions.

The first ever surgeon general's report on oral health in the United States was published in 2000. The report highlighted a "silent epidemic" of dental and oral diseases, especially among the poor, the elderly, and children. Globally, too, oral disease burden and disability, especially in poor and marginalized populations, is a huge unmet issue. Oral health is much more than the pains of a toothache. Oral diseases such as dental caries, periodontal disease, tooth loss, oral mucosal lesions, and oropharyngeal cancers are major public health problems worldwide. Poor oral health has a profound effect on general health and quality of life. The burden of oral diseases and conditions is greatest among the economically disadvantaged, which include a disproportionately large number of racial and ethnic minorities and underserved populations. The major risk factors for oral disease are known and they are common with other chronic diseases: diet, smoking, alcohol, and risky behaviors. Canto and Cruz provide an epidemiologic overview of the state of oral health care as well as discuss preventive measures initiated to reduce dental caries, including exposure to fluoride (community water fluoridation, for example, has done much to reduce dental caries), use of dental sealants, practice of good oral hygiene, and reduction in sugar intake. The unmet need for dental care is a serious problem that needs to be acknowledged and addressed.

Taking care of the health care needs of the growing geriatric population is complex, challenging, and, to some extent, costly. Adelman, Finkelstein, Mehta, and Greene present an overview of the challenges of providing high-quality care to a rapidly aging population. They examine the medical, psychological, and social components of older age and explore the needs of this heterogeneous cohort. Issues such as dementia and Alzheimer's disease, elder abuse, ageist bias, the risks of polypharmacy, and long-term care issues are discussed.

Section 4 of volume 1 focuses on population-based prevention strategies. Adolescent substance abuse (alcohol, drugs, tobacco) has been well studied over the past decades; yet, the problem remains. Prevention and control programs have received considerable attention over the past decades as well. Botvin, Griffin, and Murphy, leaders in adolescent substance abuse prevention and cessation studies, raise a number of important issues related to adolescent substance abuse, including prevalence trends and types of prevention-based program modalities used by schools, families, and communities. The authors state that the most effective approaches target salient risk and protective factors, are guided by psychosocial theories regarding the etiology of substance use and abuse, and are implemented over many years. Many school-based prevention programs, for example, focus on skill-building in the area of drug resistance as well as life-skills training. While progress has been made in the field of substance abuse prevention, continued efforts must be made in the area of skill-building to prevent adolescents and children from taking drugs in the first place.

The issue of violence has been the subject of numerous reports by private and public organizations over the past decade. The public health consequences of all forms of violence are considerable as violence is associated not just with fatalities, but also with substantial morbidity and costs. It is estimated that in 2006 the health costs of violence (both fatal and nonfatal) in the United States exceeded $70 billion. Anderson and Sidel take a global approach to the discussion of violence and its sequela, and lay out a public health approach to violence prevention. They posit that the goals of public health—to prevent disease, and injury and premature death and to promote healthy living conditions for all—are identical to the goals of violence prevention. The disciplines and methods of public health—analyzing the causes of diseases, injuries, and premature deaths and of poverty and despair and determining methods to counter them—can strengthen efforts to prevent violence. And the ability of public health workers to gain trust both nationally and internationally can bring new skills and vigor to violence prevention.

Women, especially women in resource-poor nations, are an especially vulnerable group in terms of economics and in health care. In the industrial and developing world, gender-based violence (GBV) is endemic. Not only is it a major public health and human rights problem, but also for the victims it can, and most often does, have devastating personal, health, societal, and economic consequences. Meshkat and Landes eloquently delineate the types of GBV ranging from sexual, psychological, and physical, and depict the global burden of the problem. In addressing the issue, it is important to understand that public health initiatives often are bound tightly to existing legal frameworks, and this holds especially true in the case of GBV. It is excellent that GBV is now recognized as a major global public health and human rights issue, but efforts to stem its practice still stymie those involved in the prevention and management of GBV. Much work remains both in the industrial and developing world to ensure the safety and well-being of women of all ages against all forms of GBV.

Few issues in public health have fostered as much controversy as contraception and abortion. Passions run high on both sides of the debate; religion, politics, and policy regularly clash. Henshaw, who has spent his career conducting research in this area, presents a comprehensive statistical report on the issue of contraception and abortion, and explores some of the barriers that inhibit or even prevent women from controlling their fertility. Focusing on unintended pregnancy, contraceptive use, and abortion in the United States, he clearly and concisely presents the statistical evidence showing trends and highlighting the barriers that exist to prevent women of all ages from controlling fertility. Regarding abortion, since the legalization of this procedure in 1973, it is estimated that 35 percent of women in the United States will have had at least one abortion by age 45. Regarding birth rates, recent figures show that in 2007 more babies were born in the United States than in any other year in U.S. history.[11] This increase reflects a larger population of women of childbearing age. Births to teenagers (ages 15 to 17), after declining for many years, increased, reasons for which are poorly understood. Mississippi has the nation's highest teen pregnancy rate, which was 60 percent higher than the national average.

Although tremendous advances have been made in the eradication of once-deadly diseases, the development of vaccines probably is the most significant reason for the decline in morbidity and mortality from such diseases. Perhaps the world's greatest achievement in this area is the eradication of smallpox. Rosen takes a global look at disease prevention through vaccination, presenting an historical overview and then focusing on the challenges that remain. There is a staggering disparity in vaccination efforts worldwide; millions of children are needlessly dying from preventable infections. Closing the gap will require multinational efforts and significant amounts of manpower and financial resources. The WHO and the Global Alliance for Vaccines and Immunization are deeply involved in coordinating immunization plans, especially in the resource-poor nations.

VOLUME 2

Volume 2 focuses on the determinants of health and disease. Section 1 addresses the treatment and prevention of chronic diseases. Since the mid-20th century, there has been a huge explosion in the number of individuals diagnosed with diabetes mellitus. Endocrinologist Baker's chapter focuses on the global epidemic of diabetes and discusses the public health, medical, and economic implications of dealing with this disease as well as the consequences to patients and to society. Diabetes is a growing and serious disease that affects rich and poor alike. According to the WHO, diabetes is likely to be one of the most substantial threats to human health in the 21st century. In the United States. alone, the direct medical costs of treating diabetics will be $336 billion. This does not take into account the growing proportion of overweight children and teenagers who are at high risk for developing diabetes and does not factor in immigration or the growing population of ethnic minorities who also suffer from diabetes at much higher rates than the U.S. white population. Without significant changes in public or private strategies, the burden of treating diabetics will place a significant strain on an already overburdened health care system. Ironically, and perhaps tragically, diabetes is among the most preventable of major illnesses. Clearly, as Baker discusses, much more needs to be done to stem the epidemic domestically as well as internationally. For a chance of success, prevention efforts must include a partnership between the individual and the health care provider.

Cardiovascular disease, too, is among the leading causes of morbidity and mortality globally. In 2004, according to the WHO, 17.1 million people died from cardiovascular disease, which represents 29 percent of global deaths. By 2010, cardiovascular disease is predicted to be the leading cause of death in developing countries. Kassahun and Borden explore the surge in cardiovascular disease and its risk factors worldwide, the characteristics and implications of this growth, as well as public health initiatives that can stem or even reverse this trend. They discuss the social, environmental, and cultural determinants of cardiovascular health, such as obesity, tobacco use, and access to health care that need to be addressed globally to reduce the incidence of cardiovascular disease.

The surging prevalence of obesity in the United States and around the world is growing faster than that of any other public health condition. This trend is alarming from a medical and an economic perspective. The ever-increasing prevalence of obesity has been accompanied by a host of inherently associated comorbidities. As a result, obesity is fast becoming the major cause of premature death in the industrial as well as the developing world. Cardiologists Bornstein and Cooper examine the implications of the huge explosion of overweight and obesity in the world in the 21st century. Over the past two decades, the number of overweight and obese adults, adolescents, and children has increased dramatically. Of great concern are the children and adolescents who already have early obesity-related degenerative diseases, such as hypertension, dyslipidemia, metabolic syndrome, and type-2 diabetes mellitus, as well as manifestations of early preclinical atherosclerotic cardiovascular disease that previously has not been observed in this age-group. The economic costs of obesity are examined as are preventive means of addressing the epidemic. For example, health care spending for obese American adults soared 82 percent between 2001 and 2006.[12] Health care costs related solely to obesity could easily total $344 billion in the United States by 2018, or more than one in five dollars spent on health care, if the trends continue. The central message is that if nothing is done to stem the rise in obesity, the economic, medical, and personal consequences will be even more difficult to deal with.

The global burden of asthma is explored by Shirtcliffe and Beasley from the Medical Research Institute of New Zealand. The rising global burden of chronic, noncommunicable diseases over recent decades has been labeled "the neglected epidemic." Over recent decades, asthma has become one of the most common chronic diseases in the world and is now the most common chronic disease of childhood in many countries. The authors present a comprehensive epidemiologic overview of the disease and address the probably causes of the increase of asthma worldwide, including climate change and urbanization. The economic burden of asthma is considerable both in terms of direct medical costs, such as the cost of pharmaceuticals and hospital admissions, and indirect medical costs, such as time lost from work and premature death. The GBD to governments, health care systems, families, and patients is substantial. Indeed, the authors argue that the burden of asthma in many countries is of sufficient magnitude to warrant its recognition as a priority disorder in government health strategies.

Mild to moderate hypertension is generally an asymptomatic disease. It aptly has been called the "silent killer" because it usually produces no symptoms and increases gradually and slowly over the years. People with high blood pressure usually have no idea that they have this problem, and they do not go to the doctor specifically because of elevated blood pressure. The detection and treatment of hypertension is thus a major public health challenge. Cheung and Ong focus on the growing burden of hypertension worldwide, and especially in the United States. Although hypertension is seldom curable, the more practical aim is to control the blood pressure. The authors present an epidemiologic overview of the disease and discuss the known risk factors for hypertension. Medical management and improving compliance with treatment are discussed.

Arthritis, especially osteoarthritis (OA), is a prevalent condition among most of the older population. As the baby boomers age, the number of new cases of OA are likely to increase. Perhaps not surprisingly, there has been a concomitant increase in the number of joint replacements being performed. Lyman and Nguyen focus on OA of the knee and the explosion in the number of total joint replacements being performed. While total knee replacement, in particular, is an elective procedure to treat severe arthritis of the knee, the increase in this surgery is driven both by the aging of the population as well as the obesity epidemic. Weight loss interventions may be the single most efficacious method of prevention of knee OA, but barring that, surgical intervention is increasingly being used to treat OA and enhance quality of life. The authors discuss the economic burden of OA, which is substantial (direct and indirect costs associated with OA).

Section 2 focuses on advances in cancer screening and the challenges that remain. For years, the dominant view about screening was that early detection and aggressive treatment would lead to increased longevity. Screening for cancer targets healthy, asymptomatic individuals. The purpose is to detect the disease at an early stage to initiate treatment, which hopefully will extend life. A key principle is that the potential benefits of screening should outweigh the harms of testing. The physical, psychological, and economic sequelae of follow-up testing should the screening test be positive needs to be compared with the number of lives saved as a result of screening.

Cancer is the nation's number two killer behind heart disease and accounts for nearly a quarter of annual deaths. The good news, however, is that cancer death rates and the number of new cancer cases in the United States continue to decline.[13] The conclusion drawn was that early detection and new therapies are major contributors to this effect. Almost at the same time as this report was released, a new study on the effectiveness of mammogram screening also was released. An expert panel from the U.S. Preventive Services Task Force recommended that mammography screening to detect breast cancer should be scaled back. This bombshell recommendation, in direct conflict with the recommendations from the American Cancer Society and other medical groups, caused considerable confusion, distrust, and even anger. Studies evaluating the effectiveness of the prostate-specific antigen (PSA) test to screen for prostate cancer also have yielded questionable results, making a clear recommendation for or against this test almost impossible. The American Cancer Society, a staunch defender of most cancer screening, has said that the benefits of detecting many cancers in particular prostate cancer has been overstated. The PSA prostate cancer screening test has not been shown to prevent prostate cancer deaths. The dilemma for breast and prostate screening is that it is not usually clear which tumors need aggressive treatment and which can be left alone.

Some studies focusing on routine early cancer screening found that the screening did not save lives, thus calling into question why screening was being advocated in the first place. In some cases, widespread screening increased the detection and treatment of small, slow-growing tumors that may well never have caused harm. In some cases, the tumor might regress or even disappear. While almost all of the cancer screening tests in wide use are minimally invasive, fairly inexpensive, and generally accepted by the public, none are 100 percent accurate; positive test results require further workup, which often are invasive and costly and usually lead to overtreatment. Screening does come with medical risks. In many cases, disease is not evident, such as in the case of false-positive test results.

Trevena presents a scholarly overview of the benefits and risks of screening and early detection of disease. She then examines the evidence for screening for colorectal cancer. The issue of whether an individual benefits from early detection of cancer is not as straightforward as it may seem. For some diseases, a preclinical phase may be so short that the disease is not likely to be detected by screening. Or, even if detected, options for cure may not exist. Also, not every preclinical case will progress to clinical disease. Trevena examines the screening options for colorectal cancer, including fecal occult blood testing, flexible sigmoidoscopy, colonoscopy, and a new screening option, CT colonography. She presents the pros and cons of each modality. Some countries recommend that a fecal occult blood test be used while others advocate for colonoscopy. The accuracy of the test, including false-positive results, needs to be weighed against the potential benefit in reducing colorectal mortality.

Elkin and Blinder of the Memorial Sloan Kettering Cancer Center in New York City focus on breast cancer screening. Mindful of the current mammography screening controversy, the authors present a comprehensive overview of the advances made in reducing and preventing breast cancer. Because so many of the risk factors for breast cancer are not modifiable, much attention has been devoted to other means of breast cancer prevention such as understanding the role of hormones in breast cancer etiology. Much of the chapter focuses on the current controversy in mammogram screening. The questions of when screening should be initiated, on whom, and how frequently remain controversial. The authors present a scholarly assessment of the evidence, including a discussion on the realities of false-positive results. The chapter concludes with a discussion of advances in breast cancer treatment, including surgical treatment, radiation therapy, systemic therapy, hormonal therapy, and chemotherapy.

Lung cancer, the leading cause of cancer mortality worldwide, typically exhibits symptoms only after the disease has spread to other organs, unfortunately making it difficult to cure patients with such advanced disease. The overall prognosis of this cancer is poor when compared with other cancers, such as breast or colon, and is dependent on where the cancer is located, the size and type of tumor, and the overall health status of the patient. The two types of lung cancers, small-cell lung cancer and non-small-cell lung cancer, grow and spread in different ways and also have different treatment options. To date, screening for lung cancer is not advocated for these reasons. Yet, we have known for decades that tobacco smoking is the leading cause of this cancer, and evidence is quite clear that if individuals stopped smoking (or never started), the incidence of lung cancer would be greatly reduced. Lung cancer can be prevented. Mazumdar's chapter on lung cancer prevention, screening, and treatment reviews the epidemiology of this cancer as well as focuses on the "effectiveness," "efficiency," and "efficaciousness" of treatment regimens. A national initiative for comparative effectiveness research (CER) for clinical decision making is described. A discussion of CER provides a review of ongoing research and initiatives in this area, and highlights the gaps in information and research. Overall, much works is needed to find a cure for lung cancer and in being able to bring the best possible care to patients of all race, gender, and socioeconomic status.

Controversy over prostate cancer screening and treatment options continues to play out in the lay and professional media. Nguyen and Kattan's chapter reviews the current status of prostate cancer screening and assess its benefits and potential deleterious effects, to determine ways to improve its predictive accuracy and efficacy. To better understand the controversy surrounding prostate cancer screening and perhaps offer a solution, they provide a review of current screening modalities, assess their accuracy and utility in contemporary medical practice, and suggest future directions for improvement of prostate cancer screening.

Over the past decades, the incidence of skin cancer has increased substantially. The chapter by Berwick, Erdei, Gonzales, Torres, and Flores focuses on the epidemiology and genetics of skin cancer and illustrates the growing public health burden of this particular form of cancer. Advances in screening and treatment are discussed and preventive measures are explored. The incidence of melanoma, a potentially deadly form of skin cancer, has soared over the past few decades perhaps because of an increased interest in screening for the disease. Indeed, the increase might be due to a growing tendency to identify and treat benign lesions as malignant cancers. It is quite difficult, and sometimes impossible, to tell a malignant lesion from a melanocytic nevus, a type of benign mole. The authors discuss how to protect oneself from skin cancer and provide informative information on sunscreens, tanning beds, and genetic susceptibility. Although sun exposure is the major risk factor for skin cancer, it is also necessary for synthesis of vitamin D, necessary for bone and muscle health and a possible protective factor for many diseases, including colon cancer. Given the worry about sun exposure and skin cancer, the question remains: How does one achieve favorable vitamin D levels yet also practice skin cancer prevention?

Cervical cancer, so easily and inexpensively prevented, remains a major killer among women in resource-poor nations. Without screening intervention, morbidity and mortality will continue to increase. Sankaranarayanan, Thara, Ngoma, Naud, and Keita have published groundbreaking research on the topic, and in this chapter they present a comprehensive overview of the issue, including evidence convincingly showing that screening for human papillomavirus (HPV) can yield a significant reduction in the numbers of advanced cervical cancers and deaths from this disease. They review the current status and future prospects for controlling cervical cancer in developing countries in this chapter. Low-tech screening methods (often used because most rural areas cannot realistically conduct Pap smear screening) and a single round of screening for HPV can and does result in a dramatic reduction in the incidence of advanced cervical cancer. There is a huge potential to reduce the cervical cancer burden by means of HPV vaccination. The authors acknowledge that a recommendation for HPV vaccination for adolescence women for a disease that occurs during adulthood is a major paradigm shift in cervical cancer control. Although HPV vaccination holds great promise, and has been licensed for use in more than 100 countries, there are several challenges (notably cost) for its widespread implementation through national immunization programs in high-risk developing countries. Cervical cancer reflects striking global health inequity, resulting in deaths of women in their most productive years in developing countries, with a devastating effect on the society at large. It remains as the largest single cause of years of life lost to cancer in the developing world.

Section 3 of volume 2 focuses on the treatment and prevention of infectious diseases. So much has been written about HIV/AIDS over the past two decades and so much progress has been made in extending life expectancy among those with the disease. Demars takes a broad view of the epidemic, tracing its history and focusing on the global burden of the disease. While recent trend data indicate that the incidence in Africa has appreciably slowed, dealing with the disease's sociopsychological sequela and ensuring that progress made is not eroded remain challenges both in the industrial world and the resource-poor, hard-hit part of the world.

The WHO estimates that more than 500 million individuals worldwide are infected with the hepatitis B or C virus. Hepatitis viruses are found in every part of the world and often cause infections ranging in severity from acute infections that are asymptomatic to fulminate, chronic infections, which in some instances can lead to cirrhosis and hepatocellular carcinoma or even death. Aden presents a focused discussion on the most prevalent hepatitis viruses (A, B, and C) and explains how these diseases remain an important public health concern in both the developing and the industrial world. Whereas hepatitis B is a more serious type of infection than hepatitis A, hepatitis C infection can result in serious liver damage; hepatitis C is one of the leading causes for liver transplantation. While hepatitis A and hepatitis B are vaccine preventable, no vaccine is available for hepatitis C. Risk factors, population at risk, and treatment modalities are presented.

The ebb and flow of sexually transmitted diseases (for example, chlamydia, gonorrhea, and syphilis) has long been a focus of public health practitioners. All three diseases are preventable, treatable with medication, and, in the early stages, curable. Torrone and Peterman of the CDC present an overview of the topic and focus on syphilis specifically. The authors discuss the challenges of sexually transmitted disease (STD) control focusing on trends, efforts at prevention and control, and the challenges that remain. STD control and eradication is possible, but certainly not easy.

Section 4 of volume 2 addresses the treatment and prevention of mental health illness and disease. The burden of mental health disorders in the United States is substantial with approximately half of the population meeting the criteria for one or more such disorders in their lifetime and almost one-quarter meeting the criteria in any given year.[14] Treatment costs for mental disorders are substantial, rising from $35 billion (in 2006 dollars) to nearly $58 billion, making it the costliest medical condition between 1996 and 2006.[15] The most prevalent class of disorders is anxiety disorders (for example, phobias, panic disorders, and the like) followed by impulse-control disorders, mood disorders (for example, major depressive disorders, bipolar disorders, and the like), and substance abuse disorders (for example, alcohol abuse or dependence, drug abuse or dependence, and the like). The most prevalent type of disorder is major depressive disorders. Most individuals with a lifetime mental disorder had their first onset in childhood or adolescence. Little is known about the epidemiology of child mental disorders and controversy exists about how best to treat children. Contributors to this section focus on specific mental disorders, such as depression, suicide, and substance abuse.

Depressive disorders are prevalent conditions among the general population, and the medical, public health, and economic consequences of depression are considerable. Tedeschini, Cassano, and Fava present an overview of depressive disorders and focus on the recognition, management, and treatment of these diseases. The authors stress that depression is underdiagnosed and undertreated as only half of all Americans with depression receive treatment of any kind. Despite the availability of numerous effective treatments, many depressive disorders are often misdiagnosed. Several factors contributing to the poor recognition of depression have been identified, ranging from the stigma of depression itself to the relative lack of systematic ascertainment of depressive symptoms by physicians.

Barber and Miller focus on the topic of suicide both within the Untied States as well as globally. In their informative and scholarly piece, they review the salient aspects of the epidemiology of suicide and the challenges posed by a purely clinical approach to its prevention. They outline a public health approach to suicide prevention, with an emphasis on reducing a suicidal person's access to lethal means of suicide. Their thesis clearly illustrates that although suicide is a global problem, a public health approach to prevention is still in its infancy. Public health strategies, such as changing cultural attitudes, increasing social support, improving access to high-quality treatment, and perhaps most important, reducing access to lethal means are measures that can and should be implemented.

Griffin examines the data on substance use and abuse across the life span from early adolescence to late adulthood. There is great diversity in patterns of alcohol, tobacco, and other drug use over the life course, with some individuals abstaining from use throughout their lives and others facing ongoing battles with substance abuse and dependence. The focus is primarily on substance use rather than abuse, because substance use is more prevalent than abuse in the general population and therefore has a greater public health impact. A goal of the chapter is to examine the extent to which substance use can be thought of as a developmental phenomenon not only among young people, but also throughout the life course. The implications of a life span developmental perspective to guide substance use prevention efforts are discussed. Griffin highlights a future challenge: the anticipated increase in substance use problems among the elderly and among the baby boomers, the eldest of whom will be reaching age 65 in a few short years. By taking into account how age-related developmental factors can affect substance use, we may be better able to address these and other new prevention challenges in the future.

VOLUME 3

Volume 3 shifts focus to health policy issues. In section 1, Finkel provides a historical overview of comparative health care systems illustrating why and how other industrial nations moved toward universal health care and why the United States did not. The organization, administration, financing, and delivery of health care in several countries are presented in an in-depth analysis. A critique of how health care is delivered and financed in other countries provides a stark contrast to how health care is provided and paid for in the United States.

Quality and patient safety, in addition to cost management, is an important issue in health care policy. Lazar, Dawson, Hyman, Collins, Regan, Kaplan, Green, Cook, and Graham from the New York-Presbyterian Hospital present an overview of quality assurance, quality metrics, and quality evaluation techniques. Performance improvement management methodologies designed to reduce medical errors and safeguard a safe workplace. In 1999, the IOM published a seminal report entitled *To Err Is Human,* which catalyzed an enormous shift in the understanding of medical errors. The IOM report defined an error as an event in which there is a failure of a process to achieve the intended outcome, or where an incorrect process of care was selected initially. An adverse event was defined as an injury to a patient caused by medical management rather than the patient's medical condition. The IOM report concluded that medical errors were responsible for as many as 98,000 deaths in the United States annually. Estimated annual costs of these errors were in the range of $17 billion to $29 billion. The report further opined that injuries caused by errors are inherently preventable. Lazar and colleagues state that achieving better outcomes for patients, lowering overall costs, and improving the patient experience will require the continued investment of time and money to spur innovation and create reliable effectiveness, safety, and efficiency in clinical settings. Measurement and continuous performance improvement are the mainstays of a robust organizational quality assurance program.

Until the 1980s, most people with private insurance in the United States were covered by traditional indemnity plans. As remains the case, the vast majority got their coverage through employment-based plans provided as a tax-exempt benefit. These indemnity plans delegated shopping decisions about what care to buy and where to buy it to individual consumers and their physicians and then relied on consumer cost sharing to contain costs. Specifically, plans used deductibles and coinsurance to create financial accountability for purchases; the notion was that responsibility for resulting out-of-pocket payments would create incentives for cost-conscious shopping. By design, health plans were relegated to a passive role of paying the bills, while providers were reimbursed fee-for-service on a cost basis. Such open-ended insurance schemes laid the foundation for rising costs, which the United States is now trying to reign in. Managed care was an attempt to contain costs, but has not succeeded in doing so. White discusses an alternative, consumer-oriented strategy (Consumer Directed Health Plans, CDHPs) to address the concerns and shortfalls of managed care. The basic nation of CDHPs is that by placing consumers at risk for paying for substantial amounts of care with their own money, this simultaneously will restore control over shopping decisions and increase consumers' motivation for cost-conscious shopping, while introducing savings options will mediate the accompanying increase in exposure to financial risk. White provides an in-depth discussion of CDHPs and their potential effectiveness in managing health care cost increases.

The use of health information technology (health IT) has become an exciting and important field in medicine. Ancker, Kern, Patel, Abramson, and Kaushal present a scholarly overview of the present and future uses of health IT. Health IT has been promoted widely as a potential solution to managing the massive amounts of data and information as well as serving as a cost management tool. The authors discuss the various types of health IT systems and explore the barriers to development and implementation of these technologies. Health IT offers particularly exciting possibilities for improving the quality and efficiency of health care delivery by making essential individual-level medical data more readily accessible at the point of care; improving communication among clinicians, patients, and public health agencies; and providing evidence-based clinical decision support to help clinicians practice according to optimal care guidelines.

Section 2 of volume 3 focuses on the difficult issue of health care disparities. Health status and health outcomes vary markedly among racial and ethnic groups.

According to an IOM report *Unequal Treatment: Confronting Racial and Ethnic Disparities* race and ethnicity remain a significant factor in determining whether an individual receives high-quality care and in determining health outcomes. Race has been shown to be a determinant of the characteristics and qualifications of physicians who patients see, the types of hospital to which a patient is admitted, and the types of procedures they will undergo. The explanations are complex.

Boutin-Foster focuses on diversity and the public health implications of a growing racially and ethnically diverse America. She examines the role academic medical centers can and should play in providing care to this multicultural population. An argument is made for the need to bring the issues of cultural diversity to the forefront of medical education. While progress has been made in increasing the proportion of racial and ethnic minorities in the health care field, the racial and ethnic composition of the health care workforce does not match that of the general population. Would systematic biases in treatment be reduced if the composition of the workforce resembles more closely that of the patient population? While no studies have been done to empirically answer this question, given the extent of disparities and unequal treatment (which have been researched), one could assume that it certainly would not hurt.

Section 3 of volume 3 discusses ethics and human rights issues. Atkinson explores why human rights is crucial to the work of public health, and argues that human rights is a necessary framework for public health. Her chapter explores why a human rights framework is crucial to the work of public health. The human rights framework—in concert with traditional medical ethics—articulates certain values and standards that specify how we should conduct ourselves. She presents an argument for an ethical and legal framework for moving forward the global public health agenda. She believes that the human rights framework offers us a reason to believe in the possibility of change.

Bioethicist de Melo-Martin addresses the ethically charged topic of genetic testing and public health. She presents some of the most significant ethical concerns that arise in relation to the use of genetic tests, discusses matters related to the analytic and clinical validity and utility of genetic tests, and explains how these aspects result in ethical quandaries. She then focuses on the concerns that the use of genetic tests, if such tests prove beneficial for the populations' health, might contribute to furthering existing health inequities. Finally, she discusses ethical issues related to obtaining, or omitting, informed consent and to protecting privacy and confidentiality. Ensuring that people are not unjustly discriminated against because of their genetic or health status requires careful attention to issues of privacy and confidentiality; yet, concerns about privacy need to be balanced against the legitimate public health needs. Focusing on these ethical concerns when making public-policy decisions about implementation of genetic testing and screening is necessary if we want to use these medical technologies in ways that will advance the public's health.

As chronic diseases, including cancer, surpass infectious diseases as the primary causes of death, and as individuals are living longer with their diseases, providing timely access to consistently high-quality end-of-life care has become an important international issue. How we manage the dying patient has both medical and ethical concerns. Tickoo and Glare present a comprehensive overview of the palliative care movement both in the United States as well as in Australia, England, and India. At some point, all humans have to confront the inevitability of end of life. How one prepares for the eventuality of death is a personal and individual matter. What is necessary and important, however, is that end-of-life choices be made clear and available. Providing for end-of-life care is emotionally difficult, thus making it even more imperative that all patients have the option of timely access to palliative care services that are both appropriate and cost-effective.

Section 4 of volume 3 focuses on public health practice and education. Trushin and Bang present an interesting chapter on the role of epidemiology and biostatistics in health news reporting. In their thoughtful piece focusing on the role of uncertainty in science, they provide a comprehensive overview of the mechanisms of research and statistical analysis. The scientific method is based largely on common sense, and statistical thinking involves concepts that are accessible to all: an acceptance of chance and uncertainty, an appreciation of context, an ability to detect logical and factual flaws in information and ideas, and the realization that science is a fluid process whereby new empirical evidence is accumulated every day. The true spirit of science requires a healthy skepticism, which means suspended judgment and the use of reason to evaluate the validity of research results. Science thrives on these qualities, because they lead to a search for knowledge and ensure that the scientific method remains self-correcting.

Evidence-based medicine has been incorporated into the medical school curriculum, but it also has a role in public health practice. The design and use of public health actions that are effective in promoting health and preventing disease underlie the growing field of evidence-based public health (EBPH), which emerged in the 1990s to improve the *practice* of public health. Maylahn, Brownson, and Fielding describe the concepts and principles underlying EBPH, the analytic tools to enhance the adoption of evidence-based decision making, the dissemination and implementation in public health practice, and challenges and opportunities for more widespread use of EBPH, especially through state and local health departments. Unlike solving a math problem, significant decisions in public health must balance science and art, because rational, evidence-based decision making often involves choosing one alternative from among a set of rational choices. By applying the concepts of EBPH outlined in their chapter, the authors concluded that decision making and, ultimately, public health practice can be improved.

The American Association of Medical Colleges (AAMC) is the umbrella organization for U.S. medical schools. The AAMC's position on medical curriculum has far-reaching impact. Maeshiro of the AAMC presents an informative historical overview of the tensions and barriers to integrating the disciplines of clinical medicine and public health. The challenge of incorporating public health content into the standard medical curriculum is not new. Not surprisingly, the roots of this struggle are entwined with the historical events and trends that led to the separation, or "schism" as some have described, between the practice of medicine and the practice of public health in the United States. She relates how over time the disciplines have gradually moved toward an integrated whole both at the medical school curriculum level and at the postgraduate medical training level. The rise of a specialty in preventive medicine, the development of a residency in preventive medicine, and the subsequent creation of board certification in this area are interrelated. The framework in which medical education exists (for example, accreditation criteria for both medical school and residency training, national examination content) acknowledge the need for physicians to have a population perspective.

Section 5 of volume 3 addresses some of the challenges public health faces as we move into the second decade of the 21st century. Few areas of biomedical science have aroused as much controversy as embryonic stem cell research. With advances in medical research and technology, stem cell research has proliferated around the world. Cauley addresses the stem cell debate, focusing on the medical, ethical, legal, and political aspects of the topic. He provides a scholarly overview of the short history of stem cell research and raises important questions that need to be addressed today and into the future.

Advances in computer science have opened a new area of research for global disease monitoring. McEntee, Castronovo, Jagai, and Naumova from Tufts University provide an overview of a number of advanced computational and analytical techniques that open new opportunities to examine the role of forecasting disease transmission and manifestation. They review applications of various remote sensing (RS) techniques and present the relatively nascent epidemiological applications of this technology. Public health applications of RS data are no longer new; spatial epidemiology is equally important as the strictly environmental applications for which RS was originally intended. This is not surprising because environmental studies and epidemiology are inextricably linked. Each provides information on human health conditions and the corresponding management of environmental resources. Climate and land-use change and variability can be measured remotely and corresponding effects of alterations in natural and built environments can be predicted. Their scholarly and thoughtful presentation of this new field illustrates the tremendous opportunities that can be tapped.

Smith's concluding remarks on thinking creatively about public health in the 21st century is an excellent historical wrap-up of key events in public health over the centuries. He provocatively asks what the public health field needs to do to meet the challenges. How should public health be shaped for the 21st century, both for its own sake as a critical field for the world's well-being and for the sake of the local and global public it serves? The answers to these questions, of course, are multilevel and multifaceted. He advocates that 21st-century public health should begin to look more rigorously at the multiple factors in a society that predict health outcomes. These factors include economics, housing, nutrition, sports and recreation, education, spirituality, family structure, gender relations, childcare, transportation, and whatever other factors make up an integrated human life. Those concerned with the improvement of health on a local, national, and global scale need to work collectively rather than in isolation. Health, after all, is a product of the multiple facets of society, and, as such, requires a multifaceted approach to health promotion, the prevention and treatment of disease, and, most important, the improvement of the quality of life for all people.

This is an exciting time for public health. As public health practitioners continue to work toward improvement in the health and well-being of populations around the world and focus on disease eradication and the prevention and control of diseases, injury, and disability, this increasingly is being achieved in a global context for the potential benefit of all. It is the aim of this multivolume reference text to identify and analyze the diversity of the work being conducted in the contemporary public health landscape.

The tremendous effort that went into creating this multivolume text could not have been done without the generosity of the contributing authors. My appreciation for their time, their enthusiasm, and their scholarship, and especially their friendship, cannot be underestimated.

Madelon L. Finkel, PhD
New York City

REFERENCES

1. Winslow C-EA. The untilled fields of public health. *Science*. 1920; 51:23.
2. D. Cutler D, Miller G. The Role of public health improvements in health advances: the 20th century United States. http://www.nber.org/papers/w10511. National Bureau of Economic Research working paper w10511. Published May 2004.
3. Bunker JP, Frazier HS, Mosteller F. Improving health: measuring effects of medical care. *Milbank Quarterly*. 1994; 72:225–258.
4. Ten great public health achievements—United States, 1900–1999. *MMWR*. 1999; 48(12): 241–243. http://www.cdc.gov/mmwr/.
5. World Health Organization. *The World Health Report 2003-Shaping the Future*. Geneva, Switzerland: World Health Organization; 2003.
6. Health: Confronting the Challenges. http://www.usaid.gov/our_work/global_health/home/confrontingfactsheet.html.
7. G8. G8 communiqué. http://www.g8.utoronto.ca/summit/2000okinawa/finalcom.htm. Okinawa 2000.
8. Group of Seventy-Seven. Final communiqué adopted by the thirty-fourth meeting of chairmen/coordinators of the chapters of the Group of 77. http://www.g77.org/news/pr062703.htm. June 26–27, 2003; Geneva, Switzerland.
9. Alwan A, MacLean D, Mandil A. *Assessment of National Capacity for Non-Communicable Disease Prevention and Control*. Geneva, Switzerland: World Health Organization; 2001.
10. United Nations Development Programme. Millennium Goals. http://www.undp.org/mdg.
11. National Vital Statistics Report. Births, Marriages, Divorces, and Deaths. Vol. 57, No. 12. March 18, 2009. www.cdc.gov/nchs/data.
12. Trends in health care expenditures by body mass index (BMI) category for adults in the US civilian noninstitutionalized population. http://www.meps.ahrq.gov/mepsweb/data_files/publications/st247/stat247.pdf.
13. Annual report to the nation on the status of cancer: 1975–2006, featuring colorectal cancer trends and impact of interventions (risk factors, screening, and treatment) to reduce future rates. In BK Edwards, eds. *Cancer*. Lawrenceville, GA: Surveillance Research Program, National Cancer Institute.
14. Kessler RC, Wang PS. The descriptive epidemiology of commonly occurring mental disorders in the United States. *Annu Rev Public Health*. 2008; 29:115–129.
15. The five most costly conditions, 1996 and 2006: estimates for the US civilian noninstitutionalize population. http://www.meps.ahrq.gov/mepsweb/data_files/publications/st248/stat248.pdf.

SECTION 1

HEALTH CARE POLICY

CHAPTER 1

Comparative Health Care Systems: How Does the United States Stack Up?

Madelon L. Finkel, PhD

The U.S. Congressional Budget Office (CBO) projects that without significant changes in federal policy, total spending on health care would rise to 25 percent of the gross domestic product (GDP) by 2025, and rise to 50 percent by 2082. Furthermore, the two major public programs, Medicare and Medicaid, are estimated to account for 4 percent of the GDP in 2025 and almost 20 percent by 2082.[1] The CBO has gone on record as stating that the U.S. federal budget is on an unsustainable course primarily because of the rising cost of health care. Clearly, health care represents a large and growing component of the American GDP, and some sort of "meaningful reform" clearly is needed. Of course, the devil is in the details; what constitutes "meaningful reform" is being hotly debated. In addition, and adding to the current debate about health care reform, more than 45 million Americans do not have health care insurance, primarily because they cannot afford it. Half of all bankruptcies are a result of unpaid medical bills, and this situation exists both for those with and for those without health insurance coverage. Other nations do not spend nearly as much on health care, and every major country provides universal coverage for its citizens. What are they doing "right"? And, what is the U.S. doing "wrong"? This chapter seeks to provide an overview of comparative health care systems and then focus on the U.S. system. Historical events provide insight into how each system evolved and how the U.S. system, in particular, became so dysfunctional.

WHAT CAN WE LEARN FROM OTHER COUNTRIES?

Health care systems vary according to the extent of government involvement in providing care, ranging from nationalized health care systems (such as in the United Kingdom and Sweden) to decentralized private or nonprofit institutions (such as in Germany and France). Each country had to make a decision as to how the health care system would be organized, administered, and financed. A single-payer type of health insurance, for example, characterizes the Canadian system. The United

Kingdom has the most socialized system in the world, with the government controlling all aspects of health care delivery and financing. Multipayer systems are used in France and Germany in which health care is primarily financed by publicly controlled insurers.

In terms of financing a health care system, there are many different approaches. Publicly funded health care financing relies on a publicly managed fund. In some countries, the fund is controlled directly by the government or by an agency of the government for the benefit of the entire population. In contrast, private health insurance provides coverage only to those under contractual obligation between the insured or his sponsor and an insurance company, which basically seeks to make a profit by managing the flow of funds between funders and providers of health care. In terms of administration, health care may be administered and provided by the government (United Kingdom), or may be publicly funded, but health providers are private entities (the Canadian and French system). In other compulsory insurance models, health care is financed through funds (such as in Germany), which themselves are funded from a number of places, including employees' salary deductions, employers' contributions, and so forth.

Regardless of the type of health care system in place, health care spending around the world is rising at a faster rate than overall economic growth. Almost all countries have seen an increase in health care spending as a percentage of their GDP. Health spending is also rising faster than incomes in most developed nations, which raises questions about how each will pay for future health care needs. Before getting into actual dollar amounts, it is instructive to understand how individual health care systems evolved. Post–World War II is seen to be the pivotal point in history at which decisions had to be made.

The following provides a cursory overview of selected countries' health systems. Although it is not the intent of this chapter to provide an in-depth analysis of comparative health care systems, it is useful and important to highlight historical events that helped shape each individual nation's health care systems. Doing so both provides a point of comparison and illustrates what the United States might learn from other countries. In Europe, as in Canada, the guiding philosophy was, and still is, based on the principle of social solidarity, which implies that health care should be financed by individuals on the basis of their ability to pay, but it should be available to all who need it on roughly equal terms. Each of the countries discussed below mandates that individuals—regardless of economic status, employment status, age, sex, or any other demographic factor for that matter—must be covered by the state insurance scheme. Health care coverage is portable and comprehensive in scope of benefits. Nobody is denied coverage based on an inability to pay. All provide freedom of choice of providers.

GREAT BRITAIN

In Great Britain, during the early 1940s, Winston Churchill and his government made the decision to move millions of people from the cities to the countryside in the days before declaring war on Germany. Moving a large segment of the population to the countryside, however, necessitated that local social services be built up. Hospitals and physicians had to be available and a means to pay for their services had to be put in place. The government established a national Emergency Medical Service to supplement the local services, and hundreds of hospitals were built, essential medical services (laboratory, radiology, ambulances, and so forth) were upgraded, and the Ministry of Health oversaw the operation of these services. As the war progressed, the government was compelled to provide free hospital treatment for civilians as well as for those in the military. During the German Blitz, most of the private hospitals and clinics were destroyed. Few individuals could afford to pay for private health care. As a result, the government ended up paying for medical care and doctors received a government salary for the portion of their time spent caring for patients.

While this emergency wartime health care system was intended to be temporary, after the war, both patients and providers alike did not want to see the new system discontinued. Sir William Beveridge was asked to prepare a postwar government plan for the provision of health care. The Beveridge Report on British Social Security called for comprehensive health care based on a tax-based national health service.[2] The report proposed widespread reform to the social welfare system, including the creation of the National Health Service (NHS). The National Health Service Act 1946 came into effect on July 5, 1948, and created the NHS in England and Wales; a separate NHS was created for Scotland at the same time. The NHS is accountable directly to the central government's Department of Health and Social Security, as well as to Parliament. The main principle was that a free, comprehensive health service should be available to all British citizens and legal residents, regardless of income. The system was very much a pragmatic outgrowth of postwar recovery efforts in war-damaged Britain.

A major characteristic of the NHS universal health care system is that it is universal, comprehensive, and paid for by tax-based financing.[3] Funding for the NHS is met from tax contributions paid by all persons over the age of 18 and employers in the United Kingdom. The system employs the physicians and nurses and owns most of the hospitals and clinics. The NHS also pays directly for the health care expenses. More than 1 million individuals are employed in some capacity by the NHS, and more than 2,500 hospitals and other health care organizations are included in the system. Essentially, the NHS is a single-payer system, in which the government is the nation's only health care purchaser. Individuals have the freedom to choose a provider, a general practitioner (GP), practicing in their geographic area.

Since its inception, the British NHS has followed a structured pattern, but that is not to say that reform efforts have not been initiated. As the costs of the system soared, as waiting time for hospital admissions increased, and as hospitals and health centers were showing signs of age and distress, the Thatcher government's response was privatization. In 1989, the NHS was reorganized to increase the private sector's role. The Conservative Party advocated the transfer of ownership to the private sector and tried to introduce more competitive market forces.[4] These initiatives were made on the basis of limited evidence as to whether the private sector was more efficient than the public sector.

Surveys showed little public support for the replacing the government-managed NHS with a mixed private-public health insurance program.[5] When the Blair Labour government gained control, the NHS system was in need of reform. The system was inefficient, waiting lists for nonurgent procedures were quite long, costs were rising, and facilities needed upgrading. The Blair government allocated more money to the system, established the National Institute for Clinical Excellence as part of a modernization program, and created Strategic Health Authorities (SHAs), which are responsible for managing, monitoring, and improving local services in their regions. SHAs would be responsible for developing plans for improving health services in the local area, ensuring that the services are of high quality, and making sure that national priorities are integrated into local health service plans.

Furthermore, the Blair government established local Primary Care Trusts (PCTs), designed to organize and manage specific areas of medicine, such as mental health, primary care, ambulance services, acute care (hospitals), and social services. Collectively, PCTs are responsible for spending around 80 percent of the total NHS budget. PCTs have their own budgets and set their own priorities, within the overriding priorities and budgets set by the relevant SHA they belong to and the Department of Health (DH). Essentially, the PCT is responsible for planning primary care and community health services in its catchment area, and it contracts with hospitals and hospital consultants for specialty care as well as implementing quality improvement activities.

All physicians must belong to a trust, whether they practice in primary or specialty medicine. Every person in the United Kingdom has the right to choose to register with any GP of their choice practicing in their area. If the GP has contracted to provide NHS services, as virtually all do, then all consultations with the GP will be free of charge to the patient. While far from perfect, the British tax-based system in the 21st century does provide coverage to all. It is free at point of delivery, ensures choice of providers, and is comprehensive in scope. But, there is a chronic shortage of specialists in every field and there are the legendary long waiting lists, which stem from chronic underfunding and an undersupply of personnel and equipment. The NHS is well designed but chronically underprovisioned. Britain spends less of its GDP on health care spending than other nations yet faces massive deficits. The estimated cost of the NHS in England (the most populous part of the United Kingdom) in 2008 is £91.7 billion. The government has painful choices to make between cutting expenditures and raising taxes.[6] No other country has adopted the British system; each has implemented a unique universal system to reflect its specific needs and circumstances.

FRANCE

The 21st-century French health care system evolved from the 19th-century mutual aid societies. The 19th century had been marked by the rapid rise of the mutual benefit movement, which is still an important force in French political life. Manufacturers and unions formed collective insurance funds, which were financed through a self-imposed payroll tax; there were no set premiums. After World War II, the de Gaulle government, like the British government, had to focus on rebuilding the nation; money was limited and the pressing needs of society so great that the government was not willing or able to craft a new health care system.

The 21st century system of social security, including statutory health insurance, was established in 1945. With the end of the war, France established the *Sécurité Sociale*, an expanded program of health care and pension benefits. The postwar government built on what already existed and expanded the payroll tax-funded system to cover all wage earners, their families, and retirees. (Self-employed and the uninsured were included decades later.) Although controlled by the French government, "social partners" (the trade unions and employer representatives) became active players in managing the French health care system.

The French National Health Insurance (NHI) scheme is an integral part of France's social security system, which ensures that all residents automatically be enrolled with an insurance fund based on their occupational status; health insurance is compulsory. The *Sécurité Sociale* is characterized as having universal coverage funded by payroll tax–financed insurance primarily through more than 140 independent, nonprofit, local insurance funds. Health insurance funds are not permitted to compete by lowering health insurance premiums or attempting to micromanage health care. Employer payroll taxes finance half of the NHI expenditures; "general social contributions" levied by the government on all earnings, including investment income, covers the rest. Employers, employee contributions, and personal income taxes fund the system. Of note is the fact that the working population has 20 percent of its gross salary deducted to fund the social security system.

The system is a public-private mix of hospital and ambulatory care. It is characterized as a solo-based, fee-for-service private practice for ambulatory care and public hospital system for acute institutional care. Patients are free to choose their hospital and their physician and are reimbursed under the NHI.[7] Nine out of 10 Frenchmen purchase supplementary health insurance to cover other benefits not reimbursed under the NHI. For ambulatory care, all health insurance plans operate on the traditional indemnity model—that is, reimbursement for services rendered. In the inpatient hospital services sector, there are budgetary allocations as well as per diem reimbursements. Physicians are private practitioners and are paid directly by the patient on the basis of a national fee schedule. Patients are then reimbursed by their local health insurance fund. The overwhelming number of practitioners comply with the *Tarif de convention* (tariff references), which sets reimbursement prices. Tariff references are the fixed rates to be used by doctors and are set by the national convention. Medical practitioners and clinics and hospitals that are not *conventions* have to display their prices. Public hospitals are paid on the basis of annual global budgets that are negotiated every year. Proprietary hospitals, which any insured citizen can go to, are reimbursed on a negotiated per diem basis.

As is the case with other peer nations, France is coping with rising health care costs. The deficit of the *Sécurité Sociale* is a concern to the government, which periodically considers reducing the amount of reimbursement to providers. As a result, more individuals are turning to *l'assurance complémentaire* (complementary insurance). This health insurance covers all or part of the costs not reimbursed by the national health system.

The French system is an interesting model for the United States. It is highly regarded and was ranked as the number one health care system in the world by the World Health Organization (WHO) in 2000. It provides universal coverage yet allows physicians to be private small business owners. It incorporates the private insurance sector yet is government administered. Individuals are guaranteed access to specialists and hospitals without going through a gatekeeper. There is no rationing of care to speak of. Although far from perfect, the system is highly regarded by the French, as consumer and provider satisfaction is consistently high.

GERMANY

Germany has the world's oldest universal health care system, with origins dating back to Otto von Bismarck's Health Insurance Act of 1883. Germany's system is almost elegant in its simplicity, as described by health economist Uwe Reinhardt.[8] The system is decentralized (regionalized) with private practice physicians providing ambulatory care, and independent, mostly nonprofit hospitals providing the majority of inpatient care. Approximately 91 percent of the population is covered by a Statutory Health Insurance plan, which is financed by a payroll tax; the individual's premium is not a per capita levy but is income based. The plan provides a standardized level of coverage through any one of approximately 1,100 public or private sickness funds. Insurance payments are based on a percentage of income, divided between employee and employer.[9] Standard insurance is funded by a combination of employee contributions, employer contributions, and government subsidies on a scale determined by income level. Higher income workers sometimes choose to pay a tax and opt out of the standard plan, in favor of private insurance.[10]

The system is characterized by employer-employee financing rather than funding obtained solely from general taxes. Mandated coverage and employer and employee contributions have been the mainstay of the system from the beginning. The premiums paid by individuals and employers are collected by the government, which essentially serves as a risk-pooling entity for the entire system. Physicians and hospitals are paid by the sickness funds based on negotiated reimbursement rates. Although the national government sets national standards, the regions are powerful forces in shaping the federal legislation of standards for their region. The sickness funds, for example, traditionally have been allowed to set their own premium rates.

The German system includes portability of benefits should one move from one region of the country to another. Furthermore, health insurance remains unchanged for all workers during unemployment (unemployment insurance pays the premiums for unemployed individuals as their contributions to the national health insurance are paid for by a federally administered statutory unemployment insurance fund). An employee's nonworking spouse is covered automatically by the employee's premium, and retirees and the elderly are covered as well (pension funds share with the elderly in financing their premiums, which are set below actuarial costs for the elderly). Premiums for children are covered by the government out of general revenues.

The guiding principles of the German health care system (solidarity, decentralization, and nonstate operations) have not changed much since its inception. There is freedom of choice of providers and sickness funds; there is professional autonomy; there are comprehensive benefits; there are no waiting lines so to speak. Yet, as is true with every other nation, health care costs have been rising and there is a shortage of nurses. The most important topics for current and future reforms are financing and reimbursement, health technology assessment, and the fragmentation of health care between sectors and payers and collectivism versus competition.[11]

CANADA

The Canadian single-payer system is a universal health care system that is provincially based. That is, each of the 10 provinces and 3 sparsely populated northern territories is responsible for administering and financing health care for its legal citizens. Just after the end of the war in 1946, the first Canadian province, Saskatchewan, introduced near-universal health coverage. Saskatchewan, a rural farming province, had long suffered a shortage of doctors. It also had a long history of government involvement in providing health care—for example, in the early 20th century, the province established a municipal doctor program in which a town would subsidize a doctor to practice there, which laid the foundation for the single-payer system to be in place in the 21st century. In 1950, the province of Alberta introduced a similar program and later other provinces followed suit.

The passage of the Hospital Insurance and Diagnostic Services Act of 1957 (the HIDS Act) provided further impetus for provinces to establish their own health care systems. The act outlined five conditions for a health care system: public administration, comprehensiveness, universality, portability, and accessibility, and provided up to 50 percent of the costs of a health program for any provincial government that agreed to adopt these conditions. By 1961, all 10 provinces had some sort of health care system in place under the HIDS Act. Thus, a significant proportion of health care already was controlled and paid for by the provincial government. The HIDS Act served to lay the foundation for the Canada Health Act of 1984, which specified the conditions and criteria with which the provincial and territorial health insurance programs had to conform to receive federal money. These criteria require universal coverage for all "insured persons" and for all "medically necessary" hospital and physician services without copayments.

Ottawa provides funding for specific programs, but the provinces individually organize and administer their own health care system. To receive money from the federal government, each province has only to comply with a few conditions: operate a nonprofit insurance plan, provide comprehensive benefits, ensure that the plan is universal in scope to all insured persons of the province, ensure portability should insured people move between provinces, and be accessible.[12] Under the Canadian plans, physicians are small businessmen largely working with a high degree of autonomy under a fee-for-service system. Bills are submitted directly to the single payer, which greatly reduces the administrative overhead in administering the program. Individuals have freedom of choice of providers.

No system is perfect, and the Canadian system is no exception. There are waiting lists, varying considerably by procedure and province. Costs have increased and there is evidence of cost shifting. For example, inpatients receive full coverage for pharmaceuticals. Once they are discharged, these costs need no longer be paid for from public funds. Some provinces will pay for these costs, but others do not. As such, two-thirds of Canadians have some sort of supplementary private health insurance.

SWITZERLAND

Although the above countries' approaches to health care delivery and financing encompasses variations of a public-private mix, Switzerland, a confederation of states, has a system that might be more palatable for the United States. Health care is regulated by the Federal Health Insurance Act of 1994. In 1996, Switzerland mandated that individuals purchase health insurance covering a range of benefits that are set out in detail in the Federal Act. Since it had no experience with a public system, the private nonprofit insurance industry filled the void. In this case, purchase is made from nonprofit private insurers who compete in the market place. The basic benefit package is set by law and is deemed to be quite generous; there is freedom of choice of providers. The government provides subsidies for those who cannot afford coverage.[13]

The compulsory insurance can be supplemented by a private insurance policy that would provide coverage for some of the treatment categories not covered by the basic insurance or to improve the standard of room and service in case of hospitalization. Although the level of premium can vary from one company to another, they must be identical within the same company for all insured persons of the same age-group and region, regardless of sex or state of health. This does not apply to complementary insurance in which premiums are risk-based.

Although a small and fairly homogeneous nation, Switzerland provides universal coverage, mandates that everyone purchase insurance from nongovernmental insurers, and delivers care without long waiting lists. Of course, there are issues such as containing rising costs but this system has been viewed as a model for the United States that might be acceptable to both Republicans and Democrats.

IMPLICATIONS FOR THE UNITED STATES

The countries discussed above each had to decide how best to provide health care coverage to their citizens. Each made the decision to provide, indeed mandate, affordable health care to its legal citizens. In terms of funding the health care system, each took a different path: Great Britain relies on a tax-based system; France collects general revenues and also levies a mandatory payroll tax to fund its insurance system. Germany relies primarily on work-based social insurance contributions as well as federal taxes. Canada funds its system through a national and provincial general revenue scheme, and Switzerland mandates that everyone purchase health care coverage from nongovernmental insurers. None is superior to the others; each "works," although cost control efforts and efficiencies in administration and organization clearly are necessary in every system.

In terms of satisfaction with one's health care system, citizens in these countries generally tend to be pleased. They have expressed concerns about rising costs but, by and large, people are satisfied with their system, and none reported that they would want the U.S. system to replace their own. A survey addressing this issue found that while the British were the most satisfied with their health care system, there were problems with wait times. Canadians, also very satisfied with their health care system, reported difficulties in seeing a specialist due to shortages of physicians. Wait times also topped the list of public concern.[14]

Regarding ability to get care in a timely manner or ability to see a doctor also in a timely manner, every country limits or rations health care to some extent. The United States is no exception, even for those with health care coverage. What other countries do not have is a burdensome, bloated administrative structure. Whereas the administrative costs for private insurance in the United States is approximately

25 cents on every dollar, the public programs, Medicare and Medicaid, have an administrative cost of between 4 and 8 cents per dollar. France's administrative costs are 4 cents per dollar and Canada's are 6 cents per dollar, as a point of comparison. The U.S. system is fragmented, costly, confusing, and unfair to many. In Europe, for example, nobody is denied services or care. In the United States, however, claims are denied routinely.

In terms of quality, an international comparison study found that each country performs well in some areas and poorly in others.[15] Based on 21 quality indicators, the study found that no country performed consistently better or worse than the others; each country in the study had at least one area of care where it could learn from the others. The study found that the United States performed relatively well, but because the American system is so expensive, it probably is not getting good value for its medical care dollar. More spending is not buying better outcomes.

The United States has the dubious distinction of being the only industrial country that does not have a universal health care system. Whether a government-mandated system of universal health care should be implemented in the United States remains a hotly debated political topic, with Americans divided in their views of the U.S. health care system and what should be done to improve it. What is clear, however, is that the United States spends far more per capita on health care, expends the highest proportion of its GDP on health care compared with peer nations, and has the most rapid growth rates in health spending than other nations. Little evidence indicates that the United States gets better value for its higher health care spending.[16]

OECD DATA

Data collected by the Organisation for Economic Co-operation and Development (OECD), a 30-country organization known as a premium statistical agency that publishes highly comparable statistics on a wide number of subjects including health care, are useful to make cross-national comparisons. Recent publications show that the United States continues to spend much more on health care both as a proportion of the GDP and per capita than any other OECD country, yet U.S. life expectancy is lower than would be predicted based on U.S. per capita income. Table 1.1 shows comparative data depicting total health expenditures per capita. Health spending per capita is at least 24 percent higher than in the next highest spending countries and more than 90 percent higher than in many other countries that are considered global competitors to the United States.[17] Whereas Switzerland, Sweden, and Denmark had levels of per capita health spending somewhat comparable to the United States in 1980, these countries had much lower average annual growth rates in health spending than the United States since then. This lower growth rate implies that, unlike the United States, other nations managed to control better levels of health spending.[17] Total health expenditures as a share of the GDP in the United States continues to outpace that for other comparable nations (see table 1.2).

Despite spending far more on health care, the U.S. health care system provides less access to health care resources. That is, the United States has fewer physicians, nurses, hospital beds, doctor visits, and hospital days per capita than the median OECD country.[18] What then is a plausible explanation for this situation? Analysts have concluded that U.S. prices for health resources are much higher than in other OECD countries.[19] It is well known that most newly graduated physicians have crushing tuition debt. Many medical schools in other countries do not charge tuition or, if they do, the amount is quite modest. Perhaps, then, it is not surprising that health care workers' salaries are higher in the United States than in other countries.

Other factors also account for the difference. An inpatient hospital stay in the United States is more service-intensive and more expensive than in other nations, even though the length of stay tends to be shorter in the United States. Furthermore, the fragmented, dysfunctional administrative structure in the United States does not lend itself to cost efficiencies. Anderson et al. therefore concluded that the crucial role of prices as drivers of cross-national differences in health spending is the most likely explanation for the differences.[19] Other countries rely on supply constraints to control their health care spending—that is, limiting the number of hospital beds that can be built; putting controls on the diffusion of medical technology; and limiting the number of physicians, which has led to shortages in some countries.

U.S. STATISTICS

The need for fundamental transformation of the U.S. health care system has become increasingly apparent. Research reveals a fragmented system fraught with

Table 1.1
Total Health Expenditures per Capita, United States and Selected Countries, 2003

Country	Total Health Expenditure per Capita (in U.S. dollars)
Australia	$2,886
Austria	$2,958
Belgium	$3,044
Canada	$2,998
Denmark	$2,743
Finland	$2,104
France	$3,048
Germany	$2,983
Iceland	$3,159
Ireland	$2,455
Italy	$2,314
Japan	$2,249
Luxembourg	$4,611
Netherlands	$2,909
Norway	$3,769
Sweden	$2,745
Switzerland	$3,847
United Kingdom	$2,317
UNITED STATES	$5,711

Source: Adapted from the Organisation for Economic Co-operation and Development. OECD Health Data, 2006. http//www.oecd.org/health/healthdata.

Table 1.2
Total Health Expenditures as Percent Share of GDP, United States and Selected Countries, 2003

Country	Total Health Expenditure as Percent Share of GDP
Australia	9.2
Austria	9.6
Belgium	10.1
Canada	9.9
Denmark	8.9
Finland	7.4
France	10.4
Germany	10.8
Iceland	10.5
Ireland	7.2
Italy	8.4
Japan	8.0
Luxembourg	7.7
Netherlands	9.1
Norway	10.1
Sweden	9.3
Switzerland	11.5
United Kingdom	7.8
UNITED STATES	15.2

Source: Adapted from the Organisation for Economic Co-operation and Development. OECD Health Data, 2006. http//www.oecd.org/health/healthdata.
Note: GDP = gross domestic product.

waste and inefficiency. The administrative overhead in America is huge by international standards. For example, a study of administrative costs in the U.S. and Canadian health care systems showed that Americans spent more than $1,000 per capita on administration compared with only $307 in purchasing power parity dollars spent in Canada.[20] Purchasing power parity is an economic theory that estimates the amount of adjustment needed on the exchange rate between countries in order for the exchange to be equivalent to each currency's purchasing power. Although the disparity is huge, it is important to cite that these figures are based on 1999 dollars. Most certainly the gap has widened over the years. Contributing to this excess administrative overhead is the underwriting and marketing of the complex private insurance system. Ironically, the government programs (Medicare, Medicaid, and the Veterans Administration) have a much lower administrative overhead, comparable to that seen in Canada and Europe.

The excess spending inherent in the U.S. system refers to the difference between what a country spends per person on health care and what the country's GDP per person should predict that that country would spend.[21] The United States spends nearly 40 percent more on health care per capita than its GDP per capita would predict. High spending, however, has not translated into better health. The

WHO in 2000 commissioned an analysis of the world's health care systems. Using five performance indicators to measure health systems in 191 member states, it declared that France provides the best overall health care. The United States health care system was ranked first in both responsiveness and expenditure, but 37th in overall performance and 72nd by overall level of health. In contrast, the United Kingdom, which spent just 6 percent of GDP on health services, ranked 18th.[22]

Despite spending more on health care overall and per capita, Americans do not live as long as citizens of several other industrial countries, and disparities in the U.S. system are pervasive, with widespread differences in access to care based on insurance status, income, race, and ethnicity. In all fairness, the WHO report has been heavily criticized and, perhaps as a result, the WHO no longer produces ranking because of the complexity of the task. But, the fact remains that there are real and legitimate questions regarding the access, efficiency, and quality purchased by the high sums spent in the American system compared with all others.

Health care accounts for a large slice of the U.S. economic pie. Each year, health care spending has grown at an average annual rate of almost 10 percent, often outpacing spending on other goods and services. Since 1970, health care costs have grown on average 2.4 percent faster than the GDP.[23] The high and growing cost of health care is not a new issue or a new problem. Over the past decades, the proportion of dollars devoted to health care has increased steadily, causing significant concern among individuals, businesses, and governments (federal, state, and local). Businesses, for example, find it difficult to remain economically competitive when an ever-increasing amount of money has to be allocated to pay for health insurance for their employees. Individuals are chafing because of increases in deductibles and coinsurance, and more recently, because of cost-shifting. Out-of-pocket costs have increased steadily increased. Individuals, even those with insurance, are spending more of their income each year on health care costs despite having coverage.

Health care is expected to grow faster than most other sectors of the economy. Whereas education, transportation, and agriculture tend to grow at rates close to the economy, health care has not and does not. The United States was projected to spend more than $2.5 trillion on health care in 2009 (17.6 percent of the GDP) or $7,400 per person each year. By 2018, spending on health care is estimated to be more than $4.3 trillion. Since 1970, health care spending has risen 3.4 percentage points faster than the GDP, a trend that is not economically sensible.[23] Although health spending is fairly evenly split between the private sector and the public sector, both sectors have experienced persistent and growing increases in the cost of providing health care, creating the impetus for increases in insurance premiums, higher deductibles, cost-shifting, and cost-sharing. Health insurance premium increases have consistently outpaced inflation and the growth in workers' earnings. Premiums are rising faster than overall inflation and workers' wages, and for the 160 million people who receive their health insurance through their employer, the amount paid out of pocket is also increasing.

On the public side, costs for Medicare and Medicaid have increased significantly since their inception in 1965 despite efforts at cost containment. As the baby boomer generation becomes eligible for Medicare, the future anticipated cost burden could sink the program. Moreover, the financial meltdown of 2009 has left tens of thousands of individuals without a job and thus without health care coverage. It is more than likely that many will qualify for Medicaid, thus putting additional pressure on this federal-state program. Not surprisingly, one of the major challenges in enacting health care reform is how to finance it without adding to the already huge federal budget deficit.

CONCLUSION

Equity is about fairness. In health care terms, it is about ensuring equal access to health services for those with equal need, irrespective of personal characteristics (race/ethnicity, sex, geographic area). Every developed nation in the world except the United States has a health care system that guarantees affordable health care for its citizens. For those Americans who have health insurance, the cost of purchasing insurance coverage continues to increase rapidly. Ever-increasing premiums represent a serious problem for many. A survey by the Kaiser Family Foundation found that the average premium for a family policy in 2009 was more than $13,000. In 1999, the cost was $5,800. Although premium increases have decreased from double-digit increases seen in the late 1990s and early 2000s, the 5 percent premium increase in 2009 still outpaced the 3.1 percent growth in wages. Also, premium increases are still going up faster than overall inflation and workers' wages.[23] The Kaiser report also presented some very scary numbers: if one takes the average of premium increases over the last 10 years, an annual health insurance premium in 2019, just nine years away, could top $24,000. Clearly the system cannot continue on its present path.

What we are seeing is a not-so-gradual unraveling of the employment-based system that has been in place for decades. Rising health care costs is the most significant driver of America's long-term debt and deficits. The need for reform is quite clear. How the United States got itself into this mess is the subject of the next chapter.

REFERENCES

1. Congressional Budget Office. http://www.cbo.gov/publications/collections/health.cfm.
2. Abel-Smith B. The Beveridge Report: its origins and outcomes. *Blackwell Synergy: Int Social Security Rev.* 1992;45(1/2):5–16. http://www.blackwell-synergy.com/doi/abs/10.1111/j.1468-246X.1992.tb00900.x.
3. Light DW. Universal health care: lessons from the British experience. *Am J Public Health.* 2003;93:25–30.
4. Privatization: everybody's doing it differently. *The Economist.* 1985;297:71–73.
5. Blendon RJ, Donelan K. British public opinion on national health service reform. *Health Affairs.* 1989;8(4):52–62.
6. Klein R. Britain's national health service revisited. *N Engl J Med.* 2004;350(9):937–942.
7. Rodwin VG. The health care system under French national health insurance: lessons for health reform in the United States. *Am J Public Health.* 2003;83:31–37.
8. Reinhardt UE. Global budgeting in German health care: insight for Americans. *Domestic Affairs.* 1993;94:159–194.
9. Altenstetter C. Insights from health care in Germany. *Am J Public Health.* 2003;93:38–44.
10. Universal Health Care. http://en.wikipedia.org/wiki/Universal_health_care#Germany.

11. Reinhardt UE. Health reform without a public plan: the German model. *Economix*. http://economix.blogs.nytimes.com. Published April 17, 2009.
12. Deber RB. Health care reform: lessons from Canada. *Am J Public Health*. 2003;93:20–24.
13. Reinhardt UE. The Swiss health system: regulated competition without managed care. *JAMA*. 2004;292:1227.
14. Blendon RJ, et al. Common concerns amid diverse systems: health care experiences in five countries. *Health Affairs*. 2003;22:106–121.
15. Hussey PS, et al. How does the quality of care compare in five countries? *Health Affairs*. 2004;23:89–98.
16. Anderson GF, Frogner BK. Health spending in OECD countries: obtaining value per dollar. *Health Affairs*. 2008;27(6):1718–1727.
17. Organization for Economic Cooperation and Development. OECD health data, 2006: health care spending in the United States and OECD countries. http://www.oecd.org/health/healthdata.
18. Anderson GF, Frogner BK, Reinhardt UE. Health spending in OECD Countries in 2004: an update. *Health Affairs*. 2007;26:1481–1489.
19. Anderson GF, Reinhardt UE, Hussey PS. It's the prices, stupid: why the United States is so different from other countries. *Health Affairs*. 2003;22:89–94.
20. Woolhandler S, Campbell T, Himmelstein MD. Costs of health care administration in the United States and Canada. *N Engl J Med*. 2003;349:768–775.
21. Reinhardt UE. Why does U.S. health care cost so much? Part II: indefensible administrative costs. *Economix*. www.exocnomix.blogs.nytimes.com/2008/11/21. Published November 21, 2008.
22. Blendon RJ, Kim M, Benson JM. The public versus the world health organization on health system performance. *Health Affairs*. 2001;20(3):10–20.
23. Kaiser Family Foundation. Trends in health care costs and spending. http://www.kff.org.

CHAPTER 2

Clinical Quality and Patient Safety

*Eliot J. Lazar, MD, MBA, Anthony Dawson, RN,
Dan Hyman, MD, MMM, Karen Scott Collins, MD, MPH,
Brian K. Regan, PhD, Steven Kaplan, MD,
Robert A. Green, MD, MPH, Joseph T. Cooke, MD,
and Phillip L. Graham III, MD, MPH*

INTRODUCTION

The last 40 years have seen extraordinary advances in health care, not the least of which is the development of the science of quality and patient safety. New methods of implementing and measuring improvement in the outcomes patients' experience, and the relative safety in which medical care is provided, have spawned a virtual industry devoted to these goals. Positions such as chief quality officer, patient safety officer, performance improvement specialist, or "black belt" did not exist as few as 10 to 15 years ago. Improvement methodologies such as Lean, Six Sigma, or Plan, Do, Check, and Act have evolved from a demand by health care organizations to rapidly adopt and implement new policies and procedures designed to minimize errors and improve results. Measurement approaches grow increasingly more sophisticated, although true gold standards remain elusive. New organizations seem to spring up daily, each with a slightly different perspective on just what quality and safety means. This intense focus and emphasis not only underscores society's interest in better medical care, but also has increasing financial ramifications.

Given recent efforts in this area, one would assume that improved quality and patient safety would be relatively easy to achieve, or at least simple to define. As the subsequent text will demonstrate, however, the field is anything but simple. This chapter focuses on the progress made in quality assurance and the challenges that remain. For purposes of the piece, we will use the Institute of Medicine (IOM) definition of quality: "the degree to which health services for individuals and populations increase the likelihood of desired health outcomes and are consistent with current professional knowledge."[1]

QUALITY INDICATORS

Avedis Donabedian is heralded by many as the father of quality assurance. His seminal article "Evaluating the Quality of Medical Care," published in the *Milbank Memorial Fund Quarterly*, in 1966, provided the foundation for modern approaches to the definition and measurement of contemporary clinical quality and safety.[2] Donabedian suggested that quality indicators could be characterized as measuring structure, process, or outcomes.[3] More recently, volume has been added as a fourth indicator. Ironically, in the same issue of the *Milbank Quarterly*, Odin Anderson opined that health care research had minimally affected public policy and that public health decisions were unsupported by scientific evidence.[4]

The last five years have seen an extraordinary number of quality indicators put into use, such as report cards, physician profiles, pay-for-performance, and a host of other applications. Although concerns about their validity persist, they have become a mainstay of public policy debate. Numerous entities have entered the arena of health care evaluation and clearly the discussions around health care reform include quality and access as cornerstones of future programs. Although acute care hospitals and long-term care facilities have been the focus to date, attention is being directed toward the performance of physicians and other health care providers.

DEFINING THE METRICS

If one accepts the modification of Donabedian's original construct, which categorizes quality metrics as volume, structure, outcomes, or process (VSOP), a brief discussion of the advantages and limitations of each is in order.

- **Volume:** In 1916, E. A. Codman postulated that experience was a key driver of hospital based clinical outcomes. "A hospital . . . organized to obtain the best results could not possibly allot such cases to its less experienced surgeons."[5] The basic concept is that higher volumes lead to improved quality. Although numerous papers have demonstrated that volume and quality are related, this has not been a universal finding.[6] Moreover, opinions differ as to whether institutional volume or operator volume is the more important driver, or whether excessively high volumes can erode performance. Despite these concerns, volume metrics remain in use because the data are available in administrative or financial data sets, and theoretically are easily understandable by the lay public.
- **Structure:** Structural metrics are defined by the ability to evaluate them based on yes or no answers—that is, they are binary, leading to easy aggregation and analysis. Structural metrics may be applied to institutions, programs, or practitioners. Examples may include designation as a specialty center, such as level-one trauma or cardiac surgery; qualifications including board certification; or the availability of equipment or technology, such as magnetic resonance imaging (MRI) or computerized practitioner order entry systems. Structural metrics are appealing because they are relatively easy to collect and do not require complicated data aggregation systems. Yet, the utility of structural metrics is limited, given the relative paucity of evidence indicating that they are true determinants of quality.
- **Outcomes:** In many ways, the "outcome of care" achieved by a health care institution or provider is the most critical information desired by stakeholders, especially the patient seeking to choose where to receive care and from whom. Defining outcomes and comparing them among providers is exceptionally challenging. There are confounding variables to consider when looking at even the simplest of outcome measures. For example, when evaluating mortality, does one examine the results at one week, one month, or one year? When does the time period for procedural mortality end? Depending on the methodology, various public health and systems issues may affect the results. The Center for Medicare and Medicaid Services (CMS) has adopted a 30-day mortality definition, which is designed to reduce regional and institutional variability.

Outcomes of care also are determined by a multitude of factors that include, but are not limited to, the capabilities or performance of the institution or organization as well as patient characteristics. Patient populations are different, making comparisons difficult. Risk or Severity Adjustment methodologies are employed to "normalize" the patient populations. At present no standard approach is available, and many of the adjustment algorithms are proprietary, which may pose problems for institutions trying to understand their own results and may create confusion for consumers trying to evaluate the results.

Outcomes data typically are obtained from administrative data sets, which are used primarily for billing purposes and regulatory submissions. Given the process by which data are collected, there is tremendous variability in the accuracy of administrative data. For example, the data are dependent on a process by which a medical records coder reads the medical record (often hand written) and, based on the presence of certain key words, converts the clinical narrative into numerical code. Frequently, symbols and abbreviations are not sufficiently documented. Variability in interpretation and documentation can result in significant differences in coding, which affect any subsequent risk adjustment. This is especially the case with secondary and comorbid conditions that are the basis for the majority of risk-adjustment algorithms.

Recently, the federal government mandated the inclusion of "present on admission" codes that indicate whether a particular comorbid condition was present at the time of admission versus having occurred during the inpatient stay. For example, was the patient admitted with stage II pressure ulcer, or was the pressure ulcer a result of the patient's hospitalization? The answer to this question will influence both risk-adjustment calculations as well as hospital reimbursement. Of course, some outcomes of care measures are well constructed and do provide value to health care institutions, consumers, and payers. Examples include outcomes for children with cystic fibrosis (CF) reported through the CF Foundation [7] and central line–associated blood stream infections.

- **Process Measures:** In contrast to outcomes measures, process measures assess whether particular elements of care, judged to be standard of practice, were provided to the patient. Process measures differ from outcomes measures in that they usually are abstracted and aggregated directly from the medical record rather than converted into numerical code. Data definitions are as important for process measures as they are for outcomes measures. Process measures are useful for organizations as part of their improvement efforts. Most focus on increasing the reliability and consistency of care being provided by teams working together in clinical settings.

The use of process measures for the purpose of public reporting is increasing, but it is of uncertain value to consumers, and clearly places a substantial burden on the institutions and organizations that are required to abstract them. Advancements in electronic medical records potentially will mitigate this burden; however, it is critically important that quality and patient safety leaders are involved in the design and implementation of these systems, as the usual focus is on the transactional nature of these electronic systems, rather than on data functionality. Furthermore, additional work is needed to ensure that extraction of data is both efficient and accurate.

IS MORE ALWAYS BETTER?

Over the last few years the number of quality and patient safety indicators has increased substantially. Careful attention to data definitions is critical to enhancing the value and utility of these measures to avoid excessively taxing precious organizational resources. For example, externally mandated submission of specific indicators may not be aligned with institutional focuses and priorities. Hospitals and their staff have a finite capacity for aggregating and analyzing data, particularly in times of constrained budgets. Institutional resources must be conserved and appropriately focused to achieve quality and patient safety goals. A thoughtful, evidence-based, streamlined system is needed to create and evaluate databases and registries.

In some situations, indicators are routinely collected, some over prolonged periods of time, with little variation in the results and often no attempt to act on them. Often, critical appraisal of the process or of its outcomes is lacking, thus creating a stagnant quality assurance program. We advocate the concept of determining whether an indicator is actionable—that is, whether it will drive performance improvement. Although there may be value in following some indicators even without a performance improvement intervention, it may be preferable to discontinue collection of some. Alternatively, sample size and intervals may be adjusted in an effort to conserve resources.

Careful attention to data definitions is critical to enhancing the value and utility of these measures. After all, each measure has limitations and disadvantages as well as advantages. Indeed, the recent proliferation of quality indicators may have unintended consequences—that is, creating challenges for the reporting institutions and not necessarily achieving the results a well-constructed measurement program should achieve. Numerous criteria for optimal measurement systems have been proposed, including the following: (1) the measures must be understandable to the public; (2) the measures must be related to high-priority clinical conditions; (3) the data are accessible, accurate, and permit comparisons between and among providers; and (4) an evidence-based approach to treating the condition should be embraced to ensure that the measure is then actionable.[8]

MEDICAL ERROR AND PATIENT SAFETY

Health care quality goes hand in hand with patient safety. The thrust in the 21st century is the assurance of a safe workplace for patients and for providers alike. In 1999, the IOM published a seminal report entitled "To Err Is Human: Building a Safer Health System,"[9] which catalyzed an enormous shift in our attention and understanding of medical errors. The IOM report defined an error as an event in which there is a failure of a process to achieve the intended outcome, or an incorrect process of care was selected initially. An adverse event was defined as an injury to a patient caused by medical management rather than the patient's medical condition. The IOM report concluded that medical errors were responsible for as many as 98,000 deaths in the United States annually. Estimated annual costs of these errors were in the range of $17 billion to $29 billion. The report further opined that injuries caused by errors are inherently preventable.

The IOM report was based on two seminal studies: the Harvard Medical Practice Study [10] and another by Thomas et al. focusing on adverse events in Colorado and Utah.[11] The Harvard Medical Practice Study examined more than 30,000 medical records of patients discharged from 51 different hospitals in New York State, and found that adverse events occurred in 3.7 percent of hospitalizations. The researchers postulated that more than half of these adverse events (58 percent) were preventable. In 2000, Thomas et al. published the results of a review of 15,000 hospital discharges from hospitals in Colorado and Utah. The researchers found an overall adverse event rate of 2.9 percent, of which 50 percent of the adverse events were preventable.

Similar results have been shown in other studies. A Canadian study published in 2004 found an adverse rate event of 7.5 percent across 20 hospitals in Canada; almost 40 percent were deemed to be preventable.[12] From a public health perspective, these findings are just the tip of the iceberg because almost all of the studies focus on inpatient stays. Since the majority of health care in the United States occurs in the outpatient setting, it is difficult to assess the magnitude of the problem of adverse events and preventable errors across the continuum of care. Clearly, there is a need for more studies in out-patient care settings.

PERFORMANCE IMPROVEMENT IN HEALTH CARE

The 21st-century health care system is highly complex, making it more than likely that an error or an adverse event could occur. Systems are defined as many interdependent parts working together to achieve an outcome. System failures may be attributable to both human and nonhuman factors. A number of models designed to better understand system failure have been utilized in health care settings, the most notable of which is the Reason's Swiss cheese model.[13] This approach acknowledges that systems may have multiple levels or layers of protection only one of which is required to prevent from an error reaching a patient. All too frequently each of these layers fail—that is, the holes in the slices of Swiss cheese line up, resulting in the error reaching the patient. System improvement is contingent on identification of the factors that may cause each of these layers to fail.

The recent shift in focus toward systems and how they fail has not addressed a critical issue in health care, namely, the notion of individual accountability. Paradoxically, health care as an industry has been criticized in the past for not being aggressive enough in weeding out low-quality or incompetent clinicians. A good systems approach looks beyond individual culpability. Concepts such as a blameless culture have been proposed primarily because almost all errors rarely are caused by one individual. More likely, the error occurred because of a system failure; yet, in practice, it is difficult to harmonize more aggressive action against those who deserve it while simultaneously promoting an open and transparent environment, in which the staff feel comfortable discussing and learning from their mistakes. The health care industry, however, can learn from others who have pioneered safety and quality initiatives. For example, the nuclear, aviation, and manufacturing sectors have focused on communication, team functioning, reliability, and error-reporting systems to reduce errors, resulting in excellent outcomes.

ERROR-REPORTING SYSTEMS

Mirroring corporate America, numerous approaches have been proposed to improve performance, minimize errors, and reduce unnecessary costs in the health care setting.[14] Although many of these initiatives have demonstrated substantial value, the authors believe that rarely will a single methodology sustain an organization over time. Public health leaders and health care executives, however, must exercise caution to avoid dramatically changing the methodology too frequently, thus minimizing staff buy-in because of a perception that the program will be short-lived. Avoiding the appearance of the "initiative du jour" is crucial. We believe that employing a single approach as a foundation with the addition of elements from other methodologies over time is the most effective approach. A mechanic's tool kit is a cogent analogy. Starting with a high-quality tool kit, the master mechanic will then selectively add tools from other manufacturers as needed.

To build a safer environment, many hospitals have developed voluntary adverse event and near-miss reporting systems as an important adjunct to their patient safety programs. Theoretically, these systems provide valuable information; however, a significant limitation is the absence of the "true" incidence or occurrence rate because what is being counted is simply event reports, not the events themselves. This limitation is most significant when attempting to examine trends over time or to benchmark against other institutions. Is a significant change an actual change in occurrence or simply a spike, or dip, in reporting? Although these reporting systems are critical to effective hospital safety programs, they should be employed in the context of a comprehensive patient safety program.[15] In 2001, a second IOM report, "Crossing the Quality Chasm," described six components of a quality health care system: effectiveness, efficiency, safety, patient-centeredness, equity, and timeliness.[16] These components have substantially altered our concepts of quality and safety, resulting in initiatives that were not even contemplated 10 years ago.

PERFORMANCE IMPROVEMENT METHODOLOGIES: PUTTING THEORY TO PRACTICE

Six Sigma

Six Sigma, a quality management methodology, uses statistical tools to measure processes with the ultimate goal of reducing variability and defects.[17] Six Sigma can assist an organization in identifying the source of variability, defects, or errors, thereby facilitating the development of solutions. Sigma is the measure of variation that reflects how much a process deviates from expected performance standards. The Greek letter sigma (σ) is the symbol for standard deviation. The higher the sigma value, the less variation exists. Six Sigma is equal to 3.4 defects per million opportunities, while a value of 3 Sigma is equal to 66,807 defects per million opportunities. To illustrate the importance of low variation in a process, a typical hospital operating at 3.8 Sigma (99 percent perfect) would lose approximately 20,000 lab requisitions per year. A Six Sigma hospital operating at 99.9997 percent perfection would lose only seven requisitions per year.

Six Sigma uses the Define, Measure, Analyze, Improve, Control (DMAIC) approach to implement quality improvements. DMAIC is the process by which performance teams achieve their stated goals. *Define* requires that the improvement team understands and identifies factors that are critical to quality. Teams then can develop a "charter," which serves as the project plan and typically includes the business case for improvement, statement of the problem, constraints or challenges to improvement, scope of project, players and responsibilities, and preliminary project plan. *Measure* is the phase during which process data are collected to quantify potential performance opportunities, thereby defining performance standards—that is, the values of acceptable performance. Measurement allows the team to validate data and define parameters for improvement before beginning a more complete in-depth analysis.

The *analysis* phase identifies sources of variation. An effective Six Sigma team will evaluate many potential causes of variation, preventing biases or past experience from influencing the team's thinking. Common areas for teams to investigate include *methods* (procedures or techniques), *machines* (technology and equipment), *materials* (data, instructions, forms), *measures* (data), *Mother Nature* (environmental elements), and *people* (how elements are processed together).

During the *improve* phase, teams identify an improvement strategy and pilot solutions, which if successful, will be implemented more broadly. The improvement strategy selected is highly dependent on the results of the preceding steps suggesting a sequential approach.

The final step for a Six Sigma project is *control,* which prevents the process from returning to its original state once the team completes its work. The control plan is essentially an audit and compliance functionality and should include both ongoing data monitoring as well as a defined reporting program. The success of a Six Sigma project, which can take up to six months to complete, relies heavily on the results of the control phase.

Six Sigma includes other tools that can be employed to promote change. For example, *work-out* is a highly structured, facilitated meeting designed to empower people to make decisions and drive change. A work-out approach frequently is employed to rapidly achieve consensus or to solve a complex problem. Another example, the *change acceleration process* (CAP), examines barriers to change and effectively works through those barriers to accomplish established goals.[18] CAP outlines the steps required to change a process: lead at the top, create a shared need, shape a vision, gain commitment, operationalize change, modify systems and structures, and monitor and control progress.

Lean

Lean is another management tool that has been utilized in manufacturing processes for many years, particularly in Japan. Lean thinking is based on the work of W. Edwards Deming, who is considered by many to be one of the founding fathers of the quality movement. He worked with Japanese industrialists during post–World War II Japan to change work processes. His approach was known as the 14 points, which stressed employee participation, reliance on data, and use of careful analysis to drive change.[19] In Lean, the definition of value is based solely on the customer. By minimizing steps that do not add value, waste can be removed and work completed more efficiently. Lean seeks opportunities to improve performance anywhere in the system, regardless of preestablished targets.

Lean thinking incorporates specific "tools" such as a *kaizen*, a multiday session during which the key constituents review current process and consider opportunities for improvement. A kaizen begins with the creation of a value stream map, followed by development of processes that are less wasteful. It is important to stress that health care is an industry in which the consumer (patient) pays a high price for both the value of the produce, service, or treatment and the cost of waste (medical errors, delay in care, and so on). Lean helps hospitals create value and reduce waste.

Plan, Do, Study, Act

The Plan, Do, Study, Act (PDSA) methodology is based on the work of Walter Shewhart, an engineer. PDSA can be utilized in hospital performance improvement projects of varying size and scope, from small-unit-based to pan-institutional. An advantage of PDSA is that it is both flexible and highly structured, and is adaptable to many environments.[20]

Root Cause Analysis (RCA)

Although not a performance methodology, per se, an important tool in identifying sources of error is the process of Root Cause Analysis (RCA). Currently, the most common approach in health care is to determine the underlying cause of adverse events. It is imperative to evaluate and to understand the circumstances leading up to an event that causes, or almost causes, serious harm to a patient. The RCA is a linear evaluation of the event during which staff are interviewed and both human and systems issues are identified.

Regulatory bodies often have specific requirements for RCAs, although these may differ across states and organizations. Most formats require that the institution identify corrective actions in order to reduce the risk of a similar event in the future.[21]

The value of RCAs is frequently limited in that incidents rarely have a single root cause and can occur repeatedly because of other factors not unearthed during review of the initial event. If a second similar event occurs, institutions should move to a different process.

Failure Modes Effect Analysis

Failure Modes Effect Analysis (FMEA), increasingly used in health care, differs from the RCA process in that it attempts to identify all potential risks in a particular process. In industry, design FMEAs have been widely used to examine product components; the Joint Commission (formerly the Joint Commission on Accreditation of Healthcare Organizations) now requires FMEA as a systematic, proactive method to improve safety and reliability.[22] The FMEA process involves several key steps: (1) identifying steps in the process, (2) identifying failure modes (what could go wrong?), (3) identifying failure causes (how could it go wrong?), and (4) failure effects (what would be the consequences of the failure?). FMEA methodology assigns risk to a system or process based not only on the probability of failure, but also on the impact of failure on the eventual outcome.

Tools associated with FMEA include the "Five Whys," a method for identifying the "root" of a problem. By repeatedly asking why a variation or error occurred, you can retrace the steps in a process that led to the system failure. The required components of an FMEA exercise include identification of potential failure mode;

the effects for each failure mode; a root cause analysis for the most critical effects; development, testing, and implementation of system changes to reduce risk; and monitoring the impact of changes. FMEA exercises typically involve a multidisciplinary team with varying levels of experience. At times, an outside facilitator can be brought in to keep the process flowing smoothly and to avoid intragroup conflict. FMEA tools are available on the Web site of the Institute for Healthcare Improvement.[23]

Risk Resiliency

Risk resiliency is a new approach that combines strengths of the RCA process with those of FMEA. Initially presented in 2007 at the annual meeting of the Institute for Healthcare Improvement, this method currently is being employed and evaluated at a number of health care organizations. It focuses on proactive thinking about system defenses and the adaptations required to minimize risk.[24] The process begins with identification of existing "predesigned systems" that are in place to prevent errors. The next phase of the process involves an assessment of adaptability and escalation—that is, teams are asked to consider how risk or error is recognized, whether escalation occurs, and whether environmental factors could have been identified in advance.

Before implementing any methodology, the institution's leadership must evaluate carefully the principles of the proposed approach for compatibility with the organizational culture and philosophy. Leadership must be willing to reevaluate the organizational structure, reduce hierarchical layers, and reorganize staff based on operational products or services.

QUALITY AND PATIENT SAFETY: THE KEY PLAYERS

Few fields in public health are as dynamic as quality and patient safety (Q&PS). Evolving national and regional policy, the availability of new scientific knowledge, and innovative approaches to performance improvement have resulted in the introduction of new initiatives and indicators. Health care institutions are faced with the challenge of setting strategic agendas in Q&PS, making informed decisions about participation with external entities, and coping with the financial consequences of this new environment. The resulting panoply of activities often fails to align and, at times, these activities substantially conflict with each other. This has resulted in a somewhat fragmented approach to quality measurement and has provided the impetus for an alignment of quality indicators and priority setting at the national level. Following is a brief listing of some of the relevant entities in the field of Q&PS.

Centers for Medicare and Medicaid Services

CMS's focus on quality and patient safety evolved following the publication of the 1999 IOM report "To Err Is Human: Building a Safer Health System." One result of the report was congressional authorization of "pay-for-reporting" programs, which required hospitals to submit data on 10 quality indicators, with financial consequences for nonparticipation. CMS has since added new measures and currently makes this information available through the Hospital Compare Web site. Evidence suggests that public reporting of quality data has led to an improvement in quality and patient safety, especially when linked to payment incentives, such as pay-for-performance programs.[25]

In 2006, Congress further authorized CMS to reduce payments for "hospital-acquired conditions" (for example, central-line infections). Under the prospective payment system of diagnostic-related groups (DRGs), hospitals generally are paid an average rate for each illness, regardless of actual expense. Under the DRG system, however, a case with a complication or comorbidity, such as an infection, is paid at a slightly higher rate to cover the additional costs of care. Under new rules, however, the incremental reimbursement would be prohibited if certain complications are not "present on admission" but develop in the hospital.

Peer Review Organizations

Peer Review Organizations (PROs) were established by Congress in 1984 to improve the accountability of Medicare and Medicaid programs. PROs are contracted by CMS to conduct peer reviews of clinical services provided by hospitals and individual practitioners. Specific focus areas are defined annually, although the review functions are conducted regionally. PROs cite providers for lapses of care and frequently request corrective action plans.

National Quality Forum

Established in 1999, National Quality Forum (NQF) is a "voluntary consensus standard setting body" as specified by the National Technology and Transfer Act of 1995. NQF endorses indicators and compiles "best practices."[26] The NQF is a nonprofit membership organization of several hundred members, including representation from providers, purchasers, health plans, and consumers. Consumers and purchasers hold a majority of seats on the board. NQF standards and indicators are developed by expert panels and are subject to comment by interested parties. CMS and other purchasers use NQF metrics, including the 400 indicators approved to date, as the "gold standard." NQF recognizes the need to harmonize or align measures, with the understanding that misaligned or conflicting measures will impose additional burdens on providers and lead to confusion for consumers. As such, CMS now adopts new performance measures only after they have been reviewed and endorsed through the NQF process.

Agency for Healthcare Research and Quality

The Agency for Healthcare Research and Quality (AHRQ) is an arm of the U.S. Department of Health and Human Services that funds health services research as well as studies of outcomes and effectiveness. Research goals include a means to reduce medical errors and improve patient safety as well as to develop effective methods for the delivery of quality care. AHRQ also maintains the National Guideline Clearinghouse, which is a free, Web-based compendium on specific illnesses and treatments. AHRQ provides oversight for the Patient Safety Task Force, and provides metrics and measurement tools to health care organizations.[27] AHRQ has published several sets of indicators, including the Inpatient Quality Indicators and the Patient Safety Indicators.

The Joint Commission

The Joint Commission is the primary accreditation body for hospitals and other institutional providers, deriving its authority from CMS in determining that providers are meeting the "conditions of participation" for Medicare reimbursement. Founded in 1951, the Joint Commission is an independent, nonprofit organization that accredits provider organizations in the United States by onsite surveys utilizing teams of physicians, nurses, and administrators and assesses each organization based on a comprehensive list of standards. A key element of the survey process is the concept of a "tracer" during which the course of a patient or provider is traced against the Joint Commission standards. Participating providers are required to periodically submit data to the Joint Commission regarding compliance with published standards (see their "Quality Check" Web site at www.qualitycheck.org).

The Leapfrog Group

The Leapfrog Group was created by a consortium of employers, the Business Roundtable, and is largely supported by large employers. The stated objective is to maximize employer purchasing power and to recognize and reward quality providers. By identifying "better" providers, employers hope to steer their employees to the high-quality providers.

CONCLUSION

Quality and patient safety has increasingly become a societal focus in all aspects of health care. Galvanized by the findings of the IOM reports on the topic, health care organizations have been driven by a desire (need) to ensure a high-quality, safe environment for providers and for patients. Although other industries have led the way in this area, the health care industry is rapidly adopting quality initiatives, such as Six Sigma, Leapfrog, and the like. In these competitive and economically challenging times, setting strategic priorities in quality and safety is an important driver of success.

Quality assurance is not a static entity. Through partnerships among providers, payers, government, industry, and consumers, the efforts made over the past decade or so can be improved upon. Achieving better outcomes for patients, lower overall costs, and improved patient experience will require the continued investment of time and money to spur innovation and create reliable effectiveness, safety, and efficiency in clinical settings. Measurement and continuous performance improvement are the mainstays of a robust organizational quality assurance program.

REFERENCES

1. Institute of Medicine, Committee on Quality Health Care in America. *Crossing the Quality Chasm: A New Health System for the 21st Century*. Washington, DC: National Academy Press; 2001.
2. Best M, Neuhauser D. Avedis Donabedian: father of quality assurance and poet. *Qual Saf Health Care*. 2004;13:472–473.
3. Donabedian A. Evaluating the quality of medical care. *Milbank Mem Fund Q*. 1966;44:166–206.

4. Anderson O. Influence of social and economic research on public policy in the health field. *Milbank Mem Fund Q.* 1966;44:11–48.
5. Codman EA. *A Study in Hospital Efficiency.* Iowa City: Classics of Medicine Press, 1992.
6. Helm E, Lee C, Chassin M. Is volume related to outcome in healthcare? *Ann Intern Med.* 2002;137:511–520.
7. Cystic Fibrosis Foundation. http://www.cff.org.
8. The Healthcare Association of New York State Quality Institute. *Which Quality Improvement Initiatives Are Right for Your Organization.* New York: The Healthcare Association of New York State Quality Institute; 2008.
9. Institute of Medicine. In: Kohn LT, Corrigan JM, Donaldson MS, eds. *To Err Is Human: Building a Safer Health System.* Washington, DC: National Academy Press; 2000.
10. Brennan TA, Leape LL, Laird NM, et al. Incidence and adverse events and negligence in hospitalized patients: results from the Harvard Medical Practice Study I. *N Engl J Med.* 1991;324(6):370–377.
11. Thomas EJ, Studdert DM, Burstin HR, et al. Incidence and types of adverse events and negligent care in Utah and Colorado. *Med Care.* 2000;38(3):261–271.
12. Baker GR, Norton PG, Flintoft V, et al. The Canadian Adverse Events Study: the incidence of adverse events among hospital patients in Canada. *Can Med Assoc J.* 2004;170(11):1678–1686.
13. Reason J. Human error: models and management. *BMJ.* 2000;320:768–770.
14. Pronovost P, Needham D, Berenholtz S, et al. An intervention to decrease catheter-related bloodstream infections in the ICU. *N Engl J Med.* 2006;355:2725–2732.
15. Cullen DJ, Bates DW, Small SD. Incident reporting system does not detect adverse drug events: a problem for quality improvement. *Jt Comm J Qual Improv.* 1995;21:541–548.
16. Institute of Medicine, Committee on Quality Health Care in America. *Crossing the Quality Chasm: A New Health System for the 21st Century.* Washington, DC: National Academy Press, 2001.
17. Pande P, Holpp L. *What Is Six Sigma?* New York: McGraw-Hill; 2002.
18. Smith IJ, ed. *Using Performance Improvement Tools in Healthcare Settings.* Oakbrook Terrace, IL: Joint Commission Resources; 2007.
19. Going *Lean in Health Care.* IHI Innovation Series white paper. Cambridge, MA: Institute for Healthcare Improvement; 2005. (Available on www.IHI.org)
20. Walter Shewhart-The Grandfather of Total Quality Management. http://www.skymark.com/resources/leaders/shewart.asp#
21. Percapio KB, Watts BV, Weeks WB. The effectiveness of root cause analysis: what does the literature tell us? *Jt Comm J Qual Patient Saf.* 2008;34:391–398.
22. Failure Mode and Effects Analysis. Info Center. http://www.fmeainfocentre.com.
23. Institute for Healthcare Improvement. http://www.ihi.org.
24. Frey K, Hyman D, Resar R. Evaluation of the safety system surrounding adverse events. http://www.ihi.org. Published 2007.
25. Lindenauer PK, Remus D, Roman S, et al. Public reporting and pay for performance in hospital quality improvement. *N Engl J Med.* 2007;356:486–496.
26. Leape LL, Berwick DM, Bates DW. What practices will most improve safety? evidence-based medicine meets patient safety. *JAMA.* 2002;288(4):501–507.
27. Agency for Healthcare Research and Quality. http://www.ahrq.gov.

CHAPTER 3

Consumer-Directed Health Plans, Managed Care, and Future Directions in the Organization of Health Care Payment Systems
William D. White, PhD

INTRODUCTION

Health care is not only expensive, but also highly variable—that is, it often is difficult to predict the need for medical care. Health insurance provides a way to mediate risk and provide financial access to care. A central challenge for insurance schemes, however, is how to meet the goals of mediating risk and ensuring access to care while containing costs. One response is to turn to regulatory solutions and public systems of control. In private insurance markets in the United States, however, the approach has been to rely on market-based strategies whose premise is that costs can be constrained by creating incentives for cost-conscious shopping, but also being mindful that insulating consumers from the financial consequences of purchasing decisions may distort their behavior, leading to the inefficient use of care and increasing costs. To design more efficient and effective payment schemes, it is important to focus on who should pay, and how much each party should pay.

Until the 1980s, most people with private insurance in the United States were covered by traditional indemnity plans. As remains the case in the 21st century, the vast majority of individuals got their coverage through employment-based plans provided as a tax-exempt benefit. These indemnity plans delegated shopping decisions about what care to buy and where to buy it to individual consumers and their physicians and then relied on consumer cost-sharing to contain costs. Specifically, plans used deductibles and coinsurance to create financial accountability for purchases; the notion was that responsibility for resulting out-of-pocket payments would create incentives for cost-conscious shopping. By design, health plans were relegated to a passive role of paying the bills, while providers were reimbursed fee-for-service on a cost basis.[1]

Indemnity insurance substantially mediated financial risks for consumers compared with direct cash out-of-pocket payment, which was the primary method of paying for health care services in the United States until the 1930s. It also was associated with rapidly rising costs, however. Critics argued that a key factor in this rapid cost growth was the design of indemnity plans and their reliance on consumers to shop for care. In particular, they offered two major critiques. The first was that existing levels of cost-sharing created inadequate motivation for consumers to shop for care—that is, that deductibles and coinsurance were too low to provide incentives for aggressive shopping. The second critique was that individual consumers were ill equipped to be effective shoppers because they faced prohibitively high costs in gathering and evaluating the price and quality information needed for informed shopping.[1] Some critics also raised concerns about consumers' judgment in responding to economic incentives, noting the possibility of myopic, short-sighted, "pennywise, pound foolish" behavior, such as putting off preventive services like screening tests that could yield large potential long-run benefits in order to realize short-term savings.[2]

One solution to the problem focuses on increasing the amount of consumer cost-sharing. Simply increasing consumers' exposure to out-of-pocket payments, however, conflicted with the goal of mediating risk. Instead, beginning in the early 1980s, the policy response was to alter dramatically market organization by shifting responsibility for shopping away from consumers and toward health plans. Under the banner of what has come to be known as "managed care," the rationale for this shift was twofold. First, the plans would act as more motivated shoppers than individual consumers because they would realize the full amount of any costs savings. Second, plans would be more effective shoppers than consumers because they would be able to realize economies of scale in gathering and evaluating information. A corollary claim was that if plans took over shopping for care, this would reduce the need for traditional consumer cost-sharing to contain costs, thus allowing additional mediation of risk.[3]

Managed care enrollments grew rapidly in the 1990s. In the 21st century, most Americans with private health insurance have coverage through a Managed Care Organization (MCO), such as a Health Maintenance Organization (HMO) or Preferred Provider Organization (PPO). The design of these MCOs varies considerably. But most combine relatively low levels of consumer cost-sharing with two major types of strategies seeking to constrain consumer choice. The first strategy is to impose constraints on *where* consumers can buy care and their choices of physicians and hospitals. MCOs typically selectively contract with individual providers on the basis of price and quality. They then use financial incentives to "steer" enrollees to providers in their contracting "network," where these incentives usually are framed in negative terms. Thus, HMOs usually "refuse" to reimburse for services from "out-of-network" providers unless specially authorized, leaving the consumer to foot the bill in full out of pocket. PPOs "allow" use of out-of-plan providers, but reimburse for these providers' services at substantially reduced levels—for example, if Hospital A is not in your PPO's network, you can use it, but you must bear a much larger share of the costs than at an in-network hospital.

The second major strategy is to impose constraints on choices by consumers and their physicians about *what* care to use through administrative controls and mechanisms, such as utilization review, case management, and clinical guidelines. Again, incentives associated with these efforts usually are framed in negative terms. Thus, failure to adhere to a plan's rules can lead to "denial" of reimbursement.[4]

Although managed care currently dominates private insurance markets, in recent years, it has faced major internal issues. Since the mid-1990s, consumer "backlash" against MCO constraints on choice has been increasing.[5] At the same time, after a period of decline following expansion in MCO enrollments in the early 1990s, growth in private health insurance premiums has reaccelerated.[6] Together, these trends have lead to a reexamination of strategies associated with managed care.

One response has been to seek to modify managed care strategies from within. Many MCOs have responded to consumer dissatisfaction by reducing constraints on choice.[7] For example, many MCOs have broadened networks to include additional hospitals and physicians, potentially reducing plan bargaining power. Many MCOs also have restructured utilization controls in two ways. First, they have sought to reduce controls on relatively low-cost services that tend to be used frequently by enrollees and often are an important source of tension without necessarily resulting in large savings. An example is dropping requirements that enrollees obtain permission from their primary care physician to get a referral to a specialist. Second, MCOs simultaneously have sought to reposition efforts to control costs for high-cost services involving major illness and to make these controls more consumer friendly. An example includes efforts to restructure case management programs for diseases like diabetes and congestive heart failure. Key themes have included increasing consumer "engagement" and developing more cooperative relationships with patients in seeking to manage their care.[8]

These measures may have eased consumer discontent. However, continuing questions remain about MCOs' future ability to contain costs. Reflecting these concerns, a second response to managed care's difficulties has been a growing interest in alternative, consumer-oriented strategies and, in particular, in what have come to be known as Consumer Directed Health Plans (CDHPs).

The thrust of CDHPs is to seek to put consumers back in charge of shopping for care. A major challenge for them is how to deal with the concerns about consumers' motivation and ability to shop that originally motivated managed care. Evoking an upbeat, pro-consumer rhetoric, CDHPs specifically seek to address these concerns through three major types of strategies. The first, signature strategy of CDHPs is to combine (1) a high-deductible catastrophic insurance policy, for example, with a stop-loss limit on total out-of-pocket spending of $10,000 or more, with (2) a tax-advantaged individual- or employer-funded savings account that can either be used to pay for current expenses or rolled over for future use. The basic notion is that by placing consumers at risk for paying for substantial amounts of care with their own money, this simultaneously will restore control over shopping decisions and increase consumers' motivation for cost-conscious shopping. Additionally, introducing savings options will serve to mediate the accompanying increase in exposure to financial risk. The second major strategy is to respond to concerns about consumers' ability to shop by providing them with Web-based price and quality informational tools to "empower" them in the marketplace. A third major strategy is to create incentives for consumers to use targeted services, such as preventive and chronic care, where the focus is on offering "carrots" to encourage the use of desired services, versus managed care's use of negative incentives as "sticks" to discourage the use of services plans deem undesirable.[9]

To date, enrollments in CDHPs have been modest; as of 2008, only 8 percent of workers with employment-based coverage were enrolled in a CDHP.[6] At least some advocates, however, have envisioned CDHPs as a vehicle for major health coverage restructuring.[10] For example, Scandien sees CDHPs and consumer-oriented strategies as a way "to begin to roll back the role of third-party payment and restore the control of resources to individual consumers."[11] Alternatively, Robinson et al. suggest that strategies associated with CDHPs may end up primarily complementing existing institutional arrangements and managed care.[12]

From a policy perspective, important questions include not only how CDHPs actually work, but also what role they could play in the organization of private (and public) health care payment systems in the future. This chapter considers the mechanics of CDHP plans and discusses possible design issues, examines how efforts to implement CDHPs have fared to date, and considers the possible implications of CDHPs for the organization of payment systems in the future.

Before proceeding, a brief note on language is in order. This chapter follows the convention in the consumer-oriented literature of describing patients as "consumers." From an economic perspective, this term has the advantage of encompassing both current and would-be buyers of services. It is used advisedly, however, because the term "consumer" is often used proscriptively in connection with arguments for increasing patients' involvement in actively "shopping" for care.[10]

PLAN DESIGN

Specifically turning to the design of CDHPs, a useful starting point is to begin by considering each of the main types of strategies associated with CDHPs.

Motivating Shopping

CDHPs seek to combine increased cost-sharing with tax-advantaged savings plans to simultaneously shift responsibility for shopping back to consumers, increase their motivation to shop, and mediate risk. To accomplish the first two of these goals (shifting responsibility for shopping and motivating shopping), CDHPs typically offer their enrollees high-deductible catastrophic insurance plans.

High-Deductible Catastrophic Plans

Catastrophic plans have similar designs to traditional insurance policies (a deductible and partial cost-sharing above this deductible up to a stop-loss limit) and when offered in the workplace, enjoy the same kind of tax advantages enjoyed by other employment-based coverage. They expose enrollees to higher levels of financial risk, however. For instance, consider a catastrophic insurance policy with a $5,000 deductible, a coinsurance rate of 20 percent, and a stop-loss limit on total expenditures of $10,000. In this case, a consumer will be fully responsible for paying for their first $5,000 of care out of pocket. Once their expenditures reach $5,000, they will be responsible for 20 percent of each additional dollar of expenditures until their total expenditures equal $10,000 ($5,000 for the deductible plus $5,000 in coinsurance payments). At this point, catastrophic provisions will apply and their insurance will pay in full for any additional expenses.

With a high deductible, consumers will be responsible for paying for substantial amounts of care with their own money and indeed, for the majority of consumers, the deductibles associated with CDHPs are likely to exceed their expected annual expenses. A direct implication is that at least until their deductible is met, consumers will be free to spend their money as they like without worrying about any administrative restrictions imposed by MCOs. Since they are fully responsible for their expenses up to their deductible, however, consumers also will have strong incentives for cost-conscious shopping. Specifically, potential savings may occur in two ways: (1) through selecting lower-cost providers; and (2) through selecting less costly treatment options. For example, the consumer chooses an X-ray over an MRI and elects to get it at a freestanding imaging center that charges less than the local hospitals.

Tax-Advantaged Savings Accounts

The problem with higher cost-sharing is that by definition it will expose consumers to higher levels of financial risk. Savings accounts can help mediate this risk by providing consumers with funds that can either be used to meet current expenses or be rolled over for future use. For consumers with employer coverage, these savings plans could compensate for the fact that less care may now be covered by tax-exempt insurance. For consumers without employer-based insurance, savings accounts provide a way to access tax advantages for health care purchases.

Looking specifically at savings options, CDHP plans usually are classified into two main types: (1) plans that provide an employer-based Health Reimbursement Account (HRA); and (2) plans that meet necessary federal requirements for an enrollee to establish an individual Health Savings Account (HSA). HRAs are funded, administered, and owned by an employer in conjunction with an employer-sponsored insurance plan. They first became available on a tax-advantaged basis following a 2002 Internal Revenue Service (IRS) ruling permitting tax-exempt employer contributions.[13] In a given year, employees can use these funds to pay for health care expenses or roll them over from year to year. They generally cannot take HRA funds with them if they leave their job, however.

Typically, an HRA-based plan is defined as a CDHP if there is a deductible of $1,000 or above for single coverage and $2,000 or above for family coverage, where total risk exposure depends on a plan's stop-loss limit. In 2008, the Kaiser/Health Research Educational Trust (HRET) Employer Survey found the average deductible for HRA plans was $1,552 for single coverage and $3,057 for family coverage and that the stop-loss limit for eligible out-of-pocket expenditures (deductible plus any copayments) averaged $2,543 for single coverage and $5,331 for family coverage. At the same time, the average HRA employer contribution was $1,249 for single coverage and $2,073 for family coverage, implying a substantial "gap" between the amount contributed and potential out-of-pocket expenditures in a given year.[6] For instance, if the HRA contribution for a family policy is $2,000 and the stop-loss limit is $5,300, the potential "gap" will be $3,300.

In contrast to HRAs, HSAs are individually owned and typically administered through an outside institution such as a bank or insurer. Under the provisions of Title XII of the Medicare Modernization Act of 2003, HSA plans may be established either in connection with an employer-sponsored health insurance plan or on an individual basis. In either case, to set up an HSA, an individual must be enrolled in a health plan that meets two types of qualifications: a deductible equal to or above a minimum floor, and a stop-loss limit equal to or below some maximum amount. If the consumer elects to set up an HSA, the individual can make direct contributions to his or her accounts (either in qualified individual or employer plans). In addition, employers can contribute to employment-based plans. In either case, contributions are triple tax advantaged. Not only are no taxes paid on money put into HSA accounts, but also earnings on account balances and withdrawals from HSAs to pay for medical care are tax exempt. Furthermore, unlike accounts such as Investment Retirement Accounts, there are no mandatory withdrawal requirements after age 65.[13]

In 2009, for a health plan to be HSA qualified for single coverage, there needed to be a minimum annual deductible of $1,150 and a maximum stop-loss limit on total out-of-pocket payments (deductible plus copayments) of $5,800. Limits for family coverage were $2,300 and $11,600, respectively. At the same time, combined contributions from individuals and their employers could not exceed 100 percent of the deductible or a maximum of $3,000 for single coverage and $5,950 for family coverage. Finally, the purchase of first dollar supplemental coverage is prohibited.[13] Consequently, the potential again exists that in any given year a substantial gap may exist between the maximum allowed contribution and maximum possible total out-of-pocket payments, placing a consumer at risk for large "gap" payments.

Stepping back and briefly considering some potential design issues with these arrangements, a key question is whether the schemes described here can deliver on their promise to either motivate shopping or mediate risk. First, consider issues with financial risk. Placing a consumer at risk for large "gap" payments may permit reductions in premiums compared with traditional insurance. However, critics such as Jost [14] argue that CDHPs may have the effect of redistributing risk toward sicker consumers, especially those experiencing serious ongoing health problems who are likely to repeatedly reach levels of spending requiring large out-of-pocket payments.

The potential for large out-of-pocket payments has at least two important implications. First, while CDHPs may offer lower premiums overall, especially if savings are achieved from reduced utilization, moving to a CDHP may impose substantial hardship for sicker enrollees. Second, to the extent consumers have the option of choosing between insurance plans, imposing substantial risks on sicker individuals may lead to problems with risk selection in insurance markets. In particular, if CDHPs tend to systematically attract healthy consumers while creating incentives for sicker consumers to turn to plans with more generous coverage, this may set off a downward spiral in which high-risk consumers gravitate to more generous plans, pushing up their rates and potentially driving them out of the marketplace.[14]

Turning to issues with incentives, consumers clearly face strong incentives for cost-conscious shopping until their deductible is met, while to a lesser extent, coinsurance continues to create incentives until a stop-loss limit is reached. What happens, however, when they anticipate exceeding this limit? Given 100 percent reimbursement for catastrophic care, there clearly is no incentive to engage in cost-conscious shopping for expenditures above this limit. Furthermore, if a consumer anticipates exceeding their stop-limit, there is no incentive for expenditures below this limit either—they will end up making out-of-pocket payments equal to their maximum limit anyway.[15] As noted, the majority of consumers in CDHPs are likely to have expenditures below their deductible. Concerns about incentive effects at high levels of expenditure are salient, however, because of the highly skewed nature of health care expenditures. Although only a small share of the population may have catastrophic expenditures, these consumers account for the majority of health care costs. For example, in 1996, the top 10 percent of patients in the United States were estimated to account for nearly 70 percent of total expenditures.[16]

At the other end of the spectrum, a related concern is how consumers with relatively modest anticipated levels of expenditures may view funds in savings accounts. If they take a long-term perspective and treat these funds as reserves against unknown future events (that is, savings for a rainy day), this might provide incentives to conserve funds. If, however, they take a short-term perspective and treat these funds as cash in hand to spend down in full each year, this will largely defeat the goal of motivating cost-conscious shopping while mediating risk. Instead, only "gap" spending is likely to be effective, raising the question of whether a smaller deductible without a savings account might not be better.[17] A particular issue for HRAs is that funds may be lost if a employee changes jobs, which might create strong incentives to spend down, especially for younger, healthier workers who may anticipate finding new employment within a few years.

Finally, even if consumers are well motivated, their ability to realize savings from competitive shopping will be limited by their ability to exercise choice in the marketplace. If they are in an MCO, their choices may be sharply constrained by the extent of their MCO's network. They can, of course, still go outside this network but reimbursement levels will be lower. Individual consumers also are unlikely to be able to negotiate as favorable rates with providers as those negotiated by their MCO.

Empowering Shopping

The primary problem consumers face in being an effective shopper is the high cost associated with gathering and evaluating price and quality information. Consumer-oriented efforts to increase the amount of information available in the marketplace through Web-based tools could be helpful. For instance, the Centers for Medicare and Medicaid Services' (CMS) "Hospital Compare" Web site posts extensive information on hospital quality indicators (see http://www.hospitalcompare.hhs.gov). Key logistical issues include what information to provide and how to support its use. To be of value to consumers, price and quality data need to be timely and relevant to a consumer's specific purchasing decisions. For example, suppose a consumer wants to compare prices for angioplasties at Hospital A versus Hospital B. One indicator of cost is average prices. From a consumer's perspective, however, the relevant "price" is not the average price, but the amount they personally can expect to pay out of pocket for this procedure given the specific reimbursement provisions of their plan. Furthermore, from a consumer's perspective, the relevant price includes not only expenses associated with the procedure, but also related services and the overall "bundled" cost likely to be involved with the relevant episode of care. Finally, quality also may be an important choice variable and simply listing a wide range of disparate, hard-to-interpret measures may be not be very informative.[18] One approach is to collapse a range of measures into a single one, but this risks imposing preference orderings that may not be consistent with those of individual consumers. A more general issue, discussed below, is the degree to which simply providing information will necessarily resolve concerns about consumers' ability to be cost-effective shoppers.

Incentives to Use Preventive and Chronic Care Services

Many CDHPs exempt preventive services from deductibles and coinsurance and pay for these services in full as long as they are provided within the plan's network. HSA legislation limits exemptions to preventive services. IRS rules for HRAs are more flexible and permit plans to also exempt routine services for enrollees with chronic illnesses like diabetes and asthma.[13]

The rationale for these exemptions is straightforward: that they will encourage utilization of preventive and chronic care services that can reduce future costs and lead to better health outcomes. For example, cancer screening may allow earlier detection, while routine management of diabetes and asthma may avoid costly hospitalizations. However, as Berenson [19] observes, this raises an obvious question: if these services are so desirable, why are consumers not using them in the first place and what does this say about their ability to shop for care? If the problem is that consumers do not understand the potential benefits of preventive and chronic care services, why not solve this problem by simply providing consumers with more information and education?

Example of the Operation of a CDHP

The mechanics of CDHPs are a bit complex; therefore, an example is useful to show how one actually works. Consider the case of Joe, who is enrolled over a three-year period in a single-coverage employer HRA CDHP. Suppose this plan is based in a PPO with a deductible of $1,000, a maximum stop-loss limit of $3,500, and an annual employer contribution of $1,000. Suppose further that in Joe's PPO, in-plan preventive services are exempt, and he would be responsible for a 20 percent coinsurance rate for expenses above his deductible for in-plan services. If he goes out of plan, the coinsurance rate is 30 percent, and some of his costs may not be eligible for reimbursement at all.[1]

Suppose in Year 1 Joe has no major health problems and spends a total of $500 on health care, all from in-plan providers, including $300 for exempt preventive services. In this case, it will be a good year for Joe. He simply will be at risk for the $200 he spent on nonpreventive services from a convenient care center. Because he has a deductible of $1,000, he will be responsible for paying the bill in full. Deducting $200 from his HRA, no out-of-pocket payments will be necessary and an HRA balance of $1,000 − $200 = $800 will be rolled over.

---

1. PPOs typically tie reimbursement to Usual and Customary Rates (UCRs) in the relevant geographic area and only reimbursement for charges up to this amount (or some percentage of it), where charges above this amount are the responsibility of the enrollee (for example, if the URC is $100 and the charge is $150, Joe would be responsible for 30 percent of $100 plus $150 − $100 = $50, or $80 total).

Note several important features of Joe's choices. First, assuming that Joe would like to preserve as large a balance as possible in his HRA for future use, there will be strong incentives in Year 1 for him to engage in cost-conscious shopping. By selecting a convenient care center, Joe is able to realize the full $100 of savings associated with this choice. Second, while Joe uses $300 worth of preventive services, if they had not been exempt and he had to pay for them himself, he might have purchased less or none of these services.

Turning to Year 2, if his employer again contributes $1,000, Joe's total HRA balance will now be $1,800. However, suppose in Year 2 Joe has major health problems—he has a heart attack early in the year and he ends up spending $21,000. Suppose Joe purchases all of his services from in-plan providers, and they are fully eligible for reimbursement. Joe will owe the first $1,000 of the cost of his care (the deductible), plus 20 percent of the cost of his care above his deductible. Without a stop-loss limit, he would be responsible for $1,000 + (0.20 × $20,000) = $5,000. Because of his plans stop-loss limit of $2,500, his out-of-pocket expenses will be limited to $3,500. This, however, still will place him at risk for an out-of-pocket expense of $3,500 − $1,800 = $1,700, and his HRA account will be zeroed out.

Although there is no change in plan rules, once Joe approaches his stop-loss limit, he will face quite different incentives for cost-conscious shopping than in Year 1. If Joe anticipates surpassing this limit, there is no incentive to worry about costs above it. He also has no incentive to worry about charges below the limit, unless he expects savings that will bring him below it. Otherwise, even if he takes actions to reduce his costs (say from $21,000 to $20,000), he will end up with total spending equal to his limit, $3,500.

Finally, suppose in Year 3 that Joe's employer again contributes $1,000 to his HRA, resulting in a new balance of this amount, and that Joe's heart continues to give him problems and he spends $8,000 on care. In this case, Joe will now owe $1,000 + (0.20 × $7,000) = $2,400, which he will need to pay in full because this is less than his stop-loss limit. He could take $1,000 from his HRA and pay the balance of $1,400 out-of-pocket. In this case, Joe may benefit from cost-conscious shopping. For example, if he switches to a lower cost in-plan provider who charges him only $7,000 instead of $8,000, a reduction of $1,000, he will be able to realize out-of-pocket savings of 20 percent × $1,000 = $200. Alternatively, suppose that Joe considers using an out-of-plan provider who also charges $8,000. In this case, he will have out-of-pocket expenses equal to his deductible plus 30 percent of charges, or $1,000 + (30 percent × $7,000) = $3,100, a $700 increase in out-of-pocket spending compared with $2,400 if he used his previous in-plan providers with identical charges. Unless Joe values his potential gain in quality more then $700, he presumably will stay in network.

Taken together, Joe's experiences over this three-year period illustrate several important features of CDHPs. First, by design, Joe is shielded from the kind of catastrophic loss that would have resulted if he had to pay for all care in full; however, in any given year, he is potentially at risk for substantial out-of-pocket expenses because of the $2,500 gap between his employer's contribution of $1,000 and his stop-loss limit of $3,500. His HRA account may reduce some of this risk exposure, especially if he is able to build up balances over time. But he still may be at risk for substantial out-of-pocket payments, especially if he has several bad years and exhausts any rollover balances. Second, Joe's incentives for cost-conscious shopping will vary with his needs for care. Third, the apparatus of managed care continues to hover in the background, where payment rules create strong financial incentives for Joe to limit his search to in-plan providers. If Joe's PPO included case management for catastrophic illness, this could add an additional level of complexity. Finally, consistent with concerns about risk selection, "Joe healthy" is more likely to be attracted to a CDHP then "Joe sick," who, if he has a choice of plans, may prefer a standard plan with lower deductibles and less overall risk exposure.

IMPLEMENTATION OF CDHPs

Enrollments

Over time, opportunities to enroll in CDHPs have grown, but participation in these types of plans remains modest. Focusing on employment-based plans, the share of firms offering their employees the option of an HRA with a family deductible of more than $2,000 ($1,000 single) for an HSA-qualified plan grew from 4 percent in 2005 to 13 percent in 2008. In 2008, these firms accounted for 25 percent of all covered workers. During the same period, enrollments in CDHP, HRA, and HSA plans rose from 2 percent of covered workers, or one worker in 50, to 8 percent, or almost 1 worker in 12.[6] These data suggest that while access to CDHPs is now available to about one-quarter of American workers, less then one-third of the eligible workers (8 percent) actually enrolled in them.

Breaking down enrollment patterns by firm size, in 2008, larger firms were somewhat more likely to offer CDHP plans than small ones (13 percent for firms with fewer than 200 workers versus 15 percent for those with 200 to 999 workers and 22 percent for firms with 1,000 or more workers). The proportional share of workers actually enrolled in CDHPs in small firms was higher than in larger ones (13 percent of employees for firms with less than 200 workers versus 5 percent for firms with 200 employees or more).[6]

At least one explanation of higher participation in CDHPs in smaller firms is that these firms are more likely to limit workers' options to a single insurance plan. For example, in 2008, 86 percent of firms with fewer than 200 employees offered a single-choice plan. Consequently, in most small firms, if a CDHP is offered, it is likely to be the only insurance option available. In contrast, in larger firms, CDHPs are likely to be offered as part of a menu of alternative plans and a consumer need not enroll in one to get coverage. Looking to the future, survey data from employers suggest that rising insurance premiums could accelerate current trends, where 60 percent of firms with CDHPs in 2008 named cost as the primary reason for offering them.[6]

Self-Selection

Studies of enrollment patterns for CDHPs find evidence that CDHP enrollees tend be more educated, have higher incomes, and have lower levels of prior health care utilization and chronic conditions. Among HSAs, one factor that may be potentially attracting older enrollees is opportunities for tax-advantaged retirement savings, especially in the case of individuals with higher incomes. When consumers have a choice, the literature suggests that people are more likely to enroll in such plans when the CDHP actively seeks to educate them about plan features. Interestingly, CDHP enrollees were considerably more likely to say they would seek to change plans if they developed a chronic condition requiring more care. For instance, in the case of Joe, he might look for a new plan if he anticipates continuing needs for care with his heart condition.[20]

These findings have several implications. First, they lend some credence to concerns about the possible market dynamics that could be associated with introducing CDHPs. Second, they suggest an important role for consumer education in promoting CDHPs. Consistent with this, 37 percent of small firms (less than 200 employees) and 71 percent of large firms (more than 200 employees) list "educating and communicating change in benefit" as the biggest challenge associated with introducing CDHPs.[6]

Empowering Shopping and the Provision of Cost and Quality Information

Efforts to implement strategies to "empower" consumers in the marketplace have focused on the provision of Web-based informational tools. Reports from the field indicate that most CDHP plans have some sort of Web presence. Interestingly, reports further suggest that, in many cases, insurers who develop Web tools in conjunction with CDHP products also tend to end up sharing these tools with all their enrollees, including those in conventional managed care plans.[18] Although plan provision of Web-based tools appears fairly widespread, existing evidence suggests that the use of these tools remains limited. For example, a 2006 Kaiser survey asked CDHP enrollees questions about information provided by their plans in a broad range of possible areas, including information on both prices and provider quality. In most cases, more than half of these enrollees did not know whether their health plan even had a relevant Web site. Furthermore, 10 percent or less of enrollees said they actually went to a plan Web site to get information on the cost or quality of providers, although a somewhat higher percentage (19 percent) indicated they used a plan Web site to look up drug prices.[20]

One factor that may explain this low level of utilization is simply that these tools are relatively new and have yet to gain much traction with consumers. But two other related contributing factors may be data quality and limitations on the kinds of shopping opportunities offered by CDHPs. Common complaints about data provided by Web tools include their timeliness and relevance as well as problems with interpreting these data. For example, price information may be outdated. In addition, it may not be useful for determining the actual amount a consumer can expect to pay if they purchase a service from a particular provider, where plans may be reluctant to post information that could reveal the prices they have negotiated with specific providers, which often is considered proprietary information. In addition, CDHPs rely heavily on MCO networks that may offer relatively limited opportunities for comparative shopping. This does not necessarily mean that consumers would not value accurate information about their potential costs of services or the quality of these services if it were made available.

Benefits Design

Cost-Sharing

As described earlier, a central goal of CDHPs has been to increase consumers' exposure to financial risk to motivate shopping. Pragmatically, an important question is whether, as currently constituted, CDHPs significantly affect risk exposure. Historically, the growth of managed care has been associated with declines in consumer cost-sharing. Since the late 1990s, however, consumer cost-sharing has been increasing in conventional managed care plans. Consumers bear the full impact of this cost-sharing because out-of-pocket expenses usually are not tax exempt. In contrast, the tax benefits associated with tax-exempt savings accounts may be substantial even for relatively low-income consumers because the exemption includes not only income taxes but also payroll taxes. In addition, stop-loss caps may be high in conventional plans.[2]

Taking into account tax considerations, Remler and Glied [21] simulate the implications of representative payment designs. Despite the rhetoric of CDHPs, they conclude many consumers in conventional plans, including those accounting for the bulk of health care expenditures, would likely see either no change or a decrease in their cost-sharing if they switched to a CDHP. This suggests that if CDHPs are really going to have much impact on incentives at the margin, substantial changes may be required in cost-sharing arrangements.[22]

Managed Care

Theoretically, a CDHP could simply offer an insurance product that includes a traditional indemnity high-deductible catastrophic plan with a savings option, informational tools, and incentives to use preventive and chronic care services. Once an enrollee reaches the stop-loss limit, however, this kind of plan would not provide any mechanism for controlling expenditures. Furthermore, it would place consumers in the position of having to buy services on their own in the open market where individual consumers without an MCO may face substantially higher prices.

Linking a CDHP to an MCO potentially could provide a solution to both problems, in which case an MCO could offer two major types of complementary services. First, linking a CDHP to an MCO can enable the CDHP to give its enrollees access to the MCO's provider network and associated price discounts. Second, it also can provide access to an MCO's tools for controlling health care utilization. The Kaiser/HERT Employer Survey does not provide information specifically on whether CDHPs are similar to managed care plans or what their relationship looks like.[6] However, the literature suggests that currently most CDHPs have close associations with MCOs, especially with PPO plans.[23] Potentially, a CDHP could simply rent access to a PPO network.

Significant business advantages for CDHPs appear to be linked to MCOs with strong, established networks. For example, two CDHPs, Definitely and Lumenos, were bought out by major insurers (United Health and WellPoint, respectively).[12] Anecdotal evidence suggests that reliance on managed care tools for controlling utilization is common. For example, a description on the Web site of a New Mexico Blue Cross Blue Shield CDHP plan site lists among its leading features: "Integrated health care management including disease management programs, prenatal program, case management services."[24]

---

2. Using data from the Kaiser/HRET 2005 survey, Remler and Glied [22] find that 21 percent of workers have no maximum on out-of-pocket spending and 55 percent either have no maximum or a maximum of $2,000 or more.

Further research on business relationships between CDHPs and MCOs clearly would be desirable. The kinds of relationships described herein suggest that important complementary relationships are evolving between CDHPs and MCOs. Looking at some of the implications of these relationships, reliance on PPO networks offers CDHPs a way to provide network access without completely eliminating a consumer's option of going out of network without plan permission, as would be the case with an HMO. If a PPO has a large network, there may be some allowance for comparative shopping. But, this is still a far cry from a model in which individual consumers are the engines of accountability in the marketplace. The flip side is that at least from the perspective of selective contracting, linking up with a CDHP seems likely to make relatively little difference in how an MCO conducts its business, leaving its basic organizational structure intact. Specifically, if a PPO is already engaged in selective contracting with hospitals and physicians, the main effect may be to increase the number of enrollees the PPO represents and give it additional clout in the marketplace.[3]

Regarding utilization controls, CDHPs and MCOs may complement each other in at least two ways. First, tools like case management may help CDHPs to control costs for enrollees whose expenditures have exceeded stop-loss limits on cost-sharing. CDHPs could conceivably develop their own tools for this purpose. If, however, MCOs already have such tools in place, economies of scale may be achieved from sharing them, especially within organizations offering multiple insurance products. Second, aspects of CDHPs may help MCOs address some of the issues created by consumer backlash. As discussed earlier, one particular source of tension with consumers has been MCO restrictions on the use of relatively low-cost, frequently used services like referrals to specialists. With many plans pulling back from using these types of controls, high-deductible plans may provide a way for MCOs to fill this gap and induce consumers to self-ration these kinds of services—for example, if you are paying the full cost of self-referring to a specialist, you may think twice before doing so.

Finally, CDHPs' use of carrots versus sticks to encourage the use of services like preventive and chronic care may offer an alternative to the kind of punitive models used by many MCOs in the past. It may be more effective to offer to "pay" consumers to enroll in a disease management program or participate in case management rather than to threaten them with penalties.

CDHP Impact on Costs and Quality

At the employer level, CDHPs generally are perceived as saving on benefits costs. Consistent with this, in 2008, 42 percent of employers in the Kaiser/HRET survey reported that CDHPs offered lower costs,[20] and, not surprisingly, insurers use this as an important selling point for their CDHP.[25] Benefits costs only include costs borne by firms and not those borne by workers. Studies on the issue show some savings, although results are not uniform and there are issues with where the cost data were obtained.[22, 26, 27]

---

3. One proviso, however, is that providers may be more reluctant to accept CDHP enrollees then conventional PPO enrollees, because CDHP enrollees may be more likely to default on copayments to providers because of greater cost-sharing.

In interesting new work, Lo Sasso, Helmchen, and Kaestner address selection issues by looking at workers at small firms that only offered a single plan in which the specific CDHP plan included separate deductibles for outpatient services and pharmacy and inpatient and outpatient surgery spending.[17] They found that for outpatient services and pharmacy, raising deductibles reduced spending, albeit modestly. At the same time, increases in deductibles for inpatient and outpatient surgery had minimal effects. The first finding is consistent with expectations that increased cost-sharing will reduce utilization, especially for consumers with moderate levels of expenditure. The second lends support to the concern that in the case of high-cost services, such as inpatient hospitalizations for which costs are likely to exceed stop-loss limits, even relatively high cost-sharing may have little impact. What is more surprising about their findings is that spending increases dollar for dollar for increases in employer contributions to HRA and HSA savings plans. Based on these results, when consumers receive additional funds, they appear to turn around and spend it on care immediately, thus raising questions about the value of accounts in mediating risk.

Regarding quality, there is a growing concern about the effects of high levels of cost-sharing on consumer purchasing decisions. A number of studies examined utilization services for employees enrolling in CDHPs compared with those who did not. A limitation with these types of studies, as noted earlier, is that there may be self-selection between consumers electing CDHPs versus other types of plans. In any case, these studies find evidence not only of lower utilization but also of a negative impact on quality. For example, Hibbard et al. examined impacts on the use of medical office visits, where evidence-based criteria were used to categorize visits into "high priority" and "low priority." They found that CDHP enrollees had fewer office visits, regardless of whether they were classified as high priority or low priority, suggesting that when cutting back services, consumers did not distinguish between the two types of visits.[28]

In another study, Greene et al. found that CDHP patients were more likely to discontinue medications for chronic conditions.[29] Survey data compared enrollees in CDHPs with those in more traditional employment-based coverage The researchers found that CDHP enrollees were more likely to say that they did not get needed services because of the costs.[20] Furthermore, recent work by Reed et al. suggests that consumers in CDHPs often took actions to reduce utilization without having a good understanding of plan rules.[30] These findings suggest that as currently structured, higher cost-sharing associated with CDHPs may have problematic effects on quality. On the positive side, Buntin et al. found evidence that enrollment in CDHPs led to more frequent use of preventive services, which is consistent with plan strategies to encourage the use of these services.[31]

DISCUSSION

There has been considerable discussion about empowering consumers in the marketplace. Whereas the basic strategy of managed care has been to shift responsibility for shopping and financial accountability away from consumers toward third-party payers, the strategy of CDHPs is to shift both back to consumers. The discussion in this chapter suggests that rather than a revolution, the introduction of CDHPs has been marked by a process of mutual accommodation, such as that discussed by Robinson [12] and Robinson and Ginsburg.[32] In practice, most CDHPs rely on MCOs to shop for care and then offer their enrollees access to a plan network, thus allowing MCOs to preserve their basic business model and continue with selective contracting intact. CDHPs also draw on managed care strategies like case management to control costs for high-cost patients whose expenditures exceed the relatively high stop-loss limits associated with these plans. At the same time, findings suggest the potential for adoption of some important features of CDHPs by conventional MCOs. For example, CDHP cost-sharing strategies offer a potential alternative for filling in at least some of the gaps left by MCOs' retreat from utilization controls.

CDHP efforts to incentivize use of preventive and chronic care also offer MCOs a model of how to reframe the rhetoric of managed care in more consumer-friendly terms while continuing to seek to manage behavior. One could argue that if current trends of integration of CDHPs and MCOs continue, distinctions between the two types of plans will become increasingly blurred. One possible scenario is that the process of integration will continue to the point at which MCOs' use of major strategies associated with CDHPs and CDHPs' use of MCO networks and utilization tools become so ubiquitous that there is no meaningful difference between them. The fact that tightly managed HMOs eschewing high levels of cost-sharing have maintained a substantial market share suggests the possibility of continued differentiation in the marketplace. As health care is actively being discussed and formulated, it will be interesting to see how CDHP will be integrated into the reformed delivery system.

REFERENCES

1. Starr P. *The Social Transformation of American Medicine*. New York: Basic Books; 1982.
2. Camerer, CF, Loewenstein G, Rabin M (eds). *Advances in Bahavioral Economics*. New York: Princeton University Press; 2004.
3. Dranove D. The case for competitive reform in health care. In: Arnould R, Rich R, White WD, eds. *Competitive Approaches to Health Policy Reform*. Washington, DC: Urban Institute Press; 1993.
4. White WD. Market forces, competitive strategies and health care regulation. *University of Illinois Law Review*. 2004;1:137–166.
5. Blendon RJ, Brodie M, Benson JM, et al. Understanding the managed care backlash. *Health Affairs*. 1998;17(4):80–94.
6. Kaiser Family Foundation, Health Research and Educational Trust. Employer health benefits 2008 annual survey. http://ehbs.kff.org/2008.html. Published September 2008.
7. Lesser C, Ginsburg P. *Back to the Future? New Cost and Access Challenges Emerge*. Washington, DC: Center for Health Systems Change; 2001. Issue Brief No.35.
8. Hurley RE, et al. Early experiences with consumer engagement initiatives to improve chronic care. *Health Affairs*. 2009;28(1):277–283.
9. Congressional Budget Office. *Consumer-Directed Health Plans: Potential Effects on Health Care Spending and Outcomes*. Washington, DC: Congressional Budget Office; 2006.

10. Herzlinger R. *Market-Driven Health Care: Who Wins, Who Loses in the Transformation of America's Largest Service Industry*. Reading, MA: Addison-Wesley; 1997.
11. Scandlen G. Consumer-driven health care: just a tweak or a revolution? informed, motivated consumers can have an impact on the entire health care system. *Health Affairs*. 2005;24(6):1554–1558.
12. Robinson JC. Managed consumerism in health care. *Health Affairs*. 2005;24(6):1478–1489.
13. US Internal Revenue Service. Health savings accounts, publication 969. http://www.irs.gov/publications/p969/ar02.html#en_US_publink100038739. Published 2009. Accessed September 27, 2009.
14. Jost TS. *Health Care at Risk: A critique of the Consumer-Driven Movement*. Durham, NC: Duke University Press; 2007.
15. White WD. Consumer directed health plans. In: Muller RM. *Encyclopedia of Health Services Research*. Thousand Oaks, CA: Sage; 2009:230–234.
16. Berk M, Moneit A. The concentration of health care expenditures, revisited. *Health Affairs*. 2001;20(2):8–18.
17. Lo Sasso A, Helmchen LA, Kaestner R. *The Effects of Consumer-Directed Health Plans on Health Care Spending*. Washington, DC: National Bureau of Economic Research; 2009. NBER Working Paper No.15106.
18. Regopoulos L, Christianson JB, Claxton G, et al. Marketwatch consumer-directed health insurance products: local-market perspectives. *Health Affairs*. 2006;25(3):766–773.
19. Berenson RA. Which way for competition? none of the above: advocates of consumer-directed care do not speak the language of the public, no matter how often they invoke "consumer sovereignty." *Health Affairs*. 2005;24(6):1536–1542.
20. Kaiser Family Foundation. *National Survey of Enrollees in Consumer Directed Health Plans*. Washington, DC: The Henry J. Kaiser Family Foundation; 2006. Report No.7594.
21. Remler DK, Glied SA. How much more cost sharing will health savings accounts bring? *Health Affairs*. 2006;25(4):1070–1078.
22. Feldman R, Parente ST, Christianson JB. Consumer-directed health plans: new evidence on spending and utilization. *Inquiry*. 2007;44(1):26–40.
23. Kongstvedt PR. *Essentials of Managed Health Care*. Sudbury, MA: Jones and Bartlett Learning; 2007.
24. New Mexico Blue Cross/Blue Shield. National Children's Dental Health Plan at Los Alamos National Laboratory. http://www.bcbsnm.com/lanl/cdhp.htm. Accessed December 16, 2009.
25. CIGNA. CIGNA Choice Fund Experience Study. http://newsroom.cigna.com/images/56/825638_ChoiceFund_Study.pdf. Published January 2009. Accessed December 18, 2009.
26. Parente ST, Feldman R, Chen S. Effects of a consumer driven health plan on pharmaceutical spending and utilization. *Health Serv Res*. 2008;43(5):1542–1556.
27. Wharam JF, Landon BE, Galbraith AA, et al. Emergency department use and subsequent hospitalizations among members of a high-deductible health plan. *JAMA*. 2007;297(10):1093–1102.
28. Hibbard JH, Greene J, Tusler M. Does enrollment in a CDHP stimulate cost-effective utilization? *Med Care Res Rev*. 2008;65(6):764.
29. Greene J, Hibbard J, Murray JF, et al. The impact of consumer-directed health plans on prescription drug use. *Health Affairs*. 2008;27(4):1111–1119.

30. Reed M, et al. High-deductible health insurance plans: efforts to sharpen a blunt instrument. *Health Affairs*. 2009;28(4):1145.
31. Buntin MB, Damberg C, Haviland A, et al. Consumer-directed health care: early evidence about effects on cost and quality. *Health Affairs*. 2006;25(6):w516–w530.
32. Robinson JC, Ginsburg PB. Consumer-driven health care: promise and performance. *Health Affairs*. 2009;28(2):w272–w281.

CHAPTER 4

Health Information Technology and Public Health

Jessica S. Ancker, MPH, PhD, Lisa M. Kern, MD, MPH, Vaishali Patel, PhD, MPH, Erika Abramson, MD, and Rainu Kaushal, MD, MPH

INTRODUCTION

All public health efforts depend on massive efforts to collect, organize, interpret, and disseminate data. A complex public health task, such as coordinating a national response to epidemic influenza, for example, requires tracking cases of the disease nationwide, analyzing the resulting data rapidly, presenting the information to policy makers, and organizing and tracking interventions, such as manufacturing and distributing vaccine. Rapid and high-quality information is similarly critical to other functions performed by local, state, and federal public health agencies, including assessing population health (through surveys, vital statistics, and specific reportable disease tracking), investigating epidemics, promoting healthy behavior through social marketing and public policy, monitoring and ensuring the quality of food and drinking water, and conducting research. In fact, all three of public health's essential functions—assessing population health, developing policy, and ensuring population health by applying these policies [1–2]—can be seen as information management tasks. To accomplish these functions, public health agencies have created information systems, such as electronic disease registries, to collect and aggregate the data.

Information is similarly essential to the practice of medicine. Clinical medicine has developed a different set of electronic information systems designed to track and collect individual patient data; these systems include electronic health records and billing systems. These clinical and public health information systems have remained separate not only because of a technical inability to exchange data between them, but also because the two communities have had different information needs and stakeholders.[3] Public health relies on group-level data on millions of people, is publicly funded, and involves nonclinician stakeholders such as public officials, schools, community health workers, and epidemiologists.[4] Public health also emphasizes prevention and often includes a focus on social and environmental determinants of disease, such as social support, sexual behavior, nutrition, and physical environment.[3]

Clinicians, on the other hand, require detailed chronological information about much smaller numbers of patients. Clinicians also need this data in real time, whereas public health data collection often takes place on a relatively slow timeline. Because most of the medical care in America is provided by the private sector, clinicians need this information not only to provide optimal care, but also to bill insurers or public payers such as Medicaid.

By the end of the 20th century and the beginning of the 21st century, at a time of rapid advances in computing power, several compelling new incentives emerged to improve data about personal and public health, to better link clinical and public health data, and to reform the practice of medicine. One of these incentives was an urgent new public focus on bioterrorism and biosurveillance, stemming from such events as the terrorist attacks of September 11, 2001, followed in the same year by the anthrax attacks (in which spores were mailed to several public figures and news organizations), and in 2003, the emergence of severe acute respiratory syndrome (SARS) as a novel infectious disease that rapidly crossed state and national boundaries.[5–6] These events raised concerns about the inadequacy of the public health information infrastructure, and created a new perceived need for much more timely and thorough biosurveillance.

Another incentive pertained to out-of-control medical cost related to U.S. medical care becoming more technology intensive, the ageing of the population, and the shifting of the national disease burden from acute infectious disease to costly chronic or long-term problems such as obesity, diabetes, and cancer.[7–9] Furthermore, national experts began to call attention to serious problems within the medical system itself and their cost and quality implications, such as medical errors, fragmented medical care, and unwarranted regional variations in medical practice.[7, 10–12] Engaging the public in their own health and health care began to be seen as a more important way to help improve both medical care quality and public health.[13]

The term health information technology or health IT describes a variety of methods for electronically managing and transmitting clinical and health information,[14] from a desktop record system in a doctor's office, to a Web site in which a patient can look up her Papanicolaou (Pap) smear results, to a nationwide data collection system for disease surveillance. Health IT has been widely promoted as potential solution to most of the issues mentioned in the preceding paragraphs: improving collection and management of health information; linking health data sets; improving communication between public health agencies, clinicians, and consumers; and facilitating improvements in medical practice particularly through the provision of clinical decision support. These health IT systems have the potential for organizing data in a structured fashion so that it can be shared seamlessly; improving communication within and between medicine, public health, and consumers; and shaping human behavior (either at the point of decisions or through feedback afterward) to prevent errors, improve quality, or facilitate decisions.

If these potentials can be realized, health IT could substantially improve public health,[13] reduce the cost of care, and enhance quality of medical care.[10, 15] Creating these systems is technically challenging and costly, however, and implementing them can alter behavior, work practices, and professional relationships. A variety of factors pose barriers to development and widespread adoption. Furthermore, evaluation research on health IT systems sometimes shows they fail to produce their posited advantages, and may even produce unanticipated adverse consequences.[16–18]

This chapter will—

- introduce several current types of stand-alone health IT systems in medicine and public health, with their demonstrated advantages as well as their unintended consequences;
- describe the goal of *interoperability*, or seamless health information exchange between these systems, and its potential for improving public health and medical care; and
- explain continuing barriers to health IT development, implementation, and interoperability, as well as policy initiatives and research aimed at overcoming these barriers.

DEFINITIONS AND TYPES OF STAND-ALONE HEALTH IT SYSTEMS

Systems Designed for Public Health

Among the health IT systems used in public health are disease surveillance systems and immunization registries. The law mandates that certain communicable diseases (such as sexually transmitted diseases) be reported to state public health agencies, which in turn provide data to the Centers for Disease Control and Prevention (CDC). The current reporting system relies on a hybrid of paper-based and electronic technologies. After diagnosing a new case, a clinician or a staff member generally must complete a form manually, and mail or fax it to the appropriate agency, where the data are reentered into databases either manually or through technologies such as optical character recognition. Not surprisingly, the system is plagued by a low compliance rate, delays in reporting, and substantial underreporting.[13] Also, as each agency builds its own database, the data may remain in isolated caches at the local, state, or federal levels.[19–20] Like disease data, vital statistics (birth and death records) are collected nationwide using a system centralized in the National Center for Health Statistics, which receives data from the individual states under a cooperative system.[20]

Electronic immunization registries are designed to manage the increasing complexity of immunization. In recent years, the number of recommended early childhood immunizations has risen in this country, and immunization schedules have become increasingly complex.[21] Public health agencies are not the only stakeholders who want to monitor immunization completeness; clinicians also need to know what other clinicians have administered, and parents need this information to ensure that children can attend school. Public electronic immunization registries are designed to address these needs. For example, New York City's Web-based immunization registry allows authorized users to enter and view data about both immunizations and results of blood lead tests for an individual child.[22] A nationwide success story regarding public immunization registries occurred after Hurricane Katrina in September 2005; within days after the storm, the Louisiana Immunization Network for Kids Statewide connected to the Houston-Harris County Immunization Registry in Texas to provide immediate access to the immunization records of children who were forced to evacuate New Orleans.[23]

Systems for Clinical Medicine

Health IT systems used in clinical medicine include electronic medical or health records (EMRs and EHRs), computerized provider order entry (CPOE), e-prescribing, and clinical decision support. An EMR is an electronic record of health-related information on an individual patient that can be created, gathered, managed, and consulted by authorized clinicians and staff. An EMR has been defined as an electronic record available to individuals within one health care organization. By contrast, electronic health records (EHRs) can be used by clinicians and staff across more than one health care organization (in other words, they are interoperable; see "Systems for Patients and Consumers" for more details).[24] Beyond this definition, however, there is considerable variation in the features offered by different EHR products. A basic EHR permits tracking of a patient's clinical and demographic data. A fully functional EHR, by contrast, also may allow clinicians to add free-text progress notes, view and manage results of laboratory tests and imaging, and use embedded functions such as computerized provider order entry and clinical decision support.

Systems for computerized provider order entry allow clinicians to place orders for lab tests, procedures, and prescriptions electronically, thus facilitating delivery to the appropriate service providers and avoiding illegible handwritten orders.[25] E-prescribing systems electronically link to pharmacies and pharmacy benefit companies, so that the prescription can be automatically delivered to the pharmacy, checked against patient-specific data at the pharmacy (such as drug allergies and other concurrent prescriptions), or checked against approved formularies.

Clinical decision support refers to a variety of techniques for helping clinicians manage the complexity of modern medicine by providing evidence-based guidance at the point of decision making in the context of patient-specific information.[26] A simple form of decision support might be a checklist that reminds a clinician of the optimal procedures to follow during the clinical encounter with a patient with a specific diagnosis. Electronic systems can provide considerably more complicated guidance, such as recommendations based on evidence-based clinical guidelines, and alerts when a patient has a documented allergy to a proposed drug or when a new prescription would lead to a drug interaction with the patient's current prescriptions.

Evidence that these types of health IT can reduce medication errors, improve adherence to clinical guidelines, and improve quality of care is fairly strong.[15] However, much of the data originates from four large academic centers using home-grown systems, so far less is known about commercial systems or about the experience in community-based practices or smaller medical centers.[15] Many other studies have been observational analyses or efficacy studies conducted under highly controlled circumstances rather than effectiveness studies in practice.[27, 28] Evidence about the overall impact of EHRs on quality of care, efficiency, and other relevant endpoints across the spectrum of health care is not yet very strong.[15, 27, 29]

Systems for Patients and Consumers

Health IT systems for patients include the personal health record (PHR) and emerging ad hoc systems of social networking. A personal health record is an electronic application that allows individuals to collect and manage their own health information. Although there have been some products that reside on a flash drive,[30] most are now Web-based. Again, as with EHRs, there is considerable variability between PHR applications.[31] One form is the so-called tethered PHR, or portal, which provides patients with a view into some of their EHR data residing with one particular health care provider or organization. Because these tethered PHRs are fully integrated into the organization's EHR, they also may provide secure messaging so patients can communicate with the provider, refill medications, and schedule appointments. They, however, cannot integrate data from other providers outside the organization. Another form of the PHR is the freestanding PHR, a product offered by a third party (two products available are hosted by software giants Google and Microsoft™) and are not integrally connected with an individual provider's system. Although these freestanding PHRs have the capability to receive downloads of data from multiple providers, providers may or may not choose to participate.[15]

It is widely expected that PHRs will be a valuable tool to engage patients in their own health care, raise their awareness of health issues more broadly, foster a sense of ownership and empowerment, and improve patient-provider communication.[13, 31–33] Small-scale studies suggest that when patients are given access to their medical record, they provide value by correcting data, providing missing data, and documenting their adherence to health maintenance procedures.[34] Stand-alone electronic decision support has been shown to be helpful to patients.[35] On the other hand, minority racial status, lack of Internet access, and lower education level are known to be associated with reduced use of PHRs,[36–37] and new users may find them confusing and difficult to understand.[38] Poor health literacy, numeracy, and computer skills impair patients' ability to make use of personal health information in electronic form.[39–42] This raises the possibility that any benefits of PHRs would be disproportionately concentrated among more advantaged, Internet-savvy patient populations. Research, however, has not yet been done to document the effects of PHR access on health or quality outcomes, or to learn how patient behavior may change with access to this information.

Social networking applications are beginning to be used by consumers not only to discuss health issues, but also to share their own health information. One example is PatientsLikeMe.com, which invites patients to input personal data (such as functional status while taking a particular medication) and then allows the patients to see the pooled data.[43] The effects of this type of communication are largely unknown. It could help people become better educated about their condition, empower them to better decisions, and provide much-needed social support. On the other hand, it might promote the spread of erroneous information. Also, people without a scientific background may not recognize the potential biases and flaws of the PatientsLikeMe.com database, which is made up entirely of self-selected patients and has not been vetted for accuracy.[43]

THE GOAL OF HEALTH INFORMATION EXCHANGE AND INTEROPERABILITY

The electronic systems described here are designed for collecting and aggregating health information, but typically they do not make it simple to share the resulting information. Nevertheless, exchanging health data—and doing so in real time—is critical to both public health and clinical medicine. Biosurveillance could be made vastly more powerful if emergency, ambulatory care, and pharmacy systems could be connected to the appropriate public health agency to enable event monitoring in near real time.[44–46] Public health would also benefit if public health agencies could better communicate alerts and results of investigations back to the clinician, ideally at the point at which they are caring for a patient for whom the alert is appropriate.[3] Monitoring over-the-counter medication sales also could provide advance warning of subclinical outbreaks.[47]

In clinical medicine, providers need rapid access to data from laboratories, pharmacies, and radiology after they order tests, prescriptions, or images. They also need to communicate with other clinicians and health care organizations because Americans change health care providers frequently [48] and see multiple providers (particularly specialists) concurrently. Transitions in care, such as discharge from the hospital to the community and emergency department visits, are especially vulnerable moments during which time key information often is lost or inaccessible.[49–50] From the patient's point of view, interoperability in the PHR is especially important because almost all patients consult multiple providers (primary care providers, specialists, dentists, oculists and ophthalmologists, allied health providers such as physical therapists, and so on) and are interested in their insurance data as well. One organization has estimated that only truly interoperable PHRs are likely to bring net value to the health care system.[31]

For all these reasons, building an infrastructure that will allow rapid and seamless electronic *health information exchange* for public health and clinical medicine has become a priority in the United States.[44, 51] The proposed National Health Information Network (NHIN) would (1) rely on fully functional EHRs and CPOE in physician office practices, nursing facilities, and hospitals; (2) connect these stakeholders to enable them to share data about individual patients; (3) allow all these stakeholders to view the results of lab and radiology tests electronically; and (4) connect providers with payers to allow automated claims submission, eligibility checks, and referral processing.[51] The CDC's Public Health Information Network (PHIN) is a national initiative to enable public health to exchange information electronically (www.cdc.gov/phin). One component is the National Electronic Disease Surveillance System (NEDSS), which is being designed to detect outbreaks rapidly by enabling electronic delivery of information from clinical systems to public health departments. One goal is to automate the process to minimize clinicians' burden in providing this information (www.cdc.gov/NEDSS). An example of a functioning public health surveillance system is the Real-time Outbreak and Disease Surveillance (RODS) system. In Pennsylvania and Utah, hospitals send RODS data in real time as they are collected at physician-patient encounters in emergency departments and pharmacy transactions.[52–53] Automated reporting of certain disease results from electronic laboratory data has been shown to be more complete and timely than the current clinician-initiated, paper-based reporting system.[54]

An important step toward making health information exchange genuinely useful is achieving *interoperability*, or the ability for different electronic systems to work together to integrate each other's data seamlessly, with as little manual involvement as possible.[31, 55] This requires internationally agreed-on *standards,* including standard terminology to ensure that words mean the same thing to all stakeholders and standard data structures to ensure that information is computer readable.[19, 44, 56] An example of a terminology standard is LOINC (Logical Observation Identifiers Names and Codes), which is a controlled set of codes to describe laboratory tests and other clinical observations. An example of a data format standard is the Health Level Seven (HL7) messaging standard, which specifies how information is packaged and sent electronically so that individual components of the message can be recognized by the computer software and interpreted accurately. Such standards mean the difference, for example, between e-mailing a PDF (portable document format) file of the patient's hemoglobin A1c level, and sending an electronic message such that the data would appear in the appropriate field of the EHR. Sending information regarding a PDF file is an example of so-called machine-organizable data exchange; the information is sent electronically, but human operators are needed to manually reenter the data into the electronic system or read it and make a decision on the basis of it. By contrast, machine-interpretable data exchange allows the data itself to be integrated into the record and used for electronic decision support or other purposes without the need for human involvement.

A key concept in interoperability is that data should be entered once and then reused multiple times. In a noninteroperable system of health IT, a clinician might open a child's EHR to enter her rubella immunization date, and then switch to a Web browser to access the public immunization registry, locate the child's record there, and reenter the same information in the format required by the registry. By contrast, in an interoperable system, the data once entered into an EHR could be seamlessly uploaded to the public registry, perhaps automatically to avoid burdening the clinician.

BARRIERS TO DEVELOPMENT, ADOPTION, AND USE OF HEALTH IT

Despite the potential benefits of health IT, adoption has been slow in the United States.[14, 57–58] A survey within the American Hospital Association found that only 1.5 percent of acute care hospitals had an EHR in all clinical units, and an additional 7.6 percent had a system in at least one unit.[58] Computerized provider order entry had been implemented in 17 percent of hospitals; larger hospitals, urban hospitals, and teaching hospitals were more likely to have EHRs. As of 2005, about 23 percent of U.S. physicians in ambulatory practice used some form of basic EHR, but only 9 percent had an EHR with capabilities such as CPOE and decision support.[14] Electronic prescribing is relatively rare, especially among community-based practitioners.[59] The barriers to be overcome before health IT is likely to become widespread include financial, technical, social, and human factors.

Financial

One financial barrier is the large start-up and maintenance costs for health care organizations seeking to implement health IT. Moreover, although in theory the decision support and other functions in the EHR could save money by reducing waste and inefficiencies, such as duplicated lab tests, the financial benefits may accrue primarily to the insurer, not to the practitioner.[29] This problem, in which the costs are borne by one stakeholder while the benefits accrue to another, is known as *misalignment of incentives*. A similar misalignment may hamper adoption of PHRs in which financial benefits of improved care are likely to go primarily to the insurer, whereas the costs of the PHR might be borne by either the individual or the health care provider.[31]

Technical

Continued improvements in technical and organizational architecture are needed before many of the health information exchange and interoperability benefits can be realized. For example, different EHR vendors must agree to follow the same standards and, in fact, interpret the standards in the same way before they will be able to exchange data.

Social

An important societal barrier is the American concern that sharing health information may compromise personal privacy and put individuals at risk of consequences such as stigma, loss of a job, or loss of health insurance. One way in which this concern has manifested is the popular opposition to a universal unique identification code for medical purposes. Congress currently has restricted the Department of Health and Human Services from implementing a unique identifier.[4] Without a unique identifier, it is challenging to confirm that two records in two different EHRs refer to the same individual patient and thus it is difficult to share data horizontally across data sources and longitudinally over time.

Human Factors

Human factors such as poor usability and information design, lack of integration into ordinary workflow, and the potential for disrupting professional relationships have proven to be serious barriers to adoption.[18, 60] In one famous case, physicians at Cedars-Sinai Medical Center in Los Angeles forced a halt to the implementation of a costly new CPOE system because it took a prohibitively lengthy sequence of steps to place an order, interrupted their workflow, and threatened patient safety.[61] Similarly, interface usability issues posed a serious problem for new users of a PHR.[38]

POLICY DEVELOPMENT TO PROMOTE HEALTH IT

One way in which these barriers are being addressed is through national and state policy development. A national standards organization, HL7, is continuing to develop standards for health information and health information exchange. For example, a recent HL7 product is a functional model that EHR systems should strive to meet.[56, 62] This all-volunteer, nonprofit organization includes representatives from academia and industry. The resulting standards are not mandated, but they are widely respected and adopted. One method of trying to ensure some level of uniformity in standards used in different products is to promote certification. The Certification Commission for Health Information Technology (CCHIT), a Chicago-based nonprofit organization, was assigned the task of developing certification criteria by the U.S. Department of Health and Human Services and began certifying EHR systems in 2006.[56] Certification focuses heavily on standards for data exchange, as well as security and system reliability.

National policy is beginning to focus on the problem of misalignment of incentives. The 2009 American Recovery and Reinvestment Act (ARRA) included a provision that will give providers financial incentives if they can demonstrate "meaningful use" of certified EHRs.[63] Although specifics of how "meaningful use" will be defined are still in development, this has the potential to make major changes to the health IT landscape.

State-level policy also is addressing financial and technical barriers. For example, New York State is investing heavily in health IT through a program called Healthcare Efficiency and Affordability Law for New Yorkers (HEAL NY), which has provided seed money to local organizations that are willing to raise matching funds, and has promoted independent evaluation of the impact of the resulting technologies.[64] One major focus of this program has been to promote health information exchange, so many of the beneficiaries have been regional health information organizations (RHIOs). These organizations bring together key stakeholders within a community to encourage the sharing of health information and to build technical and governance structures for health information exchange.[26] RHIOs are likely to be an integral part of the NHIN.

AREAS OF ACTIVE RESEARCH

To ensure that the best possible options are chosen for policy, careful research is needed to identify problems, test solutions, and evaluate outcomes. Thus, *biomedical informatics* research is active and growing in importance. One important area of ongoing research is improving the usability of health IT and better integrating it with workflow.[18, 60, 65] Methods may include qualitative or quantitative usability analyses: examples include verbal protocol analysis, which analyzes a single user's actions and verbalized thoughts while working with the technology; and task analyses, which breaks down tasks to be completed by various stakeholders with the help of the health IT and assesses the results for cognitive difficulty or other problems. These methods are helpful for matching technology to individual cognitive needs as well as group dynamics.[66–67] Focus groups, semistructured interviews, ethnographic analyses, and other qualitative methods are valuable for learning about workflow and how it is affected by the introduction of IT.[68] These methods are critical for reducing resistance to the introduction of new technology by professionals [60], as well as for ensuring its suitability for patients.[69–70]

Research into health literacy, communication, and behavior change is important to understand the impact of health IT on patients. Innovative ways of representing and explaining medical information [71–72] and of guiding longer-term behavior change [73] may be needed before patients will be able to make productive use of PHRs. More information is needed to determine whether and how patients will change behavior in response to access to their medical information and online communication.[43]

Computer science methods for processing information also can have strong effects on the usability of health IT. For example, clinicians and other technology users generally find free text easiest to both input and understand. Most electronic systems force structured data input through such methods as dropdown menus, checkboxes, and controlled vocabularies, because structured data are needed for interoperable data exchange, decision support, and other health IT functions. Natural language processing research uses computer science methods to find better ways of parsing free medical text to extract structured data,[74–76] and conversely of turning structured data into readable text summaries.[77] Ultimately, these methods could make systems easier to use for humans, without compromising the computer's ability to process information. Other active areas of research using computer science methods include patient record matching and de-identifying EHR data for public health reporting and research.[78–79]

At the level of program evaluation, it is critical to learn more about the costs, effectiveness, and comparative effectiveness of health IT systems.[64, 80–83] Initial evaluation of new programs (such as health information exchange) must focus on the platform to verify that it works as planned; for example, that data are accurate and exchanged in a timely fashion. Other processes and outcomes to be measured include system usage, the financial sustainability of the business case or model, clinical and administrative impact (including, at least for some projects, impact on quality of care), unintended consequences, comprehensive return on investment, and overall success of the program.[80] To demonstrate the value of EHRs, research must focus on both economic and clinical determinants of value. Also, to date, the potential benefits of health IT have been demonstrated primarily in a few large academic centers using home-grown systems iteratively refined over many years.[15] To maximize impact on public health, the focus of evaluation research must be broadened to include the experience of the wider variety of health care organizations that now are implementing health IT systems (in most cases, commercial ones). Providers, payers, public officials, and patients cannot be expected to adopt health IT wholeheartedly without better answers to the questions of whether health IT is saving money, improving public health, and adding value to the health care system.

CONCLUSION

Health IT, particularly interoperable health information exchange, has the potential to advance public health markedly by improving the assessment of population health, collecting data to inform health policy, and implementing policy to ensure population health. Linking clinical and public health systems to create a seamless, nationwide electronic data collection system could produce a much more powerful disease surveillance system with the ability to track population health status as well as rapidly emerging biological threats. Health IT offers particularly exciting possibilities for improving the quality and efficiency of health care delivery by making essential individual-level medical data more readily accessible at the point of care; improving communication among clinicians, patients, and public health agencies; and providing evidence-based clinical decision support to help clinicians practice according to optimal care guidelines.

Major barriers, however, remain to optimizing health IT systems and implementing them. User interface issues make much health IT difficult to use, and a lack of understanding of clinical or public health workflow on the part of software developers may result in systems that interfere with ordinary work processes instead of facilitating them. Technical challenges such as the need for additional standards also remain to be overcome before many of the benefits of health IT are likely to be realized. In addition, health IT systems sometimes have unanticipated adverse consequences when implemented in the real world. As a result, there are many important opportunities for quantitative and qualitative research to improve these systems so that they live up to their potential.

In addition, more extensive evaluation research is needed to establish a firmer evidence base about the impact of health IT on population health. The value of health IT must be assessed as a function of both clinical factors, such as measured improvements in indicators of health or quality of medical care, and economic factors, such as efficiency, reduction in waste, or return on investment. When both clinical and economic effects are maximized, it will be clear that health IT is genuinely adding value to the health care system.

REFERENCES

1. Institute of Medicine. *The Future of the Public's Health in the 21st Century*. Washington, DC: National Academy of Sciences; 2002.
2. Institute of Medicine. *The Future of Public Health*. Washington, DC: National Academy of Sciences; 1988.
3. Kukafka R, Ancker JS, Chan C, et al. Redesigning electronic health record systems to support public health. *J Biomed Inform*. 2007;40(4):398–409.
4. Yasnoff W, Overhage J, Humphreys B, LaVenture M. A national agenda for public health informatics: summarized recommendations from the 2001 AMIA Spring Congress. *J Am Med Inform Assoc*. 2001;8(6):535–545.
5. Khan AS, Ashford DA. Ready or not: preparedness for bioterrorism. *N Engl J Med*. 2001;345(4):287–289.
6. Institute of Medicine. *Secret Agents: The Menace of Emerging Infections*. Washington, DC: National Academy of Sciences; 2002.
7. Institute of Medicine. *To Err Is Human: Building A Safer Health System*. Washington, DC: National Academy of Sciences; 1999.
8. Alemayehu B, Warner KE. The lifetime distribution of health care costs. *Health Serv Res*. 2004;39:627–642.
9. Yach D, Hawkes C, Gould CL, Hofman KJ. The global burden of chronic diseases: overcoming impediments to prevention and control. *JAMA*. 2004;291(21):2616–2622.
10. Institute of Medicine. *Crossing the Quality Chasm: A New Health System for the 21st Century*. Washington, DC: National Academy Press; 2001.
11. Aspden P, Wolcott J, Bootman J, Cronenwett L, eds. for Institute of Medicine. *Preventing Medication Errors: Quality Chasm Series*. Washington, DC: National Academies Press; 2007.
12. Wennberg J, Cooper M, eds. *The Dartmouth Atlas of Health Care*. Chicago, IL: American Hospital Association Press; 1999.
13. The Markle Foundation. *Connecting for Health: A Public-Private Collaborative*. New York: The Markle Foundation; 2003.
14. Blumenthal D, Glaser JP. Information technology comes to medicine. *N Engl J Med*. 2007;356(24):2527–2534.
15. Chaudhry B, Jerome W, Shinyi W, et al. Systematic review: impact of health information technology on quality, efficiency, and costs of medical care. *Ann Intern Med*. 2006;144(10):742–752.
16. Koppel R, Metlay JP, Cohen A, et al. Role of computerized physician order entry systems in facilitating medication errors. *JAMA*. 2005;293(10):1197–1203.
17. Han YY, Carcillo JA, Venkataraman ST, et al. Unexpected increased mortality after implementation of a commercially sold computerized physician order entry system. *Pediatrics*. 2005;116(6):1506–1512.

18. Ash JS, Berg M, Coiera E. Some unintended consequences of information technology in health care: the nature of patient care information system-related errors. *J Am Med Inform Assoc.* 2004;11(2):104–112.
19. Chute CG, Koo D. Public health, data standards, and vocabulary: crucial infrastructure for reliable public health surveillance. *J Public Health Manag Pract.* 2002;8:11–17.
20. O'Carroll PW, Yasnoff WA, Ward ME, Ripp LH, Martin EL, eds. *Public Health Informatics and Information Systems.* New York: Springer-Verlag; 2003.
21. Yasnoff WA, Rippen HE. The electronic health records system in population health. In: Lehmann HP, Abbott PA, Roderer NK, et al., eds. *Aspects of Electronic Health Record Systems.* New York: London Springer; 2006.
22. Papadouka V, Schaeffer P, Metroka A, et al. Integrating the New York Citywide Immunization Registry and the Childhood Blood Lead Registry. *J Public Health Manag Pract.* 2004;10:S72–S80.
23. Boom JA, Dragsbaek AC, Nelson CS. The success of an immunization information system in the wake of Hurricane Katrina. *Pediatrics.* 2007;119(6):1213–1217.
24. National Alliance for Health Information Technology. *Report to the Office of the National Coordinator for Health Information Technology on Defining Key Health Information Technology Terms.* Bethesda, MD: National Alliance for Health Information Technology; 2008.
25. Kuperman G, Gibson R. Computer physician order entry: benefits, costs, and issues. *Ann Intern Med.* 2003;139(1):31–39.
26. Hunt DL, Haynes RB, Hanna SE, Smith K. Effects of computer-based clinical decision support systems on physician performance and patient outcomes: a systematic review. *JAMA.* 1998;280(15):1339–1346.
27. DesRoches CM, Campbell EG, Rao SR, et al. Electronic health records in ambulatory care: a national survey of physicians. *N Engl J Med.* 2008;359(1):50–60.
28. Kawamoto K, Houlihan CA, Balas E, Lobach D. Improving clinical practice using clinical decision support systems: a systematic review of trials to identify features critical to success. *Br Med J.* 2005;330(7494):265.
29. Wang SJ, Middleton B, Prosser LA, et al. A cost-benefit analysis of electronic medical records in primary care. *Am J Med.* 2003;114(5):397–403.
30. Wright A, Sittig DF. Encryption characteristics of two USB-based personal health record devices. *JAMIA.* 2007;14(4):397–399.
31. Kaelber DC, Shah S, Vincent A, et al. *The Value of Personal Health Records.* Charlestown, MA: Center for Information Technology Leadership, Healthcare Information and Management System Society; 2008.
32. Tang PC, Ash JS, Bates DW, Overhage JM, Sands DZ. Personal health records: definitions, benefits, and strategies for overcoming barriers to adoption. *J Am Med Inform Assoc.* 2006;13(2):121–126.
33. Public Health Data Standards Consortium. *Electronic Health Record: Public Health Perspectives.* Baltimore, MD: Public Health Data Standards Consortium; 2004.
34. Staroselsky M, Volk LA, Tsurikova R, et al. Improving electronic health record (EHR) accuracy and increasing compliance with health maintenance clinical guidelines through patient access and input. *Int J Med Inform.* 2006;75(10–11):693–700.
35. Green MJ, Peterson SK, Baker MW, et al. Effect of a computer-based decision aid on knowledge, perceptions, and intentions about genetic testing for breast cancer susceptibility: a randomized controlled trial. *JAMA.* 2004;292:442–452.
36. Miller H, Vandenbosch B, Ivanov D, Black P. Determinants of personal health record use. *J Healthc Inf Manag.* 2007;21(3):44–48.

37. Roblin DW, Houston TK, Allison JJ, Joski PJ, Becker ER. Disparities in use of a personal health record in a managed care organization. *JAMIA*. 2009;16(5):683–689.
38. Britto MT, Jimison HB, Munafo JK, Wissman J, Rogers ML, Hersh WR. Usability testing finds problems for novice users of pediatric portals. *JAMIA*. 2009;16(5):660–669.
39. McCray AT. Promoting health literacy. *JAMIA*. 2005;12:152–163.
40. Ancker JS, Kaufman DR. Rethinking health numeracy: a multidisciplinary literature review. *J Am Med Inform Assoc*. 2007;14(6):713–721.
41. Ancker JS, Senathirajah Y, Kukafka R, Starren JB. Design features of graphs in health risk communication: a systematic review. *J Am Med Inform Assoc*. 2006;13(6):608–618.
42. Poynton T. Computer literacy across the lifespan: a review with implications for educators. *Comput Human Behav*. 2005;21:861–872.
43. Ancker JS, Carpenter K, Greene P, et al. Peer-to-peer communication, cancer prevention, and the internet. *J Health Commun*. 2009;14:38–46.
44. Biosurveillance Technical Committee. *Standards Gap and Overlap Analysis Biosurveillance Use Case: Visit, Utilization, and Lab Results Data*. Washington, DC: Healthcare Information Technology Standards Panel; 2006. Report No.Contract HHSP23320054103EC.
45. Biosurveillance Technical Committee. *Selected Standards*. Washington, DC: Healthcare Information Technology Standards Panel; 2006.
46. Lazarus R, Klompas M, Campion FX, et al. Electronic support for public health: validated case finding and reporting for notifiable diseases using electronic medical data. *J Am Med Inform Assoc*. 2009;16(1):18–24.
47. Marx M, Rodriguez C, Greenko J, et al. Diarrheal illness detected through syndromic surveillance after a massive power outage: New York City, August 2003. *Am J Public Health*. 2006;96(3):547–553.
48. Reed MC. Why people change their health care providers. *Data Bulletin: Center for Studying Health System Change*. 2000;16:1–2. http://www.hschange.com/CONTENT/81/81.pdf.
49. Smith PC, Araya-Guerra R, Bublitz C, et al. Missing clinical information during primary care visits. *JAMA*. 2005;293(5):565–571.
50. Forster AJ, Murff HJ, Peterson JF, Gandhi TK, Bates DW. The incidence and severity of adverse events affecting patients after discharge from the hospital. *Ann Intern Med*. 2003;138(3):161–167.
51. Kaushal R, Bates DW, Poon EG, Jha AK, Blumenthal D, and the Harvard Inter-Faculty Program for Health Systems Improvement NHIN Working Group. Functional gaps in attaining a National Health Information Network. *Health Affairs*. 2005;24(5):1281–1289.
52. Tsui F-C, Espino JU, Dato VM, Gesteland PH, Hutman J, Wagner MM. Technical description of RODS: a real-time public health surveillance system. *J Am Med Inform Assoc*.2003;10(5):399–408.
53. Gesteland PH, Gardner RM, Tsui F-C, et al. Automated syndromic surveillance for the 2002 Winter Olympics. *J Am Med Inform Assoc*. 2003;10(6):547–554.
54. Overhage JM, Grannis S, McDonald CJ. A comparison of the completeness and timeliness of automated electronic laboratory reporting and spontaneous reporting of notifiable conditions. *Am J Public Health*. 2008;98(2):344–350.
55. Walker J, Pan E, Johnston D, Adler-Milstein J, Bates DW, Middleton B. The value of health care information exchange and interoperability. *Health Aff (Millwood)*. 2005;Suppl Web Exclusives:W510–W518.
56. Mon D. The difference between the EHR standard and certification. *J AHIMA*. 2006;77(5):66–70.

57. Ford EW, Menachemi N, Phillips MT. Predicting the adoption of electronic health records by physicians: when will health care be paperless? *J Am Med Inform Assoc.* 2006;13:106–112.
58. Jha AK, DesRoches CM, Campbell EG, et al. Use of electronic health records in US hospitals. *N Engl J Med.* 2009;360(16):1628–1638.
59. Pagan J, Pratt W, Sun J. Which physicians have access to electronic prescribing and which ones end up using it? *Health Policy.* 2009;89(3):288–294.
60. Armijo D, McDonnell C, Werner K. *Electronic Health Record Usability: Interface Design Considerations.* Rockville, MD; 2009. Report No.09(10)-0091-2-EF.
61. Morrissey J. Harmonic divergence: Cedars-Sinai joins others in holding off on CPOE. *Mod Healthc.* 2004;24(8).
62. Health Level Seven Electronic Health Record Technical Committee. Home page. http://www.hl7.org/ehr/. Published 2006. Accessed December 5, 2006.
63. Blumenthal D. Stimulating the adoption of health information technology. *N Engl J Med.* 2009;360(15):1477–1479.
64. Kern LM, Kaushal R. Health information technology and health information exchange in New York State: new initiatives in implementation and evaluation. *J Biomed Inform.* 2007;40(6 Suppl):S17–S20.
65. Poon EG, Blumenthal D, Jaggi T, Honour MM, Bates DW, Kaushal R. Overcoming barriers to adopting and implementing computerized physician order entry systems in US hospitals. *Health Aff (Millwood).* 2004;23(4):184–190.
66. Patel VL, Kaufman DR. Cognitive science and biomedical informatics. In: Cimino JJ, Shortliffe EH, eds. *Biomedical Informatics: Computer Applications in Health Care and Biomedicine.* 3rd ed. New York: Springer; 2006.
67. Seol YH, Kaufman DR, Mendonca EA, Cimino JJ, Johnson SB. Scenario-based assessment of physicians' information needs. *Medinfo.* 2004;11(1):306–310.
68. Ventres W, Kooienga S, Vuckovic N, Marlin R, Nygren P, Stewart V. Physicians, patients, and the electronic health record: an ethnographic analysis. *Ann Family Med.* 2006;4(2):124–131.
69. Kaufman DR, Patel VL, Hilliman C, et al. Usability in the real world: assessing medical information technologies in patients' homes. *J Biomed Inform.* 2003;36:45–60.
70. Kukafka R, Khan SA, Hutchinson C, et al. Digital partnerships for health: steps to develop a community-specific health portal aimed at promoting health and well-being; *Proceedings AMIA Annual Fall Symposium.* 2007:428–432.
71. Kaufman DR, Pevzner J, Hilliman C, et al. Redesigning a telehealth diabetes management program for a digital divide seniors population. *Home Health Care Manag Pract.* 2006;18(3):223–234.
72. Ancker JS, Chan C, Kukafka R. Interactive graphics to demonstrate health risks: formative developed and qualitative evaluation. *J Health Commun.* 2009;14(5):461–475.
73. Kukafka R, Lussier YA, Eng P, Patel VL, Cimino JJ. Web-based tailoring and its effect on self-efficacy: results from the MI-HEART randomized controlled trial. *Proceedings of the AMIA Symposium.* 2002:410–414.
74. Hripcsak G, Elhadad N, Chen Y, Zhou L, Morrison F. Using empiric semantic correlation to interpret temporal assertions in clinical texts. *J Am Med Inform Assoc.* 2009;16:220–227.
75. Chen E, Stetson P, YA. L, Markatou M, Hripcsak G, Friedman C. Detection of practice pattern trends through Natural Language Processing of clinical narratives and biomedical literature. *Proceedings AMIA Annual Fall Symposium.* 2007:120–124.

76. Chen E, Hripcsak G, Friedman C. Disseminating natural language processed clinical narratives. *Proceedings AMIA Annual Fall Symposium.* 2006:126–130.
77. Elhadad N, McKeown K, Kaufman DR, Jordan D. Facilitating physicians' access to information via tailored text summarization. *Proceedings AMIA Annual Fall Symposium.* 2005:226–230.
78. Kukafka R, Ancker JS, Chan C, et al. Redesigning electronic health record systems to support public health. *J Biomed Inform.* 2007;40(4):398–409.
79. Beckwith B, Mahaadevan R, Balis U, Kuo F. Development and evaluation of an open source software tool for deidentification of pathology reports. *BMC Med Inform Decis Mak.* 2006;6(12).
80. Hripcsak G, Kaushal R, Johnson KB, et al. The United Hospital Fund meeting on evaluating health information exchange. *J Biomed Inform.* 2007;40:S3–S10.
81. Kern LM, Barron Y, Blair AJ III, et al. Electronic result viewing and quality of care in small group practices. *J Gen Intern Med.* 2008;23(4):405–410.
82. Kern LM, Barron Y, Abramson EL, Patel V, Kaushal R. HEAL NY: Promoting interoperable health information technology in New York State. *Health Aff (Millwood).* 2009;28(2):493–504.
83. Kern LM, Dhopeshwarkar RV, Barron Y, Wilcox A, Pincus H, Kaushal R. Measuring the effects of health information technology on quality of care: a novel set of proposed metrics for electronic quality reporting safe. *Jt Comm J Qual Patient Saf.* 2009;35(7):359–369.

SECTION 2

HEALTH CARE DISPARITIES

CHAPTER 5

Racial and Ethnic Diversity in Academic Medicine

Carla Boutin-Foster, MD, MS

The 21st century has been marked by a significant growth in the proportion of racial and ethnic minorities in the United States relative to the total population. Currently, approximately 30 percent of the U.S. population is classified as being a racial and ethnic minority, with blacks and Hispanics accounting for approximately 12 percent each, and Asians, Pacific Islanders, and Native Americans representing approximately 5 percent. Based on vital statistics (births, deaths) and immigration statistics, it is projected that the demographic composition of the U.S. population will undergo a seismic change over the next decades. The most dramatic change will be observed among the composition of the number and proportion of Hispanic/Latinos in the population. That is, by the year 2050, the proportion of individuals of Hispanic/Latino origin is expected to double from 12.5 percent to 24.4 percent of the total population; the black population is projected to rise from 12 percent to 14.6 percent; and the proportion of people of Asian origin is expected to double from 4 percent to approximately 8 percent.[1] The changing demographics will necessarily reflect a different, multicultural population characterized by a wide diversity in languages, cultural practices, and beliefs. And with this change, there most certainly will be new health challenges.

Studies have shown that although immigrant populations tend to be healthier than their native-born counterparts, over time, as the immigrant population adopts the health habits of the existing population, their health worsens.[2] Therefore, as more immigrant populations come to the United States and the longer they live in the United States, the greater the likelihood that will adopt health behaviors characteristic of their adopted country—that is, unhealthy eating and physical inactivity, which lead to diabetes, heart disease, asthma, and other chronic conditions.[3] Furthermore, second-generation immigrants also tend to quickly become "Americanized," which often leads to behavioral and lifestyle health conditions contributing to chronic disease development. As such, public health organizations and academic medical centers, in particular, will need to shift their focus to meet the challenges of this growing diverse minority population. One way to better meet the needs of this population is to develop a culturally diverse environment, including a new focus on research of the health care needs of minority populations and the establishment of culturally sensitive projects that are designed specifically to address the health problems of this population. Importantly, academic medical centers as well as community clinics must begin to educate and train physicians and health care providers who will care for this culturally diverse population.

The focus of this chapter is on the public health implications of a growing racial and ethnically diverse America and the role academic medical centers can and should play in providing care to this multicultural population. An argument will be made for the need to bring the issues of cultural diversity to the forefront of medical education. Moreover, a case will be made for advocating for an increase in the proportion of racial and ethnic minorities in the physician workforce. As used herein, racial group will be defined as a group of persons defined by reference to race, color (including citizenship), or ethnic or national origin. For purposes in this chapter, ethnicity refers to the relating to, or characteristic of a sizable group of, people sharing a common and distinctive racial, national, religious, linguistic, or cultural heritage.

In the United States, academic health centers have a long tradition of caring for the public, particularly the less fortunate who tend to seek care at medical center clinics. To continue to provide both clinically excellent and culturally sensitive care, academic health centers need to address the issue of race and ethnicity as well as diversity of their workforce. I argue that the workforce should mirror the composition of the patient population. To achieve this objective, there will have to be an increase in the proportion of medical students, faculty, and staff from diverse backgrounds that can feed directly into the workforce to reflect the demographic shift. History shows, however, that achieving this goal is not as simple as it seems.

HISTORICAL PERSPECTIVES ON ACHIEVING DIVERSITY IN THE PHYSICIAN WORKFORCE

By the middle of the 19th century, approximately 14 medical schools were developed specifically to train black physicians. Shortly after the Civil War, however, approximately one-half were defunct, leaving seven medical schools that admitted only black students. These schools were almost exclusively located in the South and included Howard University Medical School located in Washington, D.C.; Leonard Medical School (Shaw University) in Raleigh, North Carolina; New Orleans University Medical College in Louisiana; and, in Tennessee, Meharry Medical College in Nashville, Chattanooga National Medical College, Knoxville College Medical Department, and University of West Tennessee College of Physicians and Surgeons in Memphis.[4]

A further decrease in the number of black medical schools occurred after the release of the report by Abraham Flexner, a research scholar at the Carnegie Foundation for the Advancement of Teaching. In his 1910 report, "Medical Education in the United States and Canada: A Report to the Carnegie Foundation for the Advancement of Teaching," Flexner conducted an assessment of medical education in the United States and Canada. This report has been hailed as being the impetus for overhauling medical education in the United States and is credited with creating more rigorous scientific standards for medical schools, which were designed to improve the quality of American medical education. Based on his evaluation of the medical schools, Flexner recommended that several schools be closed. After the release of this report, only two of the seven black medical schools remained: Howard University in Washington, D.C., and Meharry University in Tennessee. Flexner argued that the other five medical schools for black students should be closed because they were "ineffectual" and in no position to make any contribution of value.[4] The Flexner report also led to the closure of the only three medical schools for women. The rationale was that women showed a decreasing inclination to enter the medical profession and that there apparently was not a strong demand for women physicians at the time.[5] In one sense, the sweeping closure of these medical schools had a substantial impact on the medical education for black students and for women. At the time, there were few medical schools that even admitted blacks and women, thus closing those schools that did accept blacks and women was particularly restrictive in training black and female physicians.

After recommending these closures, Flexner made efforts to support these schools through financial support from the Carnegie Foundation. Nonetheless, the impact of these closures cannot be minimized.[6] In the wake of these closures, with few exceptions, the majority of the overwhelmingly white medical schools were not eager to admit blacks or women. In fact, by the early 1960s, less than 3 percent of the students entering medical school were black. This situation led to the impetus for development of affirmative action policies, which were designed to redress policies of institutionalized bias well entrenched in institutions of higher education, not just in medical schools.

In 1961, President Kennedy introduced the term "affirmative action" in Executive Order 10925, an order that prohibited discrimination on the basis of race, creed, color, or ethnicity. Affirmative action was a legal attempt to correct legally sanctioned racial and gender discrimination.[7] This order mandated that projects financed through federal funding "take affirmative action" to ensure that hiring practices were free of racial bias. The assassination of President Kennedy could have torpedoed the civil rights and affirmative action movement, but newly sworn in President Johnson strongly supported Kennedy's civil rights bill introduced in Congress in 1963. This bill included provisions to ban discrimination in public accommodations, and enabled the U.S. attorney general to join in lawsuits against state governments that operated segregated school systems, among other provisions. Johnson pushed for the passage of the bill and, in 1964, the Civil Rights Act of 1964 was enacted. This act was a landmark piece of legislation in U.S. history essentially outlawing racial segregation in schools, public places, and employment.

In 1965, President Lyndon Johnson mandated via Executive Order 11246, the expansion of affirmative action to federal contractors. Under this order, the Office of Federal Contract Compliance Programs stated that any agency with 50 or more employees and that received $50,000 or more in federal funds must have a written affirmative action plan for achieving a proportion of women and racial minorities that is proportionate to their availability in the general labor pool of women and members of racial minorities.[8, 9]

These affirmative action policies did not go unchallenged and resulted in debates that spanned more than three decades. One of the earliest cases that involved a medical school was the 1978 case of *Bakke v. the University of California-Davis School of Medicine*. In this landmark case, Bakke, a Caucasian medical school applicant, charged that University of California's policy of reserving a portion of their seats in the incoming freshman medical class for minority students was in violation of Title VI of the Civil Rights Act and the Equal Protection Clause of the Fourteenth Amendment. In the landmark ruling that followed this case, Supreme Court Justice Lewis Powell opined that race could be included as one of many factors to achieve diversity, which, he concluded, was in a compelling governmental interest.[10] In contrast to the Bakke case, in *Hopwood v. the University of Texas*, the Fifth U.S. Circuit Court of Appeals ruled in 1996 against the University of Texas School of Law's use of race as a factor in deciding which applicants to admit or as a basis for admission or financial aid because it was said to be a race-based policy.[11] *Hopwood v. Texas* was the first successful legal challenge to a university's affirmative action policy in student admissions since the Bakke case. After seven years as a precedent in the Fifth Circuit, the Hopwood decision was abrogated by the U.S. Supreme Court in 2003. In *Grutter v. Bollinger*, the Supreme Court ruled in favor of the University of Michigan's Law School stating that the narrowly tailored use of race in admissions process to further a compelling interest in obtaining a diverse student body was not a violation of the Equal Protection Clause of the Fourteenth Amendment or Title VI of the Civil Rights Act. In *Gratz v. Bollinger*, however, the Court ruled against the undergraduate school stating that the use of a point system that treated groups of applicants differently based on their race was in violation the Civil Rights Act and the Fourteenth Amendment.[8]

These legal attacks against affirmative action have had a rippling effect, leading to states such as California, Connecticut, Michigan, and Nebraska to reconsider and even ban affirmative action policies. In 1996, Proposition 209, a ballot initiative for the elimination of race-conscious admissions at the state's public institutions was approved in California. In the year following that initiative, the number of minority California residents accepted to one or more California medical school fell from 233 in 1993 to 157 in 1997 and subsequently to 156 in 2001. These trends have been attributed at least in part to legal efforts dismantling affirmative action.[12]

The legal challenges to affirmative action probably have contributed to the current low enrollment of racial and ethnic minorities in medical schools and subsequently among medical school faculty. Notwithstanding, within the medical community, the issue of affirmative action has been discussed and debated. In particular, the Association of American Medical Colleges (AAMC), the umbrella organization for medical schools, has developed clearly defined policies related to affirmative action and cultural diversity. In particular, the AAMC advocates for preparing physicians and scientists to meet the nation's evolving health needs, and, more pertinent to this discussion, working toward ensuring that the nation's medical students, biomedical graduate students, residents, fellows, faculty, and the health care workforce are diverse and culturally competent. The AAMC, created to advance medical education in the United States, represents all 131 accredited medical schools in the United States and 17 in Candada; approximately 400 major teaching hospitals and health systems, including 68 Department of Veterans Affairs medical centers; and nearly 90 academic and scientific societies. Through these institutions and organizations, the AAMC represents 125,000 faculty members, 75,000 medical students, and 106,000 resident physicians.

The AAMC originally used the term underrepresented minority (URM) to recognize the under-representation of certain ethnic groups. The term URM has been most often used to refer to blacks, Hispanics/Mexican Americans, and Native Americans, including American Indians, Alaska Natives, and Native Hawaiians. The new AAMC definition, however, allows for the designation of URM to be modified based on changing demographics to refer to those racial and ethnic populations that are underrepresented in the medical profession *relative to* their numbers in the general population.[12] Based on AAMC statistics, from 1970 to 1990, URM enrollment in U.S. medical schools increased from approximately 5 percent to 11 percent and has remained steady at approximately 12 percent.[13] During this same period, however, minority representation in the U.S. population increased to 26 percent of the total population. Clearly, enrollment of URM students in medical schools has not kept pace with that of the population, which is a cause for concern.[12]

The need for improving diversity in medical schools is best illustrated by looking at statistics compiled by the AAMC.[14] Table 5.1 and table 5.2 show the distribution of medical school applicants by race and ethnicity and the proportion of U.S. medical school matriculants by race and ethnicity. In 2007, the overwhelming majority of medical school applicants were white (57 percent) and one-fifth were Asian, whereas only 7.4 percent were black, 7.1 percent were Hispanic/Latino; and Native Americans, Alaskan Natives, Native Hawaiians, and Pacific Islanders accounted for less than 1 percent of the total applicants.

Similarly, among actual medical school matriculants, blacks accounted for approximately 6.7 percent, Hispanic/Latinos 7.4 percent, Native Americans and Alaskan Natives 0.4 percent, and Native Hawaiians and Pacific Islanders 0.3 percent, whereas whites and Asians represented 60.8 percent and 19.9 percent of the total, respectively. The underrepresentation of racial and ethnic minorities in medical school enrollees and matriculants contributes to the paucity of racial and ethnic minority faculty. Racial and ethnic minorities make up only 5 percent of the total U.S. medical school faculty, and, of this, approximately 20 percent of the minority faculty is concentrated in only six medical schools. Moreover, racial and ethnic minorities are less likely to be promoted to senior academic rank and are one-third less likely to attain senior rank when compared with white faculty.[15] Thus, in addition to increasing enrollment of racial and ethnic minority medical students, increased diversity and equity is needed in medical school academic faculty and leadership.

THE CASE FOR DIVERSITY

Increasing the racial and ethnic participation in the health care workforce, especially in academic medical centers where so many poor and minority groups seek care, is important from a medical and public health perspective. The 2004 Institute of Medicine (IOM) report, "In the Nation's Compelling Interest: Ensuring Diversity in the Health Care Workforce," provides several compelling reasons for achieving diversity in the health care workforce. For example, the report states that it is essential to have diverse faculty that reflect the multicultural composition of the population. It also is important to have a diverse workforce to teach students and trainees, as well as advocates for more research to address the pressing health care issues regarding providing high quality care to all, regardless of race, color, and creed.[16] Indeed,

Table 5.1
Percentage and Number of U.S. Medical School Applicants by Race and Ethnicity, 2007

Race/Ethnicity	Percent (Number)
White	57.0 (24,136)
Asian	19.8 (8,390)
African American	7.4 (3,133)
Hispanic or Latino	7.1 (2,999)
Non-U.S. Resident or Permanent Resident (Foreign)	4.3 (1,810)
Other	4.4 (1,696)

Source: Adapted from Association of American Medical Colleges data.

one major compelling reason for diversity is the elimination of racial and ethnic disparities.

The report also states that racial and ethnic minority health care providers are more likely to serve in medically underserved communities, thereby, increasing access to care for this needy population. Racial and ethnic minority patients report greater levels of satisfaction with care provided by minority health professionals perhaps because of a perceived comfort level of being treated by a race-concordant provider. Certainly, cultural and linguistic barriers can be breached more easily if the provider can speak the same language as the patient. Evidence seems to support this assumption. A 2003 study of 252 adults in a primary care setting found that

Table 5.2
Percentage of U.S. Medical School Matriculants by Race and Ethnicity, 2006–2007

Race/Ethnicity	Percent Matriculants
Whites	
In 2006:	60.8
In 2007:	59.9
Asian	
In 2006:	18.7
In 2007:	19.9
Hispanic/Latino	
In 2006:	7.4
In 2007:	7.2
African American	
In 2006:	6.7
In 2007:	6.4
Non-U.S. or Permanent Resident (Foreign)	
In 2006:	1.6
In 2007:	1.8
Other	
In 2006:	4.8
In 2007:	4.8

Source: Adapted from Association of American Medical Colleges data.

race-concordant visits were longer, these visits were associated with greater patient satisfaction, and the physicians were more participatory.[17] Concordance may reflect a greater interest in personal beliefs, values, and the patient's community.[18]

Data from the Commonwealth Fund Minority Health Survey also found that among each race and ethnic group, respondents who were race concordant reported greater satisfaction with their physician compared with respondents who were not race concordant.[19] In another study of HIV/AIDS patients, findings showed that having race-concordant providers eliminated the disparity in initiation of protease inhibitors.[20] This is not say that patients and physicians must be racially concordant to achieve such results, rather the issue speaks to physician and patient cultural sensitivity as well as physician willingness to discuss personal and social health concerns with patients with whom they can better relate because of a similar ethnic or racial background. Clearly, efforts should be made to understand factors that contribute to a sense of greater patient satisfaction, compliance, and understanding in order to promote better understanding among all physicians, regardless of racial or ethnic background.

Dr. Louis W. Sullivan, former U.S. Secretary of Health and Human Services, established the Sullivan Alliance to increase diversity in the health professions to reduce racial and ethnic health disparities. The three main objectives of the Sullivan Alliance are to (1) raise awareness of the importance and value of achieving racial and ethnic diversity in the health professions, (2) disseminate information about "best practices" and resources that enhance diversity, and (3) stimulate academic programs in the health professions of medicine, dentistry, nursing, psychology, and public health to create new or more effectively implement existing diversity initiatives (see http://www.jointcenter.org/hpi/pages/sullivan-alliance). In 2004, the Sullivan Alliance issued its final report, "Missing Persons: Minorities in the Professions," which described increasing the diversity of medical students, residents, and faculty as an "indispensable tool in efforts to improve access to health care for underserved populations."[2, 21] This report provided the public with the foundation for achieving cultural diversity and competency among health care professions. The following sections focus on the rationale for increasing diversity in the physician workforce.

HEALTH DISPARITIES DO MAKE A DIFFERENCE

Fundamental to addressing many of the current ills in the health system is addressing the role that race and ethnicity play in health care access and outcomes. Despite significant advances in civil rights, the fact remains that when it comes to both the type and quality of health care that an individual receives, race and ethnicity must be taken into account. According to the IOM report, "Unequal Treatment: Confronting Racial and Ethnic Disparities," race and ethnicity remain a significant factor in determining whether an individual receives high-quality care and in determining health outcomes.[22] Race has been shown to be a determinant of the characteristics and qualifications of the physician that patients see, the types of hospital to which a patient is admitted, and the types of procedures they will undergo.[23–26] Upon inspection, it becomes evident that race and ethnicity are important factors that are at the core of the health care debate. Of the 47 million uninsured American, more than 50 percent are racial and ethnic minorities.

Epidemiologic studies clearly show persistent differences in health outcomes and health status among racial and ethnic groups. For example, high blood pressure is more prevalent and is associated with poorer outcomes in blacks than whites. As a consequence, blacks are nearly twice as likely to have a first stroke and more likely to die from one compared with whites.[27–29] Among adults older than age 20, racial and ethnic minorities have a higher prevalence of diabetes than whites. Racial and ethnic minorities also have poorer glycemic control. Although this may be attributed to physiologic differences, differences in treatment of patients with diabetes also have been implicated.[30, 31]

Similar disparities are observed in cancer. Although cancer death rates have declined, the rate of decline is lower in blacks. Black men have the highest incidence for prostate cancer and are more than twice as likely to die from this disease.[32] White women have the highest incidence rate for breast cancer, but black women are most likely to die from breast cancer, usually at a more advanced stage, which most likely is due to a lack of early detection or suboptimal treatment.[33] Among all racial and ethnic groups, black males and black females have a higher incidence and death rate from both colorectal and lung cancer.[34, 35] Both blacks and Latinos are more likely to experience a mental disorder than their white counterparts and are less likely to seek treatment. When they do seek treatment, they are more likely to use the emergency room for mental health care and are more likely than whites to receive inpatient care rather than outpatient care.[34] With regard to mental health, women are two times more likely to suffer from depressive symptoms than men, especially Hispanic women.[36]

Not only are outcomes different among racial and ethnic groups, but treatment, too, differs. Studies have shown disparities in pain management, with minorities less likely to have access to appropriate pain management services and treatments, less likely to have their pain documented by health care providers, and less likely to receive pain medications. URMs are more likely to use the emergency department for pain care, but they are less likely to receive adequate care. They also experience poorer health and quality of life related to pain. In one study, only 25 percent of pharmacies in nonwhite neighborhoods had opioid supplies compared with 72 percent of pharmacies in white neighborhoods.[37]

THE IMPORTANCE OF HEALTH LITERACY

Health care diversity does not exclusively refer to only black and white. Diversity also applies to language. Health literacy is a major contributor to health disparity and can contribute to and exacerbate health disparities. Health literacy refers to the ability to read and comprehend health-related materials that ensure successful functioning in the role of the patient.[38] This includes the degree to which individuals have the capacity to obtain, process, and understand basic health information and services needed to make appropriate health decisions.[39] Although the reasons for health literacy are many (for example, language barriers and poor reading skills being major contributors), the consequences are quite serious. Poor health literacy has been linked to poorer adherence to medical instructions, poorer functional status, and poorer medication adherence.[40] Patients who have low health literacy also are those patients who are more likely to have poorer health outcomes.

Because language barriers often accentuate health literacy gaps, it is so important to have bilingual personnel provide instructions and to have culturally relevant education material written at a fifth-grade reading level in different languages. Having a physician or other health care provider who can speak the patient's language can make a tremendous difference. For example, a study that looked at Russian patients with type 2 diabetes found that the introduction of a Russian-speaking provider was associated with improvements in low-density lipoprotein (LDL), mean hemoglobin A1c, and both systolic and diastolic blood pressure, and improvements in medication adherence. Interpreters are important; however, they may limit the types of information patients provide.[41, 42] Thus, having physicians who speak the same language as their patients would improve communication and, hopefully, health outcomes.

Many studies have shown that language concordance is associated with greater patient comprehension and adherence to instructions. One study, for example, found that among Asian patients, those who had language-concordant physicians rather than interpreters were less likely to have unanswered questions. Conversely, patients who used interpreters were more likely than language-concordant patients to report having questions about their care or mental health that they wanted to ask but did not. Thus, although interpreter services are helpful, patients may be less likely to ask certain questions.[41]

PROVISION OF HEALTH CARE

Diversity in the health care workforce also is important for providing medical services to racial and ethnic minority populations. Although black and Latino physicians make up approximately 7 percent of the national physician pool, they provide care for up to 25 percent of black and Latino patients. Bach et al., for example, found that black patients were more likely to be seen by black physicians, physicians who were less likely to be board certified and physicians who reported greater difficulty in securing high-quality care.[24] Other studies have found that black and Latino physicians are more likely to practice in communities that are densely populated by black and Latino residents and are more likely to care for patients who are insured by Medicaid or who are uninsured. Komaromy et al. found that black physicians practiced in areas where there were five times as many black residents than in areas where other physicians practiced. Similarly, in communities where Latino physicians practiced, the proportion of Hispanic residents was twice as high as in areas where other physicians practiced.[43] This also may be attributable to patient preference; black and Latino patients may be more likely to seek out racial and ethnically similar physicians.[44]

As the proportion of blacks and Latinos in the population increases, there undoubtedly will be more black and Latino patients. From a manpower perspective, the number of minority physicians probably will be insufficient to meet this demand. This raises the question asked by Saha: "Can the current physician workforce pool keep up with this demand?"[44] More important, how will the policies and practices change to meet this need? Increasing diversity in the medical workforce potentially can enhance and expand current health disparities research.

The root causes of health disparities are complex and require a multidisciplinary approach to developing interventions. First, medical practitioners must have a better understanding of the social determinants of health disparities—that is, lower socioeconomic status, less than high school education, insufficient access to healthy foods, and poor health literacy.[45] Social determinants of disease often lead to a myriad of health disparities that disproportionally affect racial and ethnic minorities. Second, more research in this area is needed to better understand the complex components to effect change. For starters, diverse researchers are needed who can interact with and engage community members and understand the social and political climate in which they live.

There are many challenges to conducting health disparities research, including difficulty in recruiting diverse research subjects, lack of conducive settings for interventions, insufficient resources that reduce the likelihood of sustainability, and lack of trust of research and academic institutions from the prospective participants. [46, 47] Addressing health disparities also relies on community involvement and developing grassroots efforts. Community-Based Participatory Research is a methodological approach that involves equal partnership between communities and academic researchers. This research method has been used to address many medical conditions such as diabetes, asthma, and cancer.[48, 49] As part of this, bilingual researchers are needed who can increase the representation of participants who are not fluent in English. This increased representation will enhance the generalizability of research findings and extend applicability to a broader target audience.[50, 51]

MAKING MEDICAL EDUCATION MORE DIVERSE

Having a diverse faculty also might help to recruit a diverse student body and house staff. Diversity in higher education and allied health professions training settings is associated with better education outcomes among *all* students.[52, 53] One study reported a significant association between the proportion of URMs in a class and student ratings of their ability to care for a diverse population. The higher the proportion of URMs, the greater the likelihood of students rating themselves as highly prepared to care for minority populations. In schools with the highest proportion of URMs, white students also were more likely to have strong attitudes toward endorsing equitable access to care. URM students were substantially more likely than white or nonwhite and non-URM students to plan to serve the underserved.[53, 54]

A diverse faculty whose members are able to participate in the design and development of curricula programs is needed, for example, in developing a curriculum on cultural competency. The AAMC and Liaison Committee on Medical Education (LCME) have set recommendations to ensure that medical schools integrate cultural competence training as part of their curriculum. Cultural competence training involves training students to interact and communicate effectively in cross-cultural settings. A more diverse faculty can demonstrate cultural competence in practice and in theory. Having a diverse faculty creates an environment of mutual learning in which students and health professionals can learn from each other. A study of minority faculty in other higher education settings demonstrated that faculty of color employ a broader range of pedagogical techniques compared with their white counterparts, including class discussions and writing assignments that include diverse perspectives.[54] Therefore, more racially and ethnically diverse faculty may enhance the overall quality of medical education. Such diversity most certainly would reflect the demographic realities of the population.

CHALLENGES FOR THE FUTURE

The 21st century has witnessed new threats to health care that affect the most vulnerable and disenfranchised populations. For example, Hurricane Katrina forced thousands of people to relocate, the majority of whom were poor African Americans and the elderly poor. The threats of new pandemics such as H1N1 virus or biological threats such as anthrax have provided the impetus for public health officials to develop and have in place strategies for the rapid vaccination of not only those who have access to medical care, but especially those most vulnerable populations, including the chronically ill, the poor, and children and pregnant women. There is a substantial challenge for health care facilities to quickly mobilize its workforce to identify and treat those in greatest need. For this to happen expediently, medical professionals need to have a familiarity with the population in need and an understanding of their social context. Having a diverse workforce that can reach out to this population and that has the necessary social, linguistic, and cultural skills to gain trust and entry into these communities is imperative to tackling such threats.

Ideally, a diverse workforce should be present at all levels of academic medicine, especially in positions of academic leadership where policy reform is developed. Institutions must evaluate their climate for diversity through periodic confidential surveys of all students and health professional staff and ensure that diversity in numbers is accompanied by diversity in the approach to education, patient care, and research. The task for promoting diversity cannot be relegated to just a few but must be an institutional goal that is promoted from the academic medical center's leadership, that is, from the top down. This leadership must be ready to change policies that are overtly discriminatory in nature and to review the current recruitment, promotion, and tenure practices of the institution as it relates to racial ethnic minorities and women. Individuals who are familiar enough with the organizational structure and history of diversity at the institution should lead designated central offices. Institutions should review their current affirmative action policies to ensure that they reflect national standards.

To ensure diversity in academic leadership, search committees should include representation of women and racial and ethnic minorities. Leadership should compile data showing how the proportion of underrepresented minorities and women at the institution compares with national standards. Additionally, programs should be in place to ensure that adequate pipelines of talented students from underrepresented backgrounds are available. This requires developing community partnerships with local colleges, minority-serving institutions, and historically black colleges and universities. Programs also should be in place to provide social support and proper career development once diverse students and faculty join the institution.

To ensure that a diverse body of students, residents, and faculty contributes to the academic mission, there should be forums for all members of the institution to contribute to different modalities of education, clinical care, and research. A diverse research faculty can bring skill sets that can inform novel research directions. Therefore, the institution must begin to embrace different yet methodologically sound approaches to research, such as community-based participatory research, working with community partners, and conducting research in nonacademic and nontraditional venues.

In summary a diverse workforce is essential to addressing the needs of a diverse U.S. population, enriching cultural-competency education for students, improving quality of care and access to underserved populations, and developing culturally relevant approaches to research and to addressing the most pressing public health needs. There are compelling reasons to promote health care diversity. Just about every health care organization, from the AAMC to the LCME to the government, has embraced the need for cultural diversity in the education system. Academic health centers contribute to health by upholding their tripartite mission of educating future physicians, developing innovative biomedical research, and providing quality patient care. Fulfilling this mission has become increasingly challenging in light of the ever-changing demographic landscape of the United States. Therefore, strategic planning must occur in order to make diversity in the health care workforce a priority and part of the fabric of the institution.

REFERENCES

1. US Census Bureau. US interim projections by age, sex, race, and Hispanic origin: 2000–2050. http://www.census.gov/population/www/projections/usinterimproj/. Accessed November 11, 2009.
2. Goel MS, McCarthy EP, Phillips RS, Wee CC. Obesity among US immigrant subgroups by duration of residence. *JAMA*. 2004;292:2860–2867.
3. Park Y, Neckerman KM, Quinn J, Weiss C, Rundle A. Place of birth, duration of residence, neighborhood immigrant composition and body mass index in New York City. *Int J Behav Nutr Phys Act*. 2008;5:19.
4. Harley EH. The forgotten history of defunct black medical schools in the 19th and 20th centuries and the impact of the Flexner Report. *J Natl Med Assoc*. 2006;98:1425–1429.
5. Flexner A. *Medical Education in the United States and Canada: A Report to the Carnegie Foundation for the Advancement of Teaching*. New York: Carnegie Foundation for the Advancement of Teaching; 1910. Bulletin No. 4.
6. Hoover EL. Did Flexner's Report condemn black medical schools? not so, in my opinion. *J Natl Med Assoc*. 2006;98:1432–1434.
7. Strelnick AH, Lee-Rey E, Nivet M, Soto-Greene ML. Diversity in academic medicine no. 2: history of battles lost and won. *Mt Sinai J Med*. 2008;75:499–503.
8. Smith SG, Nsiah-Kumi PA, Jones PR, Pamies RJ. Pipeline programs in the health professions, part 2: the impact of recent legal challenges to affirmative action. *J Natl Med Assoc*. 2009;101:852–863.
9. Crosby FJ, Iyer A, Sincharoen S. Understanding affirmative action. *Annu Rev Psychol*. 2006;57:585–611.
10. Regents of University of California v Bakke. 438 US 265; 1978.
11. Hopwood v Texas. 78 F3d 932; 5th Cir, cert denied. 116 S Ct 2581; 1996.
12. Cohen JJ. The predictable price of Proposition 209. *Acad Med*. 1999;74:528.
13. The American Medical Student Association, Foundation Study Group on Minority Medical Education. *Findings from Literature Search and Anecdotal Data*. Reston, VA: American Medical Student Association; 1996.

14. Association of American Medical Colleges. Diversity in medical education: facts and figures 2008. http://www.aamc.org/data/facts/.
15. Palepu A, Carr PL, Friedman RH, Amos H, Ash AS, Moskowitz MA. Minority faculty and academic rank in medicine. *JAMA*. 1998;280:767–771.
16. Institute of Medicine. *In the Nation's Compelling Interest: Ensuring Diversity in the Health Care Workforce*. Washington, DC: The National Academy Press; 2004.
17. Cooper LA, Roter DL, Johnson RL, Ford DE, Steinwachs DM, Powe NR. Patient-centered communication, ratings of care, and concordance of patient and physician race. *Ann Intern Med*. 2003;139:907–915.
18. Street RL Jr., O'Malley KJ, Cooper LA, Haidet P. Understanding concordance in patient-physician relationships: personal and ethnic dimensions of shared identity. *Ann Fam Med*. 2008;6:198–205.
19. Laveist TA, Nuru-Jeter A. Is doctor-patient race concordance associated with greater satisfaction with care? *J Health Soc Behav*. 2002;43:296–306.
20. King WD, Wong MD, Shapiro MF, Landon BE, Cunningham WE. Does racial concordance between HIV-positive patients and their physicians affect the time to receipt of protease inhibitors? *J Gen Intern Med*. 2004;19:1146–1153.
21. Missing Persons Minorities in the Professions: A Report of the Sullivan Commission on Diversity in the Healthcare Workforce. 2004. http://www.sullivancommission.org.
22. Institute of Medicine. *Unequal Treatment: Confronting Racial and Ethnic Disparities in Health Care*. Washington, DC: National Academies Press; 2003.
23. Popescu I, Vaughan-Sarrazin MS, Rosenthal GE. Differences in mortality and use of revascularization in black and white patients with acute MI admitted to hospitals with and without revascularization services. *JAMA*. 2007;297:2489–2495.
24. Bach PB, Pham HH, Schrag D, Tate RC, Hargraves JL. Primary care physicians who treat blacks and whites. *N Engl J Med*. 2004;351:575–584.
25. Brown CP, Ross L, Lopez I, Thornton A, Kiros GE. Disparities in the receipt of cardiac revascularization procedures between blacks and whites: an analysis of secular trends. *Ethn Dis*. 2008;18(Suppl 2):S112–S117.
26. Nguyen LL, Hevelone N, Rogers SO, et al. Disparity in outcomes of surgical revascularization for limb salvage: race and gender are synergistic determinants of vein graft failure and limb loss. *Circulation*. 2009;119:123–130.
27. Pickering TG. Hypertension in blacks. *Curr Opin Nephrol Hypertens*. 1994;3:207–212.
28. Cooper RS, Liao Y, Rotimi C. Is hypertension more severe among US blacks, or is severe hypertension more common? *Ann Epidemiol*. 1996;6:173–180.
29. Lindhorst J, Alexander N, Blignaut J, Rayner B. Differences in hypertension between blacks and whites: an overview. *Cardiovasc J Afr*. 2007;18:241–247.
30. Thackeray R, Merrill RM, Neiger BL. Disparities in diabetes management practice between racial and ethnic groups in the United States. *Diabetes Educ*. 2004;30:665–675.
31. Allsworth JE, Toppa R, Palin NC, Lapane KL. Racial and ethnic disparities in the pharmacologic management of diabetes mellitus among long-term care facility residents. *Ethn Dis*. 2005;15:205–212.
32. Odedina FT, Akinremi TO, Chinegwundoh F, et al. Prostate cancer disparities in black men of African descent: a comparative literature review of prostate cancer burden among black men in the United States, Caribbean, United Kingdom, and West Africa. *Infect Agent Cancer*. 2009;4(Suppl 1):S2.
33. Hershman D, McBride R, Jacobson JS, et al. Racial disparities in treatment and survival among women with early-stage breast cancer. *J Clin Oncol*. 2005;23:6639–6646.

34. Polite BN, Dignam JJ, Olopade OI. Colorectal cancer model of health disparities: understanding mortality differences in minority populations. *J Clin Oncol.* 2006;24:2179–2187.
35. Flenaugh EL, Henriques-Forsythe MN. Lung cancer disparities in African Americans: health versus health care. *Clin Chest Med.* 2006;27:431–439,vi.
36. Boutin-Foster C. An item-level analysis of the Center for Epidemiologic Studies Depression Scale (CES-D) by race and ethnicity in patients with coronary artery disease. *Int J Geriatr Psychiatry.* 2008;23:1034–1039.
37. Morrison RS, Wallenstein S, Natale DK, Senzel RS, Huang LL. "We don't carry that": failure of pharmacies in predominantly nonwhite neighborhoods to stock opioid analgesics. *N Engl J Med.* 2000;342:1023–1026.
38. Leyva M, Sharif I, Ozuah PO. Health literacy among Spanish-speaking Latino parents with limited English proficiency. *Ambul Pediatr.* 2005;5:56–59.
39. Ratzan SP. Health literacy. In: Seldon CR, Ratzan SC, Parker RM, eds. *National Library of Medicine Current Bibliographies in Medicine.* Washington, DC: National Institutes of Health/U.S. Department of Health and Human Services; 2000.
40. Gazmararian JA, Kripalani S, Miller MJ, Echt KV, Ren J, Rask K. Factors associated with medication refill adherence in cardiovascular-related diseases: a focus on health literacy. *J Gen Intern Med.* 2006;21:1215–1221.
41. Green AR, Ngo-Metzger Q, Legedza AT, Massagli MP, Phillips RS, Iezzoni LI. Interpreter services, language concordance, and health care quality: experiences of Asian Americans with limited English proficiency. *J Gen Intern Med.* 2005;20:1050–1056.
42. Mehler PS, Lundgren RA, Pines I, Doll K. A community study of language concordance in Russian patients with diabetes. *Ethn Dis.* 2004;14:584–588.
43. Komaromy M, Grumbach K, Drake M, et al. The role of black and Hispanic physicians in providing health care for underserved populations. *N Engl J Med.* 1996;334:1305–1310.
44. Saha S, Taggart SH, Komaromy M, Bindman AB. Do patients choose physicians of their own race? *Health Aff (Millwood).* 2000;19:76–83.
45. Marmot MG, Bell R. Action on health disparities in the United States: commission on social determinants of health. *JAMA.* 2009;301:1169–1171.
46. Musa D, Schulz R, Harris R, Silverman M, Thomas SB. Trust in the health care system and the use of preventive health services by older black and white adults. *Am J Public Health.* 2009;99:1293–1299.
47. Rajakumar K, Thomas SB, Musa D, Almario D, Garza MA. Racial differences in parents' distrust of medicine and research. *Arch Pediatr Adolesc Med.* 2009;163:108–114.
48. Horowitz CR, Goldfinger JZ, Muller SE, et al. A model for using community-based participatory research to address the diabetes epidemic in East Harlem. *Mt Sinai J Med.* 2008;75:13–21.
49. Lengerich EJ, Kluhsman BC, Bencivenga M, Allen R, Miele MB, Farace E. Development of community plans to enhance survivorship from colorectal cancer: community-based participatory research in rural communities. *J Cancer Surviv.* 2007;1:205–211.
50. Cohen JJ, Gabriel BA, Terrell C. The case for diversity in the health care workforce. *Health Aff (Millwood).* 2002;21:90–102.
51. Stoff DM, Forsyth A, Marquez ED, McClure S. Introduction: the case for diversity in research on mental health and HIV/AIDS. *Am J Public Health.* 2009;99(Suppl 1): S8–S15.

52. Hung R, McClendon J, Henderson A, Evans Y, Colquitt R, Saha S. Student perspectives on diversity and the cultural climate at a US medical school. *Acad Med*. 2007;82:184–192.
53. Saha S, Guiton G, Wimmers PF, Wilkerson L. Student body racial and ethnic composition and diversity-related outcomes in US medical schools. *JAMA*. 2008;300:1135–1145.
54. Umbach P. The contribution of faculty of color to undergraduate education. *Res Higher Educ*. 2006;47(3):317–345.

SECTION 3

ETHICS AND HUMAN RIGHTS

CHAPTER 6

Human Rights: A Necessary Framework for Public Health
Holly G. Atkinson, MD

In these early years of the 21st century, human rights and public health intersect in an exciting and vibrant way. By working to achieve public health goals, we actually advance a number of human rights. More importantly, by embracing human rights as an ethical and legal basis and guiding framework, we adopt the most promising and compelling strategy for moving forward a global public health agenda. Human rights are a necessary framework for informing public health, for without it, public health loses much of its transformative potential and moral focus. When left to its own devices, public health does not always improve the health of communities and their members. In fact, public health initiatives sometimes—either by acts of omission or commission—fail to protect the most vulnerable among us or even themselves commit violations of human rights. The Tuskegee Study is an appalling example of a monumental public health failure.

For 40 years, between 1932 and 1972, the U.S. Public Health Service (PHS) conducted a study on nearly 400 men in the late stages of syphilis. The specific goal of the study was to follow the progression of *untreated* syphilis in African Americans men to learn more about the natural course of the infection. The men, most of whom were illiterate sharecroppers from Alabama, were never told what disease they had, or how serious it was. Their informed consent was never sought; in fact, they were deliberately misinformed about the nature of the study. Furthermore, when penicillin became available in 1943, treatment was purposely withheld from the group. When some of the men figured out their disease and sought medication from the PHS, even then they were denied treatment. The study ended only when the Associated Press ran an exposé on the sordid affair in July 1972. The Tuskegee Study, designed to advance knowledge and contribute to public health, now ranks among the most egregious violations of human rights in the history of American medicine.[1]

This chapter explores why a human rights framework is crucial to the work of public health. First, the human rights framework—in concert with traditional medical ethics—articulates certain values and standards that specify how we should conduct ourselves. The Tuskegee episode illustrates the disastrous consequences of public health initiatives failing to respect, promote, and protect human rights. A human rights framework, however, offers more to public health than professional standards alone. The human rights framework also provides a vast armamentarium—a vision of a more just world, an agenda for change, an array of initiatives shared with civil society, benchmarks for vulnerable groups, and legal strategies to hold state actors accountable—for achieving public health goals. This chapter argues that human rights is a *necessary* framework for public health.

HUMAN RIGHTS AND THE RIGHT TO HEALTH[2]

Human rights is a concept that, while rooted in antiquity, came to the vanguard only during the 18th century, when the American and French revolutions created a new ethical standard. In justifying America's independence from England, Thomas Jefferson stated in the Declaration of Independence, "We hold these truths to be self-evident, that all men are created equal." As historian Lynn Hunt writes in *Inventing Human Rights*, "With this one sentence Jefferson turned a typical eighteenth-century document about political grievances into a lasting proclamation of human rights."[3] Thirteen years later, the Declaration of the Rights of Man and Citizen—born of the French Revolution—declared the "natural, inalienable and sacred rights of man" to be the foundation of government. Although lacking in explicit definition, the idea of the "rights of man" was here to stay, and the nature of politics was forever changed around the world.

Not until the 20th century, however, did the concept of *universal* human rights take hold, culminating as the organizing principle of the Universal Declaration of Human Rights (UDHR). The UDHR is an unprecedented document, born of the tragedies and horrors of World War II and adopted by the United Nations General Assembly on December 10, 1948.[4] The breadth, depth, and universality of human rights articulated by the UDHR stands as one of the landmark achievements of the 20th century.

How do we best define human rights today? In concept, a human right is *any basic right or freedom to which all human beings are entitled and in whose exercise a government may not interfere*. Operationally, human rights refer to "an internationally agreed upon set of principles and norms that are embodied in international legal instruments."[5] These principles and norms were generated through a painstaking, consensus-building process among member states of the United Nations, and thus human rights derive from human institutions created to serve the people.

In the 21st century, human rights advance through a system of laws designed to promote and protect fundamental individual freedoms and human dignity. Rights are categorized into five basic groups: civil, political, economic, social, and cultural rights. Human rights are principally concerned with the relationship between the individual and the state. In this regard, a human rights approach to public health offers much promise, as governments have major roles to play in promoting public health and undertaking or supporting specific public health measures.

What does the "right to health" mean? Every person has the human right *to the highest attainable standard of health*, without discrimination of any kind. The World Health Organization's (WHO) 1946 Constitution was the first to declare, that the enjoyment of the highest attainable standard of health is one of the fundamental rights of every human being. In the Constitution's Preamble, health is defined as a state of complete physical, mental and social well-being, and not merely the absence of disease or infirmity." The definition goes on to highlight the importance of health promotion, which is "the process of enabling people to increase control over and to improve their health." To do so, "an individual or group must be able to identify and realize aspirations, to satisfy needs, and to change or cope with the environment."

This right to the highest attainable standard of health, or "right to health" for short, embodies a number of specific rights, which in the 21st century—extending beyond the WHO Constitution—are spelled out in various human rights treaties and other documents and should be considered in their totality. They include the following human rights:

- the right to the highest attainable standard of physical and mental health, including reproductive and sexual health;
- the right to equal access to adequate health care and health-related services, regardless of sex, race, or other status;
- the right to equitable distribution of food;
- the right to access to safe drinking water and sanitation;
- the right to an adequate standard of living and adequate housing;
- the right to a safe and healthy environment; and
- the right to a safe and healthy workplace, and to adequate protection for pregnant women in work proven to be harmful to them.[6]

How should we make sense of these rights? How do we make good on the promise of the right to the highest attainable standard of health? In defining the overarching concept of the right to health, Mary Robinson, the former United Nations High Commissioner for Human Rights, stated the following:

The right to health does not mean the right to be healthy, nor does it mean that poor governments must put in place expensive health services for which they have no resources. But it does require governments and public authorities to put in place policies and action plans which will lead to *available and accessible health care for all in the shortest possible time*. To ensure that this happens is the challenge facing both the human rights community and public health professionals. (emphasis added)[6]

Robinson rightly affirms the centrality of the principle of *progressive* realization of human rights. This means that governments and other important actors must move as expeditiously and effectively as possible to realize a right, especially the right to health. To be sure, governments around the world do not possess the equal capacities to realize the right to health. Some governments possess an abundance of resources and thus have great ability to act on behalf of their populace. Other governments have meager resources at best, leaving them unable to promote the well-being of their citizens. Yet all too often, governments are *unwilling* to act, rather than *unable* to act. Under these circumstances, citizens and concerned groups can and should use rights language and legal instruments to hold their governments accountable.

In summary, human rights are a cohesive set of values and standards that provide us with a powerful framework to move forward the public health agenda. Human rights articulate our ideals, inspire us to act on their behest, set standards for judging health and social policy, allow for the identification of violations, provide legal concepts to hold actors accountable, and protect the most vulnerable and disenfranchised among us.

PUBLIC HEALTH AND HEALTH STATUS

Writing in *Science* magazine in 1920, C. E. A. Winslow defined public health as

the science and the art of preventing disease, prolonging life, and promoting physical health and efficiency through organized community efforts for the sanitation of the environment, the control of community infections, the education of the individual in principles of personal hygiene, the organization of medical and nursing services for the early diagnosis and preventive treatment of disease, and the development of the social machinery which will ensure to every individual in the community a standard of living adequate for the maintenance of health.[7]

In the 21st century, the American Public Health Association more succinctly states, "Public health is the practice of preventing disease and promoting good health within groups of people, from small communities to entire countries."[8] Both of these definitions underscore the two distinct aspects of public health work: the *prevention* of disease and the *promotion* of health, rather than the treatment of disease *per se*. Regardless, the focus of public health is on population health, rather than on individual health, which is the primary focus of clinical medicine.

The dichotomy between public health and individual health is an ancient one. The Greeks worshipped two divinities with distinct domains: Hygeia was the goddess of good health and represented what is now the realm of public health: cleanliness, sanitation, good health habits, and ultimately the prevention of illness. Asklepios, her father, was the god of medicine and healing, and one of the most important and widely worshipped divinities of antiquity. The original Hippocratic Oath pays homage to both Asklepios and Hygeia, "I swear by Apollo the physician, and Asklepios, and Hygeia, and Panakeia, and all the gods and goddesses, that, according to my ability and judgment, I will keep this Oath and this stipulation."[9] Although belief in these gods and goddesses has long since passed, the chasm they represent remains alive and well in the 21st century. Ironically, public health initiatives remain one of the most powerful ways to advance individual health and well-being, as well as to contribute to the development of healthy, vibrant communities.

What determines individual health status? Health is influenced primarily by five major factors—personal behavior, genetic influences, social circumstances, access to medical care, and environmental exposures. In the United States, behavior is the major determinant of health, accounting for about 40 percent of all premature deaths in the United States. Medical care, or more accurately the lack of it, plays a surprisingly small role, contributing to only about 10 percent of premature deaths in the United States. The remaining 50 percent of premature deaths is due to genetic influences (roughly 30 percent), social circumstances (15 percent), and environmental exposures (5 percent).[10] Medical science cannot yet alter genetic influences in a clinically meaningful way, but we do know that lifestyle, social factors, and environment exposures alter the manner in which genes express themselves.

The medical literature is replete with evidence linking poor health to socioeconomic disadvantage. Disease and death rates in all nations are closely linked to social standing: people in lower socioeconomic groups have more disease and die earlier than those in higher groups. To make this point, Mackenbach et al. examined data on mortality, morbidity, smoking, and obesity in relation to socioeconomic status among 22 countries in Europe.[11] In almost all of the countries, researchers found that rates of death and poorer self-assessments of health were substantially higher in men and women of lower socioeconomic status than those of higher socioeconomic status. Writing in an accompanying editorial, Berkman and Epstein note, "The universal link between social class and mortality seems remarkable, given the differing disease prevalence and risk factors in these countries. Moreover, the relationships between class and mortality are consistent for almost every cause of death, with only a few exceptions, notably certain cancers."[12]

People in lower socioeconomic groups typically have more unhealthy behaviors than those in higher socioeconomic groups. This disparity can be traced, in part, to problems that include lack of access to nutritious food, safe neighborhoods, and recreational facilities, as well as higher levels of physical and psychological stress from being socially disadvantaged. Smoking, still considered by experts to be the leading cause of preventable death worldwide, is now more prevalent among people in lower socioeconomic classes than those in the upper classes.

But even when unhealthy behaviors are removed from the equation, poor people still have worse health and higher death rates than wealthier individuals. No doubt the causes are myriad and complex, and more research is needed to understand the link between class and health. We know, for example, that education, job, income, housing, and neighborhood all have a bearing on well-being. Policies that influence the quality and availability of basic necessities of life (education, housing, jobs, and so on) have important health consequences. These factors must be taken into account when leaders of government and civil society set public policy. These concerns fall directly within the realms of both public health and human rights.

THE MILLENNIUM DEVELOPMENT GOALS AND PUBLIC HEALTH

In September 2000, building on a decade of major United Nations conferences and summits, world leaders came together at United Nations Headquarters in New York to adopt the United Nations Millennium Declaration, committing their nations to a new global partnership to reduce extreme poverty and setting out a series of time-bound targets. This declaration has become known as the Millennium Development Goals (MDGs). In 2001, 192 United Nations member states and at least 23 international organizations agreed to work together to achieve eight global development goals (see table 6.1) by the year 2015. Responding to the world's main development challenges and to the calls of civil society, the MDGs promote poverty reduction, education, maternal health, gender equality, and aim at combating child mortality, AIDS and other diseases. The MDGs acknowledge the broader social factors that contribute to health. That is, 3 of the 8 goals, 8 of the 16 targets, and 18 of the 48 indicators relate directly to health. The other interventions address broader social issues that play a significant role in promoting and protecting health and preventing disease.

Over the past decades, substantial progress has been made in improving global health.[13] For example, over the past 25 years, overall life expectancy at birth has increased by nine years to 64.5 years worldwide. Because of a host of political, economic, medical, and social factors, there are, of course, notable exceptions, such as

Table 6.1
Millennium Development Goals

Goal 1: Eradicate extreme poverty and hunger
Goal 2: Achieve universal primary education
Goal 3: Promote gender equality and empower women
Goal 4: Reduce child mortality
Goal 5: Improve maternal health
Goal 6: Combat HIV/AIDS, malaria and other diseases
Goal 7: Ensure environmental sustainability
Goal 8: Develop a global partnership for development

Source: United Nations 2000.

in Africa. Worldwide, death of children age five years or younger has decreased from 13.5 million per year in 1980 to about 9.7 million in 2005. Mortality from infectious diseases, including HIV/AIDS, tuberculosis, and malaria, also is estimated to decline over the next 20 years. And while overall maternal deaths, approximately 500,000 worldwide per year, have not declined substantially over the last two decades, new initiatives have put this extremely important health issue on the public health and women's rights agendas.

Despite promising progress, much remains to be done. What is needed now is a broad public health approach based on the right to health. The three health MDGs—goals 4, 5, and 6—with the deadline looming in 2015, will not be achieved without additional funding. None of the MDGs is expected to be achieved by the target date in Sub-Saharan Africa. Epidemics of infectious disease increasingly threaten the globe, and preparedness for these outbreaks needs to be greatly improved. Gender-based violence and pernicious discrimination against women and girls still ravage the lives of tens of million of females around the world. Chronic conditions such as heart disease, stroke, diabetes, cancer, and chronic respiratory diseases—for decades the major killer diseases in the developed world—are increasingly prevalent in the developing world. By 2030, chronic noncommunicable diseases will account for more than 75 percent of all deaths worldwide, and yet health systems have not engaged in any substantial way to address these burgeoning health problems.[14] Global environmental changes—including rapid climate change—will have considerable health consequences, including changes in drinking water quality, effects of temperature extremes, and the spread of numerous infectious agents. Finally, we have made dismal progress on addressing the underlying socioeconomic determinants of health and need to make it a primary focus of the global public health agenda.

In 2005, the WHO launched the Commission on the Social Determinants of Health to identify strategies for addressing the causes of health inequalities. As articulated by Beaglehole and Bonita:

The commission's final report stresses several important needs: to improve daily living conditions, including the circumstances in which people are born, grow, live, work and age; to tackle the inequitable distribution of power, money, and resources (the structural drivers of those conditions) worldwide, nationally and locally; and to measure and understand the problem and assess the effect of action. The report is a major contribution to global public health with its breadth of vision and strong evidence base. Achievement of the fine goals of the report depends on the willingness of WHO, its member states, other key international agencies, and civil society *to strengthen the social justice approach to health* and give greater attention to intersectoral actions. (emphasis added)[13]

We *must* take action on the social factors that influence health to decrease the health disparities and inequalities that abound around the globe. Public health initiatives that mitigate the social determinants of disease and help individuals adopt healthier lifestyles offer the best opportunity to advance health and well-being in all nations, both developed and developing.

In the end, health is an issue of justice. John Rawls's landmark theory of justice argues that "deliberate inequalities [a]re unjust unless they work to the advantage of the least well off," and require corrective social action.[15] The myriad institutional inequalities that abound in health *do not* work to the advantage of the least well off, thus these injustices need to be addressed. But by whom we might ask?

Justice is one of the four major principles that constitute the most commonly promulgated ethical foundation of medicine. But for far too long, it has taken a back seat in informing health initiatives. Medical professionals are ethically bound to address issues of injustice as they pertain to health, and yet in the 21st century, many health care workers—especially clinicians—do not consider it within their professional obligation to engage in societal issues directly effecting health and well-being. Health care professionals need to redress this imbalance. What then does justice require of the profession? When applied to the domain of health, a commitment to justice becomes a declaration of human rights, including the right to health.

THE LINKS BETWEEN HUMAN RIGHTS AND HEALTH

Health and human rights intersect in a number of important ways. Figure 6.1 explores some of these complex and overlapping linkages. First, *violations* of any number of human rights can, and often do, have serious health consequences (upper circle). The Tuskegee Syphilis Study is a blatant example that involved numerous human rights violations, which resulted in horrendous consequences for the subjects. Other examples include gender-based violence, which can lead to a host of physical and mental health problems in women. Children who are trafficked into sex work suffer untold physical and mental harm. Harmful traditional practices, such as female genital cutting and mutilation, can lead to urinary, gastrointestinal, and reproductive health problems, as well as to myriad mental health issues.

Second, by *respecting, protecting, and fulfilling human rights* (lower left circle), individuals' vulnerabilities to and the impact of ill health can be reduced. A human rights approach recognizes that personal behavior is substantially influenced by social, political, and economic circumstances, and thus stresses that governments are obliged to create healthier environments in which people can undertake that personal responsibility, for example, insuring that lower socioeconomic areas have access to fresh fruits and vegetables rather than mostly fast

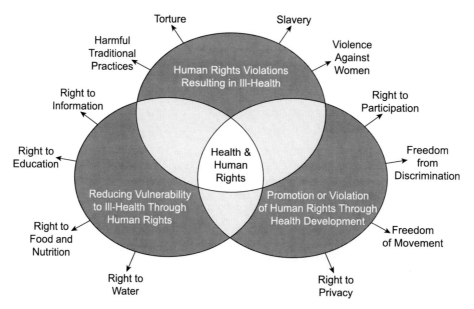

Figure 6.1 Linkages Between Health and Human Rights, from the WHO, July 2002. (*Source:* Atkinson.)

foodchains. When human rights other than the right to health are addressed, health is promoted as well. For example, access to accurate information as well as to an education promotes health and well-being.

Third, *direct efforts at health development* (lower right circle) can either promote or violate various human rights of individuals or groups, which ultimately bears on their well-being. For example, limiting women's access to reproductive health information can have a significant impact on morbidity and mortality, as well as on quality of life. People with mental disabilities often are discriminated against, which has a broad impact on their rights to employment, education, and housing, which in turn have a major impact on their health and well-being. A particular focus on human rights protection and promotion is extremely important to the design, and ultimately the outcome, of health policies and programs.

To be sure, in some situations the exercise of good public health policy necessitates infringing on some individual human rights. For example, sometimes it is appropriate to quarantine an individual to control the spread of a serious infectious disease, and thus the right to freedom of movement can be abridged. International human rights instruments do recognize that situations will arise that justifiably entail restricting certain rights. (Certain rights, however, such as the freedom from slavery or torture, never should be compromised.) To ascertain the appropriateness of restricting rights, human rights law articulates the Siracusa Principles, which state that

Public health may be invoked as a ground for limiting certain rights in order to allow a state to take measures dealing with a serious threat to the health of the population or individual members of the population. These measures must be specifically aimed at preventing disease or injury or providing care for the sick and injured.[16]

The Siracusa Principles further stipulate that before rights can be restricted, five criteria must be met:

1. the restriction is provided for and carried out in accordance with the law;
2. the restriction is in the interest of a legitimate objective of general interest;
3. the restriction is strictly necessary in a democratic society to achieve the objective;
4. there are no less intrusive and restrictive means available to reach the same objective; and
5. the restriction is not drafted or imposed arbitrarily, i.e., in an unreasonable or otherwise discriminatory manner.

The restriction of rights should be undertaken only as the last resort, with considerable justification and with safeguards in place. And when it is necessary to curtail individual rights in the service of public good, the rights should be restricted for the shortest possible time.

THE VALUE ADDED BY HUMAN RIGHTS IN PUBLIC HEALTH ARENA

How does a human rights approach to health add value to public health initiatives? First and foremost, it moves health out of the realm of being a commodity or charity into the realm of constituting moral and legal obligations of a society—especially governments—to its people. The human rights approach provides public health with (1) a guiding *framework*; (2) *strategies* for addressing inequities and disparities in health; (3) *tools* for designing, implementing, monitoring, and evaluating public health initiatives; and (4) the *foundation* for holding governments and institutions accountable.

The framework of human rights articulates internationally accepted norms and standards against which public policy can be planned, monitored, and ultimately judged. This, in and of itself, is an important step forward in human moral and legal development. For the first time in human history, we have articulated ideals that describe society's obligations to all citizens in all places at all times. These ideals and obligations are particularly inspiring and empowering to individuals who are poor, disenfranchised, or oppressed, and give them a moral *and* legal foundation on which to base their demands.

Secondly, the human rights approach offers strategies to bring about change. For example, acknowledging that education is a major socioeconomic determinant of health expands the domain of public health initiatives to include promoting and protecting the right to education. By understanding the biological and cultural role gender plays in determining health status, public health officials can use a gendered lens to analyze data, policies, and programs to achieve optimal health among women and men, as well as to reduce the profound impact of gender discrimination on women's well-being.

The human rights approach insists on designing, implementing, monitoring, and evaluating programs and policies in terms of how well they move communities toward positive health outcomes. Benchmarks and indicators can be identified to track the progressive realization of health rights. The human rights approach especially urges public health officials to consider the impact of programs and policies on vulnerable groups, such as ethnic and religious minorities, internally displaced persons, refugees of war, immigrants, prisoners, victims of sexual trafficking, and the extremely disenfranchised, such as impoverished women and children. For example, data amply demonstrate that

respect for human rights in the context of HIV/AIDS, mental illness, and physical disability leads to markedly better prevention and treatment. Respect of the dignity and privacy of individuals can facilitate more sensitive and humane care. Stigmatization and discrimination thwart medical and public health efforts to heal people with disease or disability.[17]

Finally, the human rights approach, in articulating the highest standard of health, provides a moral and legal basis for holding governments and other institutions accountable. For as Dr. Helen Potts, chief program officer of Health Programs at Physicians for Human Rights, has said, "the distinctive contribution of a human rights approach is the essential component of accountability by government[s] to the[ir] population[s]."[18] Human rights activists and public health officials, with outcomes data in hand, can press governments to take definitive steps to protect, promote, and fulfill their human rights obligations. This means establishing concrete goals, committing available resources, and executing plans in a timely way to advance health outcomes. At times, legal remedies can be sought in courts of law (for example, individuals with HIV/AIDS have petitioned the courts for access to antiretroviral drugs), while at other times, mobilization and advocacy in civil society or in the broader international arena can drive the public health agenda (for example, the International Campaign to Ban Landmines resulted in the signing of the Ottawa Treaty in December 1997 that bans government use of landmines).

The human rights approach offers an armamentarium to public health that is powerful indeed. It is particularly forceful in addressing issues of social justice and health. It gives a strong voice to the needs of the disenfranchised and vulnerable, who disproportionately suffer the negative impact of the social determinants of disease. As WHO official Ms. Helena Nygren-Krug has put it, "Linking health and human rights could act as a force for mobilizing and empowering the most vulnerable and disadvantaged. Advancing health as a human rights right means making people conscious of both their oppression and the possibility of change."[19]

THE CHALLENGES WE FACE AND THE POSSIBILITY OF CHANGE

It has been only 65 years since the right to health was articulated and subsequently codified in a number of important 20th-century documents. Since then, the concept of human rights has grown in importance around the globe. Human rights now play a central role in all major social, cultural, political, and economic discourses. Health and human rights is a nascent but rapidly growing field within both the human rights arena and the public health arena. Given the brief time this framework has informed modern thinking, the impact that human rights, particularly the right to the highest attainable standard of health, already has made on the world stage is impressive and inspiring. For example, more than 100 national constitutions worldwide establish health as a human right. And every country in the world has signed on to at least one human rights treaty that enshrines language addressing the goal of attaining the highest attainable standard of health. This is good news indeed, although much remains to be done. Although nations have articulated the right to the highest attainable standard of health, it is the particular duty of health care professionals in the public health arena to progressively *realize* the right to health in a concrete way. Our work has just begun.

How do we move forward? We need three broad initiatives: we need to teach about, advocate for, and operationalize the right to health.

- Teaching the right to health: The core curriculum of health care education, including public health schools, nursing schools, *and* medical schools, should include comprehensive instruction on health and human rights, especially the right to health. Without a deep understanding of the human rights approach, public health and medical personnel lack a powerful framework for driving the public health agenda. Young idealistic students crave this sort of instruction. They search for a way to process what they bear witness to: the deep inequities in society and health care that profoundly affect individual health. They seek a principled way to bring about meaningful change. As Len Rubenstein, former president of Physicians for Human Rights has said,

The reluctance of medical schools to address these issues is understandable: the curriculum is crowded; few faculty have experience in addressing these issues; and most of all there is distinct queasiness about bringing human rights concerns into medical education because it is somehow 'political' and therefore has no place in an education founded in scientific evidence. If the next generation of physicians is to be fully prepared to deal with the social and moral dilemmas they'll face in the coming decades, however, medical education will need to push its way through these barriers.[20] If we fail to bring about such needed education reform, we will fail yet another generation of health care workers who will, in all likelihood, see their idealism driven out by growing cynicism in the face of unattended people and unaddressed injustices the world over.

- Advocating for the right to health: All health professionals, but especially those in public health, have a primary ethical and professional responsibility for the health of the community members they serve. Because the social economic determinants of health and the full realization of human rights play such powerful roles in individual health and well-being, we have a special obligation to advocate for the right to health, and for public policy changes that address institutionalized inequities, including the lack of access to health care for the uninsured, lack of access to clean water and nutritious food, and discrimination in the provision of health services. Health advocacy initiatives need to be based on evidence and professionalism, not on individual political persuasions. The tools of medicine and science can be used to document human rights violations and to analyze the impact of the social determinants on disease. It is the data that must inform advocacy initiatives and subsequently the public debate on critical issues that deeply affects health and well-being. For public health professionals to engage effectively in advocacy work, we need to promote the attitudes of good citizenship in public health and medical education, and we need to teach advocacy skills to all health care professionals. Advocacy work requires a set of skills: the organization of people, goal setting, fact-finding, research, identification of power structures, strategizing, coalition building, taking action, and analyzing outcomes. While public health professionals already engage in many forms of advocacy, the use of a human rights framework will add even greater moral and legal authority. Advocacy for human rights offers both an inspiring and powerfully pragmatic way to increase the influence of public health professionals on public policy, especially in demanding that governments reduce health inequities and promote the health of their people—and in supporting governments as they take on these challenges.

- Operationalizing the right to health: Even though most countries have ratified at least one treaty that enshrines the right to health as an obligation of their governments to their people, vast health inequities are firmly entrenched around the world, including in prosperous countries such as the United States.[21] Only during the last decade or so have nations, human rights organizations, international organizations, and other members of civil society, including public health officials, begun the task of "operationalizing" the right to health. In essence, it means putting the concept of the right to health into *practice*. What exactly does this mean and how should we accomplish this? In reality, we are still finding our way. We are still learning. Certainly this is a highly complex and necessarily long-term endeavor. After all, the right to the highest attainable standard of health is a right that can be progressively realized only over time, given the resource constraints within any society at any time. Nevertheless, putting the right into practice entails a number of critical activities, including but not limited to the following: committing to a comprehensive governmental plan; working to strengthen health systems; conducting groundbreaking research on using a rights-based approach; advocating for essential shifts in policy; ensuring equity, equality, and nondiscrimination for the vulnerable and marginalized; setting benchmarks and standards; developing a transparent process of operating; ensuring participation by all; promoting gender equality; tracking and analyzing outcomes, especially as they pertain to disadvantaged and marginalized groups; and monitoring the progression of realizing the right to health. We are in the early years of operationalizing the right to health. Public health officials have much to contribute to this critical work.

In *The Future of Public Health*, the Institute of Medicine says: The *mission* of public health is "the fulfillment of society's interest in assuring the conditions in which people can be healthy." The *substance* of public health is "organized community efforts aimed at the prevention of disease and the promotion of health." The *organizational framework* of public health "encompasses both activities undertaken within the formal structure of government and the associated efforts of private and voluntary organizations and individuals."[22] There is one more element we should add to this compelling force for change: human rights provide us with a powerful *ethical and legal framework* for moving forward the global public health agenda. It offers us an inspiring vision, articulates an obligation, lays out an aggressive agenda, provides a framework for analysis and accountability, and ultimately commits us to dignity for all. In the end, the human rights framework offers us a reason to believe in the possibility of change.

REFERENCES

1. Tuskegee University. Research ethics: the Tuskegee syphilis study. http://www.tuskegee.edu/global/story.asp?s=1207598. Accessed December 5, 2009.
2. The full formulation of the right is "the right of everyone to the enjoyment of the highest attainable standard of physical and mental health." In this paper, "the

right to health" and "the right to the highest attainable standard of health" are used as shorthand.
3. Hunt L. *Inventing Human Rights: A History*. New York: W.W. Norton & Company; 2007:15.
4. Other important instruments and treaties that articulate human rights related to health include the International Covenant on Economic, Social and Cultural Rights; the Convention on the Elimination of All Forms of Discrimination Against Women; and the Convention of the Elimination of All Forms of Racial Discrimination; the Convention on the Rights of Persons with Disabilities; and the Convention of the Rights of the Child.
5. World Health Organization. *25 Questions and Answers on Health and Human Rights*. Geneva, Switzerland; 2002. Health and Human Rights Publication Series, Issue No.1.
6. World Health Organization. *25 Questions and Answers on Health and Human Rights*. Geneva, Switzerland; 2002. Health and Human Rights Publication Series, Issue No.1. See also Committee on Economic, Social and Cultural Rights. UN Doc E/C.12/2000/4: General Comment No. 14: the right to the highest attainable standard of health. http://www.ohchr.org/english/bodies/cescr/comments.htm. Published 2000.
7. Winslow CEA. The untilled fields of public health. *Science*. 1920;51(1306):23–33.
8. American Public Health Association. Overview. http://www.apha.org/about/. Accessed November 29, 2009.
9. Theoi Project. Hygeia: Greek goddess of good health. http://www.theoi.com/Ouranios/AsklepiasHygeia.html. Accessed November 29, 2009.
10. Schroeder SA. We can do better: improving the health of the American people. *N Engl J Med*. 2007;357:1221–1228.
11. Mackenbach JP, Stirbu I, Roskam A-JR, et al. Socioeconomic inequalities in health in 22 European countries. *N Engl J Med*. 2008;358:24682481.
12. Berkman L, Epstein A. Beyond health care: socioeconomic status and health. *N Engl J Med*. 2008;358:2509–2510.
13. Beaglehole R, Bonita R. Global public health: a scorecard. *Lancet*. 2008;372:1988–1996.
14. Fuster V, Voute J. MDGs: chronic diseases are not on the agenda. *Lancet*. 2005;366:1512–1514.
15. Kirch DG, Vernon DJ. The ethical foundation of American medicine: in search of social justice. *JAMA*. 2009;301:1482.
16. UN Commission on Human Rights. *The Siracusa Principles on the Limitation and Derogation Provisions in the International Covenant on Civil and Political Rights*. http://www.unhcr.org/refworld/docid/4672bc122.html. Published September 28, 1984. Accessed November 29, 2009. UN Doc E/CN.4/1985/4.
17. Mann J, Gruskin S, Grodin M, Annas G. *Health and Human Rights: A Reader*. Routledge, 1999. Introduction, paragraph 4.
18. Potts, H. Accountability and the right to the highest attainable standard of health. Human Rights Centre, University of Essex, 2008. (Accessed November 29, 2009 at http://www.essex.ac.uk/human_rights_centre/research/rth/docs/HRC_Accountability_Mar08.pdf.
19. World Health Organization. New WHO publication explores important links between health and human rights, an area drawing increased attention. Press Release WHO, July 2002. (Accessed November 29, 2009 at http://www.who.int/hhr/activities/q_and_a/q_a_press/en/index.html.
20. Rubenstein, LS. Viewpoint: The human rights imperative in medical education. AAMC Reporter. January 2007. (Accessed November 29, 2009 at http://www.aamc.org/newsroom/reporter/jan08/viewpoint.htm.)

21. Physicians for Human Rights. The right to equal treatment: A report by the panel on racial and ethnic disparities in medical care. PHR, September 2003. (Accessed on November 29, 2009 at http://physiciansforhumanrights.org/library/report-equaltreatment-2003.html.
22. Institute of Medicine. The Future of Public Health. National Academies Press, 1988. (Accessed November 29, 2009 at http://www.nap.edu/openbook.php?isbn=0309038308.)

CHAPTER 7

Genetic Testing and Public Health: Ethical Issues

Inmaculada de Melo-Martín, PhD, MS

INTRODUCTION

The publication in 1953 by James Watson and Francis Crick of the three-dimensional molecular structure of DNA resulted in remarkable theoretical and technological achievements during the next decades.[1] The launching of the Human Genome Project, in 1991, which culminated in the publication of the full sequence of the human genome in April 2003, has provided the impetus for an impressive advance in our knowledge of molecular science and our understanding of the genetic etiology of a variety of diseases. New developments in genomic research likely will lead to the identification of the molecular factors that underlie not just rare conditions such Tay-Sachs, Huntington's disease, and heritable breast cancer but also common multifactorial or complex diseases that represent a significant public health burden, such as cardiovascular diseases, asthma, diabetes, hypertension, cancers, obesity, and psychiatric diseases.[2–4]

This new research and knowledge has been the basis of an ever-increasing number of genetic tests that now are used under the auspices of the health care system and even ordered directly by consumers over the Internet.[5–8] Genetic testing initially was used as a resource to identify rare inherited disorders, such as Tay-Sachs and Huntington's disease, which usually affect a small percentage of the population. As more tests are developed, naturally the opportunities are expanding. New tests are being developed that detect genetic alterations that may influence more complex and common conditions, such as breast and ovarian cancer, cardiovascular diseases, colon cancer, or Alzheimer's disease.[6, 7] Currently, more than 1,000 genetic tests are available from testing laboratories. Although genetic testing and screening of a variety of human diseases are now part of medical practice, it is still not completely clear what the impact of these new molecular and genetic tools will be on public health. It is clear, however, that the incorporation of genetic tests and population screening programs as tools to improve public health raise a number of ethical concerns.

The purpose of this chapter is to examine some of these ethical issues. In the next section, I offer a brief overview of the different types of genetic tests that are available. In the second section, I present some of the most significant ethical concerns that arise in relation to the use of genetic tests. I discuss first matters related to the analytic and clinical validity and utility of genetic tests and how these aspects result in ethical quandaries. Next, I focus on the concerns that the use of genetic tests, if such tests prove beneficial for the populations' health, might contribute to furthering existing health inequities. Finally, I discuss ethical issues related to obtaining, or omitting, informed consent and to protecting privacy and confidentiality.

GENETIC TESTING AND SCREENING

Although the terms usually are used interchangeably, genetic testing and screening serve different purposes. Genetic testing targets individuals who might be at an increased risk of having a genetic disorder. They can be used to diagnose individuals with symptoms, to determine disease susceptibility in individuals who are asymptomatic, to ascertain genetic risks for offspring, as well as to guide medical treatment. [9–11] Genetic screening, on the other hand, is directed to populations to identify individuals at a higher risk for a genetic disease or condition. Several genetic screening programs, such as newborn screening for a variety of conditions, carrier screening for hemoglobinopathies, and prenatal screening to detect chromosomal abnormalities, are an established part of public health practice and research in the United States and abroad.[12–14]

Genetic tests, whether for testing or screening, usually are understood as those tests that involve the analysis of a person's chromosomes, DNA, RNA, or proteins to diagnose or rule out particular genetic disorders or to predict the likelihood of suffering such disorders in the future. These tests usually are performed on a sample of blood, but other tissues such as amniotic fluid, embryonic cells, hair, saliva, or skin also can be used. Once the tissue sample is obtained, laboratory technicians look for specific changes in chromosomes, DNA, RNA, or particular proteins that might indicate the existence of a disorder or a susceptibility to developing a particular disease.

As mentioned, genetic tests can be used for diagnostic or predictive aims. Diagnostic testing attempts to confirm whether an individual has a genetic or chromosomal condition. It usually is offered to people who show some signs of suffering a particular genetic disease or who have a family history of the disease. Diagnostic tests can be performed at any time during a person's life span. Predictive testing, on the other hand, is used to identify mutations that might increase an individual's risk of developing a disorder with a genetic basis later in life. Healthy people, with or without a family history of a particular disease, can be candidates for this type of test.

The most widespread use of genetic tests is carried out in newborn babies to identify certain diseases for which early diagnoses and treatment exist.[12] In the United States, for example, all states currently test infants for phenylketonuria (PKU) and hyperthyroidism. Also relatively common is preimplantation genetic diagnosis used in conjunction with in vitro fertilization. The embryos thus produced are then tested to identify genetic abnormalities. This testing usually is offered to couples with an increased risk of having a baby with a genetic or chromosomal disorder and is used to assess the viability of the embryos. Similarly, prenatal genetic diagnosis seeks to detect genetic or chromosomal abnormalities in developing fetuses. As in the case of preimplantation diagnosis, this test is offered to couples when there is suspicion of an increased risk of a genetic disorder. Finally, carrier testing aims to determine whether an individual carries a copy of a mutated allele that, when present in two copies, might cause a genetic disease. Often this test is offered in the context of reproductive planning to determine the risks of having a child with a particular genetic disorder.

ETHICAL ISSUES RAISED BY GENETIC TESTING AND SCREENING IN PUBLIC HEALTH

Development and implementation of new medical procedures often present ethical concerns. From the involvement of research subjects necessary to assess the safety and efficacy of such procedures, to issues related to the quality of informed consent, to effects on social justice, new biomedical developments require careful consideration of ethical implications. Genetic testing and screening thus are not unusual in this respect. Indeed, many have argued that genetic information actually brings up unique concerns because the nature of genetic data is different from other types of health information in that it is thought to provide definitive life-long health risk information, can reveal information about family members and offspring, and is highly identifiable.[15–17] The recently passed Genetic Information Nondiscrimination Act is an attempt, at least in part, to assuage some of the concerns that the use of genetic information might raise in relation to privacy and the possibility of discrimination.[18] But whether genetic information is, or is not, exceptional, it certainly is the case that the use of genetic tests presents us with important ethical concerns.[19]

THE USEFULNESS OF GENETIC TESTS

It seems clear that, if adequately implemented, both genetic testing and screening can contribute to improving the health of the population. Information on the contribution of genetic factors to disease, identification of people at higher risk for particular conditions, preventative measures, and timely treatments all could result from the suitable use of genetic testing and screening and all would foster public health goals. But, as with any other medical test, how well these goals can be furthered depends on the predictive value of genetic tests. Such assessment needs to consider the analytic validity, clinical validity, and clinical utility of the tests.[20–22]

Analytic validity refers to the ability of a test to accurately measure a particular genetic characteristic in the laboratory. Although for some genetic tests evidence indicates that the analytic validity is high, genetic and genomic technologies are complex and validation data for many of these tests are limited. Moreover, for the test to result in health benefits, clinical validity and utility need to be taken into account.[20, 21] Clinical validity describes the ability of the genetic test to reliably predict the presence or absence of a clinically defined disorder or phenotype of interest. Clinical utility refers to the ability of a test to result in improved health outcomes. The clinical utility of a genetic test then gives us information about the risks and benefits that result from its use.

Assessing analytic validity and clinical validity and utility of genetic tests is not always easy.[20, 23–25] The clinical validity and utility of genetic tests that detect highly penetrant gene mutations and polymorphisms, that is, the trait the particular mutation produces will almost always be apparent in an individual carrying such an allele and can be quite high as is the case of tests for Huntington's disease or PKU. Clinical validity and utility, however, becomes more questionable for tests that attempt to predict complex diseases, such as cardiovascular diseases, cancers, autoimmune disorders, neurodegenerative diseases, and nutritional disorders—that is, diseases that are responsible for the majority of the disease burden. This is the case because genes with reduced penetrance or variable expressivity are involved in these disorders, that is, the range of signs and symptoms that can occur in different people with the same genetic condition.[24, 26, 27]

Complex diseases or disorders result from mutations occurring simultaneously in several genes. Moreover, alleles contributing to these complex diseases are neither necessary nor sufficient to cause the particular disease. Some people might suffer the disease without having the related mutations and some people might carry the mutations but not have the disease in question. For many of these complex diseases, more than one gene at different loci contributes to the disease and those loci might interact with each other. Furthermore, modifier genes also can interact with mutations involved in the production of some diseases. The effects of interaction between an allele that might predispose toward having a particular disease and a protective allele might be especially difficult to predict with any accuracy. Similarly, epigenetic factors can modify the expression patterns of genes without altering the DNA sequence and the expression of most human diseases also involves the relations of multiple genetic and environmental factors.[28–30] Moreover, the key mutations for a particular disease might vary between different populations and thus the clinical validity of a genetic test might be limited by the particular mutations that are tested as well as in the particular populations in which the test is administered.[20, 21, 22]

Clearly, whether genetic tests have appropriate analytic validity, clinical validity, and utility raises not only scientific issues about the quality of scientific evidence, but also ethical ones. Harms to both the particular individuals using the tests and to society might result in cases in which the clinical validity and utility of these tests are questionable. Individuals obtaining information about future health states through the use of genetic tests of unproven utility might make problematic decisions about their clinical care.[31, 32] Moreover, information of unproven clinical value can result in the use of further medical tests and procedures that can produce anxiety in the patients and expose patients to unnecessary risks.[33] Because of the particular importance that we tend to attach to genetic information, these tests can result in labeling effects that can lead healthy people to see themselves as impaired.[15, 34]

Harms to society also can occur when the clinical validity and utility of these tests is questionable, which might contribute to increased costs to the health care system without appropriate benefits to offset such costs. For instance, the Advisory Committee on Heritable Disorders and Genetic Diseases in Newborns and Children recently recommended that all states screen newborns for a standard range of 29 diseases. They also included an additional 25 conditions that could be identified in the course of screening as new targets.[35] There is a paucity of studies, however, that have investigated a benefit-risk balance for many of the conditions screened.[36, 37] Thus, we might be providing genetic tests that are relatively expensive when it is unclear whether any clinical benefit is derived from the use of scarce resources. Moreover false positives that result in unnecessary treatments or further testing also contribute to increasing health care costs.

HEALTH DISPARITIES

Genetic testing and screening programs have been espoused as important tools to improve public health outcomes. What effect these tests might have on the health of the population depends not only on whether the tests are able to predict correctly the risks to health as well as on whether treatments are available or preventive measures can be put in place, but also on whether people will have access to these tests, treatments, and preventive measures. Genetic tests' prices range from $200 to more than $3,000 depending on the complexity of the test, the number of individuals tested to obtain a result that is meaningful, or the method of specimen handling.[38] For example, depending on the methodology used and the type of test performed, costs of tests for breast cancer mutations such as BRCA1 and BRCA2, range from about $300 to $3,000.[39] Obviously, under a health care system such as the one in the United States, concerns about the costs of genetic testing are relevant because cost might limit access. If it does so in significant ways, then the benefits for public health of genetic testing would be hard to realize.

Moreover, if some individuals or populations who are already disadvantaged are unable to benefit from the genetic revolution, then we run the risk of furthering injustices against them by increasing health disparities. As a significant amount of evidence shows, lack of access to effective medical technologies can contribute to an increase in heath inequities. Indeed, in spite of the improvements in the overall health of the United States, racial and ethnic minorities continue to receive a lower quality of health services and have higher rates of morbidity and mortality than non-minorities. According to the Centers for Disease Control and Prevention (CDC), for example, in 2001 the age-adjusted death rate for cancer was 25.4 percent higher for African Americans than for white Americans. The infant mortality rate among African Americans was more than twice the rate for white Americans.[40] Similarly, a recent report by the American Heart Association showed that blacks have a 1.3-times greater rate of nonfatal stroke, a 1.8-times greater rate of fatal stroke, and a 1.5-times greater rate of heart disease death than whites. Also, among the adult population over age 20, non-Hispanic blacks, Mexican Americans, American Indians, and Alaska Natives have a higher prevalence of diabetes than non-Hispanic whites.[41]

Lack of access to health care benefits affects minority populations in significant ways. Hispanic and non-Hispanic black individuals are more likely to lack health insurance than non-Hispanic white persons. In 2007, more than 10 percent of non-Hispanic whites were uninsured; the uninsured rates for blacks and Hispanics were 19.5 percent and 32.1 percent, respectively.[42] The fact that the U.S. health insurance system is primarily based on employer contributions also affects minority populations significantly. This is so because minorities have higher levels of unemployment; for example, in May 2009 the unemployment rate for Hispanics was 12.7, and for African Americans was 14.9, whereas for non-Hispanic white people it was 8.6.[43] Furthermore, more often than not minority populations tend to work full time or part time in service jobs or in temporary jobs that do not provide health insurance coverage.

But, even for those people who do have insurance, access to genetic testing is not guaranteed. At present, state laws with regard to access to, and coverage of, genetic services are limited to newborn screening and childhood genetic diseases. States do not require health insurance coverage of genetic testing for adult onset disorders. Group health insurance plans often do not cover screening tests in the absence of symptoms and thus exclude coverage of genetic testing for many diseases. Where coverage exists for genetic testing, the necessary education and counseling that should accompany such tests often are not covered by insurance.[44] Given the fact that minorities will have more difficulties having access to the possible health benefits associated with genetic testing, then it is not unreasonable to believe that these technologies might contribute to furthering existing health inequities.

INFORMED CONSENT

Shortly after the Nuremberg trials, which presented horrifying accounts of Nazi experimentations on unwilling human subjects, the issue of informed consent began to receive attention.[45] The first sentence of the Nuremberg Codes states that the voluntary consent of human subjects in research is absolutely essential.[46] At Helsinki in 1964, the World Medical Association made consent of patients and subjects a central requirement of ethical research.[47] Since then, virtually all prominent medical and research codes as well as institutional rules of ethics dictate that both physicians and investigators obtain the free informed consent of patients and subjects before performing any substantial intervention. Although obtaining free informed consent serves several goals, such as protecting patients and subjects from harm or encouraging medical responsibility in interactions with patients and subject, the most fundamental aim is to enable autonomous choices.[45, 48]

Legal, regulatory, medical, psychological, and philosophical literature tend to analyze informed consent in terms of the following elements: (1) disclosure, (2) understanding, (3) voluntariness, and (4) competence.[49] According to this understanding of informed consent, one gives free informed consent to an intervention if and only if one is competent to act, receives a thorough disclosure about the procedure, understands the disclosure, acts voluntarily, and consents to the intervention. Disclosure refers to the obligation that professionals have to offer adequate information to patients and subjects. Understanding, which may be the most important component for free informed consent, requires professionals to help patients and subjects to overcome illness, distorted information, irrationality, or other factors that can reduce a patient's grasp of the situation to which he or she has the right to give or refuse consent.

Patients and subjects need to have some basis of understanding the diagnoses, prognoses, nature, and purpose of the intervention as well as the tests' alternatives, risks, benefits, and recommendations. Voluntary action requires that people are not constrained by manipulation and coercion by other persons. Coercion occurs if and only if one person intentionally uses a credible and serious threat of harm or force to control another. One important form of manipulation in health care is informational manipulation, a deliberate act of handling information that alters patients' understanding of the situation and motivates them to do what the agent of influence plans. The way in which doctors present information by tone of voice, by framing information positively (the therapy is successful most of the time) rather than negatively (the therapy fails in 40 percent of the cases) can influence an individual's perception and, therefore, affect understanding. Finally, the criterion of competence refers to an individual's ability to perform a task. Patients or subjects are competent if they have the ability to understand the material information, to make a judgment about the evidence in light of their values, to intend a certain outcome, and freely to communicate their wishes to the professionals.

The duty to respect patients' autonomy then would seem to require that doctors obtain informed consent from their patients before they perform genetic tests. Indeed, obtaining and documenting informed consent is an essential component of the relationship between physicians and their patients. It allows patients to receive necessary information about their condition, the risks and benefits of performing such tests, the meaning and clinical usefulness of the information provided, and other possible alternatives, as well as information about existing treatments or preventive strategies.

Genetic testing and screening programs raise two different ethical issues in relation to informed consent and the respect for autonomy that such consent attempts to support. The first one relates to the quality of informed consent that is called into question because of the difficulties associated with the disclosure and understanding of genetic information. The second one pertains to genetic screening programs in particular and the mandatory nature of some of such programs, for example, newborn screening policies. In the second case, the concern is that the justification for omitting informed consent is lacking and thus that such policies are not ethically sound. In what follows, I discuss these two different concerns: quality of informed consent and mandatory programs omitting informed consent.

Disclosure of adequate information and understanding of the complexities of genetic information, as well as the psychological and social implications of performing a particular genetic test, and the indirect involvement of third parties, might make adequate informed consent difficult to obtain. As we have seen, the analytic validity as well as the clinical validity and utility of many of the genetic tests now available are difficult to ascertain and thus the quality of disclosure of pertinent information could be compromised. Perhaps if patients were somewhat knowledgeable about genetic information and genetic testing practices, problems related to disclosing and understanding the uncertainties associated with genetic tests would be assuaged.

A variety of studies, however, have revealed that members of the public have important misconceptions about genetic concepts and the use and availability of genetic technologies. Studies have shown that despite widespread efforts to popularize Mendelian genetics throughout the century, public understanding of genetic science is limited.[50–54] Some research has suggested that Mendelian explanations of inheritance are poorly accepted and understood because they conflict in a number of ways with a widespread lay understanding of inheritance that is derived from the social relationships of kinship. It might be that people do not find the Mendelian concept easy to grasp because it does not fit with what they already believe.[55] People, even when their attitudes toward genetics are positive, often lack adequate information about available genetic technologies, their use, and effectiveness, and how to have access to such technologies.[53, 56, 57]

Studies about public perception of health risks also indicate that people across all different ages, races, and socioeconomic groups, often underestimate or overestimate their risk of disease and, in general, lack adequate knowledge about risk factors.[58–61] This is problematic when people need to make decisions about whether to pursue, or not, particular genetic tests as this would depend in part on their real or perceived risk factors for a disease.

A proper estimation of risks is particularly important to make sense of genetic tests results given that genetic tests provide information about the presumed risks of suffering a particular disease. It is well known, however, that both experts and laypeople have difficulties calculating and understanding probabilities of risk and risk-related information, especially when that information is presented to them quantitatively.[62, 63] For example, people tend to believe that events are more probable when they can recall an incident of its occurrence. Also, people often disregard cumulative probabilities when they are exposed to the same risk factors over a longer time period or when they are exposed simultaneously to several risk factors. Instead, they perceive each hazard as a single, independent exposure.[62, 64]

Individuals' understanding of risk appears to be informed by particular cultural and cognitive biases.[65] People are more often than not unfamiliar with uncertainty in risk assessment and their interpretation of and responses to uncertainty depend on their personal characteristics and values all of which can be affected by the manner in which uncertainty is communicated.[66] Studies also show that recipients of genetic information related to reproductive concerns reduce probabilistic information to a dichotomous interpretation—that is, it either will or will not happen.[67] Finally, evidence suggests that people have difficulties understanding the results of genetic tests or whether the tests predict risk or diagnose disease.[68] Even when people might have sound knowledge of a particular genetic condition, they can have difficulties correctly recalling the results of genetic tests.[69]

Clearly, understanding genetic information and the implications for one's health of genetic tests is not an easy task for most people. But if this is so, then adequate informed consent might be difficult to obtain as one cannot provide such consent if the information necessary to give consent is misunderstood. A possible solution to the problems that result from insufficient or inadequate knowledge is to ensure that patients have access to recommended consultations with genetic counselors and medical geneticists. Certainly, appropriate counseling and guidance on how to interpret the results of genetic tests, on what the implications for someone's health might be, or on what the effect might be for reproductive decision making would go a long way toward limiting problems with informed consent. This possible solution has several problems, however. First, genetic counseling is expensive and many patients might not have health insurance or the financial means to pay such costs. Genetic counseling for breast cancer without the genetic testing, for instance, costs on average, more than $200, whereas counseling, testing, and disclosure of results exceeds $3,000.

Second, although the numbers of individuals graduating from counseling programs is increasing, the number of medical geneticists is not. Furthermore, it is not clear that this increase in trained genetic counselors is occurring at the rate necessary to ensure adequate and appropriate levels of support for genetic services in the future.[70]

Third, because of insufficient numbers of professionals specially trained to deal with genetic aspects of health, disease, treatment, and prevention, it is becoming apparent that primary care providers, whether physicians or nurses, will be the ones providing the necessary genetic services to their patients. For these services to be effective, however, primary care providers should have time to provide thorough counseling or to engage in lengthy discussions with patients. They should have knowledge of important genetic disorders, patterns of inheritance, genetic testing procedures, and their availability, as well as the existence of possible therapies and treatments. Practitioners also should have skills in understanding and communicating risk information. Unfortunately, evidence shows that primary care providers have inadequate knowledge of genetics, the nature of inherited disorders, and screening techniques and availability.[71–74] Moreover, primary care providers tend to view genetics as peripheral to everyday clinical concerns. They lack the skills to collect a genetic family history and lack confidence in offering advice and believe that guidelines are lacking to determine when referrals for genetic testing and services are appropriate.[75–77] Given these problems then, it is not at all clear that patients can obtain an adequate disclosure of appropriate information to provide a valid informed consent.

A different ethical concern related to the importance of obtaining informed consent for genetic tests is related to the issue of performing mandatory screening programs. As mentioned earlier, screening programs are directed at particular populations—for example, newborns or pregnant women over a particular age. Some of these screening programs are voluntary and people need to give informed consent for the tests to be performed. At times, however, such programs are mandatory; such is the case, for instance, of newborn screening.

In general, justification for mandatory screening programs for a particular disease or disorder rests on the premise that such a condition if not controlled or detected would adversely affect the individual or even the health of members of the community. This is normally the justification offered for mandatory screening of infectious diseases. In the case of genetic conditions, however, such justification is not available. Nonetheless, most U.S. states have laws making newborn screening mandatory.[78] The original rationale for mandatory policies was the urgent need for early diagnosis of some of the conditions screened—in particular for PKU—and the great benefit to the health of the babies of providing timely treatment. The recent expansion of newborn screening programs to include conditions for which no treatments exist, however, makes omitting parental informed consent controversial.[37, 79]

Justification for screening infants for conditions for which there is no available treatment, or conditions that do not need immediate treatment in the newborn period, or for which the benefits of treatment are not significant cannot be grounded on benefits to the infant but rather on possible benefits to parents or to society. But given the fact that evidence for the benefits and risks of screening of many of these conditions is not robust, arguments for possible benefits to parents or society might not be particularly compelling either. Moreover, these arguments tend to disregard the effects of false positives on the parents and the child as well as the costs to the health care system. Even if one were to agree that benefits to parents or to society are justified, I argue that this is not sufficient justification to mandate genetic screening. Arguably, screening for conditions that do not present a clear benefit to the newborn should be done on a voluntary basis and with the informed consent of the parents.

PRIVACY AND CONFIDENTIALITY

One of the primary central concerns in relation to genetic tests pertains to the confidentiality of genetic data. Clearly people see the need to secure health-related information as a way to protect their privacy, and they agree that necessary steps need to be taken by institutions and states to protect the confidentiality of such information.[80] But, as mentioned earlier, access to genetic data tends to be seen as more problematic than access to other types of health information because it is thought of as more unique, with more predictive power, immutable through the life span of the person, and with implications for other family members.[15]

There is a valid concern that unauthorized access to this data by insurance companies and employers can result in unjust discrimination against people. Insurance companies could use genetic information to make decisions about health coverage and life and disability insurance, and employers could use such information in making decisions about hiring and promotion. It is unclear whether genetic information has been used to unfairly discriminate among individuals, but it is clear that people are afraid it could be used in this manner.[81, 82] This concern is even more prevalent given the increasing use of electronic health records.[83] Indeed, it was precisely because it was thought that current legal protections for genetic health information were not sufficient that Congress passed the Genetic Information Nondiscrimination Act (GINA) of 2008. This act is intended to extend important protection against discrimination in health insurance and employment. In particular, GINA forbids health insurers from collecting and using an individual's genetic information when making determinations about eligibility and premiums. Similarly, GINA prohibits employers from using such information in making employment decisions.[84]

A variety of state laws to limit access to and the use of genetic information have been enacted. These laws protect such information against unauthorized disclosure. GINA now provides for a consistent national standard and clarifies ambiguities in existing federal law.[85] But at the same time that the GINA is intended to enhance protection against genetic discrimination in health insurance and employment, it also is expected to ease the public fears about genetic discrimination and thus facilitate genetic testing. Physicians may be more willing to offer genetic testing knowing that the results cannot be used for employment or insurance eligibility decisions.[18] Similarly, having confidence that their information will be kept confidential, individuals might be less reluctant to participate in research that collects genetic data, a growing and promising area of public health epidemiology. Of course, it is too soon to determine what the effect of GINA will be on industry practice and public opinion, whether it will protect against unjust discrimination, and whether it will promote participation in research and encourage responsible genetic testing. GINA, however, does not address issues related to access to other insurance products such as life, disability, long-term care, and mortgage insurance.[18]

A significant ethical concern about GINA is that a strict protection of privacy and confidentiality may endanger legitimate public health needs such as health surveillance and epidemiological research. Public health goals might legitimately call for research that addresses individual aspects of disease and disease prevention with the ultimate goal of improving health outcomes. Protection against discrimination might have the effect of preventing, rather than enhancing, these types of research. Indeed, a significant criticism against the privacy rule included in the Health Insurance Portability and Accountability Act (HIPAA) enacted in 1996, which was designed to safeguard access to, and use of, protected health information, is that it has slowed the research process and complicated basic medical care.[86, 87] Restrictions on legitimate genetic research might result in part from the fact that privacy and confidentiality are best protected by the requirement of informed consent. It often is difficult, however, to ascertain how researchers might use genetic data. Moreover, requirements of consent for genetic research might result in a diminished ability to recruit participants or even create serious obstacles in accessing stored tissue and genetic data sets.[88] Hence, the need to protect privacy and confidentiality, particularly through informed consent requirements, can have a deleterious effect on legitimate public health needs.

CONCLUSION

The so-called genetic revolution has been received by scientists, medical professionals, public policy makers, public health officials, and the general public with great hope. Indeed, the mapping of the human genome has been presented as the first step in solving the medical problems that afflict humans.[89] But even when one tempers the rhetorical excesses about the promises and dangers of the genetic revolution, it seems reasonable to believe that genetic tests could provide significant potential public health benefits. These benefits, however, will not be realized unless we are quite aware of the ethical concerns that these new medical technologies raise and provide assurance that such concerns are addressed adequately. Attention needs to be given to the increase in offerings of genetic tests that lack evidence of analytic validity as well as tests for which scarce evidences exists of clinical validity and utility.

The spread of genetic tests with unproven clinical validity and utility are likely to cause harm to individual patients and to society in general. Moreover, it is important to consider the social context in which new medical technologies are implemented; otherwise, we run the risk of increasing existing health care inequities. Attention to educating the public about genetics, providing a better understanding of risks of genetic testing, and ensuring that patients have access to trained medical professionals also are necessary to ensure that patients can give an adequate informed consent. Similarly, mandatory genetic screening programs need to have a clear justification to omit informed consent. Ensuring that people are not unjustly discriminated against because of their genetic or health status will require a careful attention to issues of privacy and confidentiality; yet, concerns about privacy will need to be balanced against the legitimate public health needs. Focusing on these ethical concerns when making public-policy decisions about implementation of genetic testing and screening is necessary if we want to use these medical technologies in ways that will advance the public's health.

REFERENCES

1. Watson J, Crick F. A structure for deoxyribose nucleic acid. *Nature.* 1953;171:737–738.
2. Khoury MJ, et al. Do we need genomic research for the prevention of common diseases with environmental causes? *Am J Epidemiol.* 2005;161(9):799–805.
3. Brand A, Brand H, Schulte IN, den Bäumen T. The impact of genetics and genomics on public health. *Eur J Hum Genet.* 2008;16(1):5–13.
4. Agurs-Collins T, et al. Public health genomics: translating obesity genomics research into population health benefits. *Obesity.* 2008;16(Suppl 3):S85–S94.
5. Khoury MJ, et al. A decade of public health genomics in the United States: Centers for Disease Control and Prevention 1997–2007. *Public Health Genomics.* 2008:Epub ahead of print.
6. Moyer VA, et al. United States Preventive Services Task Force: expanding newborn screening: process, policy, and priorities. *Hastings Cent Rep.* 2008;38(3):32–39.
7. Hogarth S, Javitt G, Melzer D. The current landscape for direct-to-consumer genetic testing: legal, ethical, and policy issues. *Annu Rev Genomics Hum Genet.* 2008;9:161–182.
8. Geransar R, Einsiedel E. Evaluating online direct-to-consumer marketing of genetic tests: informed choices or buyers beware? *Genet Test.* 2008;12(1):13–23.
9. Ozanne EM, et al. Identification and management of women at high risk for hereditary breast/ovarian cancer syndrome. *Breast J.* 2009;15(2):155–162.
10. Squitieri F, Cannella M, Frati L. Molecular medicine: predicting and preventing Huntington's disease. *Neurol Sci.* 2008;29(4):205–207.
11. Cram D, Pope A. Preimplantation genetic diagnosis: current and future perspectives. *J Law Med.* 2007;15(1):36–44.
12. Fernhoff PM. Newborn screening for genetic disorders. *Pediatr Clin North Am.* 2009;56(3):505–513.
13. Buckley F, Buckley SJ. Costs of prenatal genetic screening. *Lancet.* 2008;372(9652):1805.
14. Langlois S, et al. Carrier screening for thalassemia and hemoglobinopathies in Canada. *J Obstet Gynaecol Can.* 2008;30(10):950–971.
15. McGuire AL, et al. Confidentiality, privacy, and security of genetic and genomic test information in electronic health records: points to consider. *Gen Med.* 2008;10:495–499.
16. Rothstein MA. Genetic exceptionalism and legislative pragmatism. *J Law Med Ethics.* 2007;35:59–65.
17. Roche PA, Annas GJ. Protecting genetic privacy. *Nature Rev Genet.* 2001;2:392–396.
18. McGuire AL, Majumder MA. Two cheers for GINA? *Genome Med.* 2009;1(1):6.
19. Evans JP, Burke W. Genetic exceptionalism: too much of a good thing? *Genet Med.* 2008;10(7):500–501.
20. Burke W. Clinical validity and clinical utility of genetic tests. *Curr Protoc Hum Genet.* 2009;9:9–15.

21. Teutsch SM, et al. The Evaluation of Genomic Applications in Practice and Prevention (EGAPP) Initiative: methods of the EGAPP Working Group. *Genet Med.* 2009;11(1):3–14.
22. Zimmern RL, Kroese M. The evaluation of genetic tests. *J Public Health (Oxf).* 2007;29(3):246–250.
23. Rogowski WH, Grosse SD, Khoury MJ. Challenges of translating genetic tests into clinical and public health practice. *Nat Rev Genet.* 2009:Epub ahead of print.
24. Janssens AC, van Duijn CM. Genome-based prediction of common diseases: methodological considerations for future research. *Genome Med.* 2009;1(2):20.
25. Lavine G. Questions linger over utility of genetic testing. *Am J Health Syst Pharm.* 2008;65(9):793–795.
26. Shen Y, Wu BL. Microarray-based genomic DNA profiling technologies in clinical molecular diagnostics. *Clin Chem.* 2009;55(4):659–669.
27. Buchanan AV, Weiss KM, Fullerton SM. Dissecting complex disease: the quest for the Philosopher's Stone? *Int J Epidemiol.* 2006;35(3):562–571.
28. Barros SP, Offenbacher S. Epigenetics: connecting environment and genotype to phenotype and disease. *J Dent Res.* 2009;88(5):400–408.
29. Shames DS, Minna JD, Gazdar AF. DNA methylation in health, disease, and cancer. *Curr Mol Med.* 2007;7(1):85–102.
30. Moss TJ, Wallrath LL. Connections between epigenetic gene silencing and human disease. *Mutat Res.* 2007;618(1–2):163–174.
31. Henrikson NB, Bowen D, Burke W. Does genomic risk information motivate people to change their behavior? *Genome Med.* 2009;1(4):37.
32. Hunter DJ, Khoury MJ, Drazen JM. Letting the genome out of the bottle: will we get our wish? *N Engl J Med.* 2008;358(2):105–107.
33. McGuire AL, Burke W. An unwelcome side effect of direct-to-consumer personal genome testing: raiding the medical commons. *JAMA.* 2008;300(22):2669–2671.
34. Moses T. Self-labeling and its effects among adolescents diagnosed with mental disorders. *Soc Sci Med.* 2009;68(3):570–578.
35. American College of Medical Genetics. *Newborn Screening: Toward a Uniform Screening Panel and System.* Washington, DC: Health Resources and Services Administration; 2005. ftp://ftp.hrsa.gov/mchb/genetics/screeningno appendices.pdf.
36. Wilfond BS, Parad RB, Fost N. Balancing benefits and risks for cystic fibrosis newborn screening: implications for policy decisions. *J Pediatr.* 2005;147(3 Suppl):S109–113.
37. Baily MA, Murray TH. Ethics, evidence, and cost in newborn screening. *Hastings Center Report.* 2008;38:23–31.
38. Human Genome Project Information. Gene testing. http://www.ornl.gov/sci/techre sources/Human_Genome/medicine/genetest.shtml. Published September 19, 2008.
39. Lawrence WF, et al. Cost of genetic counseling and testing for BRCA1 and BRCA2 breast cancer susceptibility mutations. *Cancer Epidemiol Biomarkers Prev.* 2001;10:475–481.
40. Centers for Disease Control and Prevention. Fact sheet: racial/ethnic health disparities. http://www.cdc.gov/od/oc/media/pressrel/fs040402.htm. Published April 2, 2004. Accessed June 26, 2009.
41. American Heart Association. *Heart Disease and Stroke Statistics: 2009 Update.* Dallas, TX: American Heart Association; 2009. http://www.americanheart.org/ downloadable/heart/1240250946756LS-1982%20Heart%20and%20Stroke%20Update .042009.pdf.

42. DeNavas-Walt C, Proctor BD, Smith JC. *US Census Bureau, Current Population Reports, P60-231, Income, Poverty, and Health Insurance Coverage in the United States: 2005*. Washington, DC: US Government Printing Office; 2005.
43. US Department of Labor, Bureau of Labor Statistics. *The Employment Situation: May 2009*. Washington, DC: Bureau of Labor Statistics; 2009. http://www.bls.gov/news.release/pdf/empsit.pdf.
44. Rothstein MA, Hoffman S. Genetic testing, genetic medicine, and managed care. *Wake Forest Law Rev.* 1999;34(3):849–888.
45. Faden R, Beauchamp T. *A History and Theory of Informed Consent*. New York: Oxford University Press; 1986.
46. Nuremberg Code. *Trials of War Criminals before the Nuremberg Military Tribunals under Control Council Law No. 10, Vol. 2, Nuremberg, October 1946–April 1949*. Washington, DC: US Government Printing Office; 1949:181–182.
47. World Medical Association. World Medical Association declaration of Helsinki: ethical principles for medical research involving human subjects. Helsinki, Finland. June 1964. http://www.wma.net/e/policy/b3.htm. Accessed June 15, 2009.
48. Beauchamp T, Childress JF. *Principles of Biomedical Ethics*. 6th ed. New York: Oxford University Press; 2008.
49. National Commission for the Protection of Human Subjects of Biomedical and Behavioral Research. *The Belmont Report: Ethical Principles and Guidelines for the Protection of Human Subjects of Research*. Washington, DC: US Government Printing Office; 1978.
50. Molster C, Charles T, Samanek A, O'Leary P. Australian study on public knowledge of human genetics and health. *Public Health Genomics.* 2009;12(2):84–91.
51. Shaw A, Hurst JA. "What is this genetics, anyway?" understandings of genetics, illness causality and inheritance among British Pakistani users of genetic services. *J Genet Couns.* 2008;17(4):373–383
52. Frazier L, Calvin AO, Mudd GT, Cohen MZ. Understanding of genetics among older adults. *J Nurs Scholarsh.* 2006;38(2):126–132.
53. Catz DS, et al. Attitudes about genetics in underserved, culturally diverse populations. *Community Genet.* 2005;8(3):161–172.
54. Lanie AD, et al. Exploring the public understanding of basic genetic concepts. *J Genet Couns.* 2004;13(4):305–320.
55. Richards MP. Lay understanding of Mendelian genetics. *Endeavour.* 1998;22(3):93–94.
56. Morren M, Rijken M, Baanders AN, Bensing J. Perceived genetic knowledge, attitudes towards genetic testing, and the relationship between these among patients with a chronic disease. *Patient Educ Couns.* 2007;65(2):197–204.
57. MacDonald DJ, Sarna L, Uman GC, Grant M, Weitzel JN. Health beliefs of women with and without breast cancer seeking genetic cancer risk assessment. *Cancer Nurs.* 2005;28(5):372–379.
58. Katapodi MC, Dodd MJ, Lee KA, Facione NC. Underestimation of breast cancer risk: influence on screening behavior. *Oncol Nurs Forum.* 2009;36(3):306–314.
59. Dearborn JL, McCullough LD. Perception of risk and knowledge of risk factors in women at high risk for stroke. *Stroke.* 2009;40(4):1181–1186.
60. Burke-Doe A, Hudson A, Werth H, Riordan DG. Knowledge of osteoporosis risk factors and prevalence of risk factors for osteoporosis, falls, and fracture in functionally independent older adults. *J Geriatr Phys Ther.* 2008;31(1):11–17.
61. Nicol MB, Thrift AG. Knowledge of risk factors and warning signs of stroke. *Vasc Health Risk Manag.* 2005;1(2):137–147.

62. Visschers VH, Meertens RM, Passchier WW, de Vries NN. Probability information in risk communication: a review of the research literature. *Risk Anal.* 2009; 29(2):267–287.
63. Kahneman D, Slovic P, Tversky A, eds. *Judgment under Uncertainty: Heuristics and Biases.* Cambridge, UK: Cambridge University Press; 1974.
64. Knäuper B, et al. Motivation influenced the underestimation of cumulative risk. *Pers Soc Psychol Bull.* 2005;31:1511–1523.
65. Wildavsky A, Dake K. Theories of risk perception: who fears what and why? *Daedalus.* 1990;114:41–60.
66. Politi MC, Han PK, Col NF. Communicating the uncertainty of harms and benefits of medical interventions. *Med Decis Making.* 2007;27(5):681–695.
67. O'Doherty K, Suthers GK. Risky communication: pitfalls in counseling about risk, and how to avoid them. *J Genet Couns.* 2007;16(4):409–417.
68. Vuckovic N, Harris EL, Valanis B, Stewart B. Consumer knowledge and opinions of genetic testing for breast cancer risk. *Am J Obstet Gynecol.* 2003;189(4 Suppl):S48–S53.
69. Gordon C, Walpole I, Zubrick SR, Bower C. Population screening for cystic fibrosis: knowledge and emotional consequences 18 months later. *Am J Med Genet A.* 2003;120A(2):199–208.
70. Goodwin K. Genetic specialists trailing research boom. *State Legis.* 2009;35(2):33.
71. McInerney JD. Genetics education for health professionals: a context. *J Genet Couns.* 2008;17(2):145–151.
72. Telner DE, Carroll JC, Talbot Y. Genetics education in medical school: a qualitative study exploring educational experiences and needs. *Med Teach.* 2008;30(2):192–198.
73. Harvey EK, Fogel CE, Peyrot M, Christensen KD, Terry SF, McInerney JD. Providers' knowledge of genetics: a survey of 5915 individuals and families with genetic conditions. *Genet Med.* 2007;9(5):259–267.
74. Maradiegue A, Edwards QT, Seibert D, Macri C, Sitzer L. Knowledge, perceptions, and attitudes of advanced practice nursing students regarding medical genetics. *J Am Acad Nurse Pract.* 2005;17(11):472–479.
75. Guttmacher AE, Porteous ME, McInerney JD. Educating health-care professionals about genetics and genomics. *Nat Rev Genet.* 2007;8(2):151–157.
76. Guttmacher AE, Collins FS, Carmona RH. The family history: more important than ever. *N Engl J Med.* 2004;351(22):2333–2336.
77. Emery J, Hayflick S. The challenge of integrating genetic medicine into primary care. *BMJ.* 2001;322(7293):1027–1030.
78. National Conference of State Legislatures. Newborn genetic and metabolic disease screening. http://www.ncsl.org/IssuesResearch/Health/NewbornGeneticandMetabolicScreeningLaws/tabid/14416/Default.aspx. Published 2009.
79. President's Council on Bioethics. *The Changing Moral Focus of Newborn Screening: An Ethical Analysis by the President's Council on Bioethics.* Washington, DC: US Government Printing Office; 2008.
80. Page SA, Mitchell I. Patients' opinions on privacy, consent and the disclosure of health information for medical research. *Chronic Dis Can.* 2006;27(2):60–67.
81. Lowstuter KJ, et al. Influence of genetic discrimination perceptions and knowledge on cancer genetics referral practice among clinicians. *Genet Med.* 2008;10(9):691–698.
82. Oster E, et al. Fear of health insurance loss among individuals at risk for Huntington disease. *Am J Med Genet A.* 2008;146A(16):2070–2077.

83. Ray P, Wimalasiri J. The need for technical solutions for maintaining the privacy of EHR. *Conf Proc IEEE Eng Med Biol Soc* 2006;1:4686–4689.
84. Genetic Information Nondiscrimination Act of 2008. http://frwebgate.access.gpo.gov/cgi-bin/getdoc.cgi?dbname=110_cong_bills&docid=f:h493enr.txt.pdf. Published May 2008.
85. Tan MH. Advancing civil rights, the next generation: the Genetic Information Nondiscrimination Act of 2008 and beyond. *Health Matrix Clevel.* 2009;19(1):63–119.
86. Institute of Medicine. *Beyond the HIPAA Privacy Rule: Enhancing Privacy, Improving Health Through Research.* Washington, DC: National Academies Press; 2009.
87. Kumar S, Henseler A, Haukaas D. HIPAA's effects on US healthcare. *Int J Health Care Qual Assur.* 2009;22(2):183–197
88. Gostin LO, Nass S. Reforming the HIPAA privacy rule: safeguarding privacy and promoting research. *JAMA.* 2009;301(13):1373–1375.
89. Collins F, McKusick V. Implications of the Human Genome Project for medical science. *JAMA.* 2001;285(5):540–544.

CHAPTER **8**

Palliative Care

Roma Tickoo, MD, MPH, and Paul Glare, MD

INTRODUCTION

As chronic diseases, including cancer, surpass infectious diseases as the primary causes of death, and as individuals, thanks to advances in treatment of these diseases, are living longer with their diseases, providing timely access to consistently high-quality end-of-life care has become an important international issue. The World Health Organization (WHO) defines palliative care as "an approach which improves the quality of life of patients and their families facing life threatening illness, through the prevention and relief of suffering by means of early identification and impeccable assessment and treatment of pain and other problems, physical psychosocial and spiritual."[1] Indeed, the WHO has recognized palliative care as an important clinical and humanitarian need, particularly in places where a high proportion of patients present in advanced stages of disease usually with little chance of cure. It estimates that the quality of life of at least 100 million people globally would be improved if knowledge of 21st-century palliative care was accessible to everyone.[2]

The Center to Advance Palliative Care reported in 2008 that nearly 90 million Americans were living with serious and life-limiting illness.[3] This number is expected to more than double over the next 25 years as the population ages. Globally, the WHO has estimated that the number of global cancer deaths, for example, is projected to increase 45 percent from 2007 to 2030 (7.9 million to 11.5 million) primarily because of the increase in the aging population. Although this estimate takes into account expected declines in death rates for some cancers in developed countries, new cases of cancer in the same period are estimated to increase from 11.3 million in 2007 to 15.5 million in 2030.[4] This chapter provides an overview of the palliative care and hospice movement and explains why this is an important medical and public health issue.

WHY PALLIATIVE CARE?

Many patients and caregivers express a helpless feeling when facing a life-limiting illness. Often they have to make difficult decisions regarding the course of care, including but not limited to quality versus quantity of life. These decisions require careful communication and consideration. The Canadian Australian ethicist and academic Margaret Somerville has said "the ethical and legal tone of a society can be judged by how it treats its weakest, neediest and most vulnerable members."[5] Clearly addressing end-of-life care is an important medical, ethical, and public health issue. Yet, despite the significant advances in medical care, far less had been done to address the medical, social, and psychological needs of the dying patient. This situation is not limited to one country; rather, it is a universal issue that begs for attention. Studies had shown that most people living with a terminally fatal illness experience inadequately treated symptoms, fragmented care, poor communication with their doctors, and enormous strains on their family caregivers.[6–9] Palliative care was developed in response to these inadequacies.

Pain management is an integral component of palliative care. Some have gone so far as to call pain relief "a basic human right."[10] A growing number of statements and initiatives on the necessity for pain management reflect a "call to arms" based on three propositions. First, pain, whether acute or chronic, is inadequately addressed for a variety of cultural, educational, political, religious, and logistical reasons. Second, inadequately treated pain has major physiological, psychological, economic, and social ramifications for patients, their families, and for society. Third, it is within the capacity of all nations to significantly improve the treatment and management of pain. Indeed there is an emerging international consensus that "unreasonable failure" to treat pain is not only poor medicine, but also unethical practice and an abrogation of a fundamental human right.

Pain causes terrible suffering, yet there are inexpensive, safe, and effective medications that generally are straightforward to administer. Furthermore, international law obliges countries to make adequate pain medications available. Over the last 20 years, the WHO and the International Narcotics Control Board, the body that monitors the implementation of the United Nations drug conventions, repeatedly have reminded nations of their obligations. Unfortunately, however, little progress has been made in many countries.

Under international human rights law, governments must take steps to ensure that individuals have adequate access to treatment for their pain. At a minimum, states must ensure availability of morphine, the mainstay medication for the treatment of moderate to severe pain. Morphine is considered an essential medicine that should be available to all persons who need it. It is relatively inexpensive and widely available. Failure to make essential medicines available or to take reasonable steps to make pain management and palliative care services available might result in a violation of the right to health. In some cases, failure to ensure that patients have access to treatment for severe pain even could be construed as a violation of the prohibition of "cruel, inhuman, or degrading treatments" under Article 5 of the Universal Declaration of Human Rights.[10]

Unrelieved pain is not the only ethical imperative driving the need for access to palliative care. Many deficiencies in broader end-of-life care also demand a response.

For instance, in the early 1990s the Study to Understand Prognoses and Preferences for Outcomes and Risks of Treatment (SUPPORT) provided for the first time hard data on the problems with the care of the dying in modern hospitals.[11] Not only was pain relief shown to be inadequate, but patients' preferences for their terminal care also were ignored and their advanced directives ineffective. SUPPORT provided the impetus for the Institute of Medicine (IOM) to examine the systemwide deficiencies in end-of-life care as described in its 1997 report, *Approaching Death*.[12] The third of the seven recommendations made in this report called for systems of care to change to support the actions of individuals.

In the current context of ever-increasing patient autonomy, the sad state of terminal care has driven calls for physician-assisted suicide and voluntary euthanasia to be legalized. Fortunately not everybody sees this as an acceptable solution. In their 2002 book, *The Case against Assisted Suicide: For the Right to End-of-Life Care*, Foley and Hendin highlight the challenges to create a culture that identifies the care of the seriously ill and dying as a public health issue.[13] Neither autonomy nor compassion—the major justifications for assisted suicide—provides an adequate basis for legalizing these practices. In particular, patient autonomy is illusory when physicians do not know how to assess and treat suffering, making the only "choice" for patients either continued agony or hastened death. But, as the authors emphasize, many changes are required to American health care to ensure that patients really do have a choice. Reforming the Medicare system is advocated to allow functional disability and severity of illness to be the criteria for eligibility for the Hospice Benefit, not, as is the case, a prognosis of six months. An open public discussion with state and local officials as well as with professionals to address what we as a society can do to promote improved care of patients with serious life-threatening illness is needed.

WHAT IS HOSPICE AND PALLIATIVE CARE?

Hospice and palliative care is a philosophy of care that focuses on the palliation of a terminally ill patient. For much of its history, hospice and palliative care focused on caring for terminally ill cancer patients. Often referred to as "palliative" or "supportive" care, hospice care emphasized the management of pain and discomfort and the emotional support of the patient and family. Over the past two decades, however, noncancer diseases, such as congestive heart failure, emphysema, and Alzheimer's disease have accounted for an increasing proportion of hospice referrals. Care is rendered either on an inpatient basis or in the home setting. Palliative care concerns itself with the relief of suffering in patients with a life-limiting illness that is not amenable to cure. Palliative care is a philosophy of care that differs from mainstream health care in that it does not concern itself with *the cure of diseases* rather with *the needs of the dying*. That is, palliative medicine, a relatively new medical subspecialty,[14] focuses on improving the quality of remaining life for terminally ill patients and their family. For the purposes of this chapter, unless otherwise specified, the terms palliative care and hospice will be used interchangeably, according to the British and WHO concepts.

Palliative care, characterized by interdisciplinary teams working to meet the multidimensional needs of the dying, slowly has been integrated into the health care delivery system. This area of medicine focuses on comprehensive symptom management, coordination of care, as well as on intensive communication with the patient and the family regarding the emotional aspects of dealing with a terminal illness. The presumption of palliative care is that patients and their loved ones would benefit by a coordinated approach to end-of-life care, including pain management and a focus on patient-physician-family communication. An important outcome is that the patient and the family would be gain a better understanding of the prognosis of the disease and theoretically would be more satisfied with the care received.

The U.S. National Cancer Control Network defines palliative care as both a philosophy of care and an organized highly structured system for delivering care to persons with life-threatening or debilitating illnesses.[15] Palliative care has been defined by the WHO as an approach that improves the quality of life of patients and their families facing the problems associated with life-threatening illness, through the prevention and relief of suffering by means of early identification and impeccable assessment, treatment of pain and other problems, including physical, psychosocial, and spiritual.[1] According to the WHO, palliative care provides relief from pain and other distressing symptoms; integrates the physical, emotional, and spiritual aspects of patient care; offers a support system to help the family cope during the patient's illness; uses a team approach to address the needs of patients and families, including grief counseling and support; enhances quality of life and can positively influence the course of illness; and can be offered with other therapies that are intended to prolong life—for example, chemotherapy or radiation therapy.

In the United States, there is a unique distinction between palliative care and hospice care that primarily is driven by reimbursement issues.[16] Both place a strong emphasis on reducing pain and discomfort. Whereas palliative care is provided as part of acute care for patients with a life-threatening illness who still wish to pursue curative treatments, hospice care is specifically developed to enable patients who have acknowledged that they are dying to forego aggressive, curative treatments in lieu of receiving compassionate terminal care in their home or in a hospice facility. In other countries, especially Britain, the word "hospice" refers to an inpatient unit geographically separate from a hospital where dying patients are admitted to receive palliative or terminal care.

THE ORIGINS OF HOSPICE AND PALLIATIVE CARE MOVEMENT

The word "hospice" traces back to medieval times, when it was used to describe charitable institutions that welcomed weary travelers and pilgrims.[17] In the mid-19th century, the word was revived and adopted for residential facilities established for the care of the dying poor.[17] Such buildings existed in Britain, Australia and France, and continued to operate up until the end of World War II. In one sense, these facilities were really "proto-hospices" because they were rooted in the religious and philanthropic ideologies of the Victorian era, providing nursing and spiritual care but limited medical service,[18] but doing little to impact on the care of the dying generally.[17]

After World War II, there was a revolution in theory and practice in the care of the dying. Modern palliative care began in Britain in the 1950s and 1960s, primarily in response to the observation that resources for the care of patients dying from cancer in National Health Service (NHS) hospitals were minimal. The NHS focus was on acute care and rehabilitation and, at the same time, it had an ideological rejection of charity as a source for the provision of health care.[18–19] But several other issues were driving the development of hospice care and palliative care, as summarized by Clark.[18] These include such things as demographic changes in postwar Britain, with an aging in population and social debate about how willing families were to care for the dying in the newly constructed postwar housing. The 1960 report *Peace at Last* was highly critical of the care provided by the old "homes of the dying."[20] An awakening medical interest in pain, geriatrics, chronic illness, and the care of the dying subsequently led to the palliative care movement.[21]

Cecily Saunders, a physician who was also qualified as a nurse and social worker, is generally acknowledged to have been the driving force behind the development of the modern palliative care movement in Britain in the 1950s and 1960s.[18] Her commitment to care for the dying was driven by a personal vocation, continuing the Christian influence in modern hospice that had driven the proto-hospices decades earlier. Her work combined medical innovations in pain relief and symptom management with wider concerns of the practical and social needs of the patient as well as their spiritual needs as they approached death. The residential facility remained the focus for Dr. Saunders for delivering this new kind of comprehensive care for the dying. These residential facilities helped the palliative care concept to spread with the "bricks and mortar" of a new building being an obvious focal point for community fundraising. There was a rapid spread of these kinds of facilities across Britain over the next two decades, and by 1985, there were more than 100 such inpatient hospices. In the 1990s, the principles and practices of the inpatient hospice unit were modified for other settings, which not only included taking hospice principles into the home by means of a community team, but also into the NHS hospital via the hospital inpatient unit and consult service. By 2006, Britain had 193 hospices or other specialist inpatient units providing 2,774 beds, 20 percent of which were operated by the NHS, 314 hospital palliative care teams, 295 home care teams, and 294 day care services.[22]

In Britain, palliative care and hospice form a continuum of care. Although there has been a rapid development of palliative care, much of it occurred with little regard as to whether needs were being met by these new services,[23] although 21st-century government policy very much drives service development in Britain. (We refer to the National Institute for Clinical Excellence's guidance on cancer services: improving supportive and palliative care for adults with cancer).[24]

As the hospice concept took hold and spread around the world, it evolved to suit local conditions. The basic principles can be interpreted in widely differing cultures and with few resources other than the family values of the developing world.[17] In many countries, especially those belonging to the British Commonwealth like Australia and India, inpatient hospices similar to the British ones were established and hospital and community palliative care teams were created as well. At a national level, Australia and India are both global examples of excellent palliative care programs.

The history of Australian palliative care can be traced back to the 19th century with the arrival of the Sisters of Charity nuns who came to Sydney from Ireland to care for their compatriot female convicts who were dying in prison from tuberculosis (TB) and other infectious diseases. The Sisters of Charity founded St. Joseph's hospital in Auburn, which continued their mission of the care of the dying. Soon thereafter they founded Australia's first hospice, Sacred Heart Hospice, in Darlinghurst (Sydney) in 1890. Although run by nursing nuns, medical input was provided by family physicians.

There were two main drivers to the development of modern palliative care in Australia in the latter part of the 20th century: clinical and political. Visiting medical advocates of the palliative care movement had an impact on local physicians who became interested in advances in pain management. Politically, in 1972, Australia adopted socialized and nationalized health care. As the cost of hospital beds increased, the focus shifted reducing the length of stay of hospitalized patients, including palliative care.[25] The Australian government made community-based palliative care a priority, aiming to reduce the number of patients dying in hospital. To meet the palliative care needs of the Australian population (approximately 20 million citizens of whom some 100,000 die from diseases amenable to palliative care),[26] the federal government gives $180 million to the states to pay for palliative care services. To improve Australian palliative care further, in 2000, the Australian federal and state governments joined together with service providers and nongovernmental organizations (NGOs) interested in palliative care to formulate a framework for improving awareness of and access to quality palliative care programs.[27] An additional $60 million was made available to fund new initiatives to fill gaps in current services during the first three-year period of the program. The key platforms in the National Palliative Care strategy included support for patients, families, and caregivers throughout the community; increased access to palliative care medicines in the community; education, training, and support for the workforce; research and quality improvement for palliative care services; and methods for ensuring that these policies are being achieved or are under development as part of the program.

The evolution of modern hospice and palliative care in India began in 1986 when Dr. Louis DeSouza, a surgical oncologist, founded the first Western-style Indian Hospice, Shanti Avedna, in Mumbai, which was inspired by St. Christopher's Hospice in London. In 1993, the NGO Pain and Palliative Care Society (PPS) was founded in Calicut in the state of Kerala. Furthermore, a network of community initiatives called Neighborhood Network in Palliative Care (NNPC) was established. More than 60 units now cover a population of more than 12 million. This is probably the largest community-owned palliative care network in the world. A volunteer force is the main strength of the NNPC program. Trained volunteers work with health care professionals to provide psychological and spiritual care.

In 1996, the "CanSupport" initiative was established in Delhi. This initiative was based on the personal experience of a cancer survivor, Harmala Gupta, and its mission was to offer support to other cancer patients in India. Gupta's vision and efforts date to 1991 when she started the first cancer support group in India. She along with other cancer survivors and caregivers visited cancer clinics to provide information, assistance, and an empathetic listening ear to the dying and their family.

PALLIATIVE CARE MOVEMENT IN THE UNITED STATES

Although Calvary Hospital in New York had been established in 1899 in the image of one of the early European hospices,[17] in the United States, hospice came to represent home-based rather than institution-based care of the dying. This trans-Atlantic variance has been attributed to the consumerism movement in the 1970s that was concerned with a rediscovery of "the natural," a rising interest in thanatological subjects, and a reaction against the medicalization of death.[18] Primarily inspired by the work of Dr. Cecily Saunders, hospice in the United States was a grassroots movement outside the medical mainstream. U.S. hospice care initially was designed for cancer patients with a functional family support system and a home at which they could be cared for away from the high-tech hospital environment.

The first U.S. hospice program, the Connecticut Hospice, opened in 1974 funded by a three-year grant from the National Cancer Institute. A decade later, findings from the National Hospice Organization Study provided the impetus for the expansion of the hospice movement. The study showed that hospice was more effective and less expensive than conventional terminal care.[28] The results of the NHO study led to the recognition of hospice care by the U.S. government. The Medicare Hospice Benefit legislation legitimized end-of-life care making hospice equivalent to other reimbursable medical services. For the first time, care of the dying was institutionalized and publicly supported. Signing on for hospice care enabled a patient to receive services not normally paid for, including provision of all medical drugs and devices necessary for palliative care. Other services provided free under the benefit include professional nursing care, personal assistance with activities of daily living, various forms of rehabilitation therapy, dietary counseling, psychological and spiritual counseling for both patient and family, volunteer services, respite care, and bereavement services for the family for up to one year after the patient's death.[29] This care is provided by a multidisciplinary team under the management of a physician who may be the patient's primary physician or else a hospice physician. To qualify for this range of services, however, patients had to have a prognosis of less than six months and agree to forgo life-prolonging therapies.[30] Although this stipulation did not pose a problem when dealing with terminally ill cancer patients, patients with noncancer diagnoses, now accounting for a large part of hospice care, often lived much longer than six months. These requirements eventually led to a separation of hospice care from palliative care in the United States that is not found in other countries.

Although the hospice movement has expanded substantially, home hospice care is acknowledged to be underutilized. The reasons for this are manifold: Physicians find it difficult to prognosticate that the patient has less than six months to live,[31] or believe that hospice referral means admitting medical defeat. Patients and families have difficulty giving up hope of recovery, forgoing active treatment, or accepting the inevitability death.[32] Many find it challenging to make the abrupt cognitive and emotional shifts in transitioning from acute care to hospice care as they enter a completely new system of care that is geographically and ideologically isolated from traditional and familiar health care systems that frequently separates patients from their primary care providers. That being said, substantial progress has been made since Meier et al. identified these kind of issues and the wide range of changes needed in education and training, medication availability, and health care system reorganization needed to improve palliative care in the United States.[33] But, much work remains to be done.

Palliative care in the United States is a broad term covering all forms of prevention and treatment and suffering regardless of the diagnosis, treatment, or prognosis in a patient with a life-threatening illness even if it is potentially curable, whereas hospice is more narrowly defined as the subset of palliative care especially catering to those near death. American palliative care is a more recent development that aims to bring many of the principles of hospice, especially symptom control and attention to psychosocial and spiritual issues, to hospitalized patients while they are still receiving active treatment but without the comprehensive range of services that hospice provides,[16, 34] and has really only emerged since the 1990s.

PALLIATIVE CARE AND PUBLIC HEALTH: CURRENT STATUS AND FUTURE DIRECTIONS

Although hospice and palliative care largely began on both sides of the Atlantic as a grassroots movement, over the past 10 to 15 years, it is increasingly being viewed as a public health issue.[1–2, 23, 35–39] Advances in the treatment and management of acute and chronic diseases has led to a dramatic increase in life expectancy and a concomitant increase in the incidence and prevalence of cases of progressive, life-limiting illness. This, combined with ethical imperative to improve pain and relieve suffering in these patients, is behind the push for an expansion in palliative care services.

Using the language of the IOM's 1988 report on the future of public health,[40] one could make the cases that the physical, psychosocial and spiritual needs of dying patients and their families also falls within the "mission" and "substance" of public health and that delivery of palliative care services should fall within public health's "organizational framework." As such, there is a need for a standardized means to assess and monitor pain and suffering among those with advanced progressive terminal disease. There is a need for the formulation of palliative care policy in collaboration with community and government leaders, and there is a need to ensure that all in need have access to appropriate and cost-effective palliative care. Certainly there also must be protocols for the evaluation of effectiveness of palliative care.

The United States has done reasonably well in making palliative care part of public health. In 1983, the United States was the first nation to legislate the hospice piece of palliative care as part of mainstream medicine. The Medicare Hospice Benefit acknowledged the importance of offering hospice care to Medicare beneficiaries. Since then, there has been growing enrollment in hospice care; between 2000 and 2004, the percentage of Medicare decedents enrolling in home hospice programs increased from by almost 50 percent from 500,000 to 800,000. In 2005, more than 1.2 million Americas received hospice care.[29] In 2006, Medicare spent close to $10 billion on hospice (up from $2 billion eight years earlier), but at the same time it saved approximately $2,500 per decedent, and this number could have been closer to $7,000 with more timely referrals.[41] Evaluation studies show consistently high family satisfaction rates.[42–43] Although impressive, much more needs to be done in this area. It is estimated that at least two-thirds of deaths are amenable to palliative care,[26] yet only one-third die on hospice, thus dramatically illustrating the underuse of palliative or hospice care. Many more evaluations and cost-effectiveness studies of palliative care need to be undertaken.[44]

The development of palliative care programs, which bring hospice principles to patients ineligible for the hospice benefit because they have a "better" prognosis, has been slow. Although over the last five years palliative care programs have been implemented in U.S. hospitals,[16, 34] wide geographic variation exists making unequal access to such care a continued reality. The American Hospital Association (AHA) tracks hospital palliative care programs using its Annual Survey Database™. Along with the other 850 elements of the survey, the AHA queries all hospitals (AHA members and nonmembers) as to the presence of a palliative care program, defined as

an organized program providing specialized medical care, drugs or therapies for the management of acute or chronic pain and/or the control of symptoms administered by specially trained physicians and other clinicians, and supportive care services such as counseling on advance directives, spiritual care, and social services to patients with an advanced disease and their families.

These results have been reported by the Center to Advance Palliative Care (CAPC) in 2001, 2005, and 2008,[45–47] in the form of a "report card" scored for the percentage of hospitals in each state with at least 50 beds reporting a palliative care program. An A is awarded to states with palliative care programs in more than 80 percent of its hospitals, a B for palliative care offered in 61 to 80 percent hospitals, a C for palliative care offered in 41 to 60 percent hospitals, a D for palliative care offered in 21 to 40 percent hospitals, and an F if less than 20 percent hospitals in a state offer palliative care.

In its 2008 report, CAPC, utilizing the AHA data from 2006, found that more than 50 percent of hospitals nationwide had a palliative care program (i.e., an overall national grade of C), indicating a need for significant improvement in access to hospital palliative care.[48] Although half of the 50 states received a grade of A or B (only three states scored an A: Vermont, New Hampshire, and Montana), almost 40 percent get a grade of C, and the remainder received unacceptable grades of D and F (see appendix 8.A). While much remains to be done, just 10 years ago almost no palliative care programs were offered in U.S. hospitals. In the last five years alone, access to palliative care in American hospitals has more than doubled.

The CAPC report utilized data from the Association of American Medical Colleges, the U.S. Census, and the Dartmouth Atlas of Healthcare to examine geographic variations at the state level. Patient access to board-certified palliative medicine physicians, medical student access to clinical training in palliative medicine, and physician access to specialty-level training in palliative medicine are quantified. Findings showed that despite high access in some states, overall wide geographic variation still remains a barrier to care for many patients and families. In general, the availability of palliative care is lower in the southern states compared with the northern states. African Americans and other minorities tend to underutilize palliative care, even when they have access to it.[49] The reasons are largely speculative at this stage, but they likely are multifactorial and include historical, social, cultural, ethical, economic, legal, health policy, and medical ones. Additionally, access is lower in public and sole community-provider hospitals. Particularly worrying for the future is the fact that not all medical schools are presently affiliated with a hospital providing palliative care.

An equally serious problem is that patients and their families often are not offered palliative care as an option, and even when such a service exists and is offered, its value is discounted.[50] A recent telephone survey of 1,200 Australians representative of the general population found they most of the respondents had little understanding of palliative care.[51] Admittedly 80 percent of respondents were somewhat aware of palliative care at some level, but generally not well enough to be able to explain the concept to someone else. Respondents who knew more about palliative care had learned about it through during the care of a terminally ill family member or friend; 90 percent of them reported a positive view about palliative care and wished that they had had known about it or had their caregiver suggest it earlier. This study shows that if palliative care is not offered as an option, or discounted in value when it is offered, then it is unlikely that patients and families will request it.[50] Although no data are available for the United States, it would be most surprising if results were different from the findings from the Australia study. Raising community awareness of palliative care therefore is an important medical and public health worldwide.

Much more is known about clinicians' knowledge, skills, and attitudes toward palliative care. Multiple surveys have been done over the past 15 years, which repeatedly document deficiencies in both the medical management and psychosocial care of pain, end-of-life issues, and palliative care.[33, 52, 53] This body of data was summarized by the IOM in its 1997 report, *Approaching Death*.[12] Data from the Britain, Europe, and the United States show that up to 80 percent of dying patients are in pain, often severe, and that other symptoms like fatigue, nausea, anorexia, and breathlessness also occurred in 40 to 80 percent of cases.[54–56] Other findings also showed that undertreatment of these symptoms persist even when effective treatments are available.[57–59] Clearly, education and training of professionals must be a fundamental strategy of any public health approach to palliative care. Presently, health care professional initiatives in the area of palliative care include the American Medical Association's Educational Program in End of Life Care (EPEC) for physicians and for nurses (ELNEC) and social workers; the American College of Physicians and American Board of Internal Medicine have initiatives to enhance physicians' competency in end-of-life care and faculty development programs. Each seeks to adopt a consistent set of core principles.

In the United States, improving clinicians' knowledge, skills, and attitudes toward palliative care can succeed only if there are concomitant changes in the health care delivery system. In what would be the first federal legislation addressing comprehensive palliative care, Senators Rockefeller (D-W.Va.) and Collins (R-Maine) introduced a bill, Advance Planning and Compassionate Care Act of 2009, whose main points include workforce (physician and nurse practitioner) adequacy and loan forgiveness; National Service Corps; curricular changes; development of provider reimbursement for conversations about goals of care, and in particular support for completion of orders for life-sustaining treatment in appropriate patient populations; ensuring access to concurrent curative and hospice care for children; incentives for hospital and nursing home delivery of quality palliative care; establishment of a National Center on Palliative Care within the National Institutes of Health (NIH) as a mechanism to ensure adequate attention to the evidence necessary to deliver the highest quality of care; and an ongoing National Mortality Followback Survey to ensure a process of continuous improvement in the quality of care we deliver to this most vulnerable and needy of patient populations.

Organizational and structural characteristics of a health care delivery system can promote or inhibit palliative care for persons who are facing death.[33] Some of these organizational issues include the following:

- The difference between the United States and most other Western countries is that U.S. health care is an industry not a system,[60] and the government's role has been to regulate rather than make policy on the delivery of services.
- Cost-containment in medicine may inhibit palliative care as its patients often have long hospital stays in a highly labor-intensive, expensive clinical setting. Such patients require frequent adjustments in pain medication as well as careful management of dyspnea, delirium, or agitation. Provision of such care often leads to conflict with utilization review requirements under the current U.S. health care reimbursement system.
- Laws regulating opioid prescribing patterns can inhibit access by requiring the use of multiple-copy prescription forms, limitations on the number of tablets per prescription, and regulations for reporting on "habitual users" that stigmatize patients who need opioids and use them appropriately. Insurance companies the restrict usage of some drugs and pharmacies that refuse to stock them also contribute to this inhibition.
- The risk management approach adhered to by many hospitals views in-hospital death as an indicator of substandard delivery of health care, thus creating an incentive for medical staff.

A number of ongoing international initiatives are advocating for the integration of palliative care into national health programs. The WHO has been providing leadership in cancer pain management and palliative care for more than 20 years and advocates a public health model of policy, context, and outcomes that is based on principles of drug availability, education, and implementation.[61] In 2005, the World Health Assembly urged member states to ensure the medical availability of morphine and other opioid analgesic, and requested the WHO director general to explore mechanisms for funding cancer prevention, control, and palliative care, especially in developing countries, and to examine with the International Narcotics Control Board how to facilitate the adequate treatment of pain using opioids. The WHO has established an office for controlled substances as essential medicines, and works with such groups as the Pain and Policy Studies Group at the University of Wisconsin to develop methods and resources to achieve these changes.[62] The International Union against Cancer (UICC) supports the Global Access to Pain Relief Initiative and also included pain relief and palliative care among its immediate targets and 2020 goals in its Draft World Cancer Declaration released in 2008.

In 2006, the International Association for Hospice and Palliative Care developed a list of 34 essential medicines,[63] 14 of which already are included on the WHO Model Drugs list. Other initiatives focusing on cancer pain relief and palliative care include the International Atomic Energy Agency's Global Cancer Control Alliance to Advance Country Strategy and Action Plans; the Open Society Institute's Pain Policy Fellowship; the International Children's Palliative Care Network global advocacy agenda, and the Palliative Care as a Human Rights Initiative.[64] The International Observatory on End of Life Care (IOELC) aims to provide research-based information on palliative care in the global context. The IOELC's useful Web site (www.eolc-observatory.net) provides information on what is happening on palliative care in Eastern Europe and Central Asia.[65]

Some notable developments in the United States over the past decade include the following:

- Establishing pain as the "5th vital sign" by the Veterans Administration Health Care system in 1998;[66]
- Establishing of an International Classification of Diseases (ICD)-9 code for palliative care;[67]
- Centers for Medicare and Medicaid Services' recognition of palliative care as a subspecialty in 2004, with its own code, effective October 1, 2009;[68]
- The IOM's Report, *Improving Palliative Care in Cancer*, which highlighted the need for palliative care, especially for cancer patients;[69]
- National Quality Forum's 2008 recommendations on operational characteristics of quality palliative care programs;[70]
- The establishment of CAPC, and the recommendations associated with its Report Card;[48]
- State initiatives, such as the New York attorney general's 1998 initiative to overcome barriers to good quality end-of-life care, which included ending the regulation requiring triplicate prescribing for controlled substances and including palliative care in the curricula of the 14 New York state medical schools; and
- The American Society of Clinical Oncology's 2009 special report calling for the full integration of palliative care into comprehensive cancer care by 2020.[71]

QUALITY EFFECTIVENESS AND PALLIATIVE CARE

Palliative care services should be assessed and measured to ensure that high-quality services are being provided.[72] According to the IOM,[73] health care services, including palliative care, need to be safe, effective, patient centered, timely, efficient, and equitable. In 2006, the National Quality Forum (NQF), America's major public-private partnership organization charged with advancing the quality of health care, identified a clear set of 38 practices associated with quality palliative care, and these are presented under the IOM's quality headings.[70]

Safe

Palliative care should avoid injuries to patients from care that is intended to help them. The management of pain and other physical symptoms and psychosocial distress should adhere to opioid standards, order sets, and adverse event reporting standards. At present, the evidence base for many palliative care interventions is weak. For example, a systematic review of the WHO analgesic "ladder" approach to cancer pain management, which is based on escalating the potency of analgesics from nonopioids like aspirin or acetaminophen to strong opioids like morphine depending on the severity of pain,[74] found that despite the fact that the WHO has been promulgating the ladder for more than 20 years, the evidence for its effectiveness is meager.[75] The review found that only eight studies involving some 500 patients had been done; they all had methodological weaknesses and the results could not be combined into a meta-analysis. Some of the methodological weakness included small sample size, short-term follow-up, and variations in measuring pain. Similarly, a systematic review of morphine for cancer pain showed that despite the widespread use of morphine, there are no large-scale, well-designed studies.[76] The same applies to systematic reviews of more complex palliative care interventions.[77–78]

Effective

The NQF recommends that palliative care services should undertake various continuous improvement activities, both intermittent and continuous, for pain/nonpain symptoms, psychosocial and spiritual distress, and communication between providers and patient and surrogates. There should be continuing education in palliative care for all health care professionals as well as training and support for specialist palliative care professionals. Five of the NQF preferred practices are aimed at measuring clinical outcomes, including measuring pain and other symptoms both physical (for example, nausea, constipation, dyspnea) and psychological using standardized scales such as the Memorial Symptom Assessment Schedule,[79] as well as assessing patient satisfaction outcomes (including ability of staff to discuss hospice as an option). To be able to achieve effectiveness in all of these domains requires an interdisciplinary team of appropriately trained or certified staff, including physicians, nurses, social workers, pharmacists, and chaplains. The team should be knowledgeable in the assessment and management of symptoms, trained to assess and manage the patient's and family's emotional state, adept at discussing goals of treatment and offering advance care planning, and able to identify when the patient is transitioning to the dying phase.

Efficient

Palliative care services should avoid waste and harmful delays for those who receive and give care. With regard to avoiding waste, the palliative care service needs to be interdisciplinary and should avoid duplication. With regard to cost-savings for the health care system, the study by Morrison et al. showed that, on average, US$300 per day can be saved in directive costs through adopting palliative care, primarily via reducing laboratory and Intensive Care Unit (ICU) costs.[80] To avoid harmful delays, there needs to be a smooth transition between acute care and palliative care, and it needs to be bidirectional. The NQF requires that to the extent that existing privacy laws permit, care plans developed for the patients should be disseminated both internally and externally to all professionals involved in the patient care, especially upon transfer between care settings.

Patient-Centered

Hospice should be introduced as an option for patients with a life-limiting illness as a less aggressive approach to care. As the patient declines, end-of-life care should be modified to reflect the change in status. Care needs to be respective of and responsive to individual patient and family preferences, needs, and values and ensure that patient values guide all clinical decisions. Cultural assessment has now become an important part of high-quality, appropriate, contemporary palliative care services. The cultural assessment should include, but not be limited to, locus of decision making (individual versus family), preferences regarding disclosure of information, truth telling and decision making, dietary preferences, language, family communication, desire for support measures such as palliative care, perspectives on death, burial customs, and grieving. Professional translator services and culturally sensitive materials in the patients own language should be available. Regular patient and family conferences should be held to provide information and to discuss changes in disease status, prognosis, goals of care, advanced cancer planning and to offer support both to the patient and the family.

The patient-centered care plan needs to assess and manage the patient and family's psychological reactions to the situation (including stress, anticipatory grief, and coping); a grief and bereavement care plan; a social care plan to address the social practical and legal needs of the patient, family, and other informal caregivers; an assessment of religious spiritual and existential concerns. To formulate the best care plan, the patient and family need education on the disease, its natural history, prognosis, and the burden or benefits of any interventions. This includes educating the family on the signs and symptoms of an imminent death, when timely and as appropriate. Any treatments offered must be appropriate to patient and family. In the case of pediatric palliative care patients, the child's preference should be elicited if possible and respected.

With regard to the documentation of the goals of care, this may be in the form of an advanced directive or living will, but it is now preferable to convert them into medical orders such as the Medical Orders for Life Sustaining Therapy form, which are transferrable across care settings.[81] Initiatives such as Web-based registries or electronic personal health care records may be needed to achieve transfer of this information between care settings and to protect patient privacy and be compliant with HIPAA regulations.

Another important process component of good quality palliative care is the care of the imminently dying and his or her families. Fulfilling patient and family preferences regarding preference of place of death, ensuring that adequate doses of analgesics and sedatives are ordered to relieve pain, treating the body after death with respect, and implementing a bereavement care plan to facilitate effective grieving by the family are all important factors in any high-quality palliative care program.

Timely

Timely care means reducing wait time. Ensuring that a patient can access palliative care sooner rather than later is a very important component of palliative care. Generally speaking, in the case of cancer patients, the offer of palliative care services or referral to hospice is uniformly late, usually in the last week or two of life. Educational efforts to raise the level of awareness of palliative care are fundamental. If patients and families do not know their options, they will not ask about palliative care.

Equitable

Palliative care should not vary in quality because of personal characteristics, such as gender, ethnicity, geographic location, and socioeconomic status. U.S. health care has been differentiated from European-style health care by that fact that the ethical principle of distributive justice (that is, access to care) is trumped by the principle of autonomy (the right to choose, or in the case of end-of-life care, the right to refuse treatment). As health care reform is being debated and formulated, it is important to recognize that palliative care available to all in need must be an integrated component of any reform package. Health care providers must make a concerted effort to incorporate hospice principles into hospitals and nursing homes where the majority of Americans spend their last days of life.

One should not get the impression that little has been done; progress indeed has been made. As of 2008, of the more than 5,000 hospitals in the United States, approximately 1,314 now have palliative care programs, with 2,678 physicians and 15,133 nurses certified in palliative care. But more needs to be done. There is a strong bias within the U.S. health care system toward curative medicine, including financial incentives that encourage provision of aggressive treatment. Even if palliative care were universally available in the health care system, the 15 percent of the population lacking insurance (racial and ethnic minorities being overrepresented) could not access it. Such inequality must be addressed and changes made to ensure accessibility and equality in the provision of palliative care.

CONCLUSION

Relief of symptoms and other suffering at end of life has emerged as an important goal of medicine in the 21st century, and this domain of medical practice is now known as palliative care. Modern palliative care emerged as a grassroots movement in Australia, Britain, India, and the United States, but it is only within the last 10 to 15 years that palliative care has been integrated better into the medical system. The United States is a comparative newcomer in this area of medicine and can learn much from the organizational framework for developing palliative care services from countries like Britain, Australia, and India. In particular, these countries can provide guidance on the policy development piece regarding how governments might work with the private sector in the design and implementation of a high-quality, ethical palliative care program in America.

In the 21st century, patients and practitioners have a better appreciation of the need for and importance of treating pain and suffering at the end of life. Not only is the medical management important, but also the economic consequences of treating end-of-life patients aggressively in hospital is extremely costly. The issue will not diminish in scope given the aging of the population with its concomitant burden of chronic diseases. High-quality palliative care can do much not only to alleviate and relieve suffering, but also to contain costs.

Every one of us, be it for oneself or for one's loved ones, will at some point have to confront the inevitability of end of life. How one prepares for the eventuality of death is a personal and individual matter. What is necessary and important, however, is that end-of-life choices be made clear and available. Providing for end-of-life care is emotionally difficult, thus making it even more imperative that all patients have the option of timely access to palliative care services that are both appropriate and cost-effective. While impressive strides have been made, much more work needs to be done.

Appendix 8.A.
Results of CAPC Report Card 2008

- States Receiving A Grades
  States that are top performers (programs in 81 to 100 percent of hospitals):
  Vermont (100 percent); Montana (88 percent); New Hampshire (85 percent)
- States Receiving B Grades
  States that are on their way (programs in 61 to 80 percent of hospitals):
  District of Columbia (80 percent); South Dakota (78 percent); Minnesota (75 percent); Missouri (73 percent); New Jersey (72 percent); Oregon (72 percent); Iowa (70 percent); Maine (69 percent); Michigan (69 percent); North Carolina (69 percent); Ohio (68 percent); Colorado (67 percent); Maryland (67 percent); West Virginia (67 percent); North Dakota (67 percent); Washington (65 percent); Wisconsin (64 percent); Virginia (63 percent); Kansas (61 percent)
- States Receiving C Grades
  States in the middle (programs in 41 to 60 percent of hospitals):
  Alaska (60 percent); Delaware (60 percent); Rhode Island (60 percent); Illinois (58 percent) New York (58 percent); California (56 percent); Idaho (56 percent); Nebraska (56 percent); Utah (56 percent); Connecticut (54 percent); Indiana (54 percent); Pennsylvania (54 percent); Arizona (50 percent); Massachusetts (50 percent); Florida (49 percent); Hawaii (45 percent); Tennessee (45 percent); Arkansas (41 percent)
- States Receiving D Grades
  States that need significant improvement (programs in 21 to 40 percent of hospitals):
  Georgia (38 percent); Kentucky (37 percent); New Mexico (33 percent); Texas (33 percent); South Carolina (30 percent); Louisiana (27 percent); Wyoming (25 percent); Nevada (23 percent)
- States Receiving Failing Grades
  States with little or no access (programs in 0 to 20 percent of hospitals):
  Oklahoma (19 percent); Alabama (16 percent); Mississippi (10 percent)

Note: CAPC = Center to Advance Palliative Care

REFERENCES

1. Sepulveda C, Marlin A, Yoshida T, et al. Palliative care: the World Health Organization's global perspective. *J Pain Symptom Manage.* 2002;24:91–6.
2. Stjernsward J. Palliative care: the public health strategy. *J Public Health Policy.* 2007;28:42–55.
3. Morrison RS, Dietrich J, Meier DE. *America's Care of Serious Illness: A State-By-State Report Card on Access to Palliative Care in our Nation's Hospitals.* New York: Centre to Advance Palliative Care and the National Palliative Care Research Center; 2008:36.
4. World Health Organization. Ask the expert Online Q&A for April 1, 2008. Are the number of cancer cases increasing or decreasing in the world? http://www.who.int/.
5. Somerville M. *The Ethical Canary: Science, Society and the Human Spirit.* Toronto, Canada: Penguin Canada; 2000:254.
6. Teno JM, Clarridge BR, Casey V, et al. Family perspectives on end-of-life care at the last place of care. *JAMA.* 2004;291:88–93.
7. Covinsky KE, Goldman L, Cook EF, et al. The impact of serious illness on patients' families: Study to Understand Prognoses and Preferences for Outcomes and Risks of Treatment (SUPPORT) investigators. *JAMA.* 1994;27(2):1839–1844.

8. Addington-Hall J, McCarthy M. Dying from cancer: results of a national population-based investigation. *Palliat Med.* 1995;9:295–305.
9. Toscani F, Di Giulio P, Brunelli C, et al. How people die in hospital general wards: a descriptive study. *J Pain Symptom Manage.* 2005;30:33–40.
10. Brennan F, Carr DB, Cousins M. Pain management: a fundamental human right. *Anesth Analg.* 2007;105:205–221.
11. The SUPPORT Principal Investigators. A controlled trial to improve care for seriously ill hospitalized patients: the Study to Understand Prognoses and Preferences for Outcomes and Risks of Treatments (SUPPORT). *JAMA.* 1995; 274:1591–1598.
12. Institute of Medicine. *Approaching Death.* Washington, DC: National Academies Press; 1997.
13. Foley K, Hendin H. *The Case against Suicide.* Baltimore: Johns Hopkins University Press; 2002.
14. von Gunten CF, Lupu D. Development of a medical subspecialty in palliative medicine: progress report. *J Palliat Med.* 2004;7:209–219.
15. Levy MH, Back A, Benedetti C, et al. NCCN clinical practice guidelines in oncology: palliative care. *J Natl Compr Canc Netw.* 2009;7:436–473.
16. Meier DE. Palliative care in hospitals. *J Hosp Med.* 2006;1:21–28.
17. Saunders CM. Foreword. In: Doyle D, Hanks G, Cherny N, et al., eds. *Oxford Textbook of Palliative Medicine.* Oxford: Oxford University Press; 2004:xvii–xx.
18. Clark D, Seymour J. *Reflections on Palliative Care: Sociological and Policy Perspectives.* Buckingham, UK: Open University Press; 1999:67–78.
19. Clark D. *Cicely Saunders: Founder of the Hospice Movement. Selected Letters 1959–1999.* Oxford: Oxford University Press; 2002.
20. Bean WB. Peace at the last: a survey of terminal care in the United Kingdom: a report to the Calouste Gulbenkian Foundation 1960. *Arch Intern Med.* 1961;107:631–632.
21. Hinton JM. The physical and mental distress of the dying. *Q J Med.* 1963;32:1–21.
22. *Palliative Care Explained.* London,UK: The National Council for Palliative Care; 2009. http://www.ncpc.org.uk/palliative_care.html. Accessed September 29, 2009.
23. Franks PJ, Salisbury C, Bosanquet N, et al. The level of need for palliative care: a systematic review of the literature. *Palliat Med.* 2000;14:93–104.
24. Guidance on Cancer Services. *Improving Supportive and Palliative Care for Adults with Cancer.* London, UK: National Institute for Clinical Excellence; 2004.
25. Eagar K, Garrett P, Lin V. *Health Planning: Australian Perspectives.* Crows Nest, NSW, Australia: Allen & Unwin; 2001.
26. Rosenwax LK, McNamara B, Blackmore AM, et al. Estimating the size of a potential palliative care population. *Palliat Med.* 2005;19:556–562.
27. The National Palliative Care Strategy. *A National Framework for Palliative Care Service Development: October 2000.* Canberra, Australia: Australian Government; 2000.
28. Greer DS, Mor V, Morris JN, et al. An alternative in terminal care: results of the National Hospice Study. *J Chronic Dis.* 1986;39:9–26.
29. Gazelle G. Understanding hospice: an underutilized option for life's final chapter. *N Engl J Med.* 2007;357:321–324.
30. Lynn J. Perspectives on care at the close of life: serving patients who may die soon and their families: the role of hospice and other services. *JAMA.* 2001;285:925–932.
31. Christakis NA, Iwashyna TJ. Attitude and self-reported practice regarding prognostication in a national sample of internists. *Arch Intern Med.* 1998;158:2389–2395.

32. Wright AA, Katz IT. Letting go of the rope: aggressive treatment, hospice care, and open access. *N Engl J Med.* 2007;357:324–327.
33. Meier DE, Morrison RS, Cassel CK. Improving palliative care. *Ann Intern Med.* 1997;127:225–230.
34. von Gunten CF. Secondary and tertiary palliative care in US hospitals. *JAMA.* 2002;287:875–881.
35. Higginson IJ, Koffman J. Public health and palliative care. *Clin Geriatr Med.* 2005;21:viii,45–55.
36. Higginson I. Palliative care: a review of past changes and future trends. *J Public Health Med.* 1993;15:3–8.
37. Gomez-Batiste X, Porta-Sales J, Paz S, et al. Program development: palliative medicine and public health services. In: Walsh D, ed. *Palliative Medicine.* Philadelphia, PA: Saunders; 2008:198–203.
38. Ingleton C, Skilbeck J, Clark D. Needs assessment for palliative care: three projects compared. *Palliat Med.* 2001;15:398–404.
39. Currow DC, Abernethy AP, Fazekas BS. Specialist palliative care needs of whole populations: a feasibility study using a novel approach. *Palliat Med.* 2004;18:239–247.
40. Institute of Medicine. *The Future of Public Health.* Washington, DC: National Academies Press; 1988:40–55.
41. Taylor DH Jr. The effect of hospice on Medicare and informal care costs: the US Experience. *J Pain Symptom Manage.* 2009;38:110–114.
42. Miceli PJ, Wojciechowski SL. Impacting family satisfaction with hospice care. *Caring.* 2003;22:14–18.
43. Connor SR, Teno J, Spence C, et al. Family evaluation of hospice care: results from voluntary submission of data via website. *J Pain Symptom Manage.* 2005;30:9–17.
44. Higginson IJ, Foley KM. Palliative care: no longer a luxury but a necessity? *J Pain Symptom Manage.* 2009;38:1–3.
45. Pan CX, Morrison RS, Meier DE, et al. How prevalent are hospital-based palliative care programs? status report and future directions. *J Palliat Med.* 2001;4:315–324.
46. Morrison RS, Maroney-Galin C, Kralovec PD, et al. The growth of palliative care programs in United States hospitals. *J Palliat Med.* 2005;8:1127–1134.
47. Goldsmith B, Dietrich J, Du Q, et al. Variability in access to hospital palliative care in the United States. *J Palliat Med.* 2008;11:1094–1102.
48. Center to Advance Palliative Care. *America's Care of Serious Illness: A State-By-State Report Card on Access to Palliative Care in our Nation's Hospitals.* New York: Center to Advance Palliative Care; 2008.
49. Crawley L, Payne R, Bolden J, et al. Palliative and end-of-life care in the African American community. *JAMA.* 2000;284:2518–2521.
50. Fins JJ. *A Palliative Ethic of Care: Clinical Wisdom at Life's End.* Sudbury, MA: Jones and Bartlett Publishers; 2006.
51. Australian Government, Department of Health and Aging. *Community Attitudes towards Palliative Care: Integrated Report.* Canberra, Australia: Australian Government: 2006.
52. Von Roenn JH, Cleeland CS, Gonin R, et al. Physician attitudes and practice in cancer pain management: a survey from the Eastern Cooperative Oncology Group. *Ann Intern Med.* 1993;119:121–126.
53. Brickner L, Scannell K, Marquet S, et al. Barriers to hospice care and referrals: survey of physicians' knowledge, attitudes, and perceptions in a health maintenance organization. *J Palliat Med.* 2004;7:411–418.

54. Edmonds PM, Stuttaford JM, Penny J, et al. Do hospital palliative care teams improve symptom control? Use of a modified STAS as an evaluation tool. *Palliat Med.* 1998;12:345–351.
55. Komurcu S, Nelson KA, Walsh D, et al. Common symptoms in advanced cancer. *Semin Oncol.* 2000;27:24–33.
56. Schuit KW, Sleijfer DT, Meijler WJ, et al. Symptoms and functional status of patients with disseminated cancer visiting outpatient departments. *J Pain Symptom Manage.* 1998;16:290–297.
57. Cleeland CS, Gonin R, Hatfield AK, et al. Pain and its treatment in outpatients with metastatic cancer. *N Engl J Med.* 1994;330:592–596.
58. Reuben DB, Mor V. Nausea and vomiting in terminal cancer patients. *Arch Intern Med.* 1986;146:2021–2023.
59. Breitbart W, Rosenfeld BD, Passik SD, et al. The undertreatment of pain in ambulatory AIDS patients. *Pain.* 1996;65:243–249.
60. von Gunten CF. Financing palliative care. *Clin Geriatr Med.* 2004;20:viii,767–781.
61. Stjernsward J, Foley KM, Ferris FD. Integrating palliative care into national policies. *J Pain Symptom Manage.* 2007;33:514–520.
62. Joranson DE, Ryan KM. Ensuring opioid availability: methods and resources. *J Pain Symptom Manage.* 2007;33:527–532.
63. De Lima L, Krakauer EL, Lorenz K, et al. Ensuring palliative medicine availability: the development of the IAHPC list of essential medicines for palliative care. *J Pain Symptom Manage.* 2007;33:521–526.
64. Brennan F. Palliative care as an international human right. *J Pain Symptom Manage.* 2007;33:494–499.
65. Bath PA, Clark D, Wright M. The International Observatory on End of Life Care (IOELC): an information resource for palliative care. *Health Inform J.* 2004;10(2)121–126.
66. Kerns RD. *VHA Directive 2003-021: Pain Management.* Washington DC: Veterans Health Administration; 2003.
67. Cassel CK, Vladeck BC. ICD-9 code for palliative or terminal care. *N Engl J Med* 1996;335:1232–1234.
68. Medicare Learning Network. *MLN Matters Number MM6311: Adding a New Specialty Code for Hospice and Palliative Medicine.* Center for Medicare and Medicaid Services; 2009. www.cms.gov/mlnmattersarticles/downloads/MM6311.pdf
69. Foley KM, Gelband H. *Improving Palliative Care for Cancer: Summary and Recommendations.* Washington, DC: National Academies Press; 2001.
70. Weissman DE, Meier DE. Operational features for hospital palliative care programs: consensus recommendations. *J Palliat Med.* 2008;11:1189–1194.
71. Ferris FD, Bruera E, Cherny N, et al. Palliative cancer care a decade later: accomplishments, the need, next steps: from the American Society of Clinical Oncology. *J Clin Oncol.* 2009;27:3052–3058.
72. Ferris FD, Gomez-Batiste X, Furst CJ, et al. Implementing quality palliative care. *J Pain Symptom Manage.* 2007;33:533–541.
73. Institute of Medicine. *Crossing the Quality Chasm: A New Health System for the 21st Century.* Washington, DC: National Academies Press; 2001.
74. World Health Organization. *Cancer Pain Relief and Palliative Care.* Geneva, Switzerland: World Health Organization; 1990.
75. Jadad AR, Browman GP. The WHO analgesic ladder for cancer pain management. Stepping up the quality of its evaluation. *JAMA.* 1995;274:1870–1873.
76. Wiffen PJ, McQuay HJ. Oral morphine for cancer pain. *Cochrane Database Syst Rev.* 2007;4:CD003868. doi:10.1002/14651858.

77. Zimmermann C, Riechelmann R, Krzyzanowska M, et al. Effectiveness of specialized palliative care: a systematic review. *JAMA*. 2008;299:1698–1709.
78. Lorenz KA, Lynn J, Dy SM, et al. Evidence for improving palliative care at the end of life: a systematic review. *Ann Intern Med*. 2008;148:147–159.
79. Chang VT, Hwang SS, Kasimis B, et al. Shorter symptom assessment instruments: the Condensed Memorial Symptom Assessment Scale (CMSAS). *Cancer Invest*. 2004;22:526–536.
80. Morrison RS, Penrod JD, Cassel JB, et al. Cost savings associated with US hospital palliative care consultation programs. *Arch Intern Med*. 2008;168:1783–1790.
81. Hickman SE, Nelson CA, Moss AH, et al. Use of the Physician Orders for Life-Sustaining Treatment (POLST) paradigm program in the hospice setting. *J Palliat Med*. 2009;12:133–141.

SECTION 4

PUBLIC HEALTH PRACTICE AND EDUCATION

CHAPTER **9**

The Role of Epidemiology and Biostatistics in Health News Reporting

Paula Trushin and Heejung Bang, PhD

Medicine is a science of uncertainty and an art of probability.
—Sir William Osler

How often does a health news story make you pause and wonder what to do next? Headlines such as "Highly active compound found in coffee may prevent colon cancer,"[1] "The surprising ingredient causing weight gain,"[2] or "Three cups of brewed coffee a day 'triples risk of hallucinations,'"[3] grab the reader's attention, but are oversimplified, sensationalized,[4] and—in most cases—speak with undue authority. Barry Kramer, associate director for disease prevention at the National Institutes of Health, calls such reporting "the cure of the week or the killer of the week, the danger of the week. It's like treating people to an endless regimen of whiplash."[5] And Donald Berry, chair of the Department of Biostatistics at the M. D. Anderson Cancer Center, says that he has "seen so many contradictory studies with coffee that I've come to ignore them all."[5]

THE ROLE OF UNCERTAINTY IN SCIENCE

Science is a way of thinking and trying to understand the natural world. Advances in science are largely propelled by the scientific method, a rational and systematic mode of inquiry (based largely on common sense)[6] whereby natural phenomena can be studied through observation and experimentation. Statistics, which may be considered a tool of the scientific method, provides a theoretical basis and mathematical techniques for collecting, organizing, and analyzing data quantitatively, taking into account chance, variation, and error (defined as the difference between the computed or measured value of a factor and its actual or theoretically correct value). When used appropriately, statistics makes it possible to describe an aspect of reality and draw inferences about the relationships among variables (for a definition of "variable," see "The Meaning of Words"). Inherent in this process is the notion of "scientific uncertainty": a constant state of doubt or limited knowledge. Any meaningful attempt to understand health-related information requires an appreciation of the essential role that uncertainty plays in science, spurring the development of new ideas and leading to discovery. Statistics can help manage uncertainty by quantifying the likelihood that a particular event occurred by chance.

Like all human endeavors, the scientific method is not infallible, but it can be self-correcting over time as long as its practitioners remain open to doubt and questions about their work. Thus, disagreement and—yes—controversy are fundamental to the advancement of science.[7]

Sometimes, however, scientific controversies are manufactured for nonscientific reasons, whether political, economic, or religious. This may be done by overstating (sensationalizing) research findings; ignoring findings that do not support a particular viewpoint; casting doubt on empirical evidence, despite its strength and consistency; or arguing that legitimate differences of opinion are being suppressed.[8–12] Manufactured controversies have serious consequences. Not only can they lead to public mistrust of science and make it difficult for lay persons to appreciate legitimate differences of scientific opinion, but they also can cause public alarm, as was the case with stories linking the MMR (measles, mumps, and rubella) vaccine to autism.[10, 11, 13] Inappropriate use of scientific findings may compromise clinical practice recommendations, resulting in misdirected prevention and treatment strategies.[14]

Because the mass media influence personal health care choices, public health policies, and medical decision making, it is incumbent on everyone to develop an understanding of what statistics mean and how they are used (and sometimes misused) in health news reporting,[10, 15, 16]

This chapter will focus on statistical thinking—a broad and flexible mode of reasoning about data, variation, and chance.[17] Since there are virtually no "facts" in science, only varying degrees of certainty depending on the strength of the available evidence, statistical thinking begins with an acceptance of chance and uncertainty.[18–23] It also entails an understanding of basic principles and concepts, which we shall endeavor to explain; an appreciation of context; an ability to detect logical and factual flaws in information and ideas;[24] and the realization that science is fluid, with new empirical evidence being accumulated every day. To grasp these fundamentals, one does not have to be scientifically trained. (This chapter will not discuss the Bayesian paradigm or Bayesian statistics, which is a way of quantifying probability by factoring in prior knowledge and additional evidence.)

THE MEANING OF WORDS

A number of familiar words have scientific definitions that differ from the vernacular. They include theory, sample, uncertainty, error, bias, odds, parameter, and significance. Unless explained, words such as these hinder public understanding of science (the "homonymic obstacle"[25]). Members of the public cannot be expected to know which words have both a vernacular and a scientific definition. Therefore, scientists and journalists have a responsibility to make these distinctions clear.

Throughout this chapter, words with a distinct scientific or statistical meaning will be defined as they occur. Let us begin, however, by explaining certain key terms.

For the scientist, *a theory* does not mean a conjectural and unsubstantiated statement (as in the saying that something is "just a theory"). A scientific theory is supported by observation and experimentation, has been verified to some degree by different investigators,[26] and is used to explain and predict a natural phenomenon. If a theory is contradicted by new observations, it must be revised or replaced, but this does not mean that the underlying phenomenon has changed. As Stephen Jay Gould pointed out, "Einstein's theory of gravitation replaced Newton's in [the 20th] century, but apples didn't suspend themselves in midair pending the outcome."[27] In contrast, *a hypothesis* is a conjectural explanation for an observed phenomenon (see "Study Designs").

Risk is the estimable probability, or quantifiable likelihood, that a particular (generally negative) event will occur. In medicine, some risks, including a number of genetic disorders, are biologically determined. Many major diseases are multifactorial; however, they depend on a combination of environmental (for example, chemicals, pathogens, physical injury, social forces, lifestyle and behavior) and biological factors. For example, we can scarcely say that there is "a" cause of coronary heart disease (CHD) or lung cancer. In such cases, statistics are used to estimate the probability that a given risk factor (or set of risk factors), or an intervention, will increase, or decrease, risk.

Exposure refers to contact with a physical, chemical, or biologic influence (including a therapeutic intervention).

A *variable* is any factor or characteristic that varies, either from person to person or within a person. To be studied scientifically, a variable must be classifiable or measurable, for example, age, sex, body weight, or blood chemistry.

ASSOCIATION, CAUSATION, CONFOUNDING, AND BIAS

Association and causation, which refer to the relationship between two variables, are fundamental concepts in scientific research. An association is a correspondence or coincidence between two variables in cases in which one does not necessarily affect or alter the other.[28] In contrast, causation is defined as an act or process whereby one factor (an "independent variable") creates or produces an outcome (a "dependent variable"). An observed association (or correlation) between two events (or variables) does not mean causation. For instance, if children with larger feet are better spellers, does this mean that foot size causes orthographic proficiency? Undoubtedly not, since age is a more likely explanation for both.[29]

This introduces the notion of confounding, which refers to a confusion of effects.[30] A confounder is generally understood to be a variable, possibly unidentified or unmeasured, that (1) is associated with the exposure, either causally or non-causally; (2) has a cause-related effect on the outcome; and (3) is not a causal factor on the pathway between exposure and outcome.[31–33] For example, some observational evidence suggests an association between alcohol use and an increased risk for lung cancer. A possible confounder in this case would be cigarette smoking, which is associated both with drinking and (causally) with lung cancer. By failing to identify confounders, we may end up concluding erroneously that an association between two variables represents a cause-and-effect relationship (however unlikely it may seem in some cases).

Confounding can distort the results of a study. In extreme situations, it can even invert the direction of an association, so that an exposure appears to decrease, rather than increase, the risk for an event (or vice versa).[32]

When designing a study, researchers must try to identify and, if possible, control the variables that can confound the relationship under investigation or lead to a spurious interpretation of that relationship. Failure to do this could result in *bias*. In science, bias does not mean a prejudiced outlook. It refers to unrecognized error that systematically and consistently pervades the entire study, distorting the results. The best possible way to correct bias would be to pinpoint and eliminate any potential source(s) in the study design phase.

Frequently, the media contribute to the confusion between association and causation by oversimplifying or sensationalizing the results of scientific research.[4] This can mislead and misinform the reader.

RISK

In all fields of endeavor, history abounds with remarkable developments that have transformed human life. One such development is "mastery of risk"—the notion that the probability of future events can, to some degree, be understood, quantified, and predicted [34] by statistical means, instead of entrusted to the gods and the prophecies of oracles. There are two standard ways of quantifying risk: absolute and relative. Let us imagine a study in which 150 subjects are given drug X, an experimental treatment to prevent major cardiovascular events, and 250 subjects receive placebo (an inert substance disguised as medication). Table 9.1 illustrates how measures of absolute and relative risk would be calculated in such a scenario.[35]

Absolute Risk

Absolute risk, also called the *event rate*, is a percentage representing the number of people in a group who experience an event, such as a heart attack, in relation to the total number of people in the group. It also can be calculated by using the number of actual events in relation to the total number of possible events (that is, the total number of *at-risk* people in the group).

To assess the effectiveness of a drug or other intervention, clinical studies commonly compare the event rate with treatment (the event rate in the experimental group) versus the event rate in a similar group of untreated (control) subjects. There are two basic methods of comparison: subtraction or division.

The *absolute risk reduction* is determined by *subtracting* the experimental event rate from the control event rate: 40 percent − 10 percent = 30 percent (see table 9.1). If the intervention increases the risk for an event, however, the *absolute risk increase* is calculated in the reverse manner, also illustrated in table 9.1: 50 percent − 40 percent = 10 percent. If the event rates in both groups are the same, there will be no difference between them. Thus, a value of zero means that the intervention has no effect.

Relative Risk

Relative Risk, or *risk ratio*, represents comparison by division. To calculate the relative risk, we divide the experimental event rate by the control event rate. Based

Table 9.1
Sample Calculations of Predictive Measures (risk or odds)

Subjects	Risk Reduction (Intervention Beneficial)		Risk Increase (Intervention Harmful)	
	Experimental Group	Control Group	Experimental Group	Control Group
With Events (E)	15	100	75	100
With No Events (N)	135	150	75	150
Total (T)	150	250	150	250
Absolute Risk (Event Rate) E/T	15/150 = 10% (EER)	100/250 = 40% (CER)	75/150 = 50% (EER)	100/250 = 40% (CER[a])
Odds E/N	15/135 = 11%	100/150 = 67%	75/75 = 1	100/150 = 67%

Predictive Measure	Equation	Intervention Beneficial (Experimental Group)	Intervention Harmful (Experimental Group)
Absolute Risk Reduction	CER − EER = ARR	0.40 − 0.10 = 0.30 (30%)	NA
Absolute Risk Increase	EER − CER = ARI	NA	0.50 − 0.40 = 0.10 (10%)
Number Needed to Treat	1/ARR	1.0/0.30 = 3.33	NA
Relative Risk Reduction	ARR/CER = RRR	0.30/0.40 = 0.75 (75%)	NA
Relative Risk Increase	ARI/CER = RRI	NA	0.10/0.40 = 0.25 (25%)
Relative Risk (Risk Ratio)	EER/CER = RR	0.10/0.40 = 0.25 (25%)	0.50/0.40 = 1.25 (125%)
Odds	E/N	15/135 = 11%	75/75 = 1
Odds Ratio	E/N (EXP) / E/N (CONT)	0.11/0.67 = 0.164	1.0/0.67 = 1.5

a. The control event rate is also the baseline risk, because it represents the percentage of untreated people in the target population who are likely to experience an event.

Source: Adapted from Number needed to treat. Wikipedia, the free encyclopedia. Available at: http://en.wikipedia.org/wiki/Number_needed_to_treat. Retrieved September 28, 2009.[35]

Note: ARI = absolute risk increase; ARR = absolute risk reduction; CER = control event rate (also called the baseline risk); EER = experimental event rate; EXP = experimental group; CONT = control group; RR = relative risk; RRI = relative risk increase; RRR = relative risk reduction.

on the data in table 9.1, the relative risks for the beneficial and the harmful interventions are 0.25 and 1.25, respectively. In a clinical study, the control event rate is also called the baseline risk, because it indicates the percentage of *untreated* people in the population from which the study participants were drawn who are likely to experience an event. If the experimental and the control event rates are the same, the ratio will equal one. Thus, for the relative risk (and the odds ratio, discussed below), a value of one means that the exposure has no effect. The *relative risk reduction* is a ratio of the absolute risk difference to the baseline risk.

Relative differences are generally greater than absolute differences; thus, they may magnify the effect of a treatment or exposure. Moreover, they are nonspecific, since any baseline risk can be reduced by the same relative amount. In table 9.2, for example, absolute risk reductions of 2 percent and 24 percent both translate into a relative risk of 33 percent and a relative risk reduction of 67 percent. The potential misuse of relative numbers is illustrated by a CBS News headline announcing that "Trial AIDS Vaccine Cuts Infection Risk 31 Percent."[36] In this article, the lead paragraph describes the result as a "watershed event," but the story fails to explain that 31 percent is a relative number, and that the absolute risk reduction was just 0.3 percent. When the raw data (number of events and total number of subjects in the treatment and control groups) are given in an article, the reader can easily calculate both the experimental and the control event rates, as well as the absolute risk reduction (by simple subtraction). The calculation takes just a few minutes, yet it will contribute substantially to a more responsible understanding of the study results.

Odds Ratio

In statistics, odds refer to the probability that something will occur in relation to the probability that it will not. If the underlying risk is small (that is, the event of interest is rare), the odds ratio will approximate the relative risk. As the baseline (absolute) risk increases, however, the difference between the relative risk and the odds ratio grows larger. In most studies with a binary exposure status (exposed versus not exposed or treated versus untreated) and outcome (event versus nonevent), the data are customarily analyzed by using either the relative risk or the odds ratio. One type of observational study, however, must use the odds ratio only. This is the case-control study, which will be discussed in the following section.

Number Needed to Treat

Number needed to treat (NNT) refers to the number of patients who must be treated to prevent one (additional) event. The number needed to treat is the reciprocal of the absolute risk reduction (1 divided by the absolute risk reduction). If the absolute risk is based on the number of events, rather than the number of people with events, the recurrence of multiple events in some subjects may increase the difference between the treatment and the control groups, thereby lowering the number needed to treat and exaggerating the benefit of the intervention.

Table 9.2
Absolute versus Relative Risk

Risk for Disease					
Group I Experimental Event Rate	Group II Control Event Rate (Baseline Risk)	Absolute Risk Difference (B − A = C)	Relative Risk (A/B)	Relative Risk Reduction (C/B = D)	Absolute Risk Difference (B × D)
1.0% (10/1,000)	3.0% (30/1,000)	3.0% − 1.0% = 2.0%	33.0%	67.0%	2.0%
12.0% (240/1,000)	36.0% (360/1,000)	36.0% − 12.0% = 24.0%	33.0%	67.0%	24.0%
27.0% (270/1,000)	81.0% (810/1,000)	81.0% − 27.0% = 54.0%	33.0%	67.0%	54.0%

Note: A = experimental event rate; B = control event rate (also called "baseline risk"); C = absolute risk difference (reduction or increase); D = relative risk reduction.

STUDY DESIGNS: OBSERVATIONAL VERSUS EXPERIMENTAL

The purpose of research is to develop or contribute to generalizable knowledge.[37] When conducted in human subjects, it is known as clinical research. The two basic types of clinical research are *observational and experimental.*

Observational Studies

In observational studies (also called epidemiologic or nonexperimental studies), the researcher does not attempt to affect the outcome or control other variables that may influence the results. This type of research can be either descriptive, providing information on health-related events in populations, or analytic, in which researchers attempt to quantify the relationship between an exposure and an outcome. There are several observational research designs, distinguished chiefly by the method used to select the study sample (participants). The three basic designs—cross-sectional, cohort, and case-control—cover most observational studies, including genetic studies. Each has its advantages and disadvantages, and the decision about which one to use depends on multiple considerations.

Observational studies also can be forward looking (prospective) or backward looking (retrospective). In the former, disease-free individuals exposed and unexposed to a suspected risk factor are compared over time to determine whether an outcome develops. In the latter, subjects are identified after the outcome has occurred, and various means (for example, medical records, subject interviews) then are used to look back and see if an association between an exposure, such as cigarette smoking, and an outcome, such as lung cancer, can be identified. Because there is no need to wait for outcomes to develop, retrospective study designs are generally less costly and time-consuming than prospective designs, and they also can be useful as pilot studies in anticipation of prospective research.[38] But retrospective studies can be hampered by incomplete and unreliable data, since medical records may not be up to date and subjects may have faulty or selective memories (known as "recall bias"). With few exceptions, therefore, prospective studies are methodologically preferable to their retrospective counterparts.[39]

Because of confounding and various biases, which are part of the natural settings in which observational studies take place, evidence from this type of research generally is limited or not reliable as a basis for causal inference. As an example, let us imagine a prospective cohort study showing a lower risk for CHD among women taking antioxidant vitamins compared with those who do not. This result may be influenced by what we call the healthy user effect or bias, which means a tendency among antioxidant users to be particularly health conscious overall, with habits that include a low-fat diet, regular exercise, and proper medical care.[39] Other factors, including income level and years of education, also may confound (provide an alternative explanation for) the results if each is independently associated with antioxidant use and lower CHD risk.[40]

A case-control study is a form of observational research in which subjects are selected on the basis of outcome, rather than exposure. Consequently, subjects with the disease (cases) exceed the percentage in the population from which the study sample is drawn.[41] This means that the sample is not representative. Because a representative sample is fundamental to the prediction of risk, the data from case-control studies may only be analyzed in terms of the odds ratio.

To illustrate, let us look at a case-control investigation of hip/femur fracture (the outcome) and stroke (the exposure).[42] This study reported an odds ratio of 2.0, indicating that those who sustained a fracture were twice as likely to have suffered a stroke than their uninjured counterparts, but it cannot do the reverse and predict the risk for fracture in stroke patients.[41] Nevertheless, the following headline from *US News and World Report* implies a prospective study of risk prediction (similar headlines appeared in many other news outlets): "Stroke Doubles Risk of Hip, Thigh Fractures."[43] A more accurate (although less compelling) headline could be: "Odds of Having Had a Stroke Are Greater in Patients with Hip, Thigh Fractures."

While case-control studies are appropriate in certain situations (for example, the study of rare diseases or diseases in which there is a long lag time between exposure and outcome), their results should not be interpreted as predictive of risk for a future event. Even if the observational study described above were prospective, the headline would still be misleading because it implies that X causes Y, a claim that generally requires experimental evidence. When evaluating a health news story about clinical research, we should ask whether the study was observational or experimental and, if observational, what study design was used (see appendix 9.A).

Experimental Studies

The fundamental difference between observational and experimental research is that, in the latter, investigators can control factors that might influence the results, with the goal of being able to infer causation, quantify risk, and make probabilistic statements that could apply to like circumstances. Experimental research involving human subjects typically is conducted by means of randomized controlled trials (RCTs), a rigorous form of scientific investigation that eliminates or, via the coin-toss mechanism, controls for multiple variables that could affect the result; consequently, the finding of a strong association between an exposure and an outcome generally implies a causal relationship.[44] In the hierarchy of clinical evidence (see table 9.3),[45, 46] the results of RCTs generally are considered to be the most robust (least susceptible to error).

Each experimental study (as well as some observational studies) begins with a prespecified, well-defined hypothesis, which is a conjectural explanation for a phenomenon stated in terms that can be systematically evaluated. For example: *the antioxidant vitamins C, E, and beta-carotene reduce the risk for myocardial infarction in women between the ages of 40 to 60*. Hypotheses are generated through the application of inductive reasoning to data from observational studies, whereas hypothesis-testing studies follow the principles of reasoning by deduction. They begin with a research protocol that prespecifies all features of the study, thus ensuring that the hypothesis, methodology, endpoints (outcomes to be measured), and statistical analysis are not determined *post hoc* based on what the data show or on a desire to present the data in a favorable light. The study endpoints are classified as "primary" (the main question to be addressed) and "secondary" (all other questions).

In an experimental study, random selection of subjects helps ensure that the sample (study subjects) will be representative of the population from which it was

Table 9.3

"Viewpoints" Described by Austin Bradford Hill for Considering Whether an Observed Association May Represent a Cause-and-Effect Relationship (1965)

Condition	Explanation
Strength of the association	The lung cancer death rate in cigarette smokers was nine to ten times higher than in non-smokers, and the rate in heavy cigarette smokers was twenty to thirty times as great. With an association of this strength, the presence of an undetected cause (that is, a confounder) was unlikely.
Consistency	The association is repeatedly observed by different persons in different places, circumstances, and times.
Specificity	A single cause is linked to a single effect. However, a lack of specificity does not negate the presence of a causal relationship, since lung cancer and other diseases can result from multiple causes.
Temporality	The putative cause must precede the observed effect.
Biological gradient	The severity of the effect increases monotonically (that is, linearly) with the extent of the exposure. Also known as a dose-response curve.
Plausibility	The suspected cause is biologically plausible, based on available knowledge. This is not a necessary condition, however, because (1) current biological knowledge might not be sufficient to provide an explanation, or (2) research that conflicts with established knowledge may prompt a reconsideration of accepted beliefs and theories.
Coherence	The observed association should be compatible with existing knowledge and theories. As with plausibility, however, an association that conflicts with established knowledge is not automatically false; it may prompt a reconsideration of accepted ideas.
Experiment	Is experimental or semi-experimental[a] evidence available? Such evidence may reveal "[t]he strongest support for the causation hypothesis."
Analogy	The association may bear comparison with another circumstance. For example, if exposure to a different environmental toxin produces a similar outcome, the current situation might be analogous.

a. Semi-experimental evidence. In this context, a before-and-after time trend analysis.[56]

Source: Hill AB. The environment and disease: association or causation? *Proc R Soc Med.* 1965;58:295-300.[55]

Note:

Hill expressed his ambivalence about the usefulness of the above by saying that "[n]one of my nine viewpoints can bring indisputable evidence for or against the cause-and-effect hypothesis and none can be required as a *sine qua non*." Actually, "temporality" (that is, the cause must precede the effect) is a *sine qua non* for causality, whereas the other conditions are neither necessary nor sufficient for determining whether an observed association is causal.[57] In a 2005 paper, Rothman and Greenland concluded that there are no causal criteria in epidemiology, and that "[c]ausal inference in epidemiology is better viewed as an exercise in measurement of an effect rather than as a criterion-guided process for deciding whether an effect is present or not."[58]

drawn, so that the findings will be generalizable. For a variety of reasons, however, a representative sample may not be obtained in practice. This can introduce selection bias, potentially providing rival explanations for the outcome or making the findings less generalizable. To protect against this threat, the experimental and control groups should be as equivalent as possible with respect to "critical demographic and clinical variables" (baseline characteristics), both known and unknown, that can influence the results.[47] Such an objective may be nearly achievable only through random allocation, in which each subject has an equal chance of being assigned to one group or the other. For the same reason that a series of coin tosses is likely to yield a balanced number of heads and tails, random allocation produces groups that, on average, are balanced with regard to all variables except for the exposure (for example, treatment) being tested.[1] Thus, we can be reasonably confident that any between-group difference in outcomes is due to the exposure. Even if the groups are not perfectly balanced, randomization minimizes the possibility that subjects with a particular characteristic will be systematically assigned to the exposure or the control.[48]

Throughout the study, it is important for both groups to have equivalent experiences except for the intervention being tested, an objective that may be best achieved by concealing information on treatment allocation from subjects and investigators (a mechanism often employed in RCTs). Known as *blinding*, this helps prevent the study from being influenced by the expectations of those who receive the intervention or assess its effects. In some cases, such as a surgical procedure or an experimental drug with a high rate of adverse events, blinding may not be feasible or sustainable. It still would be possible, however, to blind the investigators during the data analysis, with the intention of protecting the integrity of the results.

Replication

Regardless of the type of study, other researchers must be able to replicate the results in independently conducted investigations. Replication establishes the credibility of the findings, extends their generalizability to other populations and contexts, contributes to the "big picture" or more complete evidence regarding an intervention, and provides support for the development of theories.[49, 50] When the findings of an observational study are successfully replicated in a hypothesis-testing study, this means that a conclusion reached deductively agrees with the results of observation and inductive inference on which the hypothesis was based.[51] Thus, in a sense, the research process is brought full circle.

If a study cannot be replicated, this sometimes may be due to methodological, rather than biological, factors, including chance, error, bias, or insufficient statistical power (that is, a sample size too small to detect the presence of an effect), either in the initial study or in the follow-up investigation.[39, 50, 52] Therefore, it is essential to examine the totality of the evidence before deciding whether to abandon a particular line of research. For example, although most placebo-controlled trials have been unable to confirm observational results suggesting that antioxidants

---

1. Every published RCT includes a table showing the distribution of baseline characteristics in the study groups. In almost all cases, the groups are expected to be balanced with regard to variables that could influence the study outcome, except for random deviation.

reduce the risk for coronary events, the totality of laboratory, animal, and epidemiologic evidence seems to indicate that oxidative stress plays an important role in atherosclerosis. Consequently, investigators are trying to understand why placebo-controlled studies of vitamins C, E, and beta-carotene have failed to show a benefit.[53]

In another example, multiple observational studies conducted over a 20-year period found that hormone replacement therapy (HRT) reduced a woman's risk for CHD. But in 2002, the Women's Health Initiative (WHI), an RCT enrolling more than 16,000 postmenopausal women, reported a greater risk for CHD among women using HRT compared with those receiving a placebo.[39] Researchers have identified multiple sources of potential bias that could explain this discrepancy. In some earlier observational studies, the healthy user effect may have accounted for the putative beneficial outcome, while in the WHI, there was a high dropout rate and a substantial rate of premature unblinding among clinicians and participants, largely because of a need to manage vaginal bleeding. Unblinding could lead to behavioral changes (for example, participants in the control arm may lose their enthusiasm and withdraw from the trial) and detection bias, which occurs when subjects known to be using the experimental medication are monitored more closely than those whose treatment allocation remains concealed. This can result in the detection of outcomes that otherwise might have gone unrecognized.[39]

Causal Inference from Observational Studies

Although well-designed RCTs are the preferred means of inferring causation and replicating results, they may not be feasible because of ethical or practical considerations. Researchers cannot knowingly randomize subjects to a harmful exposure (for example, a carcinogen) or to an investigational treatment that may be less effective than an available treatment for the target disorder. Additionally, in some cases, the time or sample size needed to test a given intervention might make an RCT prohibitively expensive or otherwise impractical (although the potential effects of some exposures or interventions, such as environmental hazards or dietary change, may only be understood over the long term). Conversely, with rare diseases, there may be too few available subjects to produce credible results. Given any of these situations, observational studies may provide a more appropriate or realistic source of evidence, despite their limitations.

The case of cigarette smoking illustrates how nonexperimental (observational) studies may, at times, permit causal inference. In the first half of the 20th century, observational evidence showed that smokers were at least nine times more likely than nonsmokers to die of lung cancer.[54] The strength of this association in multiple studies led researchers to rule out confounding variables (for example, genetic, environmental) or limitations in study design as an alternative explanation and to conclude that there was a strong causal relationship between smoking and lung cancer, despite the lack of RCT data. In this context, Austin Bradford Hill, a British epidemiologist, published a landmark paper in 1965 describing considerations that may permit us to infer causation based on an observed association between two variables (see table 9.3).[55–58] As Hill noted, "[w]hat [these 'viewpoints'] can do, with greater or less strength, is to help us to make up our minds on the fundamental

Table 9.4
Evidence Types

Grade	Type of Evidence
I	Systematic reviews and meta-analyses of randomized controlled trials (with minimal or no publication bias)
II	Randomized controlled trial(s)
III	Controlled trials without randomization
IV	Cohort studies, preferably conducted by more than one center or research group
V	Case-control studies, preferably conducted by more than one center or research group
VI	Cross-sectional surveys
VII	Case series (reports on a series of patients with outcome of interest)
VIII	Opinions of respected authorities based on clinical experience; narrative reviews; descriptive studies and case reports; or reports of expert committees
IX	Anecdotal information

Source:
Note: VI to IX grades generate hypotheses; V to I grades infer causation.

question—is there any other way of explaining the set of facts before us, is there any other answer equally, or more, likely than cause and effect?"[55]

THE IMPORTANCE OF MEASURABLE ENDPOINTS

In research, the endpoint (outcome) must be both classifiable and quantifiable. An outcome that directly measures how a patient feels, functions, or survives is called a clinical endpoint. Examples include death, loss of vision, heart attack, and onset of symptoms (for example, pain).[59] Because clinical endpoint studies often are long and costly, however, there is great interest in defining surrogate endpoints that can be quantified earlier and more conveniently.[59] A surrogate endpoint can be a laboratory measure (for example, cholesterol levels) or physical sign used as a substitute for a clinically meaningful endpoint. Changes induced by a therapy on a valid surrogate endpoint are expected to predict changes in a true clinical endpoint.[60]

While valid surrogate endpoints have the potential to reduce the size, duration, and cost of clinical trials, they are difficult to identify. Often, this is because scientists do not have a complete understanding of the causal pathway leading to the disease. For example, ventricular arrhythmias are associated with an almost fourfold increase in risk for cardiovascular death, and so it was thought that suppression of arrhythmia would predict a reduction in mortality. In the 1990s, however, three antiarrhythmic drugs approved by the Food and Drug Administration (FDA) were found to increase sudden cardiac death among subjects in placebo-controlled follow-up studies.[59] In addition, statistical methods for validating a surrogate endpoint usually require trials with sample sizes much larger than those needed to establish the clinical efficacy of a drug for FDA approval.[59] Consequently, if a biologically plausible surrogate endpoint has failed to predict a change in a clinical endpoint, one possible explanation may be that the trial was too small, suggesting that a trial with greater power (a larger sample) might be able to detect the presence of an effect.

When considering the results of a study, we must ask whether the effect of an intervention is measured in terms of a clinical endpoint or a surrogate endpoint. If the latter, further inquiry is needed to assess whether the surrogate endpoint reliably predicts the clinical outcome of ultimate interest.

INTERNAL AND EXTERNAL VALIDITY

"Validity" means how well a study measures what it proposes to measure. There are two types of validity: internal and external. Internal validity is the degree to which researchers can be reasonably confident about the finding within a particular study, for example, the outcome is the result of the variable being tested. External validity means that the results can be generalized beyond the study. There are several "threats" to internal validity, each of which may provide an alternative explanation for the observed effect of an intervention. They include the presence of confounders, selection bias (faulty samples or lack of balance between exposure and control groups that was not controlled in the statistical analysis), events outside the study that may affect the subjects' behavior, maturation (natural changes in the course of a disease or in the subjects themselves, such as growing older), instrumentation (any change in the instrument or the researchers used to measure treatment effect), experimental mortality and attrition (not death, but withdrawal of subjects from the study, particularly if it is disproportionate, for example, more men, more women, more higher risk subjects, and so on), repeated testing (improved performance due to test-taking practice, as in psychological research), contamination (use of the experimental intervention by the control subjects), and regression (a statistical phenomenon in which a variable that is extreme when first measured will be closer to the mean when measured again, regardless of the intervention being tested).

Researchers also must be mindful of threats to external validity: for example, conditions in which the observed outcome is due to the experimental situation itself, and not to the exposure or intervention being tested. If this occurs, the results may apply only to the participants in an experimental study and may not be generalizable. Threats to external validity include the experimenter effect (intervention works because of the person implementing it), and the Hawthorne effect. Named after the location of a study conducted in the 1920s, this refers to a change in the subjects' behavior simply because they know that they are being observed.

TOOLS FOR INTERPRETING THE DATA

Location versus Spread

To understand the outcome of a study, the numerical data must be summarized in a way that is both succinct and meaningful. There are two important summary statistics used to describe the data: measures of location (or central tendency) and measures of spread. The term "measure of location" refers to the location of the central, or "typical," value for a set of data. The three commonly used measures of location are the mean (average), median (middle value or 50th percentile), and mode (the value that occurs most frequently). Measures of spread (or variability around the central value) include range (highest value minus lowest value), interquartile range (the 75th percentile minus the 25th percentile), and standard deviation (a standardized measure of spread in relation to the mean). The decision about which measures of location and spread to use often depends on the presence of outliers (extreme values) or the skewness (asymmetry) of the distribution and on the type of data—for example, continuous, such as weight or height, or categorical, meaning data that are separable into mutually exclusive categories such as ethnicity or age-group.

Statistical Significance

"Significance" has a definition specific to science, especially statistical science. In common parlance, significance means importance or consequence, whereas statistical significance assesses the likelihood, or probability, that a result occurred by chance.

Evaluations of statistical significance attempt to determine the likelihood that a difference between exposure and control groups will be found when no difference actually exists (the absence of a between-group difference is called the "null hypothesis," and it is the default assumption unless contradicted by the data). The number most popularly used to express statistical significance is the "p-value" (probability value). A p-value is the probability of obtaining a statistical result at least as extreme as the one that was actually observed, assuming that the null hypothesis is true. The lower the p-value, the less likely it is that the result occurred by chance; thus, the result is deemed more significant from a statistical perspective. By convention, a p-value less than 0.05 often is considered to be a basis for rejecting the null hypothesis.[61] But a p-value greater than 0.05 does not mean that there is no difference between exposure and control; it may merely indicate that a difference has not been satisfactorily demonstrated. Given this uncertainty and potential for error, it is more appropriate to regard the p-value as a tool for quantifying the relationship between a given statistical result and the null hypothesis, rather than as a basis for summarily rejecting the latter.[61]

Just as juries sometimes convict an innocent person of a crime or let a guilty person go free, statistical analysis may produce two basic kinds of errors: a Type I error, or false positive (that is, the probability of finding a difference between exposure and control when no difference actually exists), and its converse, a Type II error, or false negative (that is, the probability of failing to detect a between-group difference when one exists). Type I and Type II errors often are denoted by α and β, respectively.

The α-level refers to a significance level agreed upon before the data are collected. This differs from the p-value, which tells us how extreme the data are. An α-level of 5 percent, a commonly accepted standard (although it is sometimes more stringent), means a 5 percent chance (5 times out of 100) of finding a between-group difference when none exists—in other words, a 5 percent chance that the result was a random occurrence and that the null hypothesis has been mistakenly rejected, resulting in a Type I error. When a significance test yields a p-value that is the same or lower than the predetermined α-level for a given study, researchers may conclude that the result would be unlikely to occur by chance if the null hypothesis were true. This is commonly termed "statistically significant."

In medicine, a Type I error often is considered relatively more serious, and thus more important to control, because the use of a treatment that we think is effective—but is actually no different from placebo or standard treatment—could result in great potential harm. It also can be argued that a Type II error (failing to recognize a meaningful clinical difference) may have similarly serious consequences. For instance, consider the possible implications of not identifying smoking as a risk factor for lung cancer, mistakenly diagnosing an HIV-infected patient as disease free, or erroneously concluding that Cox-2 inhibitors for pain relief do not increase the risk for cardiovascular events compared with other nonsteroidal anti-inflammatory drugs.[62]

The p-value is the most widely used statistical tool for drawing inferences from clinical studies,[63] yet it is subject to misuse or even abuse, in part because the demands of career advancement place researchers under pressure to establish the significance of their findings.[64] While this measure of significance has been dubbed "the almighty p-value,"[65] many scientists regret what some call the "cult of statistical significance,"[66] stating that it treats statistical models as if they were the reality, rather than a tool for the investigation of natural phenomena.[67] They also argue that emphasizing the p-value imposes a false dichotomy on the data (significant versus nonsignificant), leads to automated decision making instead of scientific reasoning, and fosters the view that those who draw different conclusions from the data may be motivated by "nonscientific" considerations.[61, 67, 68] This can inhibit the constructive controversy essential to scientific progress.

Although there is virtually no doubt about the usefulness of the p-value as a one-dimensional summary measure in decision making, careful judgment is needed to understand this powerful number adequately and use it appropriately.

Confidence Intervals

The confidence interval, which is calculated from a sample data set, presents a range of values that is likely to include the true effect (see figure 9.1). Unlike p-values, confidence intervals show us the results in terms of actual data (for example, mean values or units of measure).[69] They usually are expressed as 95 percent confidence intervals. In other words, we can feel 95 percent confident that the true effect (which is fixed) falls within this interval (which can vary), assuming the sample is properly selected.[70] If a confidence interval crosses the line of no effect ("0" for absolute risk or units of measure; "1" for ratios), it is customary to interpret this as a statistically nonsignificant result.[71] In such a case, however, we should try to understand whether the exposure and control really are equivalent, or whether a small sample size made the study incapable of detecting a meaningful difference.[71] Conversely, larger studies yield more precise confidence intervals, which can magnify the statistical significance of even minor between-group differences (for example, by producing a smaller p-value).

By presenting two numbers (an upper and a lower limit), confidence intervals broaden our focus to include an estimation of the size and strength of an intervention's effects. This takes us beyond statistical significance (a single number) and may better contribute to an assessment of the clinical significance of an intervention.[69]

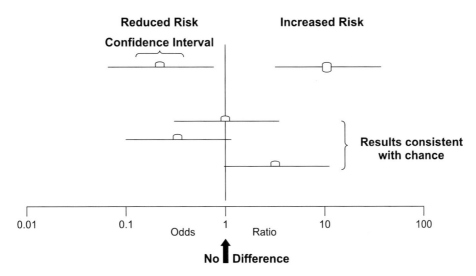

Figure 9.1 Concept of the Confidence Interval.

The margin of error, often mentioned in news reports of opinion polls, is a variant of the confidence interval. For example, if 63 percent (+/− 3 percent) of those surveyed support candidate X for mayor, this means that the true result probably lies within 3 percentage points above or below the reported result (that is, between 60 percent and 66 percent). Thus, the margin of error is usually defined as the radius of the confidence interval. Importantly, the margin of error accounts for random sampling error only, and not for error or bias from other sources, including poorly worded questions or false answers from those surveyed.

Clinical Significance

When scientists and reporters speak about the "significance" of a result, they often mean its statistical—not its clinical—significance. Unfortunately, the distinction may not be fully explained in the published research.

The concept of clinical significance was first proposed in 1984 as a way to answer the question of whether a therapy or treatment is effective.[72] Unlike statistical significance, clinical significance is not a "yes or no" concept. It involves standards of effectiveness set by a range of interested parties, including patients, physicians, and researchers.[73] For example, if a large study finds that regular screening for a particular type of cancer extends life by three days on average, the result may be statistically—but not clinically—significant.

Nuanced discussions of clinical significance are difficult to find in the mass media. Instead, relative risk reduction and the word "significant" are frequently used to emphasize the potential implications of a study, making a treatment, test, or procedure seem more effective than it is.[4]

ADDITIONAL USES OF THE DATA

Multiple Analyses

Once a study (either randomized or observational) is concluded, additional hypotheses may be tested based on the findings. These post hoc analyses often explore whether the effects of an intervention are consistent in subgroups of patients defined by baseline characteristics such as age, sex, ethnicity, or comorbid conditions.[74] For example, a drug that produces no overall benefit might be found to have a favorable effect in a particular subgroup, implying that a narrowly defined set of patients may benefit from the intervention.[44] Investigators also use multiple analyses to assess the effect of an exposure or intervention on different outcome variables.

Multiple analyses are susceptible to Type I error (false positives), because the greater the number of explorations, the greater the probability that a statistically significant result will occur purely by chance.[75] Consider the statistically strong association between reserpine, an antihypertensive drug, and breast cancer, which was reported in 1974 by the Boston Collaborative Drug Surveillance Program, a large epidemiologic study.[76] This result suggested that reserpine might have a carcinogenic effect, possibly explainable by drug-induced prolactin secretion.[77] The association was not consistently replicated, however, and 30 years later, the lead investigator bravely confessed that it was "really a chance finding" due to thousands of comparisons involving hundreds of drug exposures. True to the spirit of science, he recognized the benefit of acknowledging and learning from our mistakes.[76–78]

In addition to subgroups and outcome variables, multiple analyses commonly look at different cutpoints or categorizations. For example, if three glasses of wine a day, or seven cups of coffee, are associated with a reduced risk for some disease, we should consider the possibility that such observations or relationships might be the result of (hidden) multiple analyses. Determining whether this is so may entail some detective work on the part of those who want to understand the numbers correctly.

Statistical methods can control for Type I error in multiple analyses, typically by lowering the p-value threshold for statistical significance, so that the standard becomes more stringent (for example, using $p<0.025$ as the threshold for two analyses, rather than the standard $p<0.05$ suitable for a single analysis). This makes it harder to conclude that there is a between-group difference when none exists. Ideally, however, investigators should prespecify, or at least limit, the number of subgroup analyses or hypotheses to be tested, and reporters should distinguish between "significant results of well-planned, powerful, sharply focused studies" and those from "fishing expeditions" [79] (that is, data dredging, which means the search for statistically significant patterns or relationships in large sets of data). This can lead to unexpected findings that are also subject to Type I error.

In addition to the matter of statistical significance, the biological plausibility of post hoc arguments requires some skepticism, since the human imagination seems capable of developing a rationale for most findings, however unanticipated.[80] Thus, while multiple analyses may be useful and sometimes lead to new lines of research, the results generally are subject to future validation before they can be accepted.

Systematic Reviews and Meta-Analyses

One way of appraising current knowledge on a particular research topic and identifying areas for future study is to perform a *systematic review* of the medical literature.

Systematic reviews begin with a detailed plan for selecting the studies to be analyzed (including a comprehensive literature search of multiple databases), assessing their methodological quality, and extracting and summarizing the data, with strategies to minimize bias at each step.[81, 82] There are two kinds of systematic reviews: qualitative and quantitative. The latter, also called a *meta-analysis*, uses statistical methods to synthesize the data from several independent studies and estimate a common pooled effect, if pooling is justified.[82] Not all systematic reviews lead to a meta-analysis, but every meta-analysis should be based on a systematic review.

A meta-analysis also can evaluate the diversity (heterogeneity) of results among studies, determine whether the pooled effect of the intervention agrees with the effect in individual studies, estimate the effect with greater precision, and test hypotheses that the individual studies did not address or addressed inadequately, possibly because they were underpowered.[82, 83] Some meta-analyses use individual patient data from each study, whereas others use study-level results (for example, risk difference or odds ratio) as the unit of measure. In general, the former are considered more statistically robust and superior.[84]

Despite their utility, reviews have a number of limitations. By including only published studies, they may be biased toward favorable outcomes (see "Publication Bias"), producing an inflated appraisal or estimate of a treatment effect or an association between variables.[83] Moreover, many investigators are hesitant to perform meta-analyses that combine data from studies with different hypotheses and characteristics.[82] And perhaps most important, our confidence in the conclusions of a review depends on a basic assumption: that none of the trials is systematically flawed. If there is bias in any of the trials, it will be reinforced in a review or perpetuated and entrenched in a meta-analysis.[83] This can be particularly problematic for meta-analyses of observational studies, since the latter generally are much more susceptible to bias than RCTs.

While systematic reviews and meta-analyses make an important contribution to the medical literature, they must be evaluated carefully. In particular, caution is needed when considering meta-analyses as a basis for clinical recommendations.[82] In an era of advanced statistical methods, sophisticated computational tools, and powerful search engines, meta-analyses have become increasingly popular in medicine. But unfortunately, they are not always carefully and appropriately performed (sometimes because of shortcomings in the available data). As one team of researchers commented, by way of Mark Twain, "'There are two things you should never watch being made. The law, and sausage.'" Perhaps meta-analysis should be added to the list."[85]

Nevertheless, pooling of data in a high-quality systematic review with meta-analysis can provide a more precise estimate of the effect of an intervention or risk factor, with conclusions that are more credible than those of individual studies (see table 9.4).[46]

ASSESSING RISKS AND BENEFITS

The points covered in the foregoing discussion bring us to the fundamental question that health-related research seeks to address: how can physicians, policy planners, and patients quantify and weigh the risks and benefits of an intervention or other exposure?

When different ways of presenting the potential benefit of drug therapy to patients are compared, relative risk reduction is the most likely to prompt acceptance of treatment.[86, 87] But many physicians consider absolute risk reduction more useful for decision making—not only because relative numbers tend to magnify the treatment effect, but also because different baseline risk levels can be reduced by the same relative amount. In table 9.2, for example, absolute risk reductions of 2.0 percent, 24.0 percent, and 54.0 percent all translate into a relative risk of 33 percent and a relative risk reduction of 67 percent. Therefore, reports of relative risk reduction can be misleading unless accompanied by information on baseline risk. While absolute risk reduction may be the preferred metric for individual patient decisions, however, relative risk reduction is useful for statistical inferences because it is inclined to be more stable across patient groups.[88, 89]

Absolute numbers have limitations as well, because they do not generally account for the effects of time, age, or other variables that influence risk. A debate about how to measure risk is currently taking place over Tysabri, a powerful multiple sclerosis drug associated with a three-year risk of 0.019 percent for progressive multifocal leukoencephalopathy (PML), a neurodegenerative disease. Because the number of PML cases per 1,000 patients is slightly larger with each year of therapy, the collective event rate adjusted statistically for the effect of time is close to 1 percent, a threshold that some doctors and patients might find unacceptably high.[90] For this issue, an in-depth discussion of risks and benefits and their implications would be critical.

The Tysabri example, in which the rate of adverse events increases with duration of therapy (a consideration for all chronic conditions) or when an intervention is used in large numbers of patients, illustrates one reason why postmarketing surveillance is important. In other cases, the anticipated benefit may take decades to emerge. For example, a vaccine used in girls and young women to prevent infection with the genital human papillomavirus, which can cause cervical cancer, has been available for three years. While reports of adverse events include some that are serious, it is too soon to know whether immunization will reduce the future incidence of cancer.[91, 92] With other interventions, an effect (for example, reduced mortality) that emerges in preapproval studies may be lost over time in longer-term postmarketing trials, altering the trade-off between risks and benefits.

OTHER ISSUES THAT MAY AFFECT THE REPORTING OF RESULTS

Publication Bias

Publication bias refers to the tendency of researchers to submit, and editors to accept, studies for publication based on the strength and direction of the findings.[93] Specifically, if the findings are positive and statistically significant, or if they do not challenge accepted theory or practice, the likelihood of publication may be greater than otherwise. One meta-analysis comparing published and unpublished studies of 12 antidepressants, for example, found a bias toward the publication of positive results. Moreover, the published studies tended to report an inflated effect size.[94] This problem, which is not unique to antidepressants, highlights the need to think critically about scientific data and to avoid hyperbole in the coverage of results.

Transparency

Transparency is defined as unlimited perpetual access to scientific research (raw data, published results) and to information about the competing interests (financial and nonfinancial) of scientists and study sponsors that may influence any phase of research, from design through publication.[95] The issue of transparency is widely discussed by experts, many of whom argue that it is the best assurance of progress, quality, and benefit to patients.[96, 97] Transparency raises many complex questions, including how to protect the private data of subjects enrolled in clinical trials and safeguard intellectual property rights. Efforts to address these issues are ongoing. One important step toward achieving transparency is the Public Library of Science (PLoS), an online resource founded in 2000 by Nobel Laureate Harold Varmus and colleagues Patrick Brown and Michael Eisen. Guided by the principle that science is a public resource, PLoS and other initiatives are dedicated to making research results freely available to scientists, physicians, patients, and students around the world.[98]

CONCLUSION

More than a century ago, Benjamin Disraeli observed that "there are three kinds of lies: lies, damned lies, and statistics."

While statistical science, like all human endeavors, is subject to error or misuse, it is the most effective way yet devised of predicting the probability (risk) of events under a given set of circumstances. Thus, when we hear conflicting reports about the risks or benefits of a drug or a food product, for example, it is important to examine the validity of the study and the strength of the statistical conclusion(s).

To do this, one does not have to be a trained scientist. The scientific method is based largely on common sense, and statistical thinking involves concepts that are accessible to all: an acceptance of chance and uncertainty, an appreciation of context, an ability to detect logical and factual flaws in information and ideas, and the realization that science is a fluid process whereby new empirical evidence is accumulated every day. The true spirit of science also requires a healthy skepticism, which means suspended judgment and the use of reason to evaluate the validity of research results. Science thrives on these qualities, because they lead to a search for knowledge and help ensure that the scientific method remains self-correcting.

Physicians, policy planners, patients, and the general public depend on the media for health-related information. As such, it is imperative that research results be reported accurately and responsibly to ensure that the reader (professional or lay person) will be able to assess the risks, the benefits, and the effectiveness of a drug or other product or exposure. If the study was designed well, and if the numbers were properly generated in response to the right questions, lies and damned lies most certainly would be revealed by statistics.[99]

Appendix 9.A.
Assessment of Study Design: What to Ask

Question	Chapter Section
Is the study • observational (epidemiologic)? • experimental? If observational, is it • retrospective? • prospective? What target population does the study sample represent? • risk level (e.g., high, moderate, or low) • other characteristics What is the sample size? Is the study controlled? For example, • a randomized controlled trial (RCT)? • another type of experimental controlled trial? • an observational study with a control group (e.g., case-control)? Are the comparison groups balanced with respect to variables/characteristics that could influence or provide an alternative explanation for the results? If experimental, is the study • double blind (neither investigators nor subjects know the treatment allocation)? • single blind (investigators know the treatment allocation, but subjects do not)? • open label (no blinding is used)? Why? • blinded during the endpoint analysis only? How might each of the above potentially affect the conduct and outcome of the study? In a blinded study, was the blinding • sustained? • breached? Why? What effect could this have? How many events occurred in the • active treatment/exposure group? • control group? Have the study results been replicated or validated? If so, by • observational studies? • experimental studies? Did other studies report different or opposite results?	**Study Designs: Observational versus Experimental**
Do the results indicate • association? • causation (see Austin Bradford Hill viewpoints, table 9.3, for guidance regarding observational studies) Is the finding plausible? • implausible (e.g., likely a random occurrence)?	**Association, Causation, Confounding, and Bias**

What are the	**Association, Causation,**
• potential sources of bias or confounding?	**Confounding, and Bias**
• alternative explanations for the results?	
Are the data skewed or do they have	**Tools for Interpreting the**
any peculiar properties?	**Data: Location versus**
Is the "typical" value (measure of location)	**Spread**
reported as	
• mean?	
• median?	
• mode?	
What does this suggest about the variability of the data?	
Is the spread (variability) reported as	
• range?	
• interquartile range?	
• standard deviation?	
Does the study use	**The Importance of**
• clinical endpoints?	**Measurable Endpoints**
• surrogate endpoints?	
Are the endpoints reported in terms of	**Risk**
• absolute risk reduction?	
• relative risk reduction?	
• odds ratio?	
Are the adverse effects reported in terms of	
• absolute risk?	
• relative risk?	
If the relative risk reduction is reported,	
• is the baseline risk also presented (or can you calculate it based on the number of events and the total number of subjects in the control group)?	
• is the event rate in the experimental group also presented (or can you calculate it based on the number of events and the total number of subjects in the experimental group)?	
• can you calculate the absolute risk reduction and the number needed to treat?	
Are results reported for	**Tools for Interpreting the**
• primary endpoints?	**Data: Significance**
• secondary endpoints?	
• unexpected findings (may indicate data-dredging[a])?	
• multiple analyses?	
Are the results	
• statistically significant (what is the p-value)?	
• clinically significant?	
What does the sample size suggest about the potential for	
• statistical significance (e.g., is it too small to detect a between-group difference)?	
• clinical significance (e.g., is it large enough so that an effect with little or no clinical significance may be statistically significant)?	
Is the 95 percent confidence interval reported? Is it	
• narrow?	

- wide?
- across the "no effect" line?

What does the width/direction of the confidence interval suggest about
- the relation of the estimated effect to the "true" effect (i.e., is the result precise)?
- the statistical significance of the effect?

With multiple analyses, are they   **Additional Uses of the Data:**
- prespecified (e.g., in the protocol)?   **Multiple Analyses**
- post hoc?

Are the results of multiple analyses
- biologically/clinically plausible?
- statistically significant (with a p-value adjusted for multiple analyses or the number of analyses reported)?

Do the benefits of the intervention outweigh the risks?   **Assessing Risks and Benefits**

What is the baseline risk (control event rate)? What does it say about the patients who may benefit from the intervention? Are they at
- high risk (i.e., events are fairly common in untreated individuals)?
- low risk (i.e., events are rare in untreated individuals)?
- moderate risk?

Which of the following measures of risk are reported:
- baseline risk?
- absolute risk reduction?
- relative risk?
- relative risk reduction?

If the absolute risk reduction is not reported, can it be calculated (baseline risk × relative risk reduction)?

Is this a postmarketing study? If so, do the results alter previous risk-benefit assessments concerning the intervention?

What are the potential threats to   **Internal and External**
- internal validity?   **Validity**
- external validity?

Are the results reported in language that   **Additional Questions**
- conveys a misleading or exaggerated impression   **(not discussed in chapter)** of their importance?
- reinforces the therapeutic misconception?[b]
- supports a particular viewpoint?

Have the results been reported in
- a peer-reviewed professional journal?[c]
- an opinion piece by an expert (e.g., in a professional journal, a mass media publication)?
- a book?
- a presentation at a scientific meeting?
- an expert interview?

Is information accessible to journalists and the public on

- who funded the study?
- the researchers' industry affiliations and other potential conflicts of interest (financial and nonfinancial)?

Are titles or headlines
- overstated and misleading?
- accurate in terms of the information reported?

Do editorials, commentaries, or other opinion pieces
- use multiple sources?
- present diverse viewpoints in a fair manner?
- place the information in context?

Does the research involve
- an approved use of the drug?[d]
- an off-label use?[d]

Do reports about laboratory or animal studies make it clear that the results may not translate into benefit for humans?

---

a. Data-dredging: the search for statistically significant patterns or relationships in large sets of data. Data-dredging has a negative connotation and is sometimes called a "fishing expedition" (see Multiple Analyses).

b. Therapeutic misconception: "the defining purpose of clinical research is to produce "generalizable knowledge, regardless of whether the subjects enrolled in the trial may potentially benefit from the intervention under study or from other aspects of the clinical trial."[37] While ethical principles and stringent safeguards (e.g., informed consent) protect the rights of research subjects and prevent intentional harm, the therapeutic misconception exists when study participants do not understand the distinction between the purpose of clinical practice (to treat the patient) and clinical research (to gain knowledge).[37]

c. Reporting the results of scientific research: Publication in a peer-reviewed professional journal is the most important way of making research results known. While this does not guarantee the accuracy or validity of the results, professional journals are a more reliable source of information than other forms of dissemination.

d. Approved use: In the United States, medical products and devices are approved and regulated by the Food and Drug Administration (FDA). Although FDA-approved prescription drugs are designated for specific purposes, they may sometimes be beneficial for diseases or conditions not described in the authorized labeling. Doctors must use sound medical evidence and clinical judgment when prescribing a drug for an off-label purpose. Drug marketing/advertising for off-label use is never permitted.

REFERENCES

1. ScienceDaily. Highly active compound found in coffee may *prevent* colon cancer. http://www.sciencedaily.com/releases/2003/10/031015031251.htm. Published October 15, 2003. Accessed October 19, 2009.
2. Furtado M. The surprising ingredient causing weight gain. YAHOO!© HEALTH. http://health.yahoo.com. Published July 27, 2009. Accessed July 30, 2009.
3. Devlin K. Three cups of brewed coffee a day 'triples risk of hallucinations.' Telegraph.co.uk. http://www.telegraph.co.uk/science/science-news. Published January 14, 2009. Accessed September 27, 2009.

4. Beck M. Correlation, causation and what Welsh rugby means for the Pope. *The Wall Street Journal.* http://blogs.wsj.com/health/2009/01/27/. Published January 27, 2009. Accessed October 16, 2009.
5. von Bubnoff A. Numbers can lie: good today, but how about tomorrow? *Los Angeles Times.* Health page. http://articles.latimes.com/2007. Published September 17, 2007. Accessed February 2, 2009.
6. Angell M. *Science on Trial. The Clash of Medical Evidence and the Law in the Breast Implant Case.* London: W. W. Norton & Company; 1996.
7. Narasimhan MG. Controversy in science. *J Biosci.* 2001;26:299–304.
8. Stocking AH, Holstein LW. Manufacturing doubt: journalists' roles and the construction of ignorance in a scientific controversy. *Public Understand Sci.* 2009;18:23–42.
9. Ceccarelli L. Manufactured controversy: Science Studies Network (SSNet) Seminar; October 20, 2008; University of Washington, Seattle, WA. http://depts.washington.edu/ssnet/handout_102008.pdf. Accessed October 28, 2009.
10. Wilby P. The media's addiction to controversy can seriously damage your health. *The Guardian.* http://www.guardian.co.uk. Published August 13, 2008. Accessed April 29, 2009. Correction published on August 21, 2008. *The Guardian.*
11. Ransohoff DF, Ransohoff RM. Sensationalism in the media: when scientists and journalists may be complicit collaborators. *EFF Clin Pract.* 2001;4:185–188.
12. Greer K. Journalists forced to sensationalize science to attract readers. *Tennessee Journalist.* http://tnjn.com/2008/mar/27/journalists-forced-to-sensatio/. Published March 27, 2008. Accessed September 28, 2009.
13. Shuchman M, Wilkes MS. Medical scientists and health news reporting: a case of miscommunication. *Ann Intern Med.* 1997;126:976–982.
14. Rothman SM, Rothman DJ. Marketing HPV vaccine. Implications for adolescent health and medical professionalism. *JAMA.* 2009;302:781–786.
15. Jackson T. News skews health priorities, study claims. *BMJ.* 2003;327:688.
16. Sharma V, Dowd D, Swanson DS, Slaughter AJ, Simon SD. Influence of the news media on diagnostic testing in the emergency department. *Arch Pediatr Adolesc Med.* 2003;157:257–260.
17. Schield M. Statistical literacy and liberal education at Augsburg College. *Peer Rev* 2004. http://www.aacu-edu.org/peerreview/index.cfm. Accessed May 14, 2009.
18. University of California Museum of Paleontology. "Misconceptions about science:" understanding science. http://undsci.berkeley.edu/teaching/misconceptions.php. Retrieved May 19, 2009.
19. Martin A, Faraone SV, Henderson SW, et al. Mission statement: advancing the science of pediatric mental health and promoting the care of youth and their families. *J Am Acad Child Adolesc Psychiatry.* 2008;47:1.
20. Norton JD. Science and uncertainty. *Synthese.* 1994;99:3–22.
21. Moore DS. Statistics among the liberal arts. *J Am Stat Assoc.* 1998;93:1253–1259.
22. Campbell SK. *Flaws and Fallacies in Statistical Thinking.* Mineola, NY: Dover Publications, Inc.; 2002.
23. Feynman RP. Uncertainty in science. In: *The Meaning of It All: Thoughts of a Citizen-Scientist.* New York: Basic Books: 2005.
24. Wild CJ, Pfannkuch M. Statistical thinking in empirical enquiry. *Intl Stat Rev.* 1999;67:223–265.
25. Pellegrin P. Physics. In: Brunschwig J, Lloyd GER, eds. *The Greek Pursuit of Knowledge.* Cambridge, MA: The Belknap Press of Harvard University Press; 2000: xiii, 282–300.
26. Kuhn JE, Greenfield MVH, Wojtys EM. A statistics primer: hypothesis testing. *Am J Sports Med.* 1996;24:702–703.

27. Gould SJ. Evolution as fact and theory (abridged). In: Vetter HF, ed. *Speak Out Against the New Right*. Boston, MA: Beacon Press; 1982.
28. Parascandola M, Weed DL. Causation in epidemiology. *J Epidemiol Community Health*. 2001;55:905–912.
29. Shugan SM. Causality, unintended consequences and deducing shared causes. *Market Sci*. 2007;26:731–741.
30. Vandenbroucke JP. The history of confounding. *Soz-Präventivmed*. 2002;47:216–224.
31. Kestenbaum B. *Epidemiology and Biostatistics. An Introduction to Clinical Research*. New York: Springer Publications; 2009.
32. Szklo M, Nieto FJ. *Epidemiology: Beyond the Basics*. 2nd ed. Sudbury, MA: Jones and Bartlett Publishers; 2006.
33. Mayhall CG. *Hospital Epidemiology and Infection Control*. 3rd ed. Philadelphia, PA: Lippincott Williams & Wilkins; 2004.
34. Bernstein PL. *Against the Gods. The Remarkable Story of Risk*. New York: John Wiley & Sons, Inc.; 1998.
35. Wikipedia: The Free Encyclopedia. Number needed to treat. http://en.wikipedia.org/wiki/Number_needed_to_treat. Accessed September 28, 2009.
36. Trial AIDS vaccine cuts infection risk 31 percent. CBS News. http://www.cbsnews.com/stories/2009/09/24/health/main5334317.shtml. Published September 24, 2009. Accessed October 18, 2009.
37. Henderson GE, Churchill LR, Davis AM, et al. Clinical trials and medical care: defining the therapeutic misconception. *PloS Med*. 2007;4(11):xxe324. doi:10.1371/journal.pmed.0040324. http://www.ncbi.nlm.nih.gov/. Accessed October 25, 2009.
38. Garbe E, Suissa S. Issues to debate on the Women's Health Initiative (WHI) study. Hormone replacement therapy and acute coronary outcomes: methodological issues between randomized and observational studies. *Hum Reproduction*. 2004;19:8–13.
39. Hess DR. Retrospective studies and chart reviews. *Respir Care*. 2004;49:1171–1174.
40. Humphrey L, Chan BKS, Sox HC. Postmenopausal hormone replacement therapy and the primary prevention of cardiovascular disease. *Ann Intern Med*. 2002;137:273–284.
41. Simon SD. Understanding the odds ratio and the relative risk. *J Andrology*. 2001;22:533–536.
42. Pouwels S, Lalmohamed A, Leufkens B, et al. Risk of hip/femur fracture after stroke: a population-based case-control study. *Stroke*. 2009;40:3281–3285.
43. Edelson E. Stroke doubles risk of hip, thigh fractures. Preventive measures urgently needed, researcher says. *U.S. News & World Report*. http://health.usnews.com/articles/health/healthday/2009/08/06/stroke-doubles-risk-of-hip-thigh-fractures.html. Published August 6, 2009. Accessed August 23, 2009.
44. Moyé LA. *Multiple Analyses in Clinical Trials: Fundamentals for Investigators*. New York: Springer Publications; 2003.
45. Concato J, Shah N, Horwitz RI. Randomized, controlled trials, observational studies, and the hierarchy of research designs. *N Engl J Med*. 2000;342:1887–1892.
46. Mahid SS, Hornung CA, Minor KS, Turina M, Galandiuk S. Systematic reviews and meta-analysis for the surgeon scientist. *Br J Surg*. 2006;93:1315–1324.
47. Salmond SS. Randomized controlled trials: methodological concepts and critique. *Orthop Nurs*. 2008;27:116–122.
48. Thisted RA. What is a p-value? Department of Statistics, University of Chicago. http://galton.uchicago.edu/~thisted/Distribute/pvalue.pdf. Published May 25, 1998. Retrieved September 30, 2009.

49. Burns N, Grove SK. *Understanding Nursing Research. Building an Evidence-Based Practice.* 3rd ed. Philadelphia, PA: WB Saunders; 2002.
50. Ioannidis JPA. Large scale evidence and replication: insights from rheumatology and beyond. *Ann Rheum Dis.* 2005;64:345–346.
51. Boyer CB. *The History of the Calculus and Its Conceptual Development.* New York: Dover Publications, Inc.; 1949.
52. Boffetta P, McLaughlin JK, La Vecchia C, Lipworth L, Blot WJ. False-positive results in cancer epidemiology: a plea for epistemological modesty. *J Natl Cancer Inst.* 2008;100:988–995.
53. Steinhubl SR. Why have antioxidants failed in clinical trials? *Am J Cardiol.* 2008;101[suppl]:14DS-19D.
54. Parascandola M. Two approaches to etiology: the debate over smoking and lung cancer in the 1950s. *Endeavour.* 2004;28:81–86.
55. Hill AB. The environment and disease: association or causation? *Proc R Soc Med.* 1965;58:295–300. http://www.edwardtufte.com/tufte/hill.
56. Rothman KJ, Greenland S, Lash TL. *Modern Epidemiology.* 3rd ed. Philadelphia, PA: Lippincott Williams & Wilkins: 2008.
57. Rothman KJ, Greenland S. *Modern Epidemiology.* 2nd ed. Philadelphia, PA: Lippincott-Raven; 1998.
58. Rothman KJ, Greenland S. Causation and causal inference in epidemiology. *Am J Public Health.* 2005;95:S144–S150.
59. Fleming TR, DeMets DL. Surrogate end points in clinical trials: are we being misled? *Ann Intern Med.* 1996;125:605–613.
60. Temple RJ. A regulatory authority's opinion about surrogate endpoints. In: Nimmo WS, Tucker GT, eds. *Clinical Measurement in Drug Evaluation.* New York: J. Wiley; 1995. Quoted in Fleming TR, DeMets DL. Surrogate end points in clinical trials: are we being misled? *Ann Intern Med.* 1996;125:605–613.
61. Weinberg CR. It's time to rehabilitate the p-value. *Epidemiology.* 2001;12:288–290.
62. Graham DJ. Cox-2 inhibitors, other NSAIDs, and cardiovascular risk: the seduction of common sense. *JAMA.* 2006;296:1653–1656.
63. Lesaffre E. Use and misuse of the p-value. *Bull NYU Hosp Joint Dis.* 2008;66:146–149.
64. Drotar D. Thoughts on establishing research significance and preserving scientific integrity. *J Pediatr Psychol.* 2008;33:1–5.
65. Peck CC. The almighty p-value *or* the significance of "significance." *Present Concepts Intern Med.* 1971;4(11):1021–1024.
66. Ziliak ST, McCloskey DN. *The Cult of Statistical Significance: How the Standard Error Costs Us Jobs, Justice, and Lives.* Ann Arbor: University of Michigan Press; 2008.
67. Goodman SN. Of p-values and Bayes: a modest proposal. *Epidemiology.* 2001;12:295–297.
68. Editors. The value of p. *Epidemiology.* 2001;12:286.
69. du Prel J-B, Hommel G, Röhrig B, Blettner M. Confidence interval or p-value. *Dtsch Arztebl Int.* 2009;106:335–339.
70. Curran-Everett D. Explorations in statistics: confidence intervals. *Adv Physiol Educ.* 2009;33:87–90.
71. Simon SD. Interpreting negative studies. *J Andrology.* 2001;22:13–16.
72. Jacobson NS, Follette WC, Revenstorf D. Psychotherapy outcome research: methods for reporting variability and evaluating clinical significance. *Behav Ther.* 1984;15:336–352.
73. Jacobson NS, Truax P. Clinical significance: a statistical approach to defining meaningful change in psychotherapy research. *J Consult Clin Psychol.* 1991;59:12–19.

74. Wang R, Lagakos SW, Ware JH, Hunter DJ, Drazen JM. Statistics in medicine—reporting of subgroup analyses in clinical trials. *N Engl J Med.* 2007;357:2189–2194.
75. Young SS, Bang H, Oktay K. Cereal-induced gender selection? Most likely a multiple testing false positive. *Proc R Soc B.* 2009;276:1211–1222.
76. Lawson DH. Detection of drug-induced disease. *Br J Clin Pharmacol.* 1979;7:13–18.
77. Ross RK, Paganini-Hill A, Krailo MD, Gerkins VR, Henderson BE. Effects of reserpine on prolactin levels and incidence of breast cancer in postmenopausal women. *Cancer Res.* 1984;44:3106–3108.
78. Shapiro S. Looking to the 21st century: have we learned from our mistakes, or are we doomed to compound them? *Pharmacoepidemiol Drug Safety.* 2004;13:257–265.
79. Garcia LV. Escaping the Bonferroni iron claw in ecological studies. *Oikos.* 2004;105:657–663.
80. Ware JH. The National Emphysema Treatment Trial—how strong is the evidence? [Perspective] *N Engl J Med.* 2003;348:2055–2056.
81. Jadad A. *Randomised Controlled Trials: A User's Guide.* London: BMJ Books; 1998.
82. White PF, Watcha MF. Has the use of meta-analysis enhanced our understanding of therapies for postoperative nausea and vomiting? *Anesth Analg.* 1999;88:1200–1202.
83. Naylor CD. Meta-analysis and the meta-epidemiology of clinical research. *BMJ.* 1997;315:617–619.
84. Teramukai S, Matsuyama Y, Mizuno S, Sakamoto J. Individual patient-level and study-level meta-analysis for investigating modifiers of treatment effect. *Jpn J Clin Oncol.* 2004;34:717–721.
85. Hamer RM, Simpson PM. SAS® Tools for Meta-Analysis. http://www2.sas.com/proceedings/sugi27/p250-27.pdf. Accessed September 27, 2009. SAS® Paper No.250–27.
86. Hux JE, Naylor CD. Communicating the benefits of chronic preventive therapy: does the format of efficacy data determine patients' acceptance of treatment? *Med Decis Making.* 1995;15:152–157.
87. Carling CLL, Kristoffersen DT, Montori VM, et al. The effect of alternative summary statistics for communicating risk reduction on decisions about taking statins: a randomized trial. *PLoS Med.* 2009;6(8):e1000134. doi:10.1371/journal.pmed.1000134. www.plosmedicine.org. Accessed September 23, 2009.
88. Crewdson J. Statistics misleading, some doctors say: relative numbers skew benefit to look much larger. *Chicago Tribune.* March 15, 2002: 21.
89. Sorensen L, Gyrd-Hansen D, Kristiansen IS, Nexoe J. Laypersons understanding of relative risk reductions: randomized cross-sectional study. *BMC Med Inform Dec Making.* 2008;8:1–7. http://www.biomedcentral.com.
90. Winstein K. Medicine's dangerous guessing game. *Wall Street Journal.* http://online.wsj.com. Published September 9, 2009. Accessed September 9, 2009.
91. Slade BA, Leidel L, Vellozzi C, et al. Postlicensure safety surveillance for quadrivalent human papillomavirus recombinant vaccine. *JAMA.* 2009;302:750–757.
92. Haug C. The risks and benefits of HPV vaccination. *JAMA.* 2009;302:795–796.
93. World Health Organization. Publication bias in clinical trials due to statistical significance or direction of trial results. RHL: The WHO Reproductive Health Library. http://apps.who.int/rhl/education/MR000006_butlerpa_com/en/index.html. Accessed September 23, 2009.
94. Turner EH, Matthews AM, Linardatos E, Tell RA, Rosenthal R. Selective publication of antidepressant trials and its influence on apparent efficacy. *N Engl J Med.* 2008;358:252–260.

95. PLoS Medicine Editors. An unbiased scientific record should be everyone's agenda. *PLoS Med.* 2009;6(2):e1000038. doi:10.1371/journal.pmed.1000038. http://www.plosmedicine.org/. Accessed September 23, 2009.
96. Freedman DA, Pettiti DB. Hormone replacement therapy does not save lives. Comments on the Women's Health Initiative. *Biometrics.* 2005;62:918–920.
97. Public Library of Science. PLoS core principles. http://www.plos.org/about/principles.html. Accessed September 23, 2009.
98. Eisen MB, Brown PO, Varmus HE. PLOS Medicine: a medical journal for the internet age. *PLOS Med.* 2004;1(1):e31. http://www.ncbi.nlm.nih.gov. Accessed October 25, 2009.
99. Begley S. Lies, damned lies and . . . *Newsweek.* http://www.newsweek.com. Published July 12, 2008. Accessed September 22, 2009.

CHAPTER 10

Evidence-Based Public Health: A Fundamental Concept for Public Health Practice

Christopher M. Maylahn, MPH, Ross C. Brownson, PhD, and Jonathan E. Fielding, MD, MPH, MA, MBA

INTRODUCTION

The 30-year gain in life expectancy in the United States that occurred in the 20th century is a notable achievement.[1] Much of this increase is due to the provision of safe water and food, sewage treatment and disposal, tobacco use prevention and cessation, injury prevention, control of infectious diseases through immunization and other means, and other population-based interventions.[2] Many public health strategies have been proven to reduce risk among individuals and entire communities, yet have not been carried out. Further gains in health and longevity, as well as a reduction in health disparities, would result from widespread adoption of interventions for which there is evidence of effectiveness.[3–7]

The design and use of public health actions that are effective in promoting health and preventing disease underlie the growing field of evidence-based public health (EBPH), which emerged in the 1990s to improve the *practice* of public health. The definition of this term has evolved over time, as discussed later in the chapter. It generally is viewed as "the development, implementation, and evaluation of effective programs and policies in public health through application of principles of scientific reasoning, including systematic uses of data and information systems, and appropriate use of behavioral science theory and program planning models."[4, p. 4] Ideally, public health practitioners always should incorporate scientific evidence in selecting and implementing programs, developing policies, and evaluating progress.[8, 9]

Society pays a high opportunity cost when interventions that yield the highest health return on an investment are not implemented.[10] In practice, decisions about how to address a health issue or problem often are based on circumstances favoring a pragmatic, politically feasible approach, lack systematic planning and fail to incorporate the latest evidence about what works. These concerns were noted two decades ago when the Institute of Medicine (IOM) determined that decision making in public health

---

This chapter is reprinted, with permission, from the *Annual Review of Public Health*, Volume 30 © 2009 by Annual Reviews www.annualreviews.org.

often is driven by "crises, hot issues, and concerns of organized interest groups."[11, p. 4] Greater use of EBPH has numerous direct and indirect benefits, including access to more and higher quality information on what works, a higher likelihood of successful programs and policies being implemented, greater workforce productivity, and more efficient use of public and private resources.[4, 12, 13] Yet, in a recent survey of 107 U.S. public health practitioners, fewer than 60 percent of programs in their agencies were "evidence-based," defined as being guided by the most current evidence from peer-reviewed research.[14] Barriers to implementing EBPH include the political environment, and deficits in relevant and timely research, information systems, resources, leadership, and the required competencies.[8, 15–17]

Several concepts are fundamental to achieving a more evidence-based approach to public health practice. First, scientific information is needed about programs and policies most likely to be effective in promoting health.[4, 12, 18, 19] Evaluation research is needed to generate sound evidence and, optimally, builds on multiple studies conducted among different populations. An array of effective interventions is now available from numerous sources, including the *Guide to Community Preventive Services*,[20, 21] the *Guide to Clinical Preventive Services*,[22] Cancer Control PLANET,[23] the National Registry of Evidence-based Programs and Practices,[24] and Public Health Partners.[25] Much of this information is now widely accessible on the Internet. Second, to translate science into actual practice, the application of evidence-based interventions from the peer-reviewed literature must consider *features* of a specific "real-world" environment [4, 26, 27] and make needed adjustments, without compromising what makes the intervention work. This entails defining the processes that lead to evidence-based decision making. A combination of scientific evidence and values, resources, and context enters into decision making. Finally, widescale dissemination of proven interventions must occur more consistently at state and local levels.[28]

The focus of this chapter is on the importance of EBPH for state and local public health departments because of their responsibilities to assess public health problems, develop appropriate programs or policies, and ensure that they are implemented effectively in states and local communities.[11, 29] Government public health agencies are viewed as the primary force in organizing and mobilizing public health practice in most communities.[30] The challenges these agencies confront in applying EBPH principles in local public health practice are daunting as resources shrink, new health issues emerge, and scientific evidence to address them is slow to materialize. Often, the study aims and populations involved in published research do not match the characteristics and circumstances of a target community in which action is needed, making it problematic to assume a similar impact will occur. When a policy or public health program is launched, the intervention "dose" must be sufficient to achieve the desired change. The chapter is organized into four sections that describe: (1) the concepts and principles underlying EBPH; (2) analytic tools to enhance the adoption of evidence-based decision making; (3) dissemination and implementation in public health practice; and (4) challenges and opportunities for more widespread use of EBPH, especially through state and local health departments. It is adapted from our article published in the 2008 *Annual Review of Public Health*.[31]

TENETS OF EVIDENCE-BASED PUBLIC HEALTH

EBPH was first defined by Janicek in 1997 as the "conscientious, explicit, and judicious use of current best evidence in making decisions about the care of communities and populations in the domain of health protection, disease prevention, health maintenance and improvement."[32] Two years later, Brownson et al. described a six-stage process that enables practitioners to take a more evidence-based approach to decision making [4, 8] and provided practical guidance on how to choose, carry out, and evaluate evidence-based programs and policies. That same year, Glasziou and Longbottom posed a series of questions to enhance uptake of EBPH (for example, Does this intervention help alleviate this problem?) and identified 14 sources of high-quality evidence.[5] Kohatsu et al. broadened earlier definitions to include the perspectives of community members, fostering a more community-centered approach.[26]

An excellent resource for public health practitioners is a glossary of EBPH terminology published in 2004 by Rychetnik et al. [33] that draws on the published literature, experience gained over several years of analysis of the topic, and discussions with students. The glossary is useful in defining terms, some of which were just emerging at the time, so that they may be interpreted and applied in a consistent manner.

In summarizing these various aspects of EBPH, key characteristics include the following:

- Making decisions based on the best available peer-reviewed evidence (both quantitative and qualitative research);
- Using data and information systems systematically;
- Applying program planning frameworks (that often have a foundation in behavioral science theory);
- Engaging the community in assessment and decision making;
- Conducting sound evaluation; and
- Disseminating what is learned to key stakeholders and decision makers.

In little more than a decade, EBPH has become a fundamental concept for public health practice. Yet, the field and terminology continue to evolve. The term "evidence-informed" has been proposed to describe a process for critical appraisal of primary research studies and systematic reviews to inform effective public health practice.[34] It depends on the use of quality checklists and other tools to identify rigorous studies with valid conclusions for implementation and assessment. Within the general area of community research, what constitutes knowledge and evidence is hotly debated, or even if the notion of evidence in evaluating community interventions applies at all.[35]

Adherence to EBPH principles and methods requires a skill called "evidence based decision making"—that is, that decisions about the use of public health resources are based on the best available scientific evidence about what works and take into account stakeholder values, available resources, and the context of the problem to be addressed (see figure 10.1).[3, 4, 33, 36, 37] Knowledge of the evidence base, strong communication skills, common sense, and political acumen often are necessary. Furthermore, understanding the context in which many most public health policies and programs are implemented—in states and local communities—demands an examination of the opportunities and challenges arising in these settings.

Defining Evidence

In its most basic form, evidence involves "the available body of facts or information indicating whether a belief or proposition is true or valid."[38] The idea of

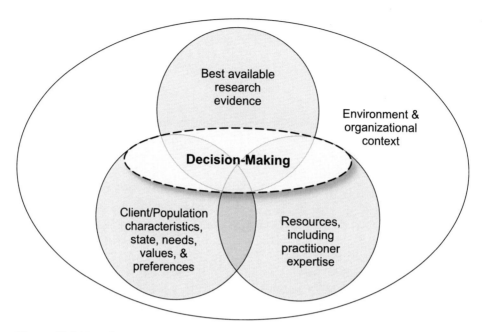

Figure 10.1 Domains that influence evidence-based decision making. (*Source:* From Spring et al.)

evidence often derives from legal settings in Western societies. Here, evidence is manifest as stories, witness accounts, police testimony, expert opinions, and forensic science.[35] The everyday use of the word evidence carries high expectations, implying that there can be no doubt if one has evidence. For a public health professional, evidence is some kind of data—including quantitative information from epidemiologic studies, results of program or policy evaluations, or qualitative data—to help make judgments or decisions. Public health evidence usually is the result of a complex cycle of observation, theory, and experiment.[39, 40] However, the value of evidence is in the eye of the beholder—its utility may vary by type of stakeholder.[41] The demand for high-quality evidence to justify a particular public health action is growing among many stakeholder groups as competition for limited resources intensifies. Yet, evidence is usually imperfect and, as noted by Muir Gray, "The absence of excellent evidence does not make evidence-based decision making impossible; what is required is the best evidence available, not the best evidence possible."[3]

There are three types of scientific evidence for public health practice.[4, 8, 33] Type 1 evidence defines the causes of diseases and the magnitude, severity, and preventability of risk factors and diseases. It suggests that "*something* should be done" about a particular disease or risk factor. Type 2 evidence describes the relative impact of specific interventions that do or do not improve health, adding "*specifically,* this should be done."[4] There are different sources of Type 2 evidence (see table 10.1). These categories emphasize the "weight of evidence" and a wider range of considerations beyond efficacy. Four categories are defined within a typology of scientific evidence for decision making: evidence-based, efficacious, promising, and emerging interventions. Type 3 evidence shows how and under what contextual conditions interventions were implemented and how they were received, thus identifying "*how* something should be done."[33] The context of an intervention is important in understanding and applying evidence from a particular study. It is more difficult to find good type 3 studies. Most of the published studies overemphasize internal validity (for example, well-controlled efficacy trials) while giving sparse attention to external validity (for example, the translation of science to the various circumstances of practice).[42, 43] Public health practitioners need this kind of information to design community-wide programs and to adjust interventions to settings different from where the evidence was obtained.

Understanding the Context for Evidence

Numerous authors have written about the role of context in informing evidence-based practice,[12, 33, 41, 44–48] but there is little consensus on its definition. One useful definition of context specifies that information is needed to adapt and implement an evidence-based intervention in a particular setting or population.[33] The context for type 3 evidence includes five overlapping domains that are included in an ecological model of health promotion (see table 10.2).[34, 49, 50] First, there are characteristics of the target population for an intervention such as their education level and health history. Next, interpersonal variables provide important clues about context. For example, a person with a family history of cancer might be more likely to undergo cancer screening. Third, organizational variables are important. For example, whether an agency is successful in carrying out an evidence-based program will be influenced by its capacity (for example, a trained workforce, agency leadership). Fourth, social norms and culture are known to shape many health behaviors. Finally, larger political and economic forces affect context. For example, a high rate for a certain disease may influence a state's political will to address the issue in a meaningful and systematic way. These contextual issues are being examined more fully in the new "realist review," which is a systematic review process that seeks to examine not only whether an intervention works but also *how* interventions work in real-world settings.[51]

Triangulating Evidence

Triangulation involves the accumulation of evidence from a variety of sources to gain insight into a particular topic,[52] and often combines quantitative and qualitative data,[4] using multiple methods of data collection or analysis in a complementary manner to determine points of commonality or disagreement.[53, 54] Although quantitative data provide an excellent opportunity to determine how variables are related for large numbers of people, these data provide few clues to understand why these relationships exist. Qualitative data, on the other hand, can explain quantitative findings. There are many examples of the use of triangulation of qualitative and quantitative data to evaluate health programs and policies including AIDS prevention programs,[55] occupational health programs and policies,[56] and chronic disease prevention programs in community settings.[57] At the state and local level, it often is necessary to use both approaches for evaluation because either one, by itself, is not sufficient.

Table 10.1
Typology for Classifying Interventions by Level of Scientific Evidence

Category	How Established	Considerations for Level of Scientific Evidence	Data Source Examples
Evidence-based	Peer review via systematic or narrative review	Based on study design and execution External validity Potential side benefits or harms Costs and cost-effectiveness	Community Guide Cochrane reviews Narrative reviews based on published literature
Effective	Peer review	Based on study design and execution External validity Potential side benefits or harms Costs and cost-effectiveness	Articles in the scientific literature Research-tested intervention programs Technical reports with peer review
Promising	Written program evaluation without formal peer review	Summative evidence of effectiveness Formative evaluation data Theory-consistent, plausible, potentially high-reach, low-cost, replicable	State or federal government reports (without peer review) Conference presentations Evaluability assessments[a]
Emerging	Ongoing work, practice-based summaries or evaluation works in progress	Formative evaluation data Theory-consistent, plausible, potentially high-reach, low-cost, replicable Face validity	Pilot studies NIH CRISP data base Projects funded by health foundations

a. A "pre-evaluation" activity that involves an assessment is an assessment prior to commencing an evaluation to establish whether a program or policy can be evaluated and what might be the barriers to its evaluation.

Source: Brownson, RC et al. *Evidence-Based Public Health.* New York: Oxford University Press, 2003.

Table 10.2
Contextual Variables for Intervention Design, Implementation, and Adaptation

Category	Examples
Individual	Education level
	Basic human needs[a]
	Personal health history
Interpersonal	Family health history
	Support from peers
	Social capital
Organizational	Staff composition
	Staff expertise
	Physical infrastructure
	Organizational culture
Socio-cultural	Social norms
	Values
	Cultural traditions
	History
Political and economic	Political will
	Political ideology
	Lobbying and special interests
	Costs and benefits

a. Basic human needs include food, shelter, warmth, safety.[49]

Source: Adapted from Ciliska, D et al. *An Introduction to Evidence Informed Public Health and a Compendium of Critical Appraisal Tools for Public Health Practice.* Hamilton, Ontario, Canada: Collaborating Centre of Methods and Tools, McAlaster University, 2008.

Audiences for EBPH

There are four overlapping user groups for EBPH. The first includes public health practitioners with executive and managerial responsibilities who want to know the scope and quality of evidence for alternative strategies, such as different program or policy approaches. In practice, however, the range of options is limited, especially because funds from federal, state, or local sources usually are earmarked for a specific purpose. Still, the public health practitioner should carefully review the evidence for alternative ways to achieve the desired health goals. The next user group is policy makers at varying geopolitical levels who must decide how to allocate the public resources for which they are stewards. This group has the additional responsibility of making policies on controversial public issues. A third audience is the stakeholders who receive or will be affected by an intervention—that is, the public, especially those who vote, as well as interest groups formed to support or oppose specific policies, such as the legality of abortion, whether the community water supply should be fluoridated, or whether adults must be issued handgun licenses if they pass background checks. The final user group is composed of researchers who may be responsible for evaluating the impact of a specific policy or program, or using evidence to answer research questions.

Similarities and Differences between EBPH and Evidence-Based Medicine

While the concept of evidence-based practice is well established in numerous disciplines including psychology,[58] social work,[59] and nursing,[60] it is probably best established in medicine. The doctrine of evidence-based medicine (EBM) started in 1992,[61] not long before the concept of EBPH was introduced. Its origins can be traced back to the seminal work of Cochrane, who noted that many medical treatments lacked scientific effectiveness.[62] A basic tenet of EBM is to deemphasize unsystematic clinical experience and place greater emphasis on evidence from clinical research. Although the formal terminology of EBM is relatively recent, its concepts are embedded in earlier efforts, such as the Canadian Task Force for the Periodic Health Examination [63] and the *Guide to Clinical Preventive Services*.[64]

Important distinctions can be made between evidence-based approaches in medicine and public health. First, the type and volume of evidence differ. Medical studies of pharmaceuticals and procedures often rely on randomized controlled trials of individuals, the most scientifically rigorous of epidemiologic studies. In contrast, public health interventions usually rely on cross-sectional studies, quasi-experimental designs, and time-series analyses. These studies sometimes lack a comparison group and require more caveats to interpret the results. EBPH has borrowed the term "intervention" from clinical disciplines, implying a specific and discrete set of actions. In public health, however, there is seldom a single "intervention," but rather a program that involves a blending of several change strategies at once. Large community-based trials can be more expensive to conduct than randomized experiments in a clinic. Population-based studies generally require a longer time period between intervention and outcome. For example, a study on the effects of smoking cessation on lung cancer mortality would require decades of data collection and analysis. Contrast that with treatment of a medical condition (for example, an antibiotic for symptoms of pneumonia), which is likely to produce effects in days or weeks, or even a surgical trial for cancer with endpoints of mortality within a few years.

ANALYTIC TOOLS AND APPROACHES TO ENHANCE THE USE OF EBPH

Typically, public health practitioners must answer a variety of questions to improve the health of the communities they serve. As a start, they will want to know the size of a particular public health problem and whether there are effective interventions to address it. Because context is important in judging whether a given strategy will work, they will need information about the community, target population characteristics, and resources available to influence the health of people living there. They must decide whether a particular program or policy is worth doing (for example, is it better than alternatives?) and whether it will provide a satisfactory return on investment, measured in monetary terms or in health impacts. Several analytic tools and planning approaches are available to help practitioners answer such questions.

Public Health Surveillance

Public health surveillance is a critical tool for those using EBPH. It involves the ongoing systematic collection, analysis, and interpretation of specific health data, closely integrated with the timely dissemination of these data to those responsible for preventing and controlling disease or injury.[65] Public health surveillance systems should have the capacity to collect and analyze data, disseminate data to public health programs, and regularly evaluate the effectiveness of the use of the disseminated data.[66] For example, measuring the prevalence of elevated levels of lead (a known toxicant) in blood in the U.S. population was used to justify eliminating lead from paint and then gasoline, and then to document the effects of these actions.[67] In tobacco control, agreement on a common metric for tobacco use enabled comparisons of the prevalence of smoking across the states and an early recognition of the doubling and then tripling of the rates of decrease in smoking in California after passage of its Proposition 99,[68] and then a quadrupling of the rate of decline in Massachusetts compared with the other 48 states.[69]

Systematic Reviews and Evidence-Based Guidelines

A systematic review is a synthesis of results from many studies on a particular topic. Reading a good review can be one of the most efficient ways to become familiar with a body of knowledge about a health issue and how to address it. The use of explicit methods (that is, decision rules) applied in a consistent manner limits bias and reduces chance effects, thus providing more reliable results upon which to make decisions.[70] One of the most useful sets of reviews for public health interventions is the *Guide to Community Preventive Services* (the *Community Guide*),[21, 71] which provides an overview of current scientific research literature through a well-defined, rigorous method. The *Community Guide* helps public health practitioners to (1) discover what interventions have been evaluated and what have been their effects; (2) select interventions of proven effectiveness; and (3) estimate their costs and likely impact. Several authors have provided "checklists" for assessing the quality of a systematic review article.[72–74] A good systematic review should allow the practitioner to understand the local contextual conditions that contribute to successful implementation.[75]

Economic Evaluation

Economic evaluation assesses the relative value of alternative expenditures on public health programs and policies. In cost-benefit analysis, all of the costs and consequences of the decision options are valued in monetary terms. More often, the economic investment associated with an intervention is compared with the health impacts, such as cases of disease prevented or years of life saved. This technique, cost-effectiveness analysis (CEA), shows the relative value of alternative interventions (that is, health return on dollars invested).[76] CEA has become an increasingly important tool for researchers, practitioners, and policy makers. The data needed in this type of analysis, however, may be difficult to obtain, especially for programs and policies designed to improve health.[77, 78]

Health Impact Assessment

Health impact assessment (HIA) seeks to estimate the probable impact of a policy or intervention on the health of the population that is carried out in nonhealth sectors, such as agriculture, transportation, and economic development.[79] Recently, Dannenberg et al. [80] reviewed 27 HIAs completed in the United States from 1999 to 2007. Topics studied ranged from policies about living wages and afterschool programs to projects about power plants and public transit. An excellent illustration is the assessment of a Los Angeles living wage ordinance.[81] Researchers used estimates of the effects of health insurance and income on mortality to project and compare potential mortality reductions attributable to wage increases and changes in health insurance status among workers covered by the ordinance. Estimates demonstrated that the health insurance provisions of the ordinance would have a much larger health benefit than the wage increases, thus providing valuable information for policy makers who may consider adopting living wage ordinances in other jurisdictions or modifying existing ordinances.

Participatory Approaches

Community-based participatory research is a relatively new paradigm that integrates education and social action to improve health and reduce disparities.[82] Participatory approaches actively involve community members in research and intervention projects [83–85] to enhance the conduct and utility of EBPH.[26] Practitioners, academicians, and community members collaboratively define issues of concern, then develop intervention strategies and evaluate their impact. This approach relies on input from stakeholders who are individuals or agencies that have a vested interest in the issue at hand.[86] In the development of health policies, for example, policy makers are especially important stakeholders.[87] Stakeholders should include those who potentially would receive, use, and benefit from the program or policy being considered. Participatory evaluation strategies may involve community groups and coalitions in identifying potential outcomes or indicators of change.[82] Participatory approaches also may present challenges in adhering to EBPH principles, especially in deciding which approaches are most appropriate for addressing a particular health problem.[88]

Active Ingredients

EBPH relies on the transferability of evidence about effective interventions to new community settings. Practitioners need to identify the most important components or "active ingredients" of an intervention, which are the essential elements that produce the desired results, and how context matters. Often, constraints require some modification of the original intervention. In these situations there is an inherent tension between fidelity (maintaining the original program design) and reinvention (changes needed for replication or adoption in a new setting or for a different population).[89] Close monitoring of the intervention is called for to be sure that it incorporates the active ingredients and that the same intermediate and long-term outcomes documented in the original research are occurring.

CHALLENGES IN THE DISSEMINATION AND USE OF EBPH

The field of EBPH has steadily matured and is now recognized by most public health professionals as an important tool in public health. Yet, the dissemination and use of effective intervention strategies, which is critically important in improving public health practice, remains a significant challenge.[90, 91] Drawing on wide experience in the clinical world, dissemination of evidence-based clinical guidelines using passive methods (for example, publication of consensus statements in professional journals, mass mailings) has been largely ineffective, resulting in only small changes in the uptake of a new practice.)[92] Similarly, single-source prevention messages generally are ineffective.[93] The dissemination and use of an evidence-based program necessitates time-efficient approaches, ongoing training, and placing a high organizational value on research-informed practice.[94] Furthermore, translation of research to practice among organizations, practitioner groups, or the general public is likely to occur in stages,[95] suggesting that the decision to adopt, accept, and utilize an innovation in EBPH is a process rather than a single act. This section addresses specific challenges standing in the way of wider dissemination of evidence-based practices and greater use of evidence-based decision making to improve the public's health.

Organizational Culture

EBPH often relies on "evidence champions" who are willing to challenge the status quo within an organization and promote scientifically proven approaches to solve health problems. New ways of making decisions and novel management strategies may be needed to achieve the desired changes. Government institutions, including public health agencies, are key users of EBPH. Yet they are not known for their organizational or budgetary flexibility, making it difficult to quickly mount a new program, alter an established way of doing business, or promote new policies in other organizations. These agencies typically are bound to rigid civil service and union-bargained requirements about how staff can be hired, remunerated, evaluated, and terminated, as well as how money can be spent. In Los Angeles County, for example, the pay scale for nutritionists and health educators is so low that it is difficult to attract even entry-level individuals. Once hired by the county, these professionals often are attracted to higher paying administrative positions that do not use their primary expertise.

An organizational climate that supports change is required for innovation,[96] but it is often not found in public health agencies. Rigid personnel systems often make it difficult to keep up with rapidly evolving technology. For example, in many health agencies, there are no suitable job classifications for a health economist or for a Web designer, making it virtually impossible to hire at competitive salaries. Within a hierarchical bureaucracy, few incentives exist to press superiors for changes in programs or approaches even when the evidence is compelling. Unlike in some private sector organizations that encourage risk taking and provide substantial monetary rewards for success, most public sector organizations have a culture that discourages "out of the box" thinking and entrepreneurship.[97] The tendency to continue doing what has been done in the past is a powerful impediment to change. In many bureaucracies, when change does occur, it is usually in small incremental steps. Continuing past practices requires less effort than working through all of the implications of a different approach based on newer evidence.

Leadership

The attitude toward EBPH among agency leadership is important because it helps to determine the organizational culture and use of finite resources. In a survey of 152 city and county health departments in the United States, one of the main predictors of strong public health system performance was the attention of organizational leadership to the science base, quality, and performance.[98] Even public health leaders who understand and embrace EBPH, however, have challenges in choosing and implementing innovative approaches. How should they choose priority opportunities for programs and policies among all those recommended based on evidence reviews? As in clinical medicine, there are more recommendations than are practical for any department to introduce. What criteria should leaders consider when selecting among options? Some worthy considerations include population-attributable disease or illness burden, preventable fraction, relative cost-effectiveness, skills of key staff, prior experience with other approaches, opportunities for leverage through partnerships with other stakeholders, and consistency with an agency's strategic plan, goals, and objectives.

Politics

Having good scientific evidence often is insufficient to convince policy makers (for example, Congress, state governors, boards of county supervisors, city councils) to initiate evidence-based changes.[99, 100] Researchers rely on experimental and observational studies to test specific hypotheses in a deliberate and systematic way [101, 102] and their influence derives from having specialized knowledge. On the other hand, policy making can happen quickly and is built on generalized knowledge and demands from stakeholders.[92, 100] Policy makers have to sell, argue, advocate, and get reelected in light of their available political capital.[78] In some cases, the evidence for a particular action does not necessarily lead to policy change.[103, 104] Public health agencies often face obstacles from other stakeholders in proposing or implementing new evidence-based practices.

Programmatic and policy changes often result in "winners" and "losers" who can be at odds in the EBPH process.[105] A contractor who financially supports an elected decision maker may have more clout than the agency, regardless of the merits. Public health agencies, because of their mission to improve the population's health, often seek to advance measures that expand the power and reach of government, raising objections from those who want less government. For example, in the debates surrounding public smoking ban proposals, public health agencies were forced to combat arguments that the smoking bans simply were a way for the government to limit personal freedoms. Overcoming this resistance often requires that public health leaders create coalitions of partners that extend well beyond the realm of public health.

The prevailing political ideology may be contrary to what science recommends, such as for water fluoridation or needle-exchange programs. The federal government recently has allowed federal funds to be used for needle-exchange programs, *two decades* after they were shown to be effective. In other cases, those without a background in scientific methods may be skeptical that a systematic review process yields a better idea of what to do about a problem than simply following advice of an individual they trust, even when the trusted advice is at variance with the best evidence.[106] Lack of skills in putting together coalitions of partners who support a particular EBPH intervention also can reduce the likelihood of convincing policy makers. Public health action that requires legislation may face opposition from local jurisdictions that could jeopardize its passage.

Public health leaders occasionally encounter situations in which the political will to implement a particular intervention exists before there is evidence to support it. A prime example is the Drug Abuse Resistance Education (D.A.R.E.) program, which is the most widely used school-based drug use prevention program in the United States reaching over 70 percent of elementary school-age children.[107] The program costs approximately $130 per student (in 2004 dollars) to implement. Systematic reviews of methodologically sound D.A.R.E. program evaluations have shown the program to be ineffective.[108]

Funding

Another challenge to implementing EBPH is the need to adhere to the requirements of the funding agencies. Most public health funding at all levels of government is categorical and restricted as to how the money may be spent—that is, "hardening of the categories,"[109] and limits the flexible use of funds to implement new evidence-based programs. Public health leaders are beginning to recognize the benefits to program integration and have articulated principles to enhance integration efforts.[110] In addition, appropriating legislation or voter initiatives may contain explicit language about restrictions, which in turn often is influenced by key stakeholders. For example, in California, no more than 20 percent of funding coming from Proposition 99, a statute in the Tobacco Tax and Health Protection Act enacted in 1988, can be used for antitobacco education in schools and communities.[111] We are not aware of any legislation or executive branch guidance that limits expenditures to evidence-based recommendations or requires that these be used whenever available. More governmental agencies appear to be referencing the best sources of evidence-based recommendations, including the *Community Guide*,[21] as important inputs into the state and local planning processes.[112] In many states, funding of tobacco control efforts is tied to the use of evidence-based strategies for tobacco use prevention and control.

Workforce Competencies

While the formal concept of EBPH is relatively new, the underlying skills are not. For example, reviewing the scientific literature for evidence or evaluating a program intervention are skills often taught in graduate programs in public health or other academic disciplines and are building blocks of public health practice. Yet, the skills and competencies of the public health workforce to carry out EBPH functions vary tremendously. The emphasis on principles of EBPH is not uniformly taught in all the disciplines represented in the public health workforce. For example, a public health nurse is likely to have had less training in how to locate the most current evidence and interpret alternatives than an epidemiologist. A recently graduated health educator with a master's degree in public health is more likely to have gained an understanding of the importance of EBPH than an environmental health specialist holding a bachelor's degree. Fewer than half of public health workers have any formal training in a public health discipline such as epidemiology or health education.[113] An even smaller percentage of these professionals have formal graduate training from a school of public health or other public health program. Currently, it appears that few public health departments have made continuing education about EBPH mandatory. Consequently, public health workers must rely on routine, on-the-job training to gain the skills required to apply the principles of EBPH.

FUTURE OPPORTUNITIES

The United States spends nearly $30 billion annually on health-related research,[114] but only a small portion of these expenditures is dedicated to research relevant to the practice of public health. Nonetheless, evidence for addressing a number of priority public health problems now exists. Unfortunately, the translation from research to clinical or community applications often occurs only after a delay of many years.[4, 28, 115] Several actions are required to accelerate the production of new evidence and the adoption of evidence-based interventions to protect and improve health in the United States.

Expanding the Evidence Base

The growing literature on the effectiveness of preventive interventions in clinical and community settings [21, 22] does not provide equal coverage of health problems. For example, the evidence for how to increase immunization levels is much stronger than how to prevent HIV infection or reduce alcohol abuse. A greater investment of resources to expand the evidence base is therefore essential. Even in cases in which we have interventions of proven effectiveness, the populations in which they have been tested often do not include subpopulations with the greatest disease and injury burden. Expanding the base of evidence requires a reliance on well-tested conceptual frameworks, especially those that pay close attention to dissemination and use of EBPH. For example, RE-AIM helps program planners and evaluators to pay explicit attention to *R*each, *E*fficacy/*E*ffectiveness, *A*doption, *I*mplementation, and *M*aintenance,[116, 117] concepts that are consistent with evidence-based interventions.

Overcoming Barriers to Dissemination and Use of EBPH

More knowledge is needed on effective mechanisms to translate evidence-based practice to public health settings. Several important questions deserve answers:

- Why have some types of evidence languished while others have been quickly adopted?
- What are cost-effective strategies to disseminate and encourage use of EBPH?
- How can funding agencies accelerate the replication and adaptation of evidence-based interventions in a variety of settings and populations?
- What specific processes best integrate community health assessment and improvement activities into health system planning efforts?
- How can we harness new tools, such as the Internet, to improve intervention effectiveness and dissemination?
- What changes in organizational culture that promote innovation and adoption of EBPH are feasible?
- How can we increase attention on external validity in the production and systematic reviews of evidence?

Engaging Leadership

Leadership is probably the most important determinant influencing the adoption of EBPH as a core part of public health practice.[98] This includes an expectation that decisions will be made on the basis of the best science, needs of the target population, and what will work locally. Baker et al. [118] examined the role of training in government workers in EBPH and the subsequent use of these methods in public health practice. Through qualitative studies, they found that the implementation of evidence-based processes strongly depends on leadership support. Encouraging leaders to embrace evidence-based public health as the underpinning of programs in their communities is vital to program success. Further research on the link between leadership and performance—and how to strengthen local public health agency capacity—was recommended by Scutchfield et al. [98] to improve local public health practice. In some cases, additional funding may be required, but usually having the will to change (rather than dollars) is the key to success. Use of EBPH should be incorporated as part of performance reviews for key public health leaders and as part of explicit goals and objectives for all program directors.

Strengthening the Public Health Workforce

To address EBPH competencies, training programs have been developed in the United States for public health professionals in state health agencies,[14, 118] local health departments and community-based organizations,[119, 120] and similar programs have been developed in other countries.[121–123] Some programs show evidence of effectiveness.[14, 120] The most common format uses didactic sessions, computer labs, and scenario-based exercises, taught by a faculty team with expertise in EBPH. The reach of these training programs can be increased by emphasizing a train-the-trainer approach.[121] Other formats have been used, including Internet based self-study,[119, 124] CD-ROMs,[125] distance and distributed learning networks, and targeted technical assistance. Training programs may have greater impact when delivered by "change agents" who are perceived as experts yet share common characteristics and goals with trainees.[126] A commitment from leadership and staff to lifelong learning is also an essential ingredient for success.[127] Training programs to address EBPH competencies should take into account principles of adult learning. These issues recently were articulated by Bryan et al.,[128] who highlighted the need to (1) know why the audience is learning; (2) tap into an underlying motivation to learn by the need to solve problems; (3) respect and build upon previous experience; (4) design learning approaches that match the background and diversity of recipients; and (5) actively involve the audience in the learning process.

The need for a competent public health workforce is consistent with numerous IOM reports calling for public health workers to be adept in policy making, communication, science translation and other advocacy skills.[11, 29, 129] Well-prepared public health professionals are essential for an effective public health system in the United States, yet this implies an adequate supply of skilled and competent workers. Thus, investments in strengthening capacity and competencies of the public health workforce are needed, as well as research to understand how this can best be accomplished. For example, the importance of epidemiologic leadership and support for public health practice led to the development of Competencies for Applied Epidemiologists in Governmental Public Health Agencies, which was designed to improve the practice of epidemiology in public health agencies. Koo et al. [130] found that these competencies map to domains other than epidemiology and also to activities and experiences outside the academic environment. The field of workforce development will be enhanced by linking such competencies to curricula in a collaborative effort between schools of public health, and local and state health departments.

More practitioner-focused training is needed on the rationale for EBPH, how to select interventions, how to adapt them to particular circumstances, and how to monitor their implementation. The Task Force on Workforce Development has recommended that the essential public health services [131] be used as a framework to build the basic, cross-cutting, and technical competencies required to address public health problems. The inclusion of EBPH principles and needed competencies [4, 132] would enhance this framework. Also, because many of the health issues needing urgent attention in local communities will require the involvement of other organizations (for example, nonprofit groups, hospitals, employers), their participation in training efforts is essential.

Enhancing Accountability for Public Expenditures

Public funds should be targeted to support evidence-based strategies. Grants made by public health agencies to outside organizations should contain language explicitly requiring the use of such strategies, when they exist, to accomplish grant objectives. While the science base for many topics is still evolving, it is irresponsible not to use existing evidence in the design and implementation of proven public health interventions. Evaluations of such efforts can thus contribute to a better understanding of what works in different settings. Simultaneously, the adoption of EBPH by the public health system as a whole and its impact on the community's health should be tracked. A central criterion in the accreditation of public health departments, soon to be implemented,[133] must be the use of best evidence in every effort to improve health and health equity.

Understanding How to Better Use EBPH to Address Disparities

To what extent does the use of specific evidence-based approaches reduce disparities while improving overall current or future health? For many interventions, there is not a clear answer to this question. Despite the Healthy People 2010 goal of eliminating health disparities, recent data show large and growing differences in disease burden and health outcomes between high- and low-income groups.[134] Most of the existing intervention research has been conducted among higher income populations, and programs focusing on elimination of health disparities have often been short-lived.[135] Yet, in both developed and developing countries, poverty is strongly correlated with poor health outcomes.[136] When enough evidence exists, systematic reviews should focus specifically on interventions that show promise in eliminating health disparities.[137, 138] Policy interventions hold the potential to influence health determinants more broadly and could significantly reduce the growing disparities across a wide range of health problems.[139]

CONCLUSION

The most significant problems affecting population health result from a complex interplay of behavioral choices, environmental influences, and genetics. Modifiable behavioral risk factors, including tobacco use, poor diet and physical inactivity, and alcohol consumption are now the leading actual causes of death in the United States.[140] Changing these behaviors and their social determinants will require effective use of public health actions for which strong evidence exists, as well as new knowledge about how to reduce the continuing health disparities between subgroups. Unintentional and intentional injuries often result in many years spent with disability or lost years of life and have large social and economic consequences. Decreasing the global burden of injuries is among the main challenges facing the public health sector in the next century.

To meet these challenges, more research is needed to find evidence for what works and how to apply this evidence in local communities. While the library of effective interventions to reduce tobacco use is filled with success stories—and many of the recommended actions have been put into place across the country—there is less certainty about how to stem the rise in obesity; for example, the sheer size of the epidemic and the dire consequences if it is not stopped calls out for evidence-based solutions that can be broadly applied. Other health threats will inevitably surface that require public health action. We must remain vigilant in monitoring the health of our communities to identify such threats and be ready to apply proven interventions to reduce risk. Underlying most of the disease and injury burden are modifiable aspects of the physical and social environments. As we look forward, to maximize public health impact and minimize health disparities, EBPH should include interventions that address such factors as the built environment, poverty, and education attainment.

The successful implementation of EBPH in public health practice is both a science and an art. The science is built on epidemiologic, behavioral, and policy research showing the size and scope of a public health problem and which interventions are likely to be effective in addressing the problem. The art of decision making often involves knowing what information is important to a particular stakeholder at the right time. Unlike solving a math problem, significant decisions in public health must balance science and art, since rational, evidence-based decision making often involves choosing one alternative from among a set of rational choices. By applying the concepts of EBPH outlined in this chapter, decision making and, ultimately, public health practice can be improved.

REFERENCES

1. Centers for Disease Control and Prevention. Ten great public health achievements: United States, 1900–1999. *MMWR*. 1999;48:241–243.
2. Centers for Disease Control and Prevention. *Public Health in the New American Health System*. Atlanta, GA: Centers for Disease Control and Prevention; 1993. Discussion Paper March, 1993.
3. Muir Gray JA. *Evidence-Based Healthcare: How to Make Health Policy and Management Decisions*. New York: Churchill Livingstone; 1997.
4. Brownson RC, Baker EA, Leet TL, Gillespie KN. *Evidence-Based Public Health*. New York: Oxford University Press; 2003.

5. Glasziou P, Longbottom H. Evidence-based public health practice. *Aust N Z J Public Health*. 1999;23:436–440.
6. McMichael C, Waters E, Volmink J. Evidence-based public health: what does it offer developing countries? *J Public Health (Oxf)*. 2005;27:215–221.
7. Fielding JE, Briss PA. Promoting evidence-based public health policy: can we have better evidence and more action? *Health Aff (Millwood)*. 2006;25:969–978.
8. Brownson RC, Gurney JG, Land G. Evidence-based decision making in public health. *J Public Health Manag Pract*. 1999;5:86–97.
9. McGinnis JM. Does proof matter? why strong evidence sometimes yields weak action. *Am J Health Promot*. 2001;15:391–396.
10. Fielding JE. Where is the evidence? *Annu Rev Public Health*. 2001;22:v–vi.
11. Institute of Medicine. *Committee for the Study of the Future of Public Health: The Future of Public Health*. Washington, DC: National Academies Press; 1988.
12. Hausman AJ. Implications of evidence-based practice for community health. *Am J Community Psychol*. 2002;30:453–467.
13. Kohatsu ND, Melton RJ. A health department perspective on the Guide to Community Preventive Services. *Am J Prev Med*. 2000;18:3–4.
14. Dreisinger M, Leet TL, Baker EA, Gillespie KN, Haas B, Brownson RC. Improving the public health workforce: evaluation of a training course to enhance evidence-based decision making. *J Public Health Manag Pract*. 2008;14:138–143.
15. Anderson J. "Don't confuse me with facts . . .": evidence-based practice confronts reality. *Med J Aust*. 1999;170:465–466.
16. Baker EL, Potter MA, Jones DL, et al. The public health infrastructure and our nation's health. *Annu Rev Public Health*. 2005;26:303–318.
17. Haynes B, Haines A. Barriers and bridges to evidence based clinical practice. *BMJ*. 1998;317:273–276.
18. Black BL, Cowens-Alvarado R, Gershman S, Weir HK. Using data to motivate action: the need for high quality, an effective presentation, and an action context for decision-making. *Cancer Causes Control*. 2005;16(Suppl 1):15–25.
19. Curry S, Byers T, Hewitt M, eds. *Fulfilling the Potential of Cancer Prevention and Early Detection*. Washington, DC: National Academies Press; 2003.
20. Briss PA, Brownson RC, Fielding JE, Zaza S. Developing and using the Guide to Community Preventive Services: lessons learned about evidence-based public health. *Annu Rev Public Health*. 2004;25:281–302.
21. Zaza S, Briss PA, Harris KW, eds. *The Guide to Community Preventive Services: What Works to Promote Health?* New York: Oxford University Press; 2005.
22. *Guide to Clinical Preventive Services*. 3rd ed. Washington, DC: Agency for Healthcare Research and Quality, 2005. http://www.ahrq.gov/clinic/gcpspu.htm. Periodic updates. Accessed October 11, 2005.
23. Cancer Control PLANET. Links resources to comprehensive cancer control: The National Cancer Institute; The Centers for Disease Control and Prevention; The American Cancer Society; The Substance Abuse and Mental Health Services; The Agency for Healthcare Research and Quality. http://cancercontrolplanet.cancer.gov/index.html. Published 2008. Accessed May 26, 2008.
24. SAMHSA's National Registry of Evidence-based Programs and Practices. US Department of Health and Human Services. Substance Abuse & Mental Health Services Administration. http://www.nrepp.samhsa.gov/. Published 2008. Accessed August 16, 2008.
25. Public Health Partners. Partners in Information Access for the Public Health Workforce. http://phpartners.org

26. Kohatsu ND, Robinson JG, Torner JC. Evidence-based public health: an evolving concept. *Am J Prev Med.* 2004;27:417–421.
27. Green LW. Public health asks of systems science: to advance our evidence-based practice, can you help us get more practice-based evidence? *Am J Public Health.* 2006;96:406–409.
28. Kerner J, Rimer B, Emmons K. Introduction to the special section on dissemination: dissemination research and research dissemination: how can we close the gap? *Health Psychol.* 2005;24:443–446.
29. Institute of Medicine. *The Future of the Public's Health in the 21st Century.* Washington, DC: National Academies Press; 2003.
30. American Public Health Association. *Local Public Health Practice: Trends and Models.* Washington, DC: American Public Health Association; 2000.
31. Brownson RC, Fielding JE, Maylahn CM. Evidence-based public health: a fundamental concept for public health practice. *Annu Rev Public Health.* 2009;30:175–201.
32. Jenicek M. Epidemiology, evidence-based medicine, and evidence-based public health. *J Epidemiol Commun Health.* 1997;7:187–197.
33. Rychetnik L, Hawe P, Waters E, Barratt A, Frommer M. A glossary for evidence based public health. *J Epidemiol Community Health.* 2004;58:538–545.
34. Ciliska D, Thomas H, Buffett C. *An Introduction to Evidence Informed Public Health and a Compendium of Critical Appraisal Tools for Public Health Practice.* Hamilton, Ontario, Canada: Collaborating Centre of Methods and Tools, McMaster University; 2008.
35. McQueen DV. Strengthening the evidence base for health promotion. *Health Promot Int.* 2001;16:261–268.
36. Spring B. OBSSR award supports training in evidence-based behavioral practice. *Outlook: A Quarterly Newsletter of the Society of Behavioral Medicine.* 2007;Winter:10.
37. Spring B, Walker B, Brownson R, et al. *Definition and Competencies for Evidence-Based Behavioral Practice.* Chicago, IL: Northwestern University; 2008. Council on Evidence-Based Behavioral Practice White Paper.
38. McKean E, ed. *The New Oxford American Dictionary.* 2nd ed. New York: Oxford University Press; 2005.
39. McQueen DV, Anderson LM. What counts as evidence? issues and debates. In: Rootman I, ed. *Evaluation in Health Promotion: Principles and Perspectives.* Copenhagen, Denmark: World Health Organization; 2001:63–81.
40. Rimer BK, Glanz DK, Rasband G. Searching for evidence about health education and health behavior interventions. *Health Educ Behav.* 2001;28:231–248.
41. Kerner JF. Integrating research, practice, and policy: what we see depends on where we stand. *J Public Health Manag Pract.* 2008;14:193–198.
42. Glasgow RE, Green LW, Klesges LM, et al. External validity: we need to do more. *Ann Behav Med.* 2006;31:105–108.
43. Green LW, Glasgow RE. Evaluating the relevance, generalization, and applicability of research: issues in external validation and translation methodology. *Eval Health Prof.* 2006;29:126–153.
44. Castro FG, Barrera M, Jr., Martinez CR Jr. The cultural adaptation of prevention interventions: resolving tensions between fidelity and fit. *Prev Sci.* 2004;5:41–45.
45. Kerner JF, Guirguis-Blake J, Hennessy KD, et al. Translating research into improved outcomes in comprehensive cancer control. *Cancer Causes Control.* 2005;16(Suppl 1):27–40.
46. Rychetnik L, Frommer M, Hawe P, Shiell A. Criteria for evaluating evidence on public health interventions. *J Epidemiol Community Health.* 2002;56:119–127.

47. Glasgow RE. What types of evidence are most needed to advance behavioral medicine? *Ann Behav Med.* 2008;35:19–25.
48. Kemm J. The limitations of 'evidence-based' public health. *J Eval Clin Pract.* 2006;12:319–324.
49. Maslov A. A theory of human motivation. *Psychol Rev.* 1943;50:370–396.
50. McLeroy KR, Bibeau D, Steckler A, Glanz K. An ecological perspective on health promotion programs. *Health Educ Q.* 1988;15:351–377.
51. Pawson R, Greenhalgh T, Harvey G, Walshe K. Realist review: a new method of systematic review designed for complex policy interventions. *J Health Serv Res Policy.* 2005;10(Suppl 1):21–34.
52. Tones K. Beyond the randomized controlled trial: a case for 'judicial review.' *Health Educ Res.* 1997;12:i–iv.
53. Denzin NK. *The Research Act in Sociology.* London, UK: Butterworth; 1970.
54. Steckler A, McLeroy KR, Goodman RM, Bird ST, McCormick L. Toward integrating qualitative and quantitative methods: an introduction. *Health Educ Q.* 1992;19:1–8.
55. Dorfman LE, Derish PA, Cohen JB. Hey girlfriend: an evaluation of AIDS prevention among women in the sex industry. *Health Educ Q.* 1992;19:25–40.
56. Hugentobler M, Israel BA, Schurman SJ. An action research approach to workplace health: integrating methods. *Health Educ Q.* 1992;19:55–76.
57. Goodman RM, Wheeler FC, Lee PR. Evaluation of the Heart to Heart Project: lessons from a community-based chronic disease prevention project. *Am J Health Promot.* 1995;9:443–455.
58. Presidential Task Force on Evidence-Based Practice. Evidence-based practice in psychology. *Am Psychol.* 2006;61:271–285.
59. Gambrill E. Evidence-based practice: sea change or the emperor's new clothes? *J Social Work Educ.* 2003;39:3–23.
60. Melnyk BM, Fineout-Overholt E, Stone P, Ackerman M. Evidence-based practice: the past, the present, and recommendations for the millennium. *Pediatr Nurs.* 2000;26:77–80.
61. Evidence-Based Medicine Working Group. Evidence-based medicine: a new approach to teaching the practice of medicine. *JAMA.* 1992;17:2420–2425.
62. Cochrane A. *Effectiveness and Efficiency: Random Reflections on Health Services.* London, UK: Nuffield Provincial Hospital Trust; 1972.
63. Canadian Task Force on the Periodic Health Examination. The periodic health examination: Canadian Task Force on the Periodic Health Examination. *Can Med Assoc J.* 1979;121:1193–1254.
64. US Preventive Services Task Force. *Guide to Clinical Preventive Services: An Assessment of the Effectiveness of 169 Interventions.* Baltimore, MD: Williams & Wilkins; 1989.
65. Thacker SB, Berkelman RL. Public health surveillance in the United States. *Epidemiol Rev.* 1988;10:164–190.
66. Thacker SB, Stroup DF. Public health surveillance. In: Brownson RC, Petitti DB, eds. *Applied Epidemiology: Theory to Practice.* 2nd ed. New York: Oxford University Press; 2006:30–67.
67. Annest JL, Pirkle JL, Makuc D, et al. Chronological trend in blood lead levels between 1976 and 1980. *N Engl J Med.* 1983;308:1373–1377.
68. Tobacco Education and Research Oversight Committee for California. Confronting a relentless adversary: a plan for success: toward a tobacco-free California, 2006–2008. In: California Department of Public Health, ed. *Health.* Sacramento, CA: California Department of Public Health; 2006.

69. Biener L, Harris JE, Hamilton W. Impact of the Massachusetts tobacco control programme: population based trend analysis. *BMJ.* 2000;321:351–354.
70. Oxman AD, Guyatt GH. The science of reviewing research. *Ann N Y Acad Sci.* 1993;703:33–34,125–133.
71. Mullen PD, Ramirez G. The promise and pitfalls of systematic reviews. *Annu Rev Public Health.* 2006;27:81–102.
72. Guyatt G, Rennie D, eds. *Users' Guides to the Medical Literature: A Manual for Evidence-Based Clinical Practice.* Chicago, IL: American Medical Association Press; 2002.
73. Kelsey JL, Petitti DB, King AC. Key methodologic concepts and issues. In: Brownson RC, Petitti DB, eds. *Applied Epidemiology: Theory to Practice.* New York: Oxford University Press; 1998:35–69.
74. Oxman AD, Cook DJ, Guyatt GH, Evidence-Based Medicine Working Group. Users' guides to the medical literature. Part 6: how to use an overview. *JAMA.* 1994;272:1367–1371.
75. Waters E, Doyle J. Evidence-based public health practice: improving the quality and quantity of the evidence. *J Public Health Med.* 2002;24:227–229.
76. Gold MR, Siegel JE, Russell LB, Weinstein MC. *Cost-Effectiveness in Health and Medicine.* New York: Oxford University Press; 1996.
77. Carande-Kulis VG, Maciosek MV, Briss PA, et al. Task Force on Community Preventive Services: methods for systematic reviews of economic evaluations for the Guide to Community Preventive Services. *Am J Prev Med.* 2000;18:75–91.
78. Brownson RC, Royer C, Ewing R, McBride TD. Researchers and policymakers: travelers in parallel universes. *Am J Prev Med.* 2006;30:164–172.
79. Harris P, Harris-Roxas B, Harris E, Kemp L. *Health Impact Assessment: A Practical Guide.* Sydney, Australia: Centre for Health Equity Training/Research and Evaluation,. Part of the UNSW Research Centre for Primary Health Care and Equity; 2007.
80. Dannenberg AL, Bhatia R, Cole BL, Heaton SK, Feldman JD, Rutt CD. Use of health impact assessment in the US: 27 case studies, 1999–2007. *Am J Prev Med.* 2008;34:241–256.
81. Cole B, Shimkhada R, Morgenstern H, Kominski G, Fielding J, Wu S. Projected health impact of the Los Angeles City living wage ordinance. *J Epidemiol Commun Health.* 2005;59:645–650.
82. Wallerstein NB, Duran B. Using community-based participatory research to address health disparities. *Health Promot Pract.* 2006;7:312–323.
83. Green LW, George MA, Daniel M, et al. *Review and Recommendations for the Development of Participatory Research in Health Promotion in Canada.* Vancouver, BC, Canada: The Royal Society of Canada; 1995.
84. Israel BA, Schulz AJ, Parker EA, Becker AB. Review of community-based research: assessing partnership approaches to improve public health. *Annu Rev Public Health.* 1998;19:173–202.
85. Cargo M, Mercer SL. The value and challenges of participatory research: Strengthening its practice. *Annu Rev Public Health.* 2008;29:325–350.
86. Soriano FI. *Conducting Needs Assessments: A Multdisciplinary Approach.* Thousand Oaks, CA: Sage Publications; 1995.
87. Sederburg WA. Perspectives of the legislator: allocating resources. *MMWR.* 1992;41(Suppl):37–48.
88. Hallfors D, Cho H, Livert D, Kadushin C. Fighting back against substance abuse: are community coalitions winning? *Am J Prev Med.* 2002;23:237–245.
89. Bauman LJ, Stein RE, Ireys HT. Reinventing fidelity: the transfer of social technology among settings. *Am J Community Psychol.* 1991;19:619–639.

90. Glasgow RE, Emmons KM. How can we increase translation of research into practice? types of evidence needed. *Annu Rev Public Health.* 2007;28:413–433.
91. Green L, Ottoson J, Hiatt R, Garcia C. Diffusion, dissemination and implementation of evidence-based public health. *Annu Rev Public Health.* In press.
92. Bero LA, Jadad AR. How consumers and policy makers can use systematic reviews for decision making. In: Mulrow C, Cook D, eds. *Systematic Reviews Synthesis of Best Evidence for Health Care Decisions.* Philadelphia, PA: American College of Physicians; 1998:45–54.
93. The Lewin Group I. *Final Report: Factors Influencing Effective Dissemination of Prevention Research Findings by the Department of Health and Human Services.* Washington, DC: The Lewin Group, Inc; 2001.
94. Dobbins M, Cockerill R, Barnsley J, Ciliska D. Factors of the innovation, organization, environment, and individual that predict the influence five systematic reviews had on public health decisions. *Int J Technol Assess Health Care.* 2001;17:467–478.
95. Rogers EM. *Diffusion of Innovations.* 5th ed. New York: Free Press; 2003.
96. Simpson DD. A conceptual framework for transferring research to practice. *J Subst Abuse Treat.* 2002;22:171–182.
97. Cohen S, Eimicke W. Understanding and applying innovation strategies in the public sector: Paper presented at 57th Annual National Conference of the American Society for Public Administration; June 29–July 3, 1996; Atlanta, GA.
98. Scutchfield FD, Knight EA, Kelly AV, Bhandari MW, Vasilescu IP. Local public health agency capacity and its relationship to public health system performance. *J Public Health Manag Pract.* 2004;10:204–215.
99. Choi BC. Twelve essentials of science-based policy. *Prev Chronic Dis.* 2005; 2:A16.
100. Choi BC, Pang T, Lin V, et al. Can scientists and policy makers work together? *J Epidemiol Community Health.* 2005;59:632–637.
101. Koepsell TD, Weiss NS. *Epidemiologic Methods. Studying the Occurrence of Illness.* New York: Oxford University Press; 2003.
102. Last JM, ed. *A Dictionary of Epidemiology.* 4th ed. New York: Oxford University Press; 2001.
103. Shulock N. The paradox of policy analysis: if it is not used, why do we produce so much? *J Pol Anal Manage.* 1999;18:226–244.
104. Almeida C, Bascolo E. Use of research results in policy decision-making, formulation, and implementation: a review of the literature. *Cad Saude Publica.* 2006;22(Suppl):S7–S19, S20–S33.
105. Abney G. Lobbying by the insiders: parallels of state agencies and interest groups. *Public Administr Rev.* 1988;48:911–917.
106. Lavis JN, Robertson D, Woodside JM, McLeod CB, Abelson J. How can research organizations more effectively transfer research knowledge to decision makers? *Milbank Q.* 2003;81: 171–172, 221–248.
107. Drug Policy Foundation. *Public Policy: Youth Drug Education/The D.A.R.E. Program.* Washington, DC: Drug Policy Foundation; 2003.
108. West SL, O'Neal KK. Project D.A.R.E. outcome effectiveness revisited. *Am J Public Health.* 2004;94:1027–1029.
109. Wiesner PJ. Four diseases of disarray in public health. *Ann Epidemiol.* 1993;3:196–198.
110. Slonim AB, Callaghan C, Daily L, et al. Recommendations for integration of chronic disease programs: are your programs linked? *Prev Chronic Dis.* 2007; 4:A34.

111. Breslow L, Johnson M. California's Proposition 99 on tobacco, and its impact. *Annu Rev Public Health.* 1993;14:585–604.
112. Brownson RC, Ballew P, Dieffenderfer B, et al. Evidence-based interventions to promote physical activity: what contributes to dissemination by state health departments. *Am J Prev Med.* 2007;33: S4–S8, S66–S73.
113. Turnock BJ. *Public Health: What it is and How it Works.* 3rd ed. Gaithersburg, MD: Aspen Publishers, Inc.; 2004.
114. Office of Management and Budget. *Budget: Department of Health and Human Services.* Washington, DC: The Executive Office of the President; 2008.
115. Balas EA. From appropriate care to evidence-based medicine. *Pediatr Ann.* 1998;27:581–584.
116. Glasgow RE, Vogt TM, Boles SM. Evaluating the public health impact of health promotion interventions: the RE-AIM framework. *Am J Public Health.* 1999;89:1322–1327.
117. Jilcott S, Ammerman A, Sommers J, Glasgow RE. Applying the RE-AIM framework to assess the public health impact of policy change. *Ann Behav Med.* 2007;34:105–114.
118. Baker EA, Brownson RC, Dreisinger M, McIntosh LD, Karamehic-Muratovic A. Examining the role of training in evidence-based public health: a qualitative study. *Health Promot Pract.* 2009;10:342–348.
119. Maxwell ML, Adily A, Ward JE. Promoting evidence-based practice in population health at the local level: a case study in workforce capacity development. *Aust Health Rev.* 2007;31:422–429.
120. Maylahn C, Bohn C, Hammer M, Waltz E. Strengthening epidemiologic competencies among local health professionals in New York: teaching evidence-based public health. *Public Health Rep.* 2008;123:35–43.
121. Brownson RC, Diem G, Grabauskas V, et al. Training practitioners in evidence-based chronic disease prevention for global health. *Promot Educ.* 2007;14:159–163.
122. Oliver KB, Dalrymple P, Lehmann HP, McClellan DA, Robinson KA, Twose C. Bringing evidence to practice: a team approach to teaching skills required for an informationist role in evidence-based clinical and public health practice. *J Med Libr Assoc.* 2008;96:50–57.
123. Pappaioanou M, Malison M, Wilkins K, et al. Strengthening capacity in developing countries for evidence-based public health: the data for decision-making project. *Soc Sci Med.* 2003;57:1925–1937.
124. Linkov F, LaPorte R, Lovalekar M, Dodani S. Web quality control for lectures: supercourse and Amazon.com. *Croat Med J.* 2005;46:875–878.
125. Brownson RC, Ballew P, Brown KL, et al. The effect of disseminating evidence-based interventions that promote physical activity to health departments. *Am J Public Health.* 2007;97:1900–1907.
126. Proctor EK. Leverage points for the implementation of evidence-based practice. *Brief Treat Crisis Interv.* 2004;4:227–242.
127. Chambers LW. The new public health: do local public health agencies need a booster (or organizational "fix") to combat the diseases of disarray? *Can J Public Health.* 1992;83:326–328.
128. Bryan RL, Kreuter MW, Brownson RC. Integrating adult learning principles into training for public health practice. *Health Promot Pract.* 2009;10(4):557–563.
129. Institute of Medicine. *Who Will Keep the Public Healthy? Educating Public Health Professionals for the 21st Century.* Washington, DC: National Academies Press; 2003.

130. Koo D, Birkhead GS, Reingold AL. Competency-based epidemiologic training in public health practice. *Public Health Rep.* 2008;123(Suppl 1):1–3.
131. Centers for Disease Control and Prevention. *CDC Taskforce on Public Health Workforce Development.* Atlanta, GA: Centers for Disease Control and Prevention; 1999.
132. Brownson R, Ballew P, Kittur N, et al. Developing competencies for training practitioners in evidence-based cancer control. *J Cancer Educ.* 2009; In press.
133. Tilson HH. Public health accreditation: progress on national accountability. *Annu Rev Public Health.* 2008;29:xv–xxii.
134. Ezzati M, Friedman AB, Kulkarni SC, Murray CJ. The reversal of fortunes: trends in county mortality and cross-county mortality disparities in the United States. *PLoS Med.* 2008;5:e66.
135. Shaya FT, Gu A, Saunders E. Addressing cardiovascular disparities through community interventions. *Ethn Dis.* 2006;16:138–144.
136. Subramanian SV, Belli P, Kawachi I. The macroeconomic determinants of health. *Annu Rev Public Health.* 2002;23:287–302.
137. Masi CM, Blackman DJ, Peek ME. Interventions to enhance breast cancer screening, diagnosis, and treatment among racial and ethnic minority women. *Med Care Res Rev.* 2007;64:195S–242S.
138. Peek ME, Cargill A, Huang ES. Diabetes health disparities: a systematic review of health care interventions. *Med Care Res Rev.* 2007;64:101S–156S.
139. Brownson RC, Haire-Joshu D, Luke DA. Shaping the context of health: a review of environmental and policy approaches in the prevention of chronic diseases. *Annu Rev Public Health.* 2006;27:341–370.
140. Mokdad AH, Marks JS, Stroup DF, Gerberding JL. Actual causes of death in the United States, 2000. *JAMA.* 2004;291:1238–1245.

CHAPTER 11

Public Health and Medical Education in the United States

Rika Maeshiro, MD, MPH

In spite of the progress of public health work the medical schools have too generally neglected or slighted the preventive side of medicine. This has had an unfortunate result. The average physician fails to see as clearly as he should that he is a vital part of the public health organization, that he is expected to discover and to report communicable diseases, to instruct his patients, to support the local authorities, to help create sound public opinion.[1]

—George E. Vincent (President, Rockefeller Foundation, 1917–1929)

HISTORICAL BACKGROUND

The challenge of incorporating public health content into the standard medical curriculum is not new. Not surprisingly, the roots of this struggle are entwined with the historical events and trends that led to the separation, or "schism" [2] as some have described, between the practice of medicine and the practice of public health in the United States. While in the mid to late 19th century some medical schools included public health in the curriculum,[3] during the first half of the 20th century trends in science, the professionalization of the medical and public health fields, and competition between private physicians and providers at public health clinics contributed to the separation of medicine and public health. Historians have described these events of the early 20th century from the "medical side" and the "public health side" of this division. Specifically, Elizabeth Fee, Roy Acheson, et al. considered the evolution of public health education as it became distinct from medical education,[4] and Kerr White reviewed how medical schools came to deemphasize epidemiology, the social sciences, and quantitative methods.[2] Both accounts reveal how some leaders of that era had concerns about distancing public health from medical training, and both considered two public health infrastructure issues that continue to be of concern. One concern relates to medical training—for example, during their training, physicians are not assured an adequate foundation in public health knowledge and skills that would facilitate collaborations with public health colleagues and solutions to societal health needs. Another relates to the inadequate numbers of physicians who choose public health as their career choice. According to White, until the late 19th century, most leaders in academic medicine embraced the care of individual patients and concern for unacceptable environmental and social conditions that endangered the public's health. In the late 1800s, physicians who had studied in Germany and Austria influenced medical education in the United States. German and Austrian medical school curricula had begun to reflect the experiences of academic, hospital-based consultants (rather than those of community-based practitioners) and the research interests of professors (rather than the health issues of the community). Theodor Billroth, a prominent Austrian surgeon of the time, documented the evolution of medical education in German-speaking countries in his 1875 publication, *The Medical Sciences in the German Universities: A Study in the History of Civilizations*, and included his critique of public health in his work:

The physician, as one of the most important members of the community, is expected not only to help in cases of individual sickness, but in community diseases as well. He is even expected to do his part in curing the stupidity and indifference of humanity. . . . The fanatical champions of public health are fighting for a goal that is too high for my myopic vision. I can admire the struggle, but I cannot become interested in it.[5]

The changing teaching priorities in Europe and the United States were driven in part by scientific discoveries, particularly in bacteriology, leading to what White describes as the "Big bug hunt": "The unquestioned message, that for each disease there was a single cause and that for most known diseases there was probably a single microbe, changed the focus of medical education, research, and practice."[2] Some described this focus as a "reductionist" [2, 3] perspective in medicine, in contrast to the broader concerns of population health and public health.

Breakthroughs in science influenced the recommendations of Abraham Flexner, author of the seminal 1910 report, *Medical Education in the United States and Canada: A Report to the Carnegie Foundation for the Advancement of Teaching*.[6] Flexner's report promoted reforms to improve medical education. He recommended that medical education be rooted in up-to-date science and be based on clinical experiences. After visiting all of the medical schools, he recommended that many close because of inadequate facilities, resources, and teaching. Because his 1910 report is associated with what evolved into the traditional medical education model (two years of basic sciences, followed by clinical experiences), and because the changes in medical education prompted by his report contributed to an inadequate number of physicians opting for public health careers, it can be perceived, perhaps mistakenly, as promoting a non-public-health orientation to medical education. In fact, the report included public health themes (for example, the training, quality, and quantity of physicians should meet the health needs of the public; physicians have societal obligations to prevent disease and promote health, and medical training should include the breadth of knowledge necessary to meet these obligations; and collaborations between academic medicine and public health communities should result in benefits to both parties).[7] As such, the report did not totally divorce public health missions from the responsibility of physicians. Flexner saw advancements in science as a basis for moving medicine toward disease prevention and a population perspective:

For scientific progress has greatly modified his ethical responsibility. His relation was formerly to his patient—at most to his patient's family; and it was almost altogether remedial. . . . But the physician's function is fast becoming social and preventive, rather than individual and curative. . . . To the intelligent and conscientious physician, a typhoid patient is not only a case, but a warning: his office it is equally to heal the sick and to protect the well.[6]

At the turn of the 20th century, the number of U.S. medical schools was declining primarily because of changes in state licensing requirements for physicians. Because longer training periods were mandated (during which no income could be earned), fewer students enrolled in medical school, and schools, particularly marginal ones, were going out of business even before the release of Flexner's findings.[8] Those that remained tended not to adopt a public health or population health perspective. Medical education reforms stemming from the 1910 report also led to a decline in the number of practicing physicians and an increase in their incomes,[9] a scenario that did not encourage many doctors to choose public health (and its lower income) as the focus of their careers.[10] Sir James Mackenzie, a Scottish cardiologist, visited U.S. medical schools in 1918, and upon visiting Johns Hopkins, felt that while their research was advancing insights into disease mechanisms, their faculty was not attuned to the needs of their patient population.[2]

Concerned that insufficient numbers of "sanitary workers" were produced through the existing education programs [3] (including postgraduate courses at medical schools [11]), the Rockefeller Foundation began to consider the training of public health workers during the second decade of the 20th century. The foundation asked Abraham Flexner, who had continued his work on medical education reform after his 1910 report, to look for a site to train health officers.[2] His recommendations led to the 1916 decision to establish schools of public health as distinct entities separate from schools of medicine. Johns Hopkins was selected as the endowed institution. Nevertheless, the discussions that led to these decisions reveal a lack of consensus regarding the separation of medical and public health training. Dr. William Welch, the dean of the Johns Hopkins School of Medicine (and future founding dean of the Johns Hopkins School of Public Health and Hygiene) and co-author of the Welch-Rose report that helped to establish schools of public health, originally had envisioned the teaching of hygiene and public health to occur within a department of the medical school, but he was not supported by his medical school faculty.[2, 8] Wickliffe Rose, the organizer of the Rockefeller Foundation's campaign against hookworm and the other co-author or the Welch-Rose report, had always preferred a national system of public health training that was separated from medical training. The Welch-Rose report was the seminal justification and blueprint for schools of public health in the United States. Its recommendations were the essential starting point for planning the future of public health and the training of its practitioners. The report called for collaboration with medical schools and hospitals to share resources, development of a method to encourage public health education for medical students and physicians ("It is of the utmost importance that education in the principles of hygiene should be available for students and graduates in medicine who are to engage in the practice of their profession."), and a grounding in basic biomedical and clinical sciences for public health students.[12] Many physicians continued to be unsupportive and suspicious of public health at this time. The prevailing belief was that efforts to control infectious diseases could pit health officers against private practitioners,[9] and the establishment of public health clinics could threaten the income of private physicians.[13]

Furthermore, the experts who developed the model for the first schools of public health had debated whether public health education should be limited to those who already had completed medical training. However, the appreciation for the multidisciplinary expertise that was required in public health and the acknowledgment that physicians were not flocking to public health practice prompted the new schools of public health to accept applicants from a variety of backgrounds (for example, engineers, statisticians, biologists), and sought to develop a discipline distinct from medicine.[10] Nonetheless, close ties were encouraged with schools of medicine primarily on the assumption that public health students would utilize medical school facilities to receive required education in "disease" and that conversely, schools of medicine would be the public health school would be "imbued with the spirit of public health."[9]

In the 1920s and 1930s, those involved in public health education continued to hope that schools of public health would promulgate "the spirit of preventive medicine" in medical schools, but the technological advances in medical diagnosis and treatment, and the new federal and state support for public health programs facilitated their separated existence.[9] Preventive medicine was taught in medical schools, but these departments typically were small and comparatively weak. In the 1930s and 1940s, preventive medicine become identified with "socialized medicine" ("social medicine" was the British term for "preventive medicine" [2]), a somewhat pejorative term and perceived as a potential economic threat to the profession. Medical schools were "more willing to express vague support for the concept of preventive medicine than to provide active advocacy or strong financial commitment to the idea."[9] More medical educators began to share and publish their concerns about improving public health education for physicians.[14] The 49th Annual Meeting of the Association of American Medical Colleges (AAMC) in October 1938, for example, featured at least four speakers who addressed the need to improve preventive medicine education in medical school.[15–18] In 1939, the AAMC appointed a Committee on the Teaching of Preventive Medicine and Public Health to design an education program in preventive medicine and public health for undergraduate medical students. During the 1944 Annual Meeting, the Committee presented its final recommendations, which addressed the organizational structure of medical schools, the curriculum, and the AAMC. Each school was to establish a Department of Preventive Medicine and Public Health, led by a full-time director, and supported by 5 to 8 percent of the medical school budget. Four percent of the total curricular time (initiated no later than the second year of medical school, and continued in each year thereafter) was to be devoted to preventive medicine and public health, and integrated into clinical teaching. The report also suggested that the preventive medicine curricula include content that would be identified in

21st-century terminology as applied biostatistics, the epidemiology and natural history of disease, the social and environmental determinants of health, and disease prevention.[18] AAMC was to support the creation of fellowships in preventive medicine and public health. None of the recommendations appear to have been applied universally.[2]

In 1949, Thomas McKeown, a British professor of social medicine, addressed the First World Conference on Medical Education and commented that medical education in Great Britain and the United States was "in danger of losing sight of the continuing importance of prevention of disease" and that the instruction provided in preventive medicine "was divorced from clinical training" and was thought to make "little impression on the student,"[2] observations that would resonate into the 21st century.

For medical educators in preventive medicine and public health, the 1940s through the 1980s were marked by expansions in scope, and related opportunities and concerns. Many departments of preventive medicine (or hygiene or public health) that had not been converted to a school of public health, merged with bacteriology departments. These departments frequently became the home for new topics that were not directly the responsibility of clinicians (for example, nutrition, environmental exposures, injury, disease screening), and they could be given responsibilities for tuberculosis, sexually transmitted infections, substance abuse, and mental illness. Later, related subjects such as health services research, planning, and evaluation and medical sociology were added to the scope, resulting in what has been described as departments of "miscellaneous medicine."[2] The Conference of Professors of Preventive Medicine (renamed the Association of Teachers of Preventive Medicine in 1953, and renamed again in the early 21st century as the Association for Prevention Teaching and Research) was established in 1942, stemming from the American Public Health Association's (APHA) subcommittee on education and medical students.[19] Members of the original group were "health officers, directors of student health services, statisticians, pathologists, bacteriologists, practitioners, and deans" who were interested in teaching public health to medical students. They agreed to meet regularly at APHA meetings and shared short presentations on public health topics. This group's meetings and activities over the ensuing four decades reflected the broad concerns of preventive medicine departments, shifting attention from quantitative skills, to clinical prevention, health services research, and health policy. Despite these efforts to enhance the public health education of physicians, and increased medical interest in the quantitative aspects of public health to meet biomedical research needs during the 1970s and 1980s,[20] U.S. educators in public health and preventive medicine approached the end of the 20th century with many of the same concerns that had been raised in the late 1930s.[18]

CONTEMPORARY PUBLIC HEALTH CHALLENGES AND IMPLICATIONS FOR MEDICAL EDUCATION

The end of the 20th century and the dawn of the 21st century found the United States confronting challenges to health and security that continued to fuel calls to improve physicians' knowledge of public health. Chronic disease prevention, health disparities, disaster preparedness and response, and health systems reform are a sample of the issues that require improved collaborations between medicine and public health.[21, 22, 23] In 1994, the American Medical Association (AMA) and the APHA embarked on the Medicine and Public Health Initiative to catalyze more effective partnerships between medicine and public health. The initiative's agenda was far-reaching, trying to address medicine and public health collaborations in communities, education, research, and health care. A 1997 publication highlighted effective examples of medicine–public health collaborations, including those in education,[24] and a second publication in 1998 [25] provided a fuller listing of case studies in medicine–public health partnerships that had been collected through the initiative. Cases listed under "Synergy 6b" focus on education and training that promote the linkages between medicine and public health.

Concerned experts in medicine and public health gathered and published a number of reports that addressed the need to better educate physicians about public health, identifying the barriers to effective education in this area and the scope of public health that should be incorporated in the medical curricula, including "The Medical School's Mission and the Population's Health" (1992),[26] "Education for More Synergistic Practice of Medicine and Public Health" (1999),[27] and "Contemporary Issues in Medicine—Medical informatics and population health: Report II of the Medical School Objectives Project" (1999).[28]

Participants at the December 1990 conference sponsored by The Royal Society of Medicine Foundation, Inc. and the Josiah Macy Jr. Foundation that resulted in "The Medical School's Mission and the Population's Health" believed that redefining the mission of medical schools would be necessary to fully embrace the public health perspective into medical education.[29] Medical schools and their faculty were directed to be "thoroughly familiar" with the distribution of health issues in populations, particularly in their institution's service area,[30] and all medical students, not just those with interest in public health, were to receive basic education in the population perspective.[31] The Josiah Macy Foundation sponsored another conference on this topic in June 1998.[27] Participants in this conference recommended flexible approaches to encouraging synergy between medical and public health schools. Specific suggestions included restructuring grand rounds to incorporate the behavioral, social, and environment determinants of the patients' problems (along with the usual assessment of the biological determinants, diagnosis, and treatment) and the development of continuing education programs on clinically relevant public health topics so that faculty would be better role models for their trainees. Epidemiology, biostatistics, health policy, and prevention were identified as the recommended public health content for medical students. The barriers to improved synergy included financial incentives that emphasized treatment and did not recognize prevention efforts, and distrust between the two disciplines.

The AAMC's "Medical School Objectives Project Report" in 1999 identified three major barriers to the improved teaching of population health: the lack of a consistent medical school department "owning" the scope of the content; lack of funding to support population health curriculum development and teaching; and the view within the academic medical community that the interest in population health was primarily a response to managed care. The experts who contributed to this report believed that public concern over the health care system and public expectations that physicians are trained to meet the health needs of the public, combined with students' expectations to be better educated in public health, and influences from the managed care movement, would help overcome these obstacles.[28]

Although not focused solely on physician training, the Institute of Medicine's (IOM) report on the public health workforce, *Who Will Keep the Public Healthy?*[32] recommended that "all medical students receive *basic* public health training in the population-based prevention approaches to health" and that "a significant proportion of medical school graduates should be *fully* trained in the ecological approach to public health at the master's of public health (MPH) level. A second report issued by the IOM in the 1990s, *Training Physicians for Public Health Careers*,[33] focused on preparing physicians who specialize in public health, but declared that all physicians "intersect with public health in many activities of their practice" and "are part of the public health system." This report divided physicians into three groups:

"All physicians"; i.e., those who can help detect and respond to epidemics, exposures, and other threats; who rely on public health guidance on topics such as international travel, immunizations, and other preventive services; and who can serve as leaders in emergency response, health promotion, tobacco control, nutrition, and other health promotion and health protection activities.
"Physicians in practices or specialties with public health needs"; i.e., infectious disease specialists investigating health-care-associated outbreaks, or pediatricians working in school health, or emergency physicians directing Emergency Medical Services.
"Public health physicians"; i.e., those who have chosen public health as their specialty and practice.

Because all medical students will become physicians practicing in at least one of these three categories, the authors reiterated the earlier IOM recommendations regarding medical education and added additional topics to the list recommended for all medical students. In particular, medical school graduates should be able to demonstrate population health competencies in the following areas:

- Assess the health status of populations using available data (for example, public health surveillance data, vital statistics, registries, surveys, electronic health records, and health plan claims data);
- Understand the role of socioeconomic, environmental, cultural, and other population-level determinants of health on the health status and health care of individuals and populations;
- Integrate emerging information on individuals' biologic and genetic risk with population-level factors when deciding on prevention and treatment options;
- Appraise the quality of the evidence of peer reviewed medical and public health literature and its implications at patient and population levels;
- Apply primary and secondary prevention strategies that improve the health of individuals and populations;
- Identify community assets and resources to improve the health of individuals and populations;
- Explain how community-engagement strategies may be used to improve the health of communities and to contribute to the reduction of health disparities;
- Participate in population health improvement strategies such as community-based interventions;

- Discuss the functions of public health systems;
- Understand the organization and financing of the U.S. health care system and effects on access, utilization, and quality of care for individuals and populations;
- Discuss the ethical implications of health care resource allocation and emerging technologies on population health; and
- Understand quality improvement methods to improve medical care and population health.

Recognizing that medical education begins with medical school, but continues through internships and residencies (graduate medical education, GME) and continuing medical education (CME), the contributors to this report addressed the continuum of medical education. The report recommended that national organizations representing medical education, public health education, and public health and preventive medicine practitioners collaborate to develop models for integrating training in public health principles and practice into physician education at both the undergraduate and graduate levels. GME programs were directed to identify and include public health concepts and skills relevant to the practice of that specialty. Medical specialty societies were urged to provide CME and self-assessment opportunities to address the elements of public health that are included in the practice of their specialty. The report also recommended that periodic recertification examinations include these elements. To help ensure the quality of these education efforts and identify potential role models, medical schools and GME programs were advised to include faculty who were trained and experienced in public health.

The Healthy People Curriculum Task Force's Clinical Prevention and Population Health Curriculum Framework [34] presented a listing of population health and clinical prevention topics that should be included in the education of all health professionals. The framework was developed by educators in medicine, nursing, pharmacy, dentistry, and physician assistant training in response to the Healthy People 2010 Objective 1-7: "Increase the proportion of schools of medicine, schools of nursing and health professional training schools whose basic curriculum for healthcare providers includes the core competencies in health promotion and disease prevention." The curriculum framework is based on the previous "[i]nventory of knowledge and skills relating to disease prevention and health promotion."[35] Although the Healthy People Objective calls for public health competencies, the interprofessional task force agreed that competency statements would be profession-specific and thus chose to identify broad topics, leaving the depth and breadth of teaching in each area to the professions.

CONTEMPORARY MEDICAL SCHOOL CURRICULA AND PUBLIC HEALTH

Incentives for curricular change in medical schools include accreditation standards, student demand, and the content of national certifying examinations. Recent trends show that these factors may be aligning to facilitate a greater emphasis on public and population health. The Liaison Committee on Medical Education (LCME) is the national accrediting authority for medical education programs at medical doctorate–granting schools in the United States and Canada, and is responsible for establishing their accreditation standards. Accreditation is a process of quality assurance in postsecondary education that determines whether an institution or program meets established standards for function, structure, and performance. The accreditation process also fosters institutional and program improvement. As of October 2009, the accreditation standards include general language regarding the inclusion of "preventive medicine" in the medical school curricula. Standard ED-11 states that "[the curriculum] must include the contemporary content of those disciplines that have been traditionally titled anatomy, biochemistry, genetics, physiology, microbiology and immunology, pathology, pharmacology and therapeutics, and preventive medicine."[36] In late 2009, the LCME released proposed revisions to Standards ED-11 and ED-15 that would include "the public health sciences" in the annotations for the proposed new structure of the standards. The potential changes were discussed during the February 2010 meeting of the LCME.

The Commission on Osteopathic College Accreditation is responsible for establishing accreditation standards for osteopathic doctorate–granting medical schools. Accreditation standards for osteopathic schools identify both preventive medicine and public health in their guidance for medical school curricula.[37] Standard 6.1 states:

The education should at least include, but not be limited to . . . principles, history and practice of osteopathic medicine, human anatomy, biochemistry, pharmacology, genetics, physiology, pathology, microbiology, physical and differential diagnosis, medical ethics and legal aspects of medicine; internal medicine, family medicine, pediatrics, geriatrics, obstetrics and gynecology, preventive medicine and public health, psychiatry, surgery, radiology.

In addition, public health is included in a discussion of Core Competencies, with Standard 6.5.1 stating a demonstration of "knowledge of professional, ethical, legal, practice management, and public health issues applicable to medical practice."[37]

Because medical schools do not share one standard data system by which curricular content can be tracked across all schools, assessing the inclusion of public health topics in current medical school curricula is imperfect. Some public health topics are included in the curriculum questions of the LCME Annual Medical School Survey, Part II.[38] Although the quality of the curriculum data is limited by its reliance on self-reporting, the survey enjoys a 100 percent response rate, and thus provides a general view of trends. Beginning in 1979, community preventive medicine, environmental health hazards, health care delivery, medical jurisprudence, nutrition, patient education, and population dynamic were among the topics included in a new question that inquired about the inclusion of subjects within the medical curriculum. The number of public health topics and the wording of the curriculum questions have changed over the years but reflect a continued interest in these issues by the LCME. In the 2008 survey, some 41 topics associated with public health were included. Over the years, great strides have been made in the inclusion of some of these topics (for example, prevention and health maintenance), but others, such as occupational medicine and health policy, remain relatively underrepresented.

Another barometer of the inclusion of public health in the medical school curriculum is reflected in the AAMC's Graduation Questionnaire, an annual survey of graduating fourth-year medical students.[39] A portion of this survey asks students about their perception of the time devoted to particular topics during medical school. The question asks "Do you believe that your instruction in the following areas was inadequate, appropriate, or excessive?" Between 2006 and 2008, more than 40 percent of respondents felt that their instruction time in occupational medicine was inadequate, and more than 45 percent felt that their instruction time in health policy was inadequate, mirroring the results of the LCME survey.

The United States Medical Licensing Examination™ (USMLE™) program is the licensure examination for graduates of LCME-accredited, doctorate-granting medical schools. The examination includes three "steps," and successful completion is intended to provide state licensing authorities evidence that the graduate has the minimum knowledge and skills required for initial licensure. Advocates of improving public health content in medical school education have been concerned that the USMLE does not include sufficient or appropriate public health content. A comprehensive review of the USMLE began in 2004.[40] The proposed changes to the examinations include efforts to assess skill in accessing relevant information, evaluating its quality, and applying it appropriately in a clinical scenario,[41] a potential opportunity to improve the quantitative public health content (biostatistics, epidemiology) of the examinations. Medical school faculty experts in public health have been invited to participate in the redesign process, providing additional opportunities to increase and improve the USMLE's public health content.

Barriers to the Effective Integration of Public Health into the Medical Curricula

Many of the obstacles to the inclusion of public health content into the medical curricula have been persistent over the years:

- Confusion about what is included public health: Within the medical community and the general public, the scope of public health can be misconstrued as medical care for the underserved or limited to services provided by government public health units. Medical school faculty and administrators who have an inaccurate or incomplete understanding of the breadth of public health may have difficulty implementing and assessing the public health content in their curricula.
- Varying terminology: Beginning in the 19th century, "public health" referred to the health of the public in broad terms, without a necessary connection to medical practice. "Sanitary reform," "sanitary engineering," and "sanitary science" are terms that are not in wide use in the 21st century, but in the 19th century, they were associated with efforts to clean up industrial environments, water, food, and city streets. "Hygiene" became associated with the German emphasis on research at the same time that "public health" reflected the British emphasis on the administrative, or practice, perspective of public health.[9] "Public health medicine," "preventive medicine," "social medicine," and "community medicine" were terms that were created to acknowledge the medical contributions to public health.[10] "Preventive medicine" is a centuries-old term that was often synonymous with public health until the 20th century when it became more closely identified with clinical preventive medicine. "Community medicine" is a 20th-century term that in the United States implies a special focus on the community aspects of health and health care delivery. In the late 20th century, "population health" became a popular term, particularly in the academic community.[42]
- Student disinterest: A 1920 survey by E. O. Jordan [43] revealed attitudes of medical students that still resonate: Insufficient knowledge of the field, lack of patient contact,

politics, lower salary, and dislike of working within a bureaucracy were reasons medical students were not interested in working in public health. Some students felt that public health was a legitimate choice for physicians ("Public health is at present a branch science of medicine."), whereas others reflected a disregard for public health ("The medical profession does not itself take public health and preventive medicine seriously.").

- Lack of role models and faculty: Medical students may not interact with public health physicians while in medical school,[44] and public health content may be taught primarily by nonphysicians, who may not effectively present the relationships between public health and clinical care.[2] Although the number of full-time faculty with MPH and other public health–related degrees grew between 1990 and 1998, a significant number of schools had few faculty with formal public health training—57 of the 125 schools, at the time of the study, had fewer than 10 faculty members with MPH degrees.[45]
- Lack of curricular time: The 1944 Final Report on the Teaching of Preventive Medicine and Public Health found that "[f]acing an already overcrowded and not entirely elastic curriculum, proponents of preventive medicine and public health have been forced to insinuate these subjects into the teaching schedule in an opportunistic rather than a systematic manner."[18] This statement continues to be true and encourages creative approaches to incorporating public health content into existing learning opportunities, rather than the creation of new courses.

Innovations in Public Health Education at Medical Schools

To respond to the need for the effective and engaging integration of public health content into the medical curricula, educators at schools across the country have developed creative curricular innovations that emphasize the clinical relevance of public health topics, engage experiential learning techniques, and involve public health partners. The innovations include introducing public health concepts during the first sessions in medical school,[46] population health case studies that incorporate local health data,[47] population health projects,[48] hospital policy projects,[49] required public health or community health clerkships,[50, 51] partnerships with academic health departments,[52, 53, 54] mock health policy hearings,[55] pandemic exercises,[56] population health "ward rounds" and grand rounds, and "community windshield tours" that have students tour the regions from which their patients come to better understand social and environmental determinants of health and to appreciate the community-based services that are available.[7]

National programs also have addressed this need through competitive grants programs to schools. The Health of the Public: Academic Challenge program was launched in 1986 to challenge academic health centers to broaden their missions to address health needs of their surrounding communities.[57] Thirty-four academic health centers were involved over 11 years with funding provide by the Pew, Rockefeller, and Robert Wood Johnson Foundations. Seven program objectives guided the projects, addressing health professions education, research, and the academic health center's interactions with their community:

- Provide basic competencies in population-based subjects, including epidemiology and preventive medicine, to all health professions students
- Provide enhanced population-based education for selected students
- Include clinical prevention knowledge and skill-building activities at all levels of health professions education

- Conduct substantive scholarly studies in subjects related to population-based medicine
- Assume institutional responsibility for maximizing the health of a defined population within available resources
- Involve the academic health center in decision making about the development and deployment of health resources
- Involve the academic health center in the social-political process as an advocate of the health of the public

Some courses and programs that were developed through this program still exist, including the MD-MPH program at Tufts and the public health course at the University of Kansas.

"Undergraduate Medical Education for the 21st Century: A Demonstration of Curriculum Innovations to Keep Pace with a Changing Health Care Environment" (UME-21) was sponsored by Health Resources Services Administration from 1997 to 2002 to support curriculum development at 18 schools to work with partners to improve medical student education in light of "new health systems," including the introduction of managed care.[58, 59] Curricular innovations were to be focused on nine content areas (that is, health systems finance, economics, organization, and delivery; evidence-based medicine; communication skills; ethics; informatics; leadership; quality measurement and improvement; systems-based care; and wellness and prevention). This initiative was unique because of the participation of more than 50 external partners, including managed care organizations, health plans, community health centers, and local health departments.

The cooperative agreement between the Centers for Disease Control and Prevention (CDC) and AAMC resulted in a national effort, the Regional Medicine-Public Health Education Centers,[60] to improve public and population health education for medical students, and later for residents. Sixteen medical schools have received funding through the cooperative agreement to enhance their public health curriculum for all of their medical students, and to achieve these improvements through partnerships with public health colleagues. At a minimum, these public health partners were to partner with their local or state health agencies. In addition to implementing the kind of curricular innovations described previously, the grantees worked with representatives from AAMC and CDC to develop "Population Health Competencies" for medical students.[7] Prior recommendations regarding relevant public health topics were transformed into competency (or learning objective) statements that facilitate curricular needs assessments and student evaluations.

An alternate approach to integrating public health content into medical education is MD-MPH programs, in which medical students can pursue their MPH degree while in medical school.[61–65] In response to student interest, the number of medical schools that offer MD-MPH opportunities has increased through the end of the end of the 20th century and into the early 21st century.[66] The MPH is offered through either a school of public health or a graduate program in public health. Although a few programs manage to schedule the dual training into four years, most programs require five years for completion.

GRADUATE MEDICAL EDUCATION AND PUBLIC HEALTH

Whereas medical school is an opportunity to introduce all medical students to the foundations of public health, residency curricula provide an important opportunity to demonstrate how public health can be integrated into specialty-specific practice, as noted in the 2007 IOM report.[33] GME, internship, and residency training that lasts three to eight years, is required after medical school to complete specialty training. Because medical school graduates no longer enter practice directly from medical school, GME has been identified as the phase of medical education that will affect how physicians will practice medicine.[67] The Accreditation Council for Graduate Medical Education (ACGME) accredits training programs that follow the MD degree. The ACGME has residency review committees (RRCs) for each of 26 specialties. RRCs are responsible for identifying program requirements for each specialty, and evaluating programs against those requirements.

In 2007, the ACGME identified six common program requirements that are to be applied across all specialty programs: patient care, medical knowledge, practice-based learning and improvement, interpersonal and communication skills, professionalism, and systems-based practice. The common program requirements and the specialty-specific program requirements affect five specialties (emergency medicine, family medicine, obstetrics, pediatrics, and psychiatry) that reflect public health content. Across these specialties, the program-specific public health requirements fell into the patient care, medical knowledge, and systems-based practice categories.[68] Family medicine and pediatric requirements reflect a comprehensive approach to identifying and integrating clinically relevant public health content. To address the need to improve public health education in medical education across all specialties, the Regional Medicine-Public Health Education Centers Initiative, supported by AAMC and CDC, was expanded to include GME in 2007. A competitive process resulted in 13 funded sites that represented a full spectrum of specialties, including emergency, family, and internal medicine, obstetrics, pediatrics, psychiatry, and surgery.[69]

THE SPECIALTY OF PREVENTIVE MEDICINE

Preventive medicine is the medical specialty with expertise in public health. Efforts to establish medical specialty board certification in preventive medicine and public health began in the mid-1940s. Representatives from the APHA, the AMA, the Canadian Public Health Association, the Southern Medical Association, and the Association of Schools of Public Health helped plan the establishment of the American Board of Preventive Medicine and Public Health, which was incorporated in 1948. The Health Officers section of the APHA felt that specialty board certification would better prepare health officers for their responsibilities.[70]

In 2007, 79 ACGME-accredited preventive medicine programs were available in the United States. Preventive medicine residencies are based in medical schools, schools of public health, hospitals, and health departments. The U.S. Army, Navy, Air Force, and CDC also offer preventive medicine residencies.[33] Current requirements for residency training include a minimum of one year of clinical training in an ACGME-accredited residency, followed by an academic year leading to an MPH or its equivalent, and a practicum requirement year. Most preventive medicine residencies do not offer the first year of clinical training, and approximately one-third of entering preventive medicine residents have completed a previous residency program. Three subspecialties include Preventive Medicine: Public Health/General Preventive Medicine (PH/GPM), Occupational Medicine, and Aerospace Medicine. PH/GPM is the specialty that is most closely associated with public health. The practicum year requirements vary by subspecialty, and PH/GPM requires a practicum experience at a public health agency for at least one month. The medical knowledge content areas for PH/GPM include: health services administration, public health practice, and managerial medicine; environmental health; biostatistics; epidemiology; and clinical preventive medicine.[71]

Preventive medicine residencies do not typically receive Medicare GME assistance, unlike most residency programs, because much of the training occurs in non-hospital settings. Consequently, many programs struggle to arrange for funding to support their residents, combining support from state and local health agencies, community health organizations, the Department of Veterans Affairs, and limited Title VII funds from the Health Resources and Services Administration.[33] As a result of these funding difficulties, some preventive medicine residency programs have been closed. The IOM report *Training Physicians for Public Health Careers* recommended strengthening the capacity of preventive medicine residency programs. The IOM suggested that federal graduate medical education funds that are not linked to clinical care support the expansion of existing PH/GPM residency programs and the creation of new programs to graduate a minimum of 400 graduates per year.

CONCLUSION

Unfortunately, the theme to improve physicians' understanding of public health is not new in medical education. Multiple generations of physicians, medical educators, and public health practitioners have voiced their concerns about how the promises of medicine, no matter how technologically sophisticated, would not be achieved without better integrated clinical care and public health systems. Foundations, medical specialty societies, and government agencies have supported a series of studies and initiatives to foster an improved appreciation for public health in all physicians (a theme that was ironically included in two historic reports—one that provided the framework for contemporary medical education and one that established public health schools separate from schools of medicine). The escalating investment in medical care, and the occasionally dubious health status indicators that are achieved fuel these concerns, along with predictions of decreased life expectancy for future generations, continued health disparities, and the threat of natural and man-made public health disasters.

The early 21st century does give cause for some optimism. The framework in which medical education exists (for example, accreditation criteria for both medical school and residency training, national examination content) appears to be acknowledging the need for physicians to have a population perspective. As reflected in the demand for MD-MPH opportunities and in student surveys, medical students are seeking public health education. The biomedical research enterprise also appears to be appreciating the need for "implementational" sciences and "translational" research, as illustrated by the National Institutes of Health's Clinical and Translational Science Awards. Much like the 1970s and 1980s, research needs may help the medical community embrace the public health sciences. In addition to the calls from special interests within the medical and public health communities, communities that are concerned about their health and health care may accelerate the decades-old efforts to heal this schism. In conclusion, "Whoever wishes to investigate medicine properly [must consider] . . . the effects of the winds, . . . waters, . . . city, . . . ground, . . . [and] the mode in which [people] live.[72]

REFERENCES

1. Vincent GE. Rockefeller Foundation President's Review: Rockefeller Foundation annual report for 1924: 27–28. http://www.archive.org/details/reportro1924rock-uoft. Accessed January 30, 2010.
2. White KL. *Healing the Schism: Epidemiology, Medicine, and the Public's Health.* New York: Springer-Verlag; 1991.
3. Viseltear AJ. The emergence of pioneering public health education programs in the United States. In: Fee E, Acheson RM, eds. *A History of Education in Public Health: Health that Mocks the Doctors' Rules.* Oxford, UK: Oxford University Press; 1991:145.
4. Fee E, Acheson RM, eds. *A History of Education in Public Health: Health that Mocks the Doctors' Rules.* Oxford, UK: Oxford University Press; 1991.
5. Billroth T. *The Medical Sciences in the German Universities: A Study in the History of Civilization.* Welch WH, trans. New York: Macmillan; 1924.
6. Flexner A. *Medical Education in the United States and Canada: A Report to the Carnegie Foundation for the Advancement of Teaching.* Boston, MA: Updyke; 1910. Carnegie Foundation Bulletin No.4.
7. Maeshiro R, Johnson I, Koo D, et al. Medical education for a healthier population: reflections on the Flexner Report from a public health perspective. *Acad Med.* 2010;85(2):211–219.
8. Starr P. *The Social Transformation of American Medicine: The Rise of a Sovereign Profession and the Making of a Vast Industry.* New York: Basic Books; 1982.
9. Fee E. Designing schools of public health for the United States. In: Fee E, Acheson RM, eds. *A History of Education in Public Health: Health that Mocks the Doctors' Rules.* Oxford, UK: Oxford University Press; 1991.
10. Fee E, Porter D. Public health, preventive medicine, and professionalization: Britain and the United States in the nineteenth century. In: Fee E, Acheson RM, eds. *A History of Education in Public Health: Health that Mocks the Doctors' Rules.* Oxford, UK: Oxford University Press; 1991.
11. Ruis AR, Golden RN. The schism between medical and public health education: a historical perspective. *Acad Med.* 2008;83(12):1153–1157.
12. Welch WH, Rose W. Institute of hygiene: being a report by Dr. William H. Welch and Wickliffe Rose to the General Education Board Rockefeller Foundation, 1915. In: Delta Omega Honorary Public Health Society, ed. *The Welch-Rose Report: A Public Health Classic.* http://www.deltaomega.org/WelchRose.pdf. Updated 1991. Accessed February 6, 2010.

13. Brandt A, Gadrner M. Antagonism and accommodation: interpreting the relationship between public health and medicine in the United States during the 20th century. *Am J Public Health.* 2000;90(5):707–715.
14. FitzGerald JG. The place of preventive medicine in the medical curriculum. *J Assoc Am Med Coll.* 1939;14:16–20.
15. Leathers WS. The integration of the teaching of preventive and clinical medicine. *J Assoc Am Med Coll.* 1939;14:21–25.
16. Russell FF. The place of preventive medicine in the medical curriculum. *J Assoc Am Med Coll.* 1939;14:26–30.
17. Mustard HS. Utilizing of health districts in the teaching of preventive medicine to medical students. *J Assoc Am Med Coll.* 1939;14:31–36.
18. Final report of the Committee on the Teaching of Preventive Medicine and Public Health. *J Assoc Am Med Coll.* 1945;20:152.
19. Barker WH, Jonas S. The teaching of preventive medicine in American medical schools, 1940–1980. *Prev Med.* 1981;10:674–688.
20. Brandt A. Collaboration and competition: tracing the historical relationship of medicine and public health in the 20th century. In: Hager M., ed. *Education for More Synergistic Practice of Medicine and Public Health.* New York: Josiah Macy, Jr. Foundation; 1999.
21. Beitsch LM, Brooks RG, Glasser JH, et al. The Medicine and Public Health Initiative: ten years later. *Am J Prev Med.* 2005;29:149–153.
22. Davis RM. Marriage counseling for medicine and public health: strengthening the bond between these two health sectors. *Am J Prev Med.* 2005;29(2):154–157.
23. McGinnis JM. Can public health and medicine partner in the public interest? *Health Aff.* 2006;25(4):1044–1052.
24. Lasker R. *Medicine and Public Health: The Power of Collaboration.* New York: New York Academy of Medicine; 1997.
25. Lasker RD, Abramson DM, Freedman GR. *Pocket Guide to Cases of Medicine and Public Health Collaboration.* New York: New York Academy of Medicine, 1998.
26. White KL, Connelly JE, eds. *The Medical School's Mission and the Population's Health.* New York: Springer-Verlag; 1992.
27. Hager M, ed. *Education for More Synergistic Practice of Medicine and Public Health.* New York: Josiah Macy, Jr., Foundation; 1999.
28. Contemporary issues in medicine: medical informatics and population health: report II of the Medical School Objectives Project. *Acad Med.* 1999;74:130–141.
29. White KL, Connelly JE. Redefining the Mission of Medical School. In: White KL, Connelly JE, eds. *The Medical School's Mission and the Population's Health.* New York: Springer-Verlag; 1992.
30. Marmot MG, Zwi AB. Measuring the burden of illness in general populations. In: White KL, Connelly JE, eds. *The Medical School's Mission and the Population's Health.* New York: Springer-Verlag; 1992.
31. Black D. Discussion. In: White KL, Connelly JE, eds. *The Medical School's Mission and the Population's Health.* New York: Springer-Verlag; 1992.
32. Gebbie K, Rosenstock L, Hernandez LM, eds. *Who Will Keep the Public Healthy? Educating Public Health Professionals for the 21st Century.* Washington, DC: National Academies Press; 2003.
33. Hernandez LM, Munthali AW, eds. *Training Physicians for Public Health Careers.* Washington, DC: National Academies Press; 2007.
34. Allan J, Barwick TA, Cashman S, et al. Clinical prevention and population health: curriculum framework for health professions. *Am J Prev Med.* 2004;27:471–476.

35. Wallace RB, Wiese WH, Lawrence RS, et al. Inventory of knowledge and skills relating to disease prevention and health promotion. *Am J Prev Med*. 1990; 6:51–56.
36. Liaison Committee on Medical Education. Functions and structure of a medical school. http://www.lcme.org/functions2008jun.pdf. Published 2008. Accessed October 19, 2009.
37. Commission on Osteopathic College Accreditation. Accreditation of colleges of osteopathic medicine: COM Accreditation Standards and Procedures (effective July 1, 2009). http://www.osteopathic.org/pdf/SB03-Standards%20of%20Accreditation%20July%202009.pdf. Accessed October 26, 2009.
38. Liaison Committee on Medical Education. Part II: annual medical school questionnaire. http://www.lcme.org/qunaires.htm. Accessed October 23, 2009.
39. Association of American Medical Colleges. 2008 medical school graduation questionnaire: final all schools summary report. http://www.aamc.org/data/gq/allschoolsreports/2008_pe.pdf. Accessed September 13, 2009.
40. US Medical Licensing Examination. Comprehensive Review of USMLE:CRU. http://www.usmle.org/General_Information/CRU/index.html. Accessed February 1, 2010.
41. Committee to Evaluate the USMLE Program. Comprehensive Review of USMLE. http://www.usmle.org/General_Information/CEUP-Summary-Report-June2008.PDF. Accessed October 19, 2009.
42. Tricco AC, Runnels, V, Sampson M, et. al. Shifts in the use of population health, health promotion, and public health: a bibliometric analysis. *Can J Public Health*. 2008;99:466–471.
43. US Public Health Service. *The Future of Public Health in the United States and the Education of Sanitarians*. Washington, DC: Government Printing Office; 1922. Public Health Bulletin. No.124:19–21.
44. Coker RE Jr, Kosa J, Back KW. Medical students' attitudes toward public health. *Milbank Mem Fund Q*. 1996;44(2):155–180.
45. Dismuke SE, Sherman L. Identifying population health faculty in US medical schools. *Am J Prev Med*. 2001;20(2):113–117.
46. Ornt DB, Aron DC, King NB, et al. Population medicine in a curricular revision at case western reserve. *Acad Med*. 2008;83(4):327–331.
47. Kekering KW, Novick LN. An enhancement strategy for integration of population health into medical school curriculum: employing the framework developed by the Healthy People Curriculum Task Force. *Acad Med*. 2008;83(4):345–351.
48. Chamberlain LJ, Wang E, Ho ET, et al. Integrating collaborative population health projects into a medical student curriculum at Stanford. *Acad Med*. 2008;83(4): 338–344.
49. Jacobsohn V, DeArman M, Moran P. Changing hospital policy from the wards: an introduction to health policy education. *Acad Med*. 2008;83(4):352–356.
50. Finkel ML, Fein O. Teaching about the changing US health care system: an innovative clerkship. *Acad Med*. 2004;79(2):179–182.
51. McIntosh S, Block RC, Kapsak G, Pearson TA. Training medical students in community health: a novel required fourth-year clerkship at the University of Rochester. *Acad Med*. 2008;83(4):357–364.
52. Keck CW. Health department-medical school collaboration. In: Hager M., ed. *Education for More Synergistic Practice of Medicine and Public Health*. New York: Josiah Macy, Jr., Foundation; 1999.
53. Novick LF, Greene C, Vogt RL. Teaching medical students epidemiology: utilizing a state health department. *Public Health Rep*. 1985;100(4):401–405.

54. Melville SK, Coghlin J, Chen DW, Sampson N. Population-based medical education: linkages between schools of medicine and public health agencies. *Acad Med.* 1996;71(12):1350–1352.
55. Blumenthal DS. Improving community health through 'hands on' approach. *Natl AHEC Bull.* 2003;20(1):22–23.
56. Finkelstein JA, McMahon GT, Peters A, et. al. Teaching population health as a basic science at Harvard Medical School. *Acad Med.* 2008;83(4):332–337.
57. Edelman N, Guttman N. Evaluation of health of the public: an academic challenge. http://www.rwjf.org/pr/product.jsp?id=17974. Accessed October 19, 2009.
58. Pascoe JM, Babbott D, Pye KL, et al. The UME-21 Project: connecting medical education and medical practice. *Fam Med.* 2004;36(Suppl):S12–S14.
59. Mahoney JE, Cox M, Gwyther RE, et al. Evidence-based and population-based medicine: national implementation under the UME-21 Project. *Fam Med.* 2004; 36(Suppl):S31–S35.
60. Maeshiro R. Public health practice and academic medicine promising partnerships: regional medicine public health education centers—two cycles. *J Public Health Manage Pract.* 2006;12(5):493–495.
61. Chauvin SW, Roedenhauser P, Bowdish BE, Shenoi S. Double duty: students' perception of Tulane's MD-MPH Dual Degree Program. *Teach Learn Med.* 2000; 12(4):221–230.
62. Boyer MH. A decade's experience at Tufts with a four-year combined curriculum in medicine and public health. *Acad Med.* 1997;72(4):269–275.
63. Stellman JM, Cohen S, Rosenfield A. Evaluation of a one-year masters of public health program for medical students between their third and fourth years. *Acad Med.* 2008;83(4):365–370.
64. Harris R, Kinsinger LS, Tolleson-Rinehart S, Viera AJ, Dent G. The MD-MPH Program at the University of North Carolina at Chapel Hill. *Acad Med.* 2008; 83(4):371–377.
65. Smith SR. Perceptions of the MD-MPH Option at Brown. *Acad Med.* 1996;71(10): 1024–1025.
66. Maeshiro R. MD-MPH opportunities at US medical schools: Poster presented at Association of American Medical Colleges Annual Meeting; April 30, 2004; Boston, MA.
67. Whitcomb ME. Flexner redux 2010: *graduate* medical education in the United States. *Acad Med.* 2009;84:1476–1478.
68. Accreditation Council for Graduate Medical Education. Common program requirements: general competencies. http://www.acgme.org/outcome/comp/GeneralCompetencies Standards21307.pdf. Accessed January 30, 2010.
69. Association of American Medical Colleges. Regional medicine-public health education centers: GME. http://www.aamc.org/members/cdc/rmphec/rmphecgme_detail.htm. Accessed February 7, 2010.
70. Ring AR. History of the American Board of Preventive Medicine. *Am J Prev Med.* 2002;22(4):296–319.
71. Accreditation Council for Graduate Medical Education. ACGME program requirements for graduate medical education in preventive medicine, 2007. http://www.acgme.org/acWebsite/downloads/RRC_progReq/380pr07012007.pdf. Accessed on February 1, 2010.
72. Hippocrates. *On Airs, Waters, and Places.* Adams F, trans. The Internet Classics Archive by Daniel C. Stevenson, Web Atomics. http://classics.mit.edu/Hippocrates/airwatpl.mb.txt. Accessed January 31, 2010.

SECTION 5

ASSURING THE HEALTH OF THE PUBLIC: PUBLIC HEALTH CHALLENGES IN THE 21ST CENTURY

CHAPTER 12

The Stem Cell Controversy: Navigating a Sea of Ethics, Politics, and Science

Ryan Cauley, MD

Sitting in the far corner of Dr. Shahin Raffi's lab at Weill-Cornell Medical College's Institute of Regenerative Medicine is a beating heart. Not a whole heart, but a piece of living heart tissue that has been produced from human embryonic stem cells. Dr. Raffi created the cells by introducing them to a series of growth factors typically present when the fetal heart develops in the womb. The heart tissue lies in a Petri dish and contracts between 60 and 70 beats per minute—normal for human cardiac tissue.

Roughly two blocks away, in New York Presbyterian Hospital's Cardiac Intensive Care Unit lies Mr. Smith, a recent recipient of a quadruple coronary bypass surgery. Severe heart disease runs in Mr. Smith's family, and despite trying to maintain a healthy diet, he has had three heart attacks in the past three years. Each heart attack has caused irreversible damage to his cardiac tissue, drastically increasing his risk for subsequent attacks and eventual death from heart disease. He now becomes so fatigued from simply walking across the room, that he tends to sit most of the time. Having exhausted all other reasonable options, a heart transplant is his only hope of living a normal life. At any given time, more than 2,500 patients are on the national heart transplant list. Of those, slightly over half will receive a new heart.[1] More than 450 of these patients will die waiting.

Few areas of biomedical science have aroused as much controversy as embryonic stem cell research. Since the derivation of the first human embryonic stem cells in 1998, the issue has been at the forefront of scientific, ethical, and political debates. Stem cells appear to offer unprecedented opportunities for developing new medical therapies for many debilitating diseases and a new way to explore fundamental questions of biology. In many ways, stem cell therapies may be the only foreseeable hope to many individuals who suffer from a variety of diseases for which there is currently no cure or effective treatment. Despite the great

---

This chapter was originally printed as Cauley, R. "The Stem Cell Controversy: Navigating a Sea of Ethics, Politics, and Science" in Finkel, M.L. *Truth, Lies, and Public Health*. Westport, CT: Praeger Publishers, 2007. Reprinted with permission.

aspirations of stem cell proponents, Dr. Raffi would be the first to admit that his heart cells are not yet ready for implantation in humans. After all, there are inherent risks in transplanting cardiac tissue derived from stem cells in someone's heart; but with more research, the future may be very bright.

With the global economy now faltering, the financial industry, politicians, physicians, and scientists envision tremendous economic benefits of a burgeoning stem cell industry. Individuals with incurable diseases envision the medical miracles that possibly could cure a multitude of diseases. Nevertheless, opponents of stem cell research still speak of the immorality of utilizing human cells, even for potential medical cures. While it would be ideal to have a rational and coherent national dialogue about this complex and controversial issue, radical viewpoints on both sides of have made it difficult to reach a compromise regarding a way forward for stem cell research.

This chapter focuses on the stem cell debate and addresses the issue from a medical, ethical, and political perspective. How close are we to curing diseases using stem cells? What are the ethical and moral issues involved in researching these cures? What political issues have arisen over the funding of stem research and how has this affected its progress? But firstly, what are stem cells anyway?

WHAT ARE STEM CELLS?

Most cells in humans are committed to becoming a single type of cell with a specific function within the body—that is, muscle cells, blood cells. In contrast, pluripotent stem cells are "uncommitted"—that is, able to become a number of different cell types, providing a number of different functions. Because pluripotent stem cells give rise to almost all of the cell types of the body, they hold great promise for both research and medical care. Pluripotent stem cells may serve as a source of generated cells and tissues for transplantation, potentially treating many diseases and conditions.

Each time these cells differentiate, they potentially can become fewer different types of cells. Stem cells that no longer can become every type of cell in the human body are called "multipotent" cells, loosely translating to "potentially many" (usually of a single cell class, like blood cells). For example, stem cells derived from adult bone marrow, where blood is made, only become blood cells, and not liver, heart or nerve cells.[2] Eventually each of the stem cells differentiates into "committed" cells. These committed cells sometimes can divide and produce copies of themselves, but they can never become any other type of cell.[3]

Although stem cells are present in the greatest quantities during human embryonic development, some stem cells still are maintained in the adult human body, albeit in very small quantities. It is thought that in most tissues these "adult stem cells" provide a source of new cells to replace those lost due to organ damage or natural cell death. These adult stem cells produce copies of themselves throughout the lifetime of the organism, providing a permanent source of cellular repair.[4] As such, adult stem cells may have limited potential compared to pluripotent stem cells derived from embryos or fetal tissue. While adult stem cells can be useful in certain therapies, it previously was thought that they may not be as potentially powerful as a truly "pluripotent" stem cell, which can become any other type of cell in the human body. Recently, however, scientists have discovered ways to "de-differentiate" or reprogram these adult cells, in an attempt to turn them back into pluripotent stem cells. By creating pluripotent cells from adult tissues, it may be possible to circumvent some of the ethical concerns of using stem cells strictly from embryonic sources. Researchers currently are studying whether or not these induced pluripotent stem cells truly are equivalent to the embryonic stem cell.

HISTORY OF STEM CELL RESEARCH

In 1953, almost by accident, research on stem cells began. While investigating the effects of cigarette papers and tobacco on laboratory mice, a young scientist named Leroy Stevens noticed a tumor in one of his lab mice. Strangely, this tumor seemed to be completely unrelated to the effects of the smoking trials. Located in the testicles of one of his adult male mice, the tumor was found to be a teratoma, or a mass of wrongly differentiated cells, containing bone, teeth, and hair. Dr. Stevens found that by injecting stem cells derived from the inner cell mass of embryonic mouse blastocysts into the testes of other mice, he could induce the formation of a teratoma. In a series of experiments, he proved that stem cells could both be derived from the embryo, and forced to differentiate when placed in a live organism.[5] A year later, in 1954, Dr. John Enders of Harvard University began to use stem cells derived from a fetal kidney to produce poliovirus. For this work, Dr. Enders later would be awarded the Nobel Prize in Medicine.

It was not until the late 1960s that the first medical therapies based on the use of stem cells became available. In 1968, several children with severe immune deficiency disorder (known commonly as the "bubble boy disorder," where no functional white blood cells are made) were successfully given bone marrow transplants. After the transplants, the children were found to be making new white blood cells, proving that the transplanted marrow both contained blood stem cells, and that these cells were capable of surviving and dividing in a new organism.[6]

In the 1970s and 1980s, embryonic stem cells derived from blastocysts were demonstrated to spontaneously give rise to a number of different cell types while allowing them to divide and replicate in a Petri dish. One of the most exciting discoveries related to stem cell research occurred in 1996 when scientists at the Roslin Institute in Scotland announced the birth of Dolly the Sheep, the first animal cloned from adult cells. To clone Dolly from her "mother," the scientists had taken skin cells from an adult sheep, extracted the genetic information and placed it into a fertilized sheep egg (with its genetic information already removed). This fertilized egg, now with Dolly's mother's genes, was then implanted in the womb of a surrogate sheep to be allowed to come to term. Several months later Dolly was born, and history was made.[7]

Researchers in the United States also were working in this nascent field. In 1998, two separate research teams led by Drs. James Thompson of the University of Wisconsin and John Gearhart of Johns Hopkins University developed the first embryonic stem cell lines. In both cases, the research was funded privately (no federal funds were used). Stem cell lines are stem cells that have been placed in a Petri dish and induced to replicate, producing a permanent source of identical stem cells. Dr. Thompson and his colleagues derived their cell line from cells taken from surplus embryos donated voluntarily by couples undergoing fertility treatment at an in vitro fertilization (IVF) clinic.[8, 9] Dr. Gearhart's cell line, from early, nonliving fetuses obtained from first trimester abortions, produced cells that could be replicated indefinitely and were shown to have the potential to grow into any tissue or organ in the body, thus holding great promise for treatment and cures. Before this time, animal embryos were the only source of embryonic stem cells.

In response to these ground-breaking studies, in 1999, the journal *Science*, in a special cover article and editorial, declared pluripotent stem cell research to be the scientific 'breakthrough' of the year.[10]

HOW ARE STEM CELL LINES MADE?

Stem cells can come from several different sources in the human body, specifically from adult organs and tissues, embryonic tissues, and most recently from umbilical cord blood, which possesses a high concentration of stem cells. Adult stem cells are taken from adult tissues, such as skin, the liver, and bone marrow rather than from embryos. As stem cells are present in greater quantities in adult bone marrow than in most other adult tissues, it is not surprising that marrow was one of the first places that adult stem cells were successfully harvested and used therapeutically.

Adult stem cells have been used therapeutically since the 1960s, when the first successful bone marrow transplants were performed. Yet stem cell lines are far more difficult to create and maintain when starting with adult stem cells. Adult stem cells can be made to divide and replicate in culture; however, scientists have found that they often cannot induce the cells to divide indefinitely. Adult cells lack a gene for "telomerase," an enzyme that allows for a cell to continue dividing. Without it, after a certain number of divisions, the cell lines simply will die.[11] Until quite recently, it had been thought that stem cells originating from adult organs could only become cells found in the organ from which the stem cell was taken. In other words, it was thought that stem cells in liver could only make liver cells, and stem cells found in the nervous system could only make nerve cells. Several experiments conducted over the past few years, however, have found that stem cells originating from one organ possibly can become cells of another organ type if encouraged in "the right way." For example, some researchers have shown that adult liver cells could be transformed relatively easily into insulin-producing pancreas cells.[12]

Embryonic tissues historically have been the most reliable source of stem cell lines. Pluripotent stem cells are found in great quantities in the human embryo. Embryonic stem cell lines can be derived from early embryos before they implant in the uterus. The greatest advantage of using embryonic stem cells is their "pluripotency," or ability to become any type of cell. A single stem cell line from an embryo therefore potentially could cure a larger range of diseases than a single adult stem cell line from an adult organ. With the recent advent of induced pluripotent stem cells, this may change. Currently, inducing adult tissues is so inefficient that it may not be ready for bedside therapy for quite some time. Although stem cell lines are difficult to create from induced adult stem cells, large numbers of embryonic stem cells can be grown relatively easily in culture. By placing the cells in Petri dishes with feeder cells (which help support the stem cells) and several chemical agents, embryonic stem cells will divide and flourish indefinitely. In fact, the first embryonic stem cell lines created during the late 1990s are healthy and continue to divide to this day.[4] With thousands of surplus embryos, the byproducts of IVF therapy, embryonic stem cells theoretically are readily available for research purposes.

Umbilical cord blood is a new and potentially exciting source of adult stem cells. The blood, which is now often collected from the umbilical cord after birth, is typically rich in several different types of adult stem cells (although the majority are blood stem cells). As the collection procedure is painless and quick, it is possible that this could be a major source of stem cells in the future. In fact, in 2003, Congress passed the Cord Blood Stem Cell Act to establish a national network to prepare, store, and distribute the cells. Just after this act was passed, nongovernmental organizations such as the National Bone Marrow Donation Center and the Red Cross also began to set up national cord blood banking programs to encourage the donation of cord blood and to take advantage of this rich source of cells.[5]

Inducing adult cells to become pluripotent stem cells always had been the goal of stem cell researchers hoping to avoid the ethical arguments over the use of embryonic stem cells. In a landmark study Takahashi and Yamanaka [13] found that by introducing several key genes into adult mouse cells they could create "induced pluripotent stem cells" (or iPS cells). As these iPS cells were created from adult cells, they immediately were hailed as a means of eliminating the use of embryos in stem cell therapy and research. With this possibility in mind, iPS cells quickly became a favorite of the conservative movement and opponents of embryonic stem cell research.[14] While iPS cells potentially could reduce the reliance on embryonic stem cells, the most important aspect of iPS cells is actually their possible ability to create cells for use in personalized or customized medicine. Until this time, the only means of creating cells that were identical to the patients they were meant to treat was through therapeutic cloning. By using "personalized stem cells" to cure disease, physicians could avoid the use of potentially toxic antirejection drugs.[15] For stem cell researchers, the development of personalized stem cell lines always has been the holy grail of stem cell treatment.

STEM CELL RESEARCH AND CLONING

One goal of stem cell research is to provide cells that could be implanted in humans to repair damaged organs and tissues. The range of diseases that could be helped by this type of therapy is tremendous. Many considerations need to be taken into account, however, when placing foreign material in any human being. First and foremost, there is the consideration of the possibility of rejection. The human body has an excellent immune system that is built to recognize foreign material. When a foreign organ is transplanted into an individual, the individual's immune system will work to attack and destroy the organ. For this reason, organs must be "matched" to their recipient to minimize the chance of rejection. Using a series of complex tests, doctors can tell the likelihood of a certain individual rejecting a given organ. Of course, except in the case of identical twins, no donor is going to completely genetically match a recipient. Therefore, doctors have discovered that by using a cocktail of medications they can suppress or "turn off" the immune system so that the transplanted organ can survive. As these types of immune suppression therapies can wreak havoc on an individual, leaving them more at risk of infection and some cancers, they are used only when absolutely necessary.

In stem cell therapies, a foreign body, albeit a much smaller one, is being transplanted into an individual. If the stem cell line is not a complete genetic match for the recipient, there will be an immune response that will reject the foreign stem cells. It is therefore of utmost importance to either (1) have stem cells that will be a complete genetic match for the recipient, or (2) have a sufficient number of unique stem cell lines available that a near perfect match can be made. In this vein, scientists have begun to conceive of ways to produce stem cell lines that satisfy these criteria. One possibility for creating genetically identical stem cells is therapeutic cloning.

Cloning is a time-intensive and expensive process. Theoretically, only one human egg is required to create each new stem cell line. However, therapeutic cloning is actually quite a bit more difficult than this implies. Using current techniques, only 1 percent of eggs that have been injected with new genetic information go on to become stem cell lines. This means that for each stem cell line that is created, more than 100 eggs will be needed. Each egg will need to be donated by women willing to undergo the painful procedure of egg harvesting. Although doctors are now making great strides in increasing the yield of stem cell lines from cloned eggs in mouse studies, much work still is being done to continue to improve the process.

Through the use of therapeutic cloning, it is possible to produce embryonic stem cell lines that are perfect genetic matches for patients. Reaching this goal would mean being one step closer to realizing the tremendous therapeutic potential that embryonic stem cells appear to offer for the future. The stakes are high and the pressure to be the first to produce stem cell lines by cloning cells can lead some to take irresponsive action. The biggest scandal to date occurred in South Korea.

Scientist Dr. Hwang Woo Suk and his colleagues of Seoul National University published a paper in the acclaimed journal *Science* in 2004 claiming to have produced stem cell lines by cloning cells derived from adult patients.[16] The researchers alleged that these cell lines were genetically identical to the patients from whom they were cloned, and therefore perfect for future stem cell therapy. Scientists around the globe became ecstatic, as their goal of using genetically identical stem cells for "personalized medicine" seemed closer than ever to being realized. Dr. Hwang's apparent accomplishments were received by the medical establishment as a harbinger of future success in embryonic stem cell research. His experiments were deemed to be proof of the success of stem cell research and were used to justify increases in state and private spending. But, in December 2005, Dr. Hwang admitted to falsifying his experimental records and abruptly resigned from his university post.[17] A panel of investigators found that Dr. Hwang's laboratory had no record of ever having successfully created a genetically identical stem cell line through the use of cloning.

Despite Dr. Hwang's unfortunate falsification of his records, many other stem cell researchers have pressed on in the quest to create human stem cells through the use of therapeutic cloning. The process of therapeutic cloning to create stem cell lines is still its infancy; thus far, no study has reported the successful creation of a stem cell line from an embryo derived through somatic cell nuclear transfer (SCNT) or therapeutic cloning.[18] However, a number of scientists have been able to use therapeutic cloning to create early human embryos.[19] Although none of these human embryos have been implanted in a human uterus to create a child, they appear able to progress though early stages of development. If these embryos could be developed further, they theoretically could become a source for embryonic stem cells that are identical to the donor of its genetic information.

INDUCED PLURIPOTENT STEM CELLS: THE FUTURE OF STEM CELL RESEARCH?

Since the discovery of pluripotent stem cells, the direction of stem cell research often has been dictated by political and ethical controversy. It is thought that with therapeutic cloning, stem cells could be created that are identical to the individuals they will be used to treat. When utilizing stem cells that are identical to the patient, it likely would not be necessary to give potentially dangerous drugs to suppress the immune system and avoid rejection. With many religious leaders opposed to the use of therapeutic cloning in the production of new stem cell lines, new ways of creating pluripotent stem cells for use in personalized medicine have been investigated.

In a landmark study in 2006, Takahashi and Yamanaka discovered a way of reprogramming adult cells to become iPS cells, effectively avoiding the arguments over the use of cloning or embryos to produce stem cells. To create these pluripotent stem cells, Takahashi and Yamanaka used four genes known to be critical in allowing pluripotent stem cells to divide indefinitely. By inserting these genes into the DNA of a type of adult mouse cell called a "fibroblast," these adult cells began to exhibit characteristics of pluripotent stem cells. These iPS cells were found to have the crucial ability to differentiate into other cell types, a feature unique to stem cells.[13] The cells expressed genes typically found only in pluripotent stem cells and even could contribute to development when they were injected into mouse embryos (as stem cells are typically able to do). For all intensive purposes, it appeared that these cells were pluripotent stem cells. Since these initial mouse studies, Takahashi, Yamanaka, and others have created induced pluripotent stem cells using adult cells from a human.[20]

In the ensuing years, a number of researchers began to find significant differences between these iPS cells and embryonic stem cells. One of the major sources of these differences is thought to be something known as "epigenetics." Epigenetics is a recent discovery in the field of cell biology. It always had been thought that all genetic information was determined by the sequence of genes in the DNA. However, researchers began to notice that some genes were turned "on" or "off" not only by other genes (such as gene sequences in the DNA known as "promoters" or "repressors"), but also by factors that occur after the DNA sequence was completed. It was found that DNA could be changed after it was made, allowing a cell to pass on genetic information that was not contained purely in the sequence of DNA (the precise order of bases that make up a gene). In fact, the term "epigenetics" literally means "outside of genetics." Cells that may appear to have the same gene sequence, and thus the same genetic information, may in fact have different sets of genes epigenetically turned on or off, effectively resulting in different cells.

For stem cells to replicate, they need to have certain specific genes turned "on." In the process of creating iPS cells, however, it is not known how the epigenetics of a cell are affected. Since the process of reprogramming described by Takahashi and Yamanaka involves only the introduction of new genes, it changes only the cells genetic sequence. Epigenetically, no changes are made. As genes can be turned off due to epigenetics, not reprogramming the cells epigenetically makes little sense. Without reprogramming all aspects of the cells genetic material, we never will be able to create cells that are truly identical to embryonic stem cells.

The successful formation of stem cell lines from iPS cells is startlingly low: 0.0006–3 percent,[21] versus 50–69 percent from early embryos.[22] This low rate of return makes it costly and difficult to reliably create stem cell lines from iPS cells. Currently, embryos remain a much more reliable and easier source of pluripotent stem cells. It has been found that epigenetics may be one reason that the reprogramming process is so inefficient. Clearly, embryonic stem cells are in a different epigenetic state than iPS cells, which largely possess the epigenetic state of an adult cell.[23] For this reason, many of the induced stem cells likely have many embryonic genes epigenetically "turned off." For these cells to successfully transform into stem cells, it is thought that random events causing epigenetic changes may be required to "turn on" the necessary genes. As these random events occur at a low rate, it becomes a long and arduous process to successfully create iPS cells.

Genes typically found in stem cells often are found in tumor cells. Some scientists have been concerned that the injection of tumor genes into normal cells may increase the likelihood that they could become cancerous. Recent studies have concentrated on reducing this risk by decreasing the number of cancer-related genes used to produce iPS cells. Researchers are continuing to find ways to reduce the risks of iPS cells so that they may be used safely in future therapies. Despite these worries, iPS cells remain one of the most likely sources of stem cells for use in personalized medicine, and an extremely important discovery in the field of stem cell research.[24]

THE POTENTIAL OF STEM CELL RESEARCH

Millions of people suffer from a wide range of diseases, many of which are either difficult to treat or are incurable with current medical therapies. The potential use of stem cell therapy to affect a cure, or ameliorate symptoms, is fueling research. It is hoped that with more focused studies, stem cell treatments will be found for a great number of diseases. One reason for hope is that a number of diseases already are being treated successfully with stem cell–based therapies. One of the best examples of this cell-based treatment is leukemia. A sometimes-devastating blood cancer, Leukemia often is treated through the use of radiation or chemotherapy, followed by bone marrow transplants. Research has shown that stem cells from cord blood are a viable alternative to bone marrow as a source of new blood stem cells. In fact, it recently was suggested that cord blood stem cells might not have to be as closely genetically matched to a recipient to avoid detection and rejection by the patient's immune system.[25] As cancer patients often do not have relatives that would be suitable genetic matches for bone marrow donation, cord blood from unrelated donors potentially could be a life-saving alternative. Since this discovery, transplants of stem cells from cord blood have begun to replace bone marrow transplants in the treatment for leukemia, often with great success.[26]

Recent animal trials have shown partially restored eyesight in mammals with macular degeneration, the most common cause of blindness in human beings (essentially due to older age).[27] Research is focusing on isolating adult stem cells from a blind individual and reimplanting these cells in a patient's retina. If successful, this technique could revolutionize the way physicians treat blindness. Much work still needs to be done, of course, to ensure that this kind of therapy will be feasible.

Spinal cord trauma always has been one of the most difficult injuries for physicians to treat. Unlike the cells of our skin, which can divide and replace themselves when the skin is cut or damaged, nerve cells normally are not capable of regeneration. For many years it was thought that spinal cord cells never would be capable of repair, leaving little hope for people with spinal cord injuries.

In 2009, the Geron Corporation became the first group to receive clearance from the Federal Drug Administration (FDA) for a human trial of embryonic stem (ES) cell therapy. The trial is a phase I multiphase study to assess the safety of ES cells in treating patients with new spinal cord injuries. At first, the study will use patients with spinal cord injuries to the thoracic spine that are between 7 and 14 days old. In the future they also will attempt to treat older injuries or those outside of the thoracic spine.

The repair of heart tissue often has been seen as a holy grail for cardiac researchers. Nearly 700,000 Americans died of heart disease in 2002, now the leading cause of death in the United States.[28] At present, it is impossible to completely reverse the heart damage that inevitably occurs during a myocardial infarction, the major cause of cardiac-related deaths. If heart tissue could be replaced or repaired, it would be possible to greatly reduce the catastrophic nature of this illness. As is the case with spinal cord damage, stem cells offer one of the most promising therapies for the repair of cardiac tissue. The current therapy for people with pacemaker damage is the implantation of an electronic pacemaker. As with any heart surgery, the implantation of an artificial pacemaker poses a considerable amount of risk to patients, and it can lead to many more cardiac complications than a natural pacemaker. If the heart's pacemaker could be repaired using ES cells, it is possible that the result would be far more stable and reliable than the current electronic therapies.

In another exciting study, researchers at Weill-Cornell Medical College and Memorial Sloane-Kettering Cancer Institute found that congenital heart defects could be repaired in utero using ES cells.[29, 30] Congenital heart defects can be highly lethal for newborns and often are difficult to surgically repair at birth. Amazingly, these researchers found that congenital heart defects could be partially repaired simply by injecting ES cells into the afflicted fetal mouse's mother. After being injected, the ES cells were found to secrete certain growth factors and chemical signals that caused the offspring's own heart cells to regenerate themselves.

Among those suffering from Parkinson's disease (PD), a neurodegenerative disorder primarily characterized by the loss of nerve cells within the brain that secrete the neurotransmitter dopamine, stem cell research is viewed as a mean of alleviating a host of symptoms, including tremors, muscle rigidity, and a general slowing of physical movement. This debilitating neurodegenerative disease affects more than 5.5 million Americans. ES cells have been viewed as being useful in treating those with Parkinson's disease. Currently, there are two main types of therapy: dopamine-boosting medication and deep brain stimulation. Medication, which had been the primary mode of therapy, mainly focuses on increasing the amount of dopamine in the brain.

The main dilemma in PD is the loss of dopamine secreting neurons; therefore, to treat PD, scientists must first be able to create these neurons from ES cells. Takagi et al., of Kyoto University in Japan, were the first to do so at the end of 2004. When these newly created dopamine-secreting neurons were implanted in monkeys with symptoms of Parkinson's disease, tremors were significantly reduced.[31]

Diabetes currently affects more than 16 million Americans. As obesity rates skyrocket in the United States, adult onset diabetes mellitus is increasingly prevalent.[32] Diabetes can lead to a host of problems throughout a person's life, including blindness, loss of limb function, heart disease, and kidney failure. Current diabetes therapies are based on the replacement of insulin through the use of pills or an injection, depending on how much insulin is needed. To match insulin dosage with blood glucose levels (which fluctuate throughout the day), diabetics often are required to test their glucose levels several times each day. The goal is to maintain this delicate balance of insulin and glucose to keep glucose levels as close to normal as possible. Stem cells are being considered as a means to help diabetics better regulate their insulin. As diabetes is the result of losing a single specific type of cell, stem cell therapy to replace this cell population is an optimal treatment. A number of different sources for insulin-producing cells exist.[33] Adult pancreatic stem cells were one of the first sources of cells capable of insulin replacement. However, these cells are in very low numbers within the pancreas, and they do not replicate once removed, making them a difficult source for therapy. Bone marrow stem cells sometimes can produce insulin, and some even will differentiate into fully fledged beta cells.[34, 35] Although they currently differentiate into beta cells very inefficiently, they may be a good source of cells if the right growth factors are identified. More research will need to be done to investigate their potential. In October 2005, three scientists at the University of Wisconsin announced that they had produced synthetic beta islet cells using embryonic stem cells in rats.[36] If human embryonic stem cells could be made to efficiently transform into beta cells capable of producing insulin, and responding to the level of sugar in the blood like real pancreatic beta cells, diabetes and all of its complications would be things of the past.

President Ronald Reagan's death from Alzheimer's disease triggered an outpouring of support for ES cell research. But, in contrast to Parkinson's disease, diabetes, and spinal injuries, Alzheimer's disease involves the loss of huge numbers and varieties of nerve cells in the brain. The complexity of the brain makes stem cells an unlikely therapy for this disease.

Despite the stunning advances in stem cell research, much more needs to be understood before individuals can maximally benefit from all of these potential stem cell therapies. Early research results are extremely promising, but ethical, political, and legal issues have clouded the debate. Detractors of ES cell research tend to play down the scientific merits of stem cell use and focus on the more difficult ethical and moral issues. The crux of the matter is that the extraction of human stem cells to create a stem cell line currently requires the destruction of a harvested embryo. The stem cell debate is now focused on the status of the embryo. Is it a living "human being"? Should embryos be destroyed for the sake of future advances in medical science?

CHALLENGES IN STEM CELL RESEARCH

Since the landmark study by Takahashi and Yamanaka in 2006, a second source of pluripotent stem cells has seemed within reach. The induction of pluripotent stem cells from harvested adult cells is an exciting alternative source of personalized stem cells to therapeutic cloning, a source that is fraught with potential ethical concerns. However, the insertion of genes into the adult cells to "reprogram" them back to pluripotency has caused some scientists to worry about an increased risk of cancer formation. The genes used to reprogram these cells are essentially "cancer genes," giving the cells the ability to copy themselves indefinitely. Without any form of regulation, this ability to replicate may cause the induced pluripotent stem cells to be even higher risk of causing teratoma or tumor formation than traditional pluripotent stem cells derived from embryos.[37] Researchers have now focused on eliminating the need to use cancer genes used in the reprogramming process. If a method can be found to induce pluripotency in adult cells without inserting potentially dangerous genes it would go a long way to ease fears of tumor formation.

Aside from the possible dangers of inducing disease through stem cell transplantation, there are a number of legal and regulatory factors that could prove difficult to overcome. As stem cells can be harvested from individuals, there is the very intriguing legal question of ownership. Who owns a stem cell? The scientist? The donor? The recipient? These are questions that have been dealt with for some time by sperm banks, organ donation, and egg surrogacy; however, they will arise again with the advent of human stem cell treatments.[37] Along with the question of ownership is the issue of privacy. Like other organ or tissue donations, a stem cell always can be traced back to an individual through the genetic code. For donors of embryos, bone marrow, or cord blood, it will be especially important to have protections in place to ensure that privacy is upheld. The federal government and the NIH currently are examining these issues.

ETHICAL ISSUES

The human embryonic stem cell debate is often framed as part of a larger discussion on the definition of human life and the role of medical science in maintaining it. The extraction of human embryonic stem cells to create a stem cell line currently requires the destruction of the harvested embryo. Although much research is being done on inducing adult cells to become pluripotent stem cells, the challenging nature of this process likely will ensure that embryos will be a major source of stem cell lines in the near future. As a result, the question of the embryo's moral status often is considered the most controversial question in the stem cell research debate. At the center of the dialogue is the question of an embryo's "personhood." Do embryonic stem cells represent a life? That is, are the pluripotent stem cells human and do they have the same rights as born humans? Are pluripotent embryonic stem cells morally protected entities or are they more like other disposable tissues gleaned from the human body?[38] In essence the debate focuses on when life begins, a question for which there is no easy answer.

A current method of avoiding this controversy has been to find ways to extract stem cells without harming or destroying a human embryo. It has been thought that by discovering benign harvesting techniques, stem cell research could be unhampered by the ethical and religious debates surrounding the question of the embryos personhood and human right to life.

Several new methods for producing embryonic stem cell lines have shown great promise. The use of Pre-implantation Genetic Diagnosis (PGD) for the harvesting of embryonic stem cells is a benign procedure that has been used by IVF clinics for many years to determine the genetic health of embryos before their implantation in the mother's uterus. By using this technique, IVF clinics can avoid using embryos that are predisposed to developing lethal genetic diseases such as Tay-Sachs, Huntington's, Muscular Dystrophy, and Cystic Fibrosis. Since two days after the meeting of the sperm and the egg an embryo consists of only eight cells, by using special techniques, it is possible to remove a single cell while allowing the remaining cells to develop into a human being.[22]

Alexander Meissner and Rudolf Jaenisch of the Whitehead Institute for Biomedical Research recently suggested another alternative for creating stem cell lines without causing the destruction of an embryo: Alternative Nuclear Transfer (ANT), which is designed to create a modified cell that is incapable of fully developing into a human individual.[39] Meissner and Jaenisch believe that if the cell cannot become a human, it cannot be considered to possess personhood.

The response to both of these alternative techniques has been highly varied. After the announcement of the new methods in the journal *Nature*, a spokesman from the U.S. Conference of Catholic Bishops stated that while the two reported techniques still raise some ethical questions, they do represent "a step in the right direction."[40] Some social conservative leaders, such as Rep. Roscoe G. Bartlett of Maryland, a self-described pro-life advocate, believe that "except for the small minority in the pro-life community that doesn't even support IVF therapy, [these techniques] circumvent all of the ethical arguments against stem cell research."[41] Other leaders, like Dr. John Shea, medical advisor to the Campaign for Life Coalition, came out against these techniques, saying that the PGD technique does not benefit the child and thus cannot be used without the child (embryo's) consent.[42] Similarly, Tony Perkins of the Family Research Council, wrote that "it is not clear what effect [PGD] would have on the children born after having had one of their cells removed."[43]

The debate will continue until the answers to a number of important questions can be found. What if stem cells could be produced without embryo loss? Would this then make a difference? As it happens, a small biotech company says that it has found a way to produce human embryonic stem cells without destroying an embryo.[44] Researchers at Advanced Cell Technology grew a colony of stem cells, leaving the embryo unharmed, from a single cell removed from an embryo that had only 8 to 10 cells. Presently, physicians routinely remove a cell from an eight-cell embryo to screen for chromosomal abnormalities before implantation. Hence, logic has it that deriving stem cells from this method adds no additional risk since a diagnostic screening procedure already relies on this technique.

Many questions need to be answered: Would this new technique satisfy those who believe that it is unethical to remove a cell purely for stem cell research? Would this technique satisfy those who believe that life is being destroyed? For those who believe that a single cell removed from an early embryo may have the potential to produce life, this new technique probably will not change their mind. For those who are proponents of stem cell research, what this newest development shows is that stem cells can be produced without destroying an embryo and does not destroy the potential for life.

THE POLITICS OF STEM CELL RESEARCH

With the inherent ethical and moral issues of stem cell research so difficult to resolve, the political debate over stem cell research has raged from its inception. At the end of the 1992 Presidential Campaign, Bill Clinton announced his intention to overturn the de facto prohibition of research on human embryos that had been put in place by President George H. W. Bush. On June 10, 1993, the newly elected President Clinton signed legislation authorizing the NIH to begin to conduct and fund human embryo research. But, worrying that federal funds could be abused for research on human cloning, he issued an executive order in 1994 to prohibit the creation of human embryos for research purposes. To many ethicists, scientists, and politicians, this executive order was deemed insufficient to make sure that the considerable funds of the NIH would not be misused. Therefore, in the summer of 1995, members of Congress decided to attach a rider to the Health and Human Services Appropriations Act that was used to fund the NIH each year. The "Dickey-Wicker amendment," as it became known, prohibited the NIH from using appropriated funds for the creation of human embryos for research purposes. The amendment defined a human embryo as being an organism capable of becoming a human being when implanted in a uterus.[45] Using this broad language, it initially was thought that the act prevented the use of federal funds for almost any research related to human embryonic stem cells.

In 1998, after the initial successes of the research groups from the University of Wisconsin and Johns Hopkins, the Clinton administration decided to reevaluate its position on the support of embryonic stem cell research. The NIH requested a legal opinion from the Department of Health and Human Services (DHHS) on whether federal funds could be made available to researchers working with the human ES cells produced by the groups of Wisconsin and Johns Hopkins. In January 1999, Harriet Rabb, the general counsel of DHHS, found that the Dickey-Wicker amendment could not apply to human embryonic stem cells. The Dickey-Wicker amendment officially defines a human embryo as being an *organism* capable of becoming a human being when implanted in a uterus. Because an ES cell cannot develop into a human being even when implanted in a uterus, Rabb determined that it could not be considered a human embryo. According to this logic, the DHHS maintained that despite the amendment, it could fund any research related to human ES cells, as long the cells *initially* were created with private funding.[3] That is, after careful consideration, DHHS concluded that because human pluripotent cells are not embryos, current federal law does not prohibit DHHS funds from being used for research utilizing these cells.

In April of 1999, NIH director Harold Varmus appointed an oversight committee to begin drafting guidelines and oversight for the federal funding of ES cell research. The working group included scientists, clinicians, ethicists, lawyers, patients, and patient advocates. By February 2000, more than 50,000 comments had been received by experts in fields as far ranging as medicine, philosophy, ethics, biology, and neuroscience. Finally, in summer 2000, NIH published the final set of guidelines, NIH Guidelines for Research Using Human Pluripotent Stem Cells, in the *Federal Register*, which became effective on August 25, 2000.[46] The purpose of the NIH Guidelines was to set forth procedures to help ensure that NIH-funded stem cell research was conducted in an ethical and legal manner. Among other stipulations, the guidelines prescribed that for studies using human pluripotent stem cells derived from human embryos, NIH funds may be used only if the cells were derived from frozen embryos that were created for the purpose of fertility treatment, were in excess of clinical need, and were obtained after the consent of the donating couple.

The Clinton administration's guidelines for stem cell research were actually relatively conservative in comparison to the policies of other developed countries. In accordance with the Dickey-Wicker amendment, which had been renewed on every DHHS appropriations bills since 1997, the guidelines only allowed federal funding for studies using stem cells derived from embryos created for the purposes of *in vitro* fertilization, and only if they were in excess of the clinical need for such embryos. In addition, it was decided that the NIH could not fund any research that actually involved the derivation or creation of ES cells, as this was explicitly barred by the Dickey-Wicker amendment.[47]

Furthermore, the Clinton administration decided to outlaw the use of NIH funds for research involving ES cells derived using therapeutic cloning (or SCNT), even if the actual derivation of the cells was performed with private funds.[48] SCNT is the most well-researched technique that potentially could create embryonic stem cells that are genetically identical to an individual. That is, the cloned cell is used to create a stem cell line (not to create a new human being) that would be a perfect genetic match for a patient. Stem cells that are created by this method would likely avoid immune rejection, the primary concern of tissue transplantation. Without the ability to use therapeutic cloning, scientists utilizing federal funding would not be able to participate in research related to the "personalized medicine" that had become the ultimate goal for many stem cell researchers.

With the new guidelines in place, the NIH began to accept grant applications from research projects using human ES cells. The first review of these grants was supposed to occur by April 2001, several months after the Clinton administration left office. In mid-April, however, the DHHS decided to postpone the meeting until the incoming Bush administration could review the department's policies. After several months of review, on August 9, 2001, President George W. Bush announced the first federal funding of human embryonic stem cell research. Funding, however, would be available only to researchers using the 78 human ES cell lines that had been created before that date. President Bush believed that the government could explore the promise and potential of stem cell research without crossing a fundamental moral line. Of the 78 cell lines that were originally eligible for federal funding, only 15 are currently available. The remainder of the eligible stem cell lines was either unavailable or unsuitable for research. With so few lines actually available, relatively few federal dollars actually have been spent on human stem cell research.

During the U.S. presidential election of 2008, stem cell research again rose to the forefront of national political debate. Both major party candidates for president, then Democratic senator Barack Obama and Republican senator John McCain, announced their strong support for increasing federal funding of embryonic stem cell research. Mr. Obama even declared that soon after assuming office he would repeal the Bush administration's 2001 executive order preventing the use of federal funds for research involving embryonic stem cell lines created after August 9, 2001.[49] Although neither candidate made explicit the degree to which they would increase funding, proponents of stem cell research were ecstatic to receive the support of both major party candidates.

In January 2009, upon the inauguration of Mr. Obama as president, supporters of stem cell research received a significant boost. On March 9, 2009, just weeks after he was sworn into office, he officially repealed the 2001 Bush executive order, laying the groundwork for federal funding of new embryonic stem cell lines. In the executive order, the president stated,

for the past eight years, the authority of the Department of Health and Human Services, including the National Institutes of Health (NIH), to fund and conduct human embryonic stem cell research has been limited by Presidential actions. The purpose of this order is to remove these limitations on scientific inquiry, to expand NIH support for the exploration of human stem cell research, and in so doing to enhance the contribution of America's scientists to important new discoveries and new therapies for the benefit of humankind.[50]

As of the writing of this chapter, Congress was just beginning to reexamine the issue of stem cell research. The Dickey-Wicker amendment, which bans the use of federal funds to create embryos for research purposes, is under examination. Rep. Diana DeGette (D-Col.), a staunch supporter of stem cell research, is planning on reintroducing the Castle-DeGette bill by the summer of 2009 to officially sanction the use of federal funds for embryonic stem cell research on stem cell lines created after 2001.[51] The broad language used by President Obama in his executive order has given the NIH the power to redefine the specific federal funding guidelines for stem cell research, effectively returning science to the scientists.

Since the election of Mr. Obama in November 2008, the scientific community has hoped for a major increase in the federal funding of stem cell research. The NIH budget for the fiscal years 2008 and 2009 was just over $29 billion. In 2008, stem cell research accounted for $938 million, but only $88 million was given to researchers working with human embryonic stem cell lines.[52] It is not yet clear how much the federal funding of stem research would change over the course of the year.

The Obama administration used broad language in its executive order calling for the use of federal funds for stem cell research, effectively allowing the NIH to determine the details of the new federal funding policy. The NIH was due to release new guidelines outlining these new funding policies in the summer of 2009. As of yet the U.S. Congress has not yet passed a bill to complement the strongly worded executive order released by the Obama administration in March 2009. The Dickey-Wicker amendment, which still outlaws the use of federal funds for embryos created solely for research purposes, may need to be repealed or amended in order for the NIH to legally fund some of the most promising stem cell research. Therapeutic cloning (SCNT), for example, in which the genetic material of an adult patient is injected into a human egg to create a personalized stem cell line, would not be legal under the Dickey-Wicker amendment.

Rep. Diana DeGette, one of the original sponsors of the pro stem cell research Castle-DeGette bill twice vetoed by former President Bush, stated that "in consultation with experts," the sponsors of a new bill "are reviewing past legislative efforts to assess what needs to be done [legislatively] going forward."[49] The congressional climate has changed dramatically since the original Castle-DeGette bill, with a great majority of congressional leaders now supporting the research. Currently, stem cell research proponents have high hopes that Congress will move swiftly to allow for significant funding increases in the year 2009. Whether or not the federal government will be able to support the use of therapeutic cloning, or even the creation of embryonic stem cell lines from embryos created specifically for research, remains a question. All 78 embryonic stem cell lines that currently are eligible for federal funding were created from excess embryos donated from in vitro fertilization clinics. Even with the new executive order, the only ES cell lines eligible for federal funding will continue to be those created from donated surplus IVF embryos. Without congressional action and a more permanent change in federal law, this would continue to be a significant limitation for researchers interested in creating personalized stem cell lines for therapeutic interventions free of immune rejection.

WHERE DO WE GO FROM HERE?

Few areas of biomedical science have aroused as much controversy as ES cell research. Since the derivation of the first human ES cells in 1998, the issue has been at the forefront of scientific, political, and ethical debate. Proponents tend to emphasize the considerable therapeutic potential of stem cell research while opponents speak of the immorality of using human cells for this purpose. Yet, to those individuals suffering from debilitating diseases for which stem cells may offer a cure, such as Parkinson's disease, diabetes, and spinal cord injuries, they view the use of ES cells as the best means to treat or even cure their illness.

Stem cell research involves such unprecedented opportunities to improve medical science that it is hard not to be overwhelmed by its sheer potential. The major legal, ethical, religious, and political hurdles continue to fuel the debate. Both proponents and opponents make cogent arguments for and against ES cell research. What is needed is a scientific resolution to the moral dilemmas, with input from both science and medical ethics. Yet, given the scope of the issue, it is unlikely that the issue will be resolved quickly, and the broader application of ES cell research to those who potentially could benefit is still a hope and a dream. Hopefully researchers will continue to discover new ways of creating and using stem cells, making their future even brighter.

REFERENCES

1. United Network of Organ Sharing. UNOS Scientific Registry. www.UNOS.org. Accessed May 29, 2009.
2. Prosper F, Verfaillie CM. Human pluripotent stem cells from bone marrow. In: Chiu A, Rao MS. *Human Embryonic Stem Cells*. Totowa, NJ: Humana Press; 2003: 89–112.
3. Fischbach GD, Fischbach RL. Stem cells: science, policy, and ethics. *J Clin Invest*. 2004;114:1364–1370.
4. Bongso A, Lee EH. Stem cells: their definition, classification, and sources. In: Bongso A, Lee EH, eds. *Stem Cells: From Bench to Bedside*. NJ: World Scientific; 2005: 1–13.

5. Parson A. Proteus effect: stem cells and their promise in medicine. Washington, DC: Joseph Henry Press; 2004.
6. Van Bekkum DW. Bone marrow transplantation. *Transplant Proc.* 1977;9:147–154.
7. Usdin S. Ethical issues associated with pluripotent stem cells. In: Chiu A, Rao MS, eds. *Human Embryonic Stem Cells.* Totowa, NJ: Humana Press; 2003:3–26.
8. Thompson JA, et al. Embryonic stem cell lines derived from human blastocysts. *Science.* 1998;282:1145–1147.
9. Shamblott MJ, et al. Derivation of pluripotent stem cells from cultured human primordial germ cells. *Proc Natl Acad Sci U S A.* 1998;95(23):13726–13731.
10. Breakthrough of the year. *Science.* 1999;286(5448):2221–2416.
11. Wilmut I, Paterson LA. Stem cells and cloning. In: Sell S, ed. *Stem Cells Handbook.* Totowa, NJ: Humana Press; 2004.
12. Horb ME, et al. Experimental conversion of liver to pancreas. *Curr Biol.* 2003;13:105–115.
13. Takahashi K, Yamanaka S. Induction of pluripotent stem cells from mouse embryonic and adult fibroblast cultures by defined factors. *Cell.* 2006;126:663–676.
14. Kastenberg, ZJ. and Odorico, JS. Alternative sources of pluripotency: science, ethics and stem cells. *Transplant Rev.* 2008;22:215–222.
15. Wilmut I. The first direct reprogramming of adult human fibroblasts. *Cell Stem Cell.* 2007;1:593–594.
16. Hwang SW, et al. Patient-specific embryonic stem cells derived from human SCNT blastocysts. *Science.* 2005;308(5729):1777–1783.
17. Cyranoski D. South Korean scandal rocks stem cell community. *Natl Med.* 2006;12:4.
18. Cervera RP, Stojkovic M. Commentary: somatic cell nuclear transfer: progress and promise. *Stem Cells.* 2008;26:494–495.
19. French AJ, et al. Development of human cloned blastocysts following somatic cell nuclear transfer with adult fibroblasts. *Stem Cells.* 2008;26:485–493.
20. Yu J, et al. Induced pluripotent stem cell lines derived from human somatic cells. *Science.* 2007;318:1917–1920.
21. Silva J, et al. Nanog promotes transfer of pluripotency after cell fusion. *Nature.* 2006;441:997–1001.
22. Chung Y, et al. Embryonic and extraembryonic stem cell lines derived from single mouse blastomeres. *Nature.* 2006;439:216–219.
23. Hochedlinger K, Plath K. Epigenetic reprogramming and induced pluripotency. *Development.* 2009;136:509–523.
24. Condic ML, Rao M. Regulatory issues for personalized pluripotent cells. *Stem Cells.* 2008;26:2753–2758.
25. O'Brien TA, et al. No longer a biological waste product: umbilical cord blood. *Med J Aust.* 2006;184:407–410.
26. Advani AS, Laughlin MJ. Umbilical cord blood transplantation for acute myeloid leukemia. *Curr Opin Hematol.* 2009;16:124–128.
27. Young MJ. Stem cells in the mammalian eye: a tool for retinal repair. *APMIS.* 2005;113:845–857.
28. Centers for Disease Control and Prevention. CDC Statistics. www.cdc.gov/nchs/fastats/lcod.htm. Published June 20, 2006.
29. Fraidenreich D, et al. Rescue of cardiac defects in id knockout embryos by injection of embryonic stem cells. *Science.* 2004;306(5694):247–252.
30. Fraidenreich D, Benezra R. Embryonic stem cells prevent developmental cardiac defects in mice. *Nature Clin Practice Cardiovasc Med.* 2006;3:S14–S17.
31. Takagi Y, et al. Dopaminergic neurons generated from monkey embryonic stem cells function in a Parkinson primate model. *J Clin Invest.* 2005;115:102–109.

32. Boyle JP, et al. Projection of diabetes burden through 2050. *Diabetes Care*. 2001; 24:1936–1940.
33. Jones PM, et al. Cell based treatments for diabetes. *Drug Discov Today*. 2008;13:888–893.
34. Tang DQ, et al. In vivo and in vitro characterization of insulin-producing cells obtained from murine bone marrow. *Diabetes*. 2004;53:1721–1732.
35. Karielli O, et al. Generation of insulin-producing cells from bone marrow mesenchymal stem cells by genetic manipulation. *Stem Cells*. 2007;25:2837–2844.
36. Wisconsin Technology Web site. http://www.wisctechnology.com/article.php?id-2340. Accessed July 6, 2006.
37. Ahrlund-Richter L, et al. Isolation and production of cells suitable for human therapy: challenges ahead. *Cell Stem Cell*. 2009;4:20–26.
38. Green RM. *The Human Embryo Research Debates: Bioethics in the Vortex of Controversy*. New York: Oxford University Press; 2001.
39. Meissner A, Jaenisch R. Generation of nuclear transfer-derived pluripotent ES cells from cloned cdx2-deficient blastocysts. *Nature*. 2006;439(7073):212–215.
40. Studies may calm stem cell qualms. Associated Press. October 16, 2005.
41. Wade N. Stem cells with ethics. *New York Times*. October 16, 2005.
42. Bush's stem cell policy received with mixed emotions. http://www.lifesite.net.
43. Perkins T. Embryonic stem cell studies raise questions, not cures. *Washington Update*. October 16, 2005.
44. Stem cell without embryo loss. *New York Times*. August 26, 2006: A35.
45. Bonnicksen AL. *Crafting a Cloning Policy: From Dolly to Stem Cells*. Washington DC: Georgetown University Press; 2002: 77–79.
46. National Institutes of Health. The need for guidelines to govern research using pluripotent stem cells. http://www.nih.gov/news/stemcell/index.htm.
47. Wertz DC. Embryo and stem cell research in the United States: history and politics. *Gene Therapy*. 2002;9:674–678.
48. Casell JH. Lengthening the stem: allowing federally funded researchers to derive human pluripotent stem cells from embryos. *Univ Mich J Law Reform*. 2001;34:547–572.
49. Holden C. A fresh start for embryonic stem cells. *Science*. 2008;322:1619.
50. Obama B. Presidential Executive Order: Removing barriers to responsible scientific research involving human stem cells. White House Press Release. March 9, 2009.
51. Holden C. For congress and NIH, Headaches ahead on stem cells. *Science*. 2009;323:1552–1553.
52. National Institutes of Health Research Portfolio Online Reporting Tool. Estimates of funding for various research, condition, and disease categories. http://www.HHS.gov. Published January 15, 2009.

CHAPTER 13

Application of Novel Analytical Tools in Global Disease Monitoring: Remote Sensing in Public Health Research and Practice

Jesse C. McEntee, MA, Denise Castronovo, MS, Jyotsna S. Jagai, MS, MPH, PhD, Kenneth K. H. Chui, MS, MPH, PhD, and Elena N. Naumova, PhD

INTRODUCTION

Epidemiological research typically aims to characterize disease occurrence in terms of geographic space, temporal pattern, and human behavior. Community-based or hospital-based biomonitoring that tracks these three dimensions of disease incidence require the power of sophisticated analytical tools to extract useful information from multisourced databases. Such tools may include statistical and mathematical modeling, simulation techniques, Geographic Information Systems (GIS), and dynamic mapping. They enhance traditional methods of epidemiologic investigations, allow effective use of emerging or underutilized data sources, and facilitate comprehensive approaches to data visualization across space and time. They help to better understand the causes of disease dynamics; combine traditional surveillance data, hospital records, and vital statistics with novel sources of data that describe environment, social infrastructure, and cultural background; and eventually track progress in alleviating disease risks and effects. During the past decade, public health professionals have accrued skill in informatics, modeling, mobile communication, and GIS analysis that can facilitate linking disease risk and environmental variables as well as enhance active disease control and prevention.

    This chapter provides an overview of a number of advanced computational and analytical techniques that open new opportunities to examine the role of environmental drivers and forecast disease transmission and manifestation. We review applications of various remote-sensing (RS) techniques and present the relatively nascent epidemiological applications of this technology. Although our review provides an in-depth examination of a number of remote sensing techniques for monitoring disease, we acknowledge that it is not a comprehensive review of *all* techniques in existence in the 21st century. The particular focus of this article is on remote sensing applications relating to satellite-retrieved data in order to answer research questions in the field of public health. We will first illustrate the utility of novel technologies, practical applications, and examples. Then we will delineate key principles in data acquisitions and analyses. Finally, we will highlight future directions for public health research.

WHAT IS REMOTE SENSING?

The American Society for Photogrammetry and Remote Sensing states that remote sensing techniques are used to gather and process information about an object without direct physical contact.[1] RS emerged in the 1960s and 1970s as a result of intensified wartime investment in aerial photo interpretation.[2] Before 1972, all remotely sensed images were either obtained from ground sensors or aerial cameras on planes. On July 23, 1972, the *Landsat 1* land-surface observation satellite system began recording Earth resource data, which changed everything.[1] Traditionally used to observe land cover information about objects and geographic areas on the Earth's surface by measuring electromagnetic energy emitted from these areas, RS increasingly has been used by geographers and epidemiologists to measure environmental variables that have direct pertinence to the spread of infectious disease. Using RS to predict epidemics of infectious disease has been shown to be cost-effective and helpful.[3, 4] The framework for utilizing remotely sensed data in epidemiology involves linking measures of radiation, typically obtained by satellite, to measures of the geographic distribution of a disease and its vector.[5]

On February 16, 2005, a global initiative was implemented in which 61 countries agreed to implement the Global Earth Observation System of Systems (GEOSS), which aims to bring together countries' global Earth Observation System (EOS) hardware and software to streamline format, ensure compatibility, and incorporate shared international resources, such as ocean buoys, satellites, and weather monitoring stations.[6] EOS data are used to measure characteristics of air, water, and land through the use of visible and nonvisible radiation. The GEOSS effort represents a heightened awareness of the potential value of remotely sensed imagery in a number of fields, such as the biological sciences, urban planning, and public health.

Remotely sensed imagery is obtained through measurement of reflectance. Depending on the wavelength that is measured, a number of precise data values can be obtained and inputted into computer algorithms that subsequently are used to measure land use values.[7] Spatial epidemiology aims to analyze the spatial distribution of disease data to identify risk populations and possible causal factors.[8] RS technology, for example, could serve to provide a more accurate identification of disease-carrying vector habitat.

Key Principles of Remote Sensing Data

Public health research and practice utilize a wide variety of health outcomes that originate from large data systems, including vital statistics records, hospitalization claims, local, regional, and national registry of diseases, diagnostic data repositories, and surveillance systems. Typically, each source has its own population coverage, timeliness, and ability to properly reflect disease presence (see figure 13.1). These important characteristics have to be taken into account when analyzed to detect systematic patterns and particular aberrations. Technological advancements in compiling and exchanging large volumes of data reveal new potential for

Measures of Health

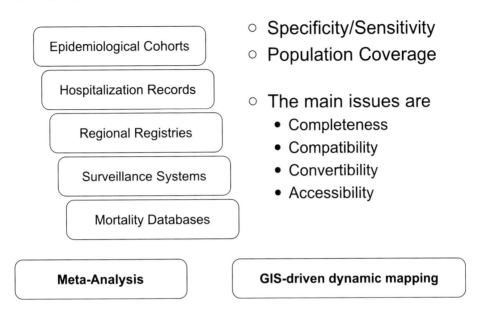

Figure 13.1 Measures of Health.

knowledge mining and retrieval.[9] This process also reveals the need for better understanding of limitations and requirements for a new generation of disease-tracking systems.

Worldwide disease tracking systems historically are supported by a network of hospitals, outpatient clinics, and diagnostic facilities and are operated in cooperation with local and regional public health institutions. Overall, the established infrastructure facilitates consistent improvement of data quality, essential for reliable disease monitoring. The major data sources that form the basis for many national surveillance systems strive to ensure a complete and comprehensive coverage of a population.

The most recent lessons of remote-sensing data (RSD) utilization in public health practice and research can be summarized as following. Initially, *conceptual support* is needed for a study, followed by *compatibility* of health outcome measures and exposure measures derived from RS. Ideally, there should be complete uninterrupted temporal overlap in health and exposure data. Such temporal *completeness* expands the array of applicable analytical techniques; many statistical methods for time-series data have serious limitation if there are gaps in the time-series. Poor overlap in time periods of available data for health outcomes and exposure measure may lead to a substantial reduction in statistical power to detect an effect because the sample size available for the analysis will be smaller in a joint time-series. Typically, time-referenced health outcome data are recorded as daily, weekly, monthly, quarterly, or annual counts of health-related events. The temporal period of RSD depends on orbits of satellites; therefore, the measurements are collected in corresponded temporal scales, for example, every 10 or 16 days. Therefore, to properly link RSD with health outcome it is important to ensure *convertibility of time units* and perform a basic time unit alignment. Finally, the *spatial alignment* has to be carefully addressed; health outcome data need to be georeferenced to ensure proper selection of the target or catchments areas for abstracting RSD.[10]

Public Health Applications of Remote Sensing

Pavlovsky [11] was the first to explicitly state that diseases are found only where the environmental habitat requirements of the parasite, host, and vector are satisfied. As obvious as it may seem, this logical inference began to form what is known in the 21st century as spatial epidemiology. Efforts to illustrate this assertion continue today. To effectively use RS to monitor or predict infectious disease, the disease's habitat must be known. Conversely, a disease's habitat may be revealed through the analysis of remote sensing data given known patterns of outbreak. Some researchers have cited the inadequacy of current infectious disease surveillance and response systems and the corresponding benefits of improving these systems, such as advanced surveillance and modeling that can predict the temporal and spatial risks of epidemics using environmental data.[3, 12, 13, 14] For example, remotely sensed data can be converted into vegetation, land surface temperature (LST), atmospheric moisture (also referred to as cold cloud duration [CCD]), soil moisture, rainfall, and sea surface temperature (SST) indexes, which in turn can be used to track infectious diseases for public health purposes.[15]

MAJOR TYPES OF RS INDEXES

Variations in vegetation cover on the Earth's surface are indicative of different biological, meteorological, and human-induced conditions. Orthophotos of the Earth's surface can be incredibly revealing in illustrating what types of vegetation lie below. In 1971, for example, an early NASA flight yielded strong empirical evidence of a relationship between *Aedes sollicitans* (salt marsh mosquitoes) and water hyssop (wetland plant species) using color, color-infrared and multiband sensor, and film combinations.[13] In the 21st century, the normalized difference vegetation index (NDVI) is the most commonly used vegetation index in epidemiological studies because of its ability to be an indicator of moisture regime (NDVI is most commonly used to measure chlorophyll or "greenness" [16]) and its ability to be derived from satellite sensors that produce a regular and frequent time-series (see figure 13.2).[10, 17]

NDVI values are directly affected by both the time of year due to plant senescence as well as the types of vegetation in the study. If study areas that contain less than 20 percent ground cover are unable to yield accurate NDVI values, this could be a major limiting factor in using NDVI to study urban areas. Although debate exists over appropriate application of NDVI data, it remains not only the most commonly used vegetation index, but also the most widely used RS variable in epidemiological studies. This wide use could be attributed to the fact that vegetation often is referenced as representing the combined impact of rainfall, temperature, humidity, topography, soil, water availability, and human activities. Vegetation readings are independent of height aboveground, which makes it a desirable proxy because this can vary between the top surface of biomass and the enclosed climate.[18]

NDVI Background

○ Normalized Difference Vegetation Index:

- Low values (<0.1) correspond to barren areas of rock, sand, or snow
- Moderate values (0.2-0.3) represent shrub and grassland
- High values (0.6-0.8) are typical for tropical rainforests

NDVI Mean 1992-1996: TALA Research Group, Oxford University

Figure 13.2 NDVI Background.
Source: Hay et al., (2006) *Advances in Parasitology*, 62, 37–77.

Other tools include Spectral Vegetation Indexes (SVIs) and the Global Vegetation Moisture Index (GMVI), which also are used to provide information on vegetation water content at the canopy level. NDVI should not be used for this purpose because it should not be assumed that in all species plant chlorophyll content is related to water content.

An example of the use of these techniques is illustrated by the Bavia et al. study designed to identify the landscape epidemiology of American *Visceral Leishmaniasis* (VL) in Bahia, Brazil.[19] Using NDVI and climate data on rainfall and temperature as well, their GIS consisted of political maps of the study area, georeferenced maps of the 33 municipal study areas, ground-collected vegetation information, NDVI values for municipalities, and disease prevalence information. Using geospatial methods, statistical analysis yielded correlations that could be used to estimate the spatial distributions of VL.

Kitron and Kazmierczak [16] used similar techniques to map Lyme disease distribution in Wisconsin. Specifically, they collected county-level data on tick distribution, human population density, Lyme disease case distribution, and proportion of wooded areas to assess measurement techniques used in the explanation of tick distribution in Wisconsin. The researchers used NDVI data to measure "greenness" in the spring and fall to find associations between county-level NDVI values, tick distribution, human population density, number of cases by county of exposure and residence, and incidence rates. Significant correlations between NDVI values and human exposure and tick distribution were found in northern regions of the state. This correlation decreased in southern sections of the state, becoming negatively correlated in highly populated deforested areas.

These two studies represent typical applications of NDVI in attempting to use RS data for epidemiological purposes. Although other methods exist, correlating NDVI data to other variables involved in disease placement (typically disease vectors and hosts) and their habitat is quite common.

Land Surface Temperature and Diurnal Temperature Difference

Different land, soil, and geologic compositions emit radiance differently across thermal spectrums, which therefore indicates a range of temperatures that may be suitable for certain diseases and their vectors. A number of studies have successfully correlated either LST or temperature difference to environmental variables that could be used to measure disease distribution. Malone et al., for example, found that temperature difference maps could be used to determine water table levels. They concluded that surface water may be an environmental determinant of *S. mansoni* infection risk in the Nile Delta.[20]

Sea Surface Temperature

Although multiple studies exist that use SST for epidemiological applications, only a few use remotely sensed SST data. One study that has made a notable contribution is by Lobitz et al.[21] Because SST has been shown to be related to phytoplankton concentration and sea surface height (SSH), researchers investigated whether a temporal trend exists between remotely sensed image availability and timing of the disease being studied—cholera in this case. By superimposing cholera incidence plots on SST and SSH data maps, researchers found a consistent annual bimodal cycle trend with certain years of outbreaks occurring on a level of statistical significance. The real-world application of this finding is vital to the future of cholera monitoring techniques, especially in vulnerable areas such as Bangladesh (the location of the Lobitz et al. study). A temporal lag was found between the time when SST increased, SSH rose, and the cholera outbreak occurred; this remotely sensed data could be used to predict future outbreaks.

Strong and McClain [22] found that using remotely sensed data was a reliable source of SST data, which they verified by examining data from stationary as well as drifting buoys. Remotely sensed SST data has proven useful in monitoring the environmental phenomenon El Niño, which causes considerable economic damage to South American countries when the global trade winds relax in the central and western Pacific as a result of changes in the marine food chain.[1]

Rainfall Indexes

Hay and Lennon [23] established that rainfall was more effectively predicted by remotely sensed sources than interpolation methods. Others have used this as a rational basis for using CCD as a proxy for rainfall because the CCD pixels in a remotely sensed image represent the time that that particular location was covered by rain clouds.[15] Some researchers simply use CCD as another remotely sensed variable to find relationships, such as Thompson et al.'s study of meningitis in Africa.[24] Most studies use CCD as a proxy for rainfall and therefore as measure of suitable habitat for disease vectors.

The Use of Novel Analytical Approaches to Understand Seasonality of Waterborne Infection

Waterborne infections are caused by pathogens ingested with contaminated drinking or recreational water. Cholera, typhoid, and emerging infectious diseases caused by waterborne pathogens (*Cryptosporidium, Campylobacter, Giardia*, rotavirus, norovirus, *E. coli*, and potentially *Salmonella* and *Shigella*) are examples of waterborne diseases. These pathogens (protozoa, bacteria, viruses) of human and animal waste and feces naturally are present in water bodies; however, their concentration, pathogenicity, and the effect on human health might change dramatically because of natural and man-made changes in the environment. For example, cryptosporidiosis is a diarrheal illness caused by protozoan, which are spread though water and food contaminated with human or animal waste and feces. Although cryptosporidiosis is self-limiting in immunocompetent people, it can be life threatening to immunocompromised individuals, such as those with AIDS and the malnourished.

Considering the nature and etiology of waterborne diarrheal infections, it is likely that seasonal patterns of diseases, such as cryptosporidiosis can be predicted with RSD on a global scale. Cryptopsporidiosis typically manifests through a low endemic level and well-pronounced seasonal outbursts, indicating a strong effect of meteorological and environmental factors. Studies conducted in tropical climates, for example, have found an increase in cryptosporidiosis incidence during the rainy season.[25–27] In the temperate climate of Massachusetts, cryptosporidiosis peaks about six weeks after ambient temperature reached its annual maxima.[28] The seasonal patterns in cryptosporidiosis incidence can be affected substantially by seasonal variations in exposure level associated with water quality, access to clean water, as well as wildlife and agricultural activities.

Jagai et al. [10] conducted a meta-analysis to examine how an increase in cryptosporidiosis relates to precipitation and ambient temperature and to investigate the potential use of NDVI as a proxy for exposure to *Cryptosporidium parvum*. Included in the analysis were more than 60 locations worldwide, representing a wide diversity of climates, that reported monthly cryptosporidiosis incidence over one year or longer. The study showed that an increase in temperature and precipitation predicted an increase in cryptosporidiosis; the strength of relationship varied by climate subcategory. In moist tropical locations, for example, precipitation is a strong seasonal driver for cryptosporidiosis whereas in mid-latitude and temperate climates, temperature is the driver. Cryptosporidiosis infection rates increased after heavy rainfall because of an elevated presence of recreational and drinking water.

This example provides a quantitative link between the incidence of cryptosporidiosis and meteorological parameters on a global scale and illustrates a strong potential for NDVI as a suitable proxy for exposure to *Cryptosporidium parvum*, especially in the humid mid-latitude climate zones. Of course, extreme meteorological events, such as heavy rainfall, droughts, and heat waves, may substantially alter a seasonal pattern in disease incidence. In warm and wet locations, expected precipitation can serve as a reliable predictor for incidence of cryptosporidiosis with one month lead time. Weather forecasting on a local and global scale can be useful for disease forecasting, so public health measures for disease prevention can be better targeted and focused. Because the mean NDVI is strongly associated with temperature in specific geographic regions, it is very likely that RSD and indexes reflecting vegetation water content in particular can be very useful for predicting the incidence of waterborne infections on a large geographic scale and RSD can be applied to a variety of waterborne diseases and infections caused by thermosensitive pathogens.

CHALLENGES OF RSD APPLICATIONS

The major challenge in using RSD data in public health application is our ability to achieve proper temporal and spatial alignment. In the examples presented in this chapter, each study location had specific challenges in gathering data: large urban areas and coastal regions needed to be properly treated in the data extraction process, NDVI values obtained from different sources have different time and image resolution, and access to complete data can be a challenge as well. In using RSD, it is crucial to develop methodologies for uniform study area identification and relevant data abstraction. This is one of the many challenges facing emerging fields of RS analysis.

That being said, perhaps the greatest challenge facing the remote sensing community is the potential discontinuation of the *Landsat* series of satellites. For more than 30 years *Landsat* images have informed decisions on relationships between land use, water quality, agricultural production, vegetation health, and epidemiology. In the *Strategic Plan for the U.S. Integrated Earth Observation System*, the authors acknowledge the benefits of *Landsat* as well as the funding maladies, but they offer no pragmatic solution other than a vague need for global observation systems.[29][1] A functional EOS relies on complete data sets, including not only remotely sensed data, but also data on disease monitoring, population characteristics, food production, and natural disasters.

Although *Landsat* faces a set of funding issues that most likely will be remedied by a government contract with a commercial entity, some experts have encouraged international cooperation to account for data gaps.[30] The 1992 Land Remote Sensing Policy Act assessed the potential of four different avenues for continuing *Landsat* and national RS operations. Included were an assessment of private sector funding for RS systems, establishment of an international consortium for RS systems, a solely U.S.-funded and -managed RS system, and a cooperative effort between the U.S. government and commercial entities for future RS systems. The 1992 Act's goals became more important, however, when *Landsat 7* suffered a severe malfunction in 2003, thus disrupting data continuity until 2011 when the *Landsat Data Continuity Project Mission* is scheduled to launch.

FULL INTEGRATION IN PUBLIC HEALTH RESEARCH AND PRACTICE

Integration of remote sensing-related resources, including personnel, technology, and data, has yet to occur. For instance, though multiple strategies exist that examine RS data and disease location, the general public as well as organizations that could benefit from this research, have yet to be made aware of its existence and

---

1. According to this document, "the development of the Strategic Plan addresses the first goal of the Interagency Working Group on Earth Observations and serves as the initial step towards the development and implementation of the US Integrated Earth Observation System" (Interagency Working Group on Earth Observations 2005, 10).

successes.[31] In addition, new RS technologies have yet to be applied widely in many fields that could benefit, simply because of the difficulty of learning how to use the technology. Communication, interpretation, and cooperation are elements that must be improved for RS and GIS systems to be truly integrated across disciplines. Improved environmental monitoring is needed to realize not only geologic and natural system application, but also health-related data recording, such as cancer registries. Cromley [32] recommended that the distribution of GIS data meet the needs of the larger research community and the general public. Greater communication between epidemiologists and software programmers, as suggested by Graham et al. [33] certainly would help. Most important, not only is expert-oriented support for spatial analysis and RS techniques needed, but societywide changes must be made that pervade not only these respective fields, but also the institutions that influence them. The *Strategic Plan for the U.S. Integrated Earth Observation System* set forth a four-point plan for this type of integration:

1. Policy and Planning Integration: To maximize synergies brought about by unforeseen applications of earth observations research (research and operational oriented).
2. Issue and Problem-focused Integration: Align multiple societal benefit areas (e.g. climate disasters, agriculture) in order to pool resources as well as successfully communicate results across interest areas in common, consistent, and understandable terms.
3. Scientific Integration: Integrate information about Earth process modeling across scientific sub-disciplines, which involves comparison of data analysis processes as well as data that is collected through satellites and *in situ* measurements.
4. Technical Systems Integration: Coordinate observation system technology and data management systems, which result in research and operation applications.[29]

These recommendations address the major overarching issues standing in the way of a truly integrated EOS. Although the report from which these issues originated does a fairly adequate job of describing these points, no clear policy guidelines are provided. This omission, in combination with a lack of government funding in RS technologies, indicates an overall lack of priority on RS-related technologies, which takes the form of inadequate funding in both execution of and research into developing new technologies. Public health fields, including epidemiology are perhaps most severely affected by potential gaps in data availability, accessibility, and data quality because creation and utilization of risk-based knowledge requires careful validation between in situ and satellite measurements.

FUTURE DIRECTIONS FOR PUBLIC HEALTH APPLICATIONS OF RS

Currently, there are two primary purposes of applying RS in the field of public health. The first set of applications deals with disease-vector habitat identification. These applications involve identifying suitable habitat for disease vectors; these types of studies usually take place in stable environments in which conditions are static and/or are highly predictable and account for the majority of the studies reviewed in this paper. The second type of application involves natural phenomena and aberrations for which the conditions being studied are either for identification of vector habitats or direct environmental impacts of these events on human health (for example, effects of volcanic ash on human cardiovascular systems). The events

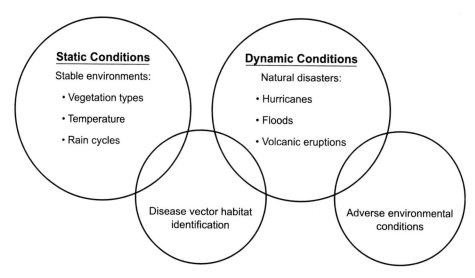

Figure 13.3 Interrelationship of RS and Public Health.

are typically dynamic and unpredictable. As illustrated in figure 13.3, both types of applications can involve disease-vector habitat identification.

In addition to studying the direct relationships along the transmission pathway and potential interaction between environment and human activities, RS would be valuable for other secondary purposes. For instance, RS can provide information on susceptibility or vulnerability of a geographic entity to certain infectious disease.[34] Examples include assessments of the risk of wild fire,[35] earthquake, flood, and landslide.[36] Another valuable use of RS would be locating and assessing physical destruction brought about by natural disasters, such as hurricanes,[37] floods,[38] landslides,[39] and forest fires,[40] so that emergency aids and long-term redevelopment efforts can be directed to the correct location.

CONCLUSION

Applications like Google Earth, Google Maps, Bing Maps, and NASA World-Wind have allowed people with little technical knowledge of GIS or RS to use these technologies for everyday purposes like finding the quickest route to the grocery store or discovering a bird's-eye view of cities halfway around the world. For RS to be securely financed, public awareness of this field and the corresponding environmental and public health applications must be enhanced. User-friendly graphic interfaces that allow people to measure and see the average temperature of the Earth's surface or watch clouds that moved over Europe a few hours ago from the perspective of a geostationary weather satellite could educate people about the benefits of this technology and therefore generate political support. The RS community must make greater efforts to show how and why this technology is important.

Public health applications of RS data are no longer new; spatial epidemiology is equally important as the strictly environmental applications for which RS was originally intended. This is not surprising, because environmental studies and epidemiology are inextricably linked. Each provides information on human health

Toward Interdisciplinary Understanding

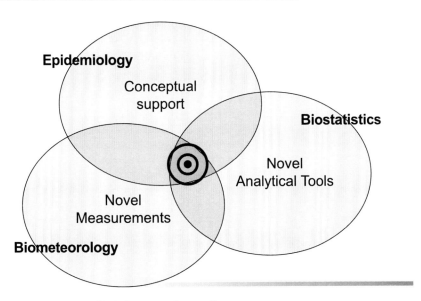

Figure 13.4 Toward Interdisciplinary Understanding.

conditions and the corresponding management of environmental resources. Climate and land use change and variability can be measured remotely and corresponding effects of alterations in natural and built environments can be predicted. Despite the uncertainty involved in forming sound habitat-parasite-host-vector connections, we expect that the promise offered by RS eventually will outweigh current fiscal concerns expressed, for example, by politicians. A globally shared and managed EOS would provide monitoring and predictive capabilities to help people around the world deal with disease, climate variability, and natural disasters. Although RS has many technical challenges, perhaps the most urgent problem is not one of scientific rigor or data availability, but rather one of social and political will to make an international effort toward the greater good.

Examples presented in this chapter indicate that future developments of novel approaches in public health are driven by a strong movement toward interdisciplinary research. New challenges to human, animal, and ecosystem health are demanding novel solutions: new diseases are emerging from new configurations of humans, domestic animals, and wildlife; new pressures on once-robust and resilient ecosystems are compromising their integrity; synthetic compounds and engineered organisms, new to the natural world, are spreading unpredictably around the globe. Globalization also is providing opportunities for infectious organisms to gain access to new hosts, changing in distribution and virulence. Many are calling for interdisciplinary health research to better understand the complex nature of the problems facing the world today (see figure 13.4). The most important requirements of interdisciplinary research include the desire, ability, and capacity to form, test, and utilize a common language that supports the development of novel hypotheses.

A necessary part of interdisciplinary research is asking questions in progressive steps during the process of insight, communication, persuasion, agreement, and decision, while considering the strengths and weaknesses of individual disciplines in terms of what each discipline can contribute to the solution. Novel sources of information and novel ways of knowledge synthesis should be embraced as a means to enhance the health of the population, globally or locally.

REFERENCES

1. Jensen JR. *Remote Sensing of the Environment: An Earth Resource Perspective.* Upper Saddle River, NJ: Prentice Hall, 2002.
2. American Society for Photogrammetry and Remote Sensing. http://www.asprs.org/society/about.html. Published 2007. Accessed April 9, 2007.
3. Myers MF, et al. Forecasting disease risk for increased epidemic preparedness in public health. In: Hay SI, Randolph SE, Rogers DJ, eds. *Remote Sensing and Geographical Information Systems in Epidemiology.* 2nd ed. London, UK: Elsevier Science Ltd; 2000:309–330.
4. Susser M, Susser E. Choosing a future for epidemiology Part 1: eras and paradigms. *Am J Public Health.* 2006;86(5):668–673.
5. Curran PJ, Atkinson PM, Foody GM, Milton EJ. Linking remote sensing, land cover and disease. In: Hay SI, Randolph SE, Rogers DJ, eds. *Remote Sensing and Geographical Information Systems in Epidemiology.* 2nd ed. London, UK: Elsevier Science Ltd; 2000: 37–80.
6. US Environmental Protection Agency. Global earth observation system of systems. http://epa.gov/geoss/. Published 2007. Accessed April 9, 2007.
7. Schmidt CW. Terra cognita: using earth observing systems to understand our world. *Environ Health Perspect.* 2005;113(2):A98–104.
8. Tran A, Gardon J, Weber S, Polidori L. Mapping disease incidence in suburban areas using remotely sensed data. *Am J Epidemiol.* 2002;156(7):662–668.
9. Ford TE, et al. Using satellite images of environmental changes to predict infectious disease outbreaks. *Emerg Infect Dis.* 2009;15(9):1341–1346.
10. Jagai JS, Castronovo DA, Monchak J, Naumova EN. Seasonality of cryptosporidiosis: a meta-analysis approach. *Environ Res.* 2008;109:465–478.
11. Pavlovskii EN. *Natural Nidality of Transmissible Diseases with Special Reference to the Landscape Epidemiology of Zooanthroponoses.* Urbana, IL: University Illinois Press; 1966.
12. Hay SI, Packer MJ, Rogers DJ. The impact of remote sensing on the study and control of invertebrate intermediate hosts and vectors for disease. *Intern J Remote Sensing.* 1997;18(14):2899–2930.
13. Hugh-Jones M. Applications of remote sensing to the identification of the habitats of parasites and disease vectors. *Parasitol Today.* 1989;5(8):244–251.
14. Epstein PR, Chikwenhere GP. Environmental factors in disease surveillance. *Lancet.* 1994;343:1440–1441.
15. Hay SI. An overview of remote sensing and geodesy for epidemiology and public health application. In: Hay SI, Randolph SE, Rogers DJ, eds. *Remote Sensing and Geographical Information Systems in Epidemiology.* 1st ed. London, UK: Elsevier Science Ltd; 2000:1–35.
16. Kitron U, Kazmierczak JJ. Spatial analysis of the distribution of Lyme disease in Wisconsin. *Am J Epidemiol.* 1997;145(6):558–566.

17. Tucker CJ, Gatlin JA, Schneider SR, Kuchinos MA. Monitoring vegetation in the Nile Delta with NOAA-6 and NOAA-7 AVHRR imagery. In: *Remote Sensing of Arid and Semi-Arid Lands*. 1982:973–987.
18. Daniel M, Kolar J, Zeman P. GIS tools for tick and tick-borne disease occurrence. *Parasitol.* 2004;129:S329–S352.
19. Bavia ME, et al. Remote sensing and geographic information systems and risk of American visceral leishmaniasis in Bahia, Brazil. *Parassitol.* 2005; 47(1):165–169.
20. Malone JB, et al. Geographic information systems and the distribution of Schistosoma mansoni in the Nile delta. *Parasitol Today.* 1997;13(3):112–119.
21. Lobitz B, et al. Climate and infectious disease: use of remote sensing for detection of vibrio cholerae by indirect measurement. *Proc Natl Acad Sci U S A.* 2000;97(4):1438–1443.
22. Strong AE, McClain EP. Improved ocean surface temperatures from space: comparisons with drifting buoys. *Bull Am Meteorol Soc.* 1984;65(2):138–142.
23. Hay SI, Lennon JJ. Deriving meteorological variables across Africa for the study and control of vector-borne disease: a comparison of remote sensing and spatial interpolation of climate. *Trop Med Intern Health.* 1999;4(1):58–71.
24. Thomson MC, et al. Potential of environmental models to predict meningitis epidemics in Africa. *Trop Med Intern Health.* 2006;11(6):781–788.
25. Adegbola RA, Demba E, De Veer G, Todd J. Cryptosporidium infection in Gambian children less than 5 years of age. *J Trop Med Hyg.* 1994;97:103–107.
26. Newman RD, et al. Longitudinal study of Cryptosporidium infection in children in northeastern Brazil. *J Infect Dis.* 1999;180:167–175.
27. Perch M, et al. Seven years' experience with Cryptosporidium parvum in Guinea-Bissau, West Africa. *Ann Trop Pediatr.* 2001;21(4):313–318.
28. Naumova EN, et al. Seasonality in six enterically transmitted diseases and ambient temperature. *Epidemiol Infect.* 2007;135(2):281–292.
29. Interagency Working Group on Earth Observations and the National Science and Technology Council Committee on Environmental and Natural Resources. *Strategic Plan for the US Integrated Earth Observation System*. Washington, DC: Executive Office of the President; 2005.
30. Williamson RA, Baker JC. Current US remote sensing policies: opportunities and challenges. *Space Policy.* 2004;20(2):109–116.
31. Kuhn K, et al. *Using Climate to Predict Infectious Disease Epidemics*. Geneva, Switzerland: World Health Organization; 2005.
32. Cromley EK. GIS and disease. *Annu Rev Public Health.* 2003;24:7–24.
33. Graham AJ, Atkinson PM, Danson FM. Spatial analysis for epidemiology. *Acta Trop.* 2004;91(3):219–225.
34. Chuvieco E, et al. Development of a framework for fire risk assessment using remote sensing and geographic information system technologies. *Ecolog Model.* 2009; In Press. doi:10.1016/j.ecolmodel.2008.11.017
35. Chandra S. Application of remote sensing and GIS technology in forest fire risk modeling and management of forest fires: a case study in the Garhwal Himalayan Region. *Geo-inf Disaster Manage.* 2005;1239–1254.
36. Tralli DM, et al. Satellite remote sensing of earthquake, volcano, flood, landslide and coastal inundation hazards. *ISPRS J Photogramm Remote Sensing.* 2005;59:185–198.
37. Frickel S, Campanella R, Vincent MB. Mapping knowledge investments in the aftermath of Hurricane Katrina: a new approach for assessing regulatory agency responses to environmental disaster. *Environ Sci Policy.* 2009;12(2):119–133.

38. Fritz HM, et al. Hurricane Katrina storm surge distribution and field observations on the Mississippi Barrier Islands. *Estuar Coast Shelf Sci.* 2007;74(1–2):12–20.
39. Metternicht G, Hurni L, Gogu R. Remote sensing of landslides: an analysis of the potential contribution to geo-spatial systems for hazard assessment in mountainous environments. *Remote Sensing of Environment.* 2005;98(2/3):284–303.
40. Dlamini WM. Characterization of the July 2007 Swaziland fire disaster using satellite remote sensing and GIS. *Appl Geogr.* 2009;29(3):299–307.

CHAPTER 14

Thinking Creatively about Public Health for the 21st Century
Barry H. Smith, MD, PhD

THE DEVELOPMENT OF PUBLIC HEALTH AS A FIELD

Writing in 1920, one of the statesmen and founders of the field of public health in the United States, C-E. A. Winslow, defined public health as "the science and art of preventing disease, prolonging life and promoting health through the organized community efforts . . . and the development of social machinery which will ensure to every individual in the community a standard of living adequate for the maintenance of health."[1] This definition has proven to be a useful one over the past 90 years, helping to bring together a modern and professional discipline, but public health activities have a history that dates back thousands of years with roots in every Eastern and Western civilization. Whenever and wherever people have come together, there have been issues of preventing disease and maintaining or improving the health of communities, both large and small.

From the beginnings of human civilization, peoples of different cultures and geographies have recognized that polluted water and improper waste disposal were associated with disease. The relation of human behavior to health was also recognized long ago, with the eating of certain foods, the use or abuse of alcohol and other substances, and sexual relations being associated with disease under particular circumstances and often at specific times. Various early religions and cultural traditions, including those of the Han Chinese (Huangdi, the Yellow Emperor, *Huangdi Neijing*); Indians (Buddhism and Hinduism, Sushruta *Samhita*); Hebrews (*Torah*); Greeks (*Corpus Hippocraticum*); Muslims; Christians; and Incas provided and enforced rules designed to protect the health of individuals in these and other areas and likely were among the first organized "public health" efforts. The Romans understood the importance of proper human waste disposal; the Chinese experimented with variolation around 1,000 BCE to try to stop a smallpox epidemic; and Medieval Europe developed burning techniques and quarantine rules to stop the spread of the Black Plague and other diseases based on the then-prevalent miasma theory.

Cholera in pandemic form ravaged Europe from 1829 to 1851, but it was an outbreak in London in 1854 that led Dr. John Snow to develop epidemiology, one of the cornerstones of public health in the 21st century. The long-overlooked observation of microorganisms by Leeuwenhoek (1680) was rightly given preeminence by Pasteur's elaboration of the germ theory of disease in the 1880s. These advances, along with other public health measures, including the building of latrines and sewers, the regular collection of garbage and its incineration or placement in landfills, the provision of clean water, and the removal of standing water to prevent mosquitoes from breeding for diseases such as dengue fever and yellow fever, brought tremendous benefits to the more developed world, with a marked decrease in infectious diseases and an increase in life span. This was much less true for the poorer (developing) areas of the world, a subject to which we will return shortly.

New York City's statistics provide dramatic evidence of just how significant this increase has been in developed, especially urban, areas. Figure 14.1, from the Bureau of Vital Statistics of the New York City Department of Health and Mental Hygiene's Summary of Vital Statistics 2007 shows the deaths per 1,000 population from 1800 through 2007 for the City of New York. Striking is the decrease in the death rate from 1890 to 1920. The conquest of infectious diseases such as yellow fever, cholera, typhoid, and diphtheria, among others, accounts for a large measure of this success.[2] A new decrease in death rates from 1990 through 2007 is apparent, if not quite as striking as the earlier decrease. During this period, life expectancy for a New Yorker born in 2000 is 77.6 (for females, 80.2 years and males, 74.5 years). This overall figure is 5.2 years longer that of a decade earlier and 0.6 years longer than the national average.[3]

During this second period of decline in the death rates, an infectious disease of a new and different sort, HIV/AIDS, was a leading cause of death, but in the 10 years from 1991 to 2001 New York City deaths associated with AIDS dropped by 66 percent. A 70 percent decline in homicide deaths and a 52 percent decrease in deaths of infants less than one year of age were the greatest contributing factors to the decline in the death rate. Notably, two of the three major reasons for the death rate decline, and even the third as well, relate directly to human behavioral patterns, clearly indicative of the changing nature of public health concerns.

A rather different, but nonetheless encouraging, story of increase in life expectancy is that of India—a vast country with a population approaching 1.2 billion. India's overall life expectancy is projected to increase from the current 64.7 years to 75.6 years by 2050, not very different from the current U.S. figure of 77.5 years.[4]. In the state of Kerala, it is already 73 years overall. The Indian infant mortality rate (IMR) has fallen from 59 per 1,000 live births in 2003 to 32 per 1,000 live births in 2008, a dramatic improvement, but still high compared with that of New York City in 2007 (5.4). Improved control of infectious diseases, better nutrition, and rising literacy among women have all been factors, among others, in these encouraging statistics.

The striking progress against many of the then-existing communicable diseases was a great triumph for public health. With that progress came new foci for public health, especially in the developed world, as well as countries such as India and Brazil where development has taken place rapidly. One clear new focus was on chronic diseases, such as heart disease, diabetes, hypertension, stroke, and cancer. Beyond this, however, was the much broader issue of health maintenance and promotion. For example, Dr. Sara Josephine Baker in New York City worked with poor

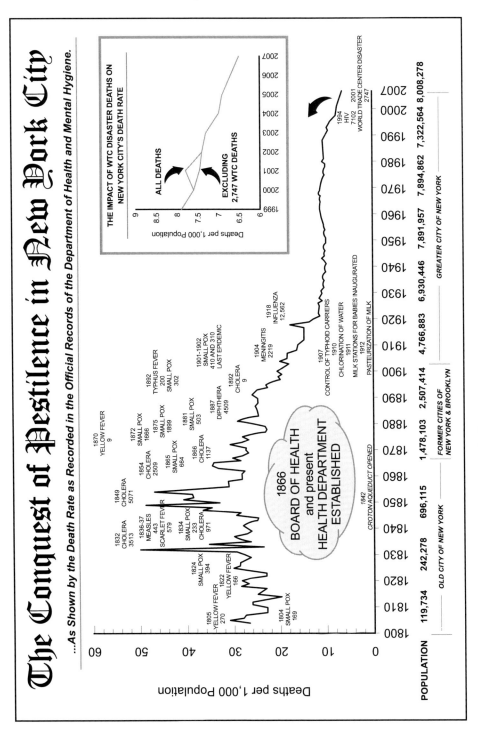

Figure 14.1 The Conquest of Pestilence in New York City.

people and their babies to keep them healthy and to reduce infant mortality rates, and the benefits of her pioneering work are continuing to make a contribution to infant health and mortality. Over the course of the 20th century the control of infectious diseases; vaccination programs for diseases such as polio, smallpox, typhoid, diphtheria; mumps, measles, and rubella; the use of seat belts in cars; regulations and education concerning the importance of use of bicycle helmets; occupational safety regulations and health screening; family planning; fluoridation of drinking water; antismoking campaigns; exercise and healthy diet promotion; and increased screening for chronic disease risks and signs led to a dramatic increase in life span and a much healthier population. With these successes, public health was beginning to mature into a field with a much broader range of interests and questions than it had in the past. The field increasingly focused on population health and its determinants rather than individual health, risk factors, and behavioral change.

Although the positive impact of public health in the 20th century was unquestionable, the end of the century and the beginning of the 21st century saw a host of new challenges. The developed world was not immune to these challenges, while the developing world struggled with many of the old infectious disease and malnutrition problems as well as new problems. Multi-drug-resistant tuberculosis, avian flu, H1N1 swine flu, and the increase of chronic diseases, such as heart disease and diabetes, and are found in both the developed and the developing world. The developing world has to contend with the rapidly rising prevalence of the chronic diseases and the new infectious disease challenges, while still fighting diseases such as polio, cholera, and malaria that have been eradicated in the developed world. All countries also continue to struggle with inequalities within their populations such that, for example, IMR was 10 per 1,000 live births in 2007 in Mississippi,[5] compared with 5.8 per 1,000 live births in New York City.[2] In India in 2006, the under-five mortality rate was 29.7 per 1,000 deaths for mothers with the highest level of education and 94.7 per 1,000 for those with the lowest. The highest and lowest wealth quintiles showed a similar, approximately threefold, difference.[6]

With the advent of the 21st century, it was now clear that health is a global issue with the health of one region dependent on the health of all the others. Because many emerging diseases as well as noncommunicable diseases do not honor nation-state boundaries, the interdependence of all humanity is evident. Consistent with and underscoring this, the new challenges have been increasingly global in nature, whether directly or indirectly. Considering the challenges of emerging infectious diseases such as HIV/AIDS, severe acute respiratory syndrome (SARS), and the H1N1 flu; epidemic type 2 diabetes; childhood and adult obesity; respiratory disease, including asthma secondary to air pollution; adolescent pregnancy; violence; terrorism and bioterrorism; medical care and drug costs; lack of access to health care; natural disasters; and global climate change, the message is clear. The continued growth of the world's population, with some of the least developed areas experiencing the greatest growth rates, makes the problems more difficult because of the enormous numbers of people needing help.

HEALTH: A BROADENING PERSPECTIVE AND NEW CHALLENGES

The public health field has changed along with the changes in global health challenges. A critical change, for example, has been the broadening definition of health. As the Constitution of the World Health Organization (WHO) puts it, "Health is a state of complete physical, mental and social well-being and not merely the absence of disease or infirmity."[7] One important way in which the field has changed its emphasis is to shift from a concern with individual behaviors such as the use of tobacco, to risk factors in populations. The subfield of population health took off in the 1980s and has concerned itself with issues of poverty, inequality, and education. These were spelled out in what have come to be known as the "social determinants of health." According to WHO, "the social determinants of health are the circumstances in which people are born, grow up, live, work and age, and the systems put in place to deal with illness. These circumstances are in turn shaped by a wider set of forces: economics, social policies, and politics."[8] Specific factors that are determinants of health include the following:

1. Income and social status
2. Social support networks
3. Education and literacy
4. Employment working conditions
5. Social environments
6. Physical environments
7. Life skills
8. Personal health practices and coping skills
9. Health childhood development
10. Biology and genetic endowment
11. Health services
12. Gender
13. Culture

A more strictly "social" list drawn up in Canada [9] includes the following:

1. Aboriginal status
2. Early life
3. Education
4. Employment and working conditions
5. Food security
6. Gender
7. Health care services
8. Housing
9. Income and its distribution
10. Social safety net
11. Social exclusion
12. Unemployment and employment security

From the nature of the above lists, it is easy to see how these determinants shape the health inequities that exist, whether within a given country or between countries. Recognizing this, the WHO established the Commission on Social Determinants of Health (CSDH) in 2005 to propose ways to reduce health inequities by working through the social determinants. Although medical care has changed vastly since 1900, McKinlay and McKinlay in 1987 [10] estimated that only 10 to 15 percent of the increase in longevity since that time is due to improved health care, at least in the developed nations. Similarly, it was not improvements in individual behavior that produced these results. It was much more the improvements in daily life that were responsible. Key elements, consistent with the above lists, included education, early childhood, food processing and availability, health and social services, employment security and conditions—all social determinants of health.

Changes in the public health field have not come easily or without cost. In its 1988 report, "The Future of Public Health," the U.S. Institute of Medicine (IOM) stated, "In recent years there has been a growing sense that public health as a profession, as a governmental activity, and as a commitment of society is neither clearly defined, adequately supported, nor fully understood . . . current capabilities for effective public health action are inadequate."[11] The report defined the core functions of public health as (1) assessment: surveillance of disease and injury (trends, causes, needs); (2) policy development: evidence-based decision making, strategic approaches, and comprehensive public health policies—with broad community involvement; and (3) assurance: implementing legislative mandates and fulfilling statutory responsibilities, providing essential services and access to those services, with subsidies for those needing them.

The challenges facing public health in the 21st century are thus enormous, including, as they do, the original challenges of fighting infectious diseases, but also much more than that, that is, striving to achieve for the people of the world that "complete state of physical, mental, and social well-being and not merely the absence of disease or infirmity" proposed by WHO as the "health" part of public health.[7] Paraphrasing the IOM report referenced above, public health's mission is to create the conditions within which people can be healthy. Alternatively, in Henry Taylor's words, "Public Health shapes the context within which people and communities can be safe and healthy."[12]

TWENTY-FIRST-CENTURY CHALLENGES

The challenges for the field of public health are enormous and difficult to specify and communicate to a public that is accustomed to issues and results that are both defined, and easy to grasp, at least in United States. The issues must be seen as affecting one's personal life and should not require sacrifice on the part of that person or group of people. A new treatment or drug for a particular disease is easy to understand. Prevention of a potential problem is much less obvious. Surveillance is not glamorous and the effects of new health policies may be years, if not decades, away. Unfortunately, the support of the public for the public health field is critical and currently that support is not as strong as it should be. This is a problem that must be addressed.

At the same time, as stated clearly and explicitly in a recent IOM report entitled, *The U.S. Commitment to Global Health: Recommendations for the Public and Private Sectors*, released in May 2009, the United States and the world have a unique and critical opportunity to improve the health of all people in all nations.[13] The knowledge, innovative technologies, and tools are there, but, as the report points out, a wide gap exists between what is possible and what actually is being done in disadvantaged communities and nations. The report calls for action in four areas: (1) generating and sharing knowledge regarding problems endemic to poor countries; (2) investing in people, institutions, and capacity building in resource-poor settings; (3) increasing U.S. financial investments in global health; and (4) ensuring that the United States is a respectful partner and leader in this effort. The report recognizes that the global health enterprise in the United States involves both many governmental and nongovernmental sectors and disciplines.

Not only must the U.S. government be committed, but also foundations, universities, nonprofit entities, and commercial units must be committed. Of course, much of what is called for is already happening, but the integration of the many disparate efforts to produce the greatest possible impact remains to be achieved. Implicit in the report is the need to educate and engage the public so that the U.S. commitment is deeply rooted and supported by a large segment of the population. The seriousness of the lack of U.S. public understanding of, and support for, public health is emphasized by the IOM report. Without the understanding and support of the public, the full potential of the U.S. global health effort will not be realized. The same is likely to be true in every country around the world.

Another significant issue is the divergence of public health from its molecular, biologically based cousin, mainstream medicine. If medicine has become more and more molecular in its approach and outlook, public health has become more "social" and more holistic in its approach and guiding principles. With its emphasis on populations, it is clearly operating on a broader and quite different stage than that of individual patients with health problems that require interventions from one or more medical specialists. Public health was originally a department within a medical college and still is in many schools in the 21st century. In the United States, approximately 50 independent schools of public health are members of the American Association of Schools of Public Health. Outside the United States, and, in countries such as India, Departments of Community Health have been established. This divergence of the conceptual base of public health from that of contemporary medicine is understandable, but its long-term effects are unlikely to be in the best interests of the health of the people or the further development of the fields of public health or medicine. Ultimately, the two disciplines are interdependent and complementary. Bringing them back together is an important task. Public health should take the initiative in this regard.

Relevant to this point is the fact that the Bill and Melinda Gates Foundation, for example, has made an enormous and broad-based commitment to global health.[14] The Foundation's Global Health program emphasizes the importance of scientific innovation and discovery. It lists three priority areas: (1) the discovery of new insights to fight serious diseases and other problems affecting developing countries; (2) development of effective and affordable vaccines, medicines, and other health tools; and (3) delivery of proven health solutions to those who need them most. Undergirding these efforts, of course, is a strong foundation of technology. The field of public health must shape the ways in which these new solutions are delivered to the people who need them and integrated meaningfully into their lives, providing education that is culturally sensitive and finding ways to deliver such solutions effectively over "the last mile." The people need to take ownership of the solutions, if this effectiveness is to be achieved.

A third obvious problem for public health is the sheer magnitude of the human population and its needs. United Nations projections [15] indicate that the world population will have grown from 6.1 billion in 2000 to 8.9 billion in 2050—a 47 percent increase or the addition of 57 million people a year on average. This means adding a population the current size of Italy every year between now and 2050. The report goes on to note that the 50-year increase will be more than twice the current population of China and more than double that of the combined current population of all the developed regions of the world. Adding to the challenges is the fact that most of the demographic increase will take place in the less developed regions of the world. These regions will increase their population by 58 percent, while the developed regions increase by only 2 percent, according to the projections.[15] Africa is projected to add 1 billion to its population, with the continent's share of the global population rising from 13 percent to 20 percent. In other words, 99 percent of the population increase will occur in regions where public health systems are the weakest or nonexistent. Beyond that, there is the dramatic shift of people from rural areas to densely packed urban centers with an associated shift in disease patterns and the opportunities for emerging diseases to spread rapidly.

The population problem has another important aspect: the changing global demographics, with aging being the most prominent of these. The growth rate of the over 65 population around the world is expected to be 2.4 percent, with a higher figure (3 percent) seen in developing regions. Put another way, the percentage growth of the population over 65 will increase by 84.8 percent from 2000 to 2050, but by 344 percent in developing regions over this same period. The percentage of the total population over 65 will have risen from 5.2 percent in 1950 to 15.9 percent by 2050.[15] The point is not to belabor the projected numbers, but rather to emphasize the size of the problem. The chronic illnesses of the aging population are far more complex and expensive to manage than communicable diseases. Noncommunicable diseases are projected to account for more than 75 percent of all deaths by 2030 [16] and an increasing percentage of these problems will be seen in the over 65 population. Given the struggles the world already has meeting the needs of the present population burden, it is clear that the difficulties are only going to grow. The resources needed to meet the challenges are unlikely to grow at the pace required to even keep up with the problems. It would appear that many aspects of the disease burden are far outpacing the systems designed to control them.

RESPONDING TO THE CHALLENGES

If the above analysis is correct, then what does the public health field need to do to meet the challenges facing it? How should public health be shaped for the 21st century, both for its own sake as a critical field for the world's well-being and for the sake of the local and global public it serves? The answers to these questions are multilevel and multifaceted. What I will attempt to do here is suggest some of the directions and actions public health as a field must consider if it is to fulfill its potential to contribute to the public good and further develop itself as the exciting, vital field it should be.

First of all, recognizing the numbers presented above, it is clear that there will never be enough public health professionals, medical personnel, and financial resources to meet the challenges. The sheer size and continuing growth of the global human population that is adding 57 million people to the world every year, seems to be a highly discouraging fact. How can we possibly cope with this? We need to radically change our thinking about such numbers. Yes, they represent a burden to the system, but they also bring us a solution. The people are not the problem. They are a major part of the solution. The "people" whom public health is designed to serve must be integrated into public health as actors and not simply passive recipients or objects of the field's efforts.

How is this integration to be achieved? First of all, traditional thinking about the "people" as passive recipients of the knowledge held by public health experts must be changed. I emphasize this point because biases from within the field are deep and subtle, and ultimately they are limiting and harmful. To emphasize what I mean, I recount a conversation I had in an Asian country with a Ministry of Health official. When asked for her evaluation of the status of public health programs in her country, she responded that the country had excellent health programs. After I replied that that was good to hear, the official replied, "But they don't work." Puzzled, I asked, "How can that be? The programs are excellent, but they don't work?" Her reply was quick. "That's easy. The people don't follow our instructions. They are lazy. They are stupid. You can't trust them." Perhaps that is an extreme example, but it is also an honest one, even if wrong—and it is a widespread view. We need to change our way of thinking.

Amartya Sen in his book, *Development as Freedom*, makes the point that poverty is not really the problem for poor people. The problem is the denial of opportunities for them to exercise their innate abilities to solve problems using local knowledge and skills bred of experience in a particular environment and set of challenges.[17] This does not mean that the "people" have all the knowledge, answers, or tools required to promote their own health or prevent disease, but it does mean that they can be the ones to turn the knowledge into action, belief, and behavioral change, and practice within their communities. The "people" are the ones to integrate the external ("expert") knowledge, priorities, beliefs, and practices into local priorities and realities.

How do we engage the "people" in public health? Crucial to achieving this is to get them to take ownership of the problems and make a commitment to be actively involved in the solution(s). They must see a given issue as a priority for them and not for someone else. One approach is the one utilized by the Dreyfus Health Foundation (DHF). It is Problem Solving for Better Health® (PSBH®).[18,19, 20] It involves asking people to think about the two or three most important (from their point of view) problems in their community or region. These should be problems that they believe they can do something about as individuals or in small groups. Implementing a solution must also fit within what is possible for them to do and it must be a solution that they have created. It may be informed by knowledge that has come from an external source, but it must ultimately belong to the individual who has made a commitment to solving the problem and has detailed the implementation of the solution.

PSBH® is a tool for the individual to use and consists of the scientific method adapted to community-level needs and issues. It includes a series of steps, which begin with (1) defining the problem precisely (nature, size, cause(s), contributing factors); (2) prioritizing it from the point of view of the community and asking if it can, in fact, be addressed by an individual (at least initially); (3) identifying and sorting out possible solutions, choosing one and asking a "good question";[1] (4) developing an action plan (including background and rationale, good question, hypothesis, methods, and evaluation); and (5) taking action.[19] As a tool, PSBH must be met with a strong commitment to making a positive change, a blend of the intellect and passion. It is about stimulating community organization to achieve change and working to achieve a strong sense that it is realistic to expect it.[18, 20]

PSBH® is a means for helping to organize a community.[21] It has its own intrinsic strength and applicability, and it is intended to sow the seeds of a transformative process in that community. It is about creating change in a self-sustaining, dynamic, and forward-looking approach to continuous community improvement, with a strong emphasis on improving individual and family quality of life. It is not magic and certainly not the only approach to community organization and short- and long-term transformation, but it is a time-tested and proven means of achieving such goals. It serves to bring out what 21st century public health must do if it is to bring the "public" into public health and make the much larger impact it is going to have to make if health is to improve from where it is now and not remain as it is or deteriorate. Put another way, the public must take active ownership of the solutions, thereby ensuring their implementation, effectiveness, and sustainability.

Effective organization of communities at the grassroots level is not simple. It requires hard work and a consistent forward-looking plan that has at its heart local individuals and teams within communities. They must incorporate the transformative process into the very fabric of their community. Public health shares many things in common with political processes and should incorporate lessons from this discipline into its own planning. Examples of effective "community" organization can be found in post-1949 China, with both good and less good results, as well as Barack Obama's recent presidential campaign in the United States and Dr. Thomas Frieden's campaigns for tobacco control and trans fat reductions in New York City. With regard to his presidential campaign, Barack Obama, with a skillful use of the Internet, built a 13-million-strong grassroots network. He indicated that this network would play a critical role as the "Organizing for America" group to achieve the goals for his agenda once in the White House. Public health as a field must build similar grassroots-led networks and find ways to help them become self-sustaining and autoreplicating. The Web site www.whatispublichealth.org and sticker campaign "This Is Public Health," put together by the Association of Schools of Public Health, is one example of what can be done to help build such networks. Just as studies of populations have become important parts of public health, the engagement of populations as active agents for health promotion and prevention is a vital piece that must be added for the 21st century.

Public health professionals also should recognize that they might be part of the problem. Although it is not particularly palatable and some of the terminology bears the stamp of the 1970s, Paulo Freire's *Pedagogy of the Oppressed* makes the point clearly.[22] Freire points out that the oppressed (the "poor") live an existential duality that means that they are at once themselves and at the same time living with an image of themselves that has been provided by their "oppressors." The internalized image

---

1. The "good question" is as follows: Will doing **What With Whom** (and **Where**) for **How Long** achieve the **Desired Objective** (quantifiable and measurable goal)?

drawn from the oppressors is one of ignorance, lack of capability, and good for nothingness. This leads to fatalistic and self-deprecatory attitudes among poor individuals about their situation. Freire quotes poor individuals who say:

The peasant begins to get courage to overcome his dependence when he realizes that he is dependent. Until then, he goes along with the boss and says, What can I do? I am only a peasant.[22, p. 61]

The peasant feels inferior to the boss because the boss seems to be the only one who knows things and is able to run things.[22, p. 63]

Freire also adds an admonishment to those who seek to help the oppressed:

Those who authentically commit themselves to the people must re-examine themselves constantly. The conversion [to a true humanist] is so radical as to not allow of ambiguous behavior. To affirm this commitment but to consider oneself the proprietor of revolutionary wisdom—which must then be given to (or imposed on) the people—is to retain the old ways. The man or woman who proclaims devotion to the cause of liberation yet is unable to enter into communion with the people, whom he or she continues to regard as totally ignorant, is grievously self-deceived. The convert who approaches the people but feels alarm at each step they take, each doubt they express, and each suggestion they offer, and attempts to impose his "status," remains nostalgic towards his origins.[22, pp. 60–61]

At all stages of liberation, the oppressed must see themselves as women and men engaged in the ontological and historical vocation of becoming more fully human ... action on the side of the oppressed ... must be action with the oppressed. Those who work for liberation must not take advantage of the emotional dependence of the oppressed. ... Using their dependence to create still greater dependence is an oppressor tactic.[22, pp. 65–66]

Unfortunately, often with the best of intentions, many of our public health professionals' efforts have been beset and greatly diminished by the sense that they are the "experts" bringing knowledge and enlightenment to those who have none of their own. Education in public health will have to teach its young would-be professionals that the new reality and techniques must be quite different than those of the past.

Problem-solving education of the kind I have described is essential for both public health professionals and individuals.. In such education, as Freire puts it, "people develop their power to perceive critically the way they exist in the world with which and in which they find themselves; they come to see the world not as a static reality, but as a reality in process, in transformation."[22, p. 83] For the public health professional, the conversion is a radical one in the direction of humility and listening. For the poor individual, such education is liberation. Both the professional and the oppressed are beings in the "process of becoming—as unfinished, uncompleted beings in and with a likewise unfinished reality."[22, p. 84] Mutual transformation in space and time is the common theme.

A second issue for public health as a field is its growing separation from mainstream curative or healing medicine. Although medicine has taken a decided turn toward the molecular, genomic, and highly specialized practice, public health has moved in the direction of dealing with populations and the associated societal factors that promote or inhibit the achievement of population health. The two disciplines must find new ways to work together. If this does not happen, the losses to the public benefit will be much larger than they need to be and both fields will suffer. This is not to say that the two disciplines must do the same work. Instead, they must use the information and concepts each generates from their respective analytical platforms to enhance and make the work of the other more effective. For example, genomic information about populations with respect to metabolism and susceptibility to disease can be combined with the delivery of more appropriate and better-targeted public health information in mass campaigns.

Dr. Victor Herbert, the nutritionist, told me a story of his work in East Africa with folic acid to reduce the prevalence of anemia. To his surprise, he found that while he did indeed reduce anemia with his folate program, he also increased the incidence of malaria, because it turned out, perhaps not surprisingly in retrospect, that folate-poor erythrocytes were less attractive targets for the malarial parasite. The molecular science should have informed the public health campaign to reduce anemia, and the public health results should have helped drive the molecular understanding of real-world malaria. That is but one small example of a principle that requires emphasis in 21st-century public health. HIV/AIDS, hepatitis, diabetes, and cancer incidence and prevalence patterns offer other examples of the value of bringing public health and contemporary evidence-based medical practice and research together.

Exactly how to bring these two disciplines closer together, especially where the public can benefit in significant ways, is an important question. The first reaction to this question is to say that it is already happening, but the evidence does not indicate that this is so. There are at least two approaches to this. In the United States, the first is the utilization of an existing body, such as the IOM, to promote such cross-talk and cross-fertilization. This might be coupled with a programmatic effort by the U.S. Association of Schools of Public Health to promote such interchange. The American Association of Public Health and American Medical Association might provide another locus for interaction. The National Institutes of Health (U.S. Department of Health and Human Services) support for such a program could help put it on a sound, formal footing. A similar effort in the European Union or at the WHO level also could be valuable. At whatever level it takes place, there must be a solid, even passionate, commitment to identifying the areas in which such interactions could make a difference and staying with them until there is a practical product. It will not be easy, but it is crucial.

Perhaps more practical and important for the long run is an increased emphasis on integrating public health issues and thinking into medical and nursing school education. From the other side, more of contemporary medicine's approaches to health could be injected into the education of public health students. Based on our experience with PSBH® around the world, it could be a tool to bring medical and nursing and public health students together and also introduce both to the thinking of the other discipline. There is no reason why every medical and nursing student, however specialized, cannot contribute to the public health aspects of the diseases treated, especially where prevention and health promotion are possible. Practical problem solving can show future doctors and nurses what they can do beyond the usual clinical therapeutics to promote family and public health. The public health professional's awareness of the generally more narrow clinical treatment concerns of medicine means that data collection and policy issues may be much better addressed over time. There is everything to gain and nothing to lose.

Yet another challenge for 21st century public health is an enhanced ability to deal with the complex interactions among various sectors of society that end up affecting health. Health is a product of society. A well-functioning community or society will produce better health than one that is marginally functional or fully dysfunctional. Public health and medicine, for understandable and practical reasons, have more often than not focused on particular habits, diseases, or conditions, such as tobacco, lipid profiles, or currently, the obesity epidemic and type 2 diabetes, and their accompanying knowledge, attitudes, beliefs, and practices in the public.

Twenty-first century public health should begin to look more rigorously at the multiple factors in a society that predict health outcomes. These factors include economics, housing, nutrition, sports and recreation, education, spirituality, family structure, gender relations, childcare, transportation, and whatever other factors make up a whole, integrated human life. A chart of the multiple influences that ultimately define the level of health and quality of life for one community in the Mississippi Delta,[2] a DHF PSBH® program site, makes these multiple influences and resources clear (see figure 14.2). The fact is that people cannot be described by a disease label, such as diabetes, HIV/AIDS, tuberculosis, peripheral vascular disease, or whatever else comes from the diagnoses medicine provides. The total human being is much

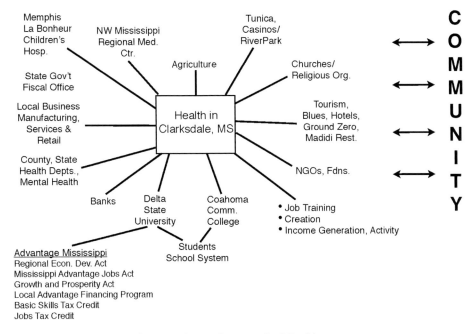

Figure 14.2 Multiple Influences that Define Level of Health.

---

2. The Mississippi Delta, which is the geographic region extending from just below Memphis, Tennessee, to Vicksburg, Mississippi, is one of the poorest regions in the United States, with Mississippi itself ranking 50th in both economic and health terms of all the U.S. states.[23] It is also a place of great people and great promise.

more than one or more medical diagnoses or behavioral habits and practices. A more effective public health discipline can bring the multiple factors contributing to people's total well-being, health, and quality of life together to predict outcomes both qualitatively and quantitatively. As a result, it can plan interventions that are more likely to be successful in promoting health and preventing disease. It also will draw on multiple resources, many of which do not seem to have a direct relationship to health, to achieve the health goals that have been set. Achieving this new analytical and predictive power will require new mathematical approaches, perhaps with elements taken from chaos theory [24] and the sophisticated navigational systems involving satellites and computers for data collection and analysis program that already have been developed.[25] Developing and embracing these techniques must be a priority for public health. Without such techniques, public health cannot fulfill its responsibilities for assessment, policy development, and assurance.

Public health of the 21st century will be an increasingly important part of the approach to ensuring better health and better quality of life for all people. The challenges are tremendous, but so are the opportunities. To achieve its full potential, public health must bring the "public" into the process. Schools of medicine, dentistry, nursing, and public health need to integrate their curricula better and reach out to schools in other sectors to find new and better ways to achieve better health. All concerned with the improvement of health on both a local and national and global scale need to work collectively rather than in isolation from one another. Health, after all, is a product of the multiple facets of society, and, as such, requires a multifaceted approach to health promotion, the prevention and treatment of disease, and, most important of all, the improvement of the quality of life for all people.

REFERENCES

1. Winslow C-EA. The untilled fields of public health. *Science.* 1920; 51(1306):23–33.
2. New York City Department of Health and Mental Hygiene. Summary of vital statistics 2007: the City of New York. http://www.nyc.gov/html/doh/html/vs/vs.shtml. Published 2008.
3. New York City Department of Health and Mental Hygiene. Summary of vital statistics 2007: the City of New York. http://www.nyc.gov/html/doh/html/vs/vs.shtml.
4. World Health Organization. World health statistics 2008. http://www.who.int/countries/ind/en.
5. Mississippi State Department of Health, Office of Health Data and Research. 2008 Mississippi infant mortality report. http://www.msdh.state.us.ms/msdhsite/_static/resources/3109.pdf. Published 2008.
6. World Health Organization. World health statistics 2008. http://apps.who.int/whosis/database/core/core__select__process.
7. World Health Organization. Constitution of the World Health Organization. 45th ed. http://www.who.int/governance/eb.constitution/en. Published 2006.
8. World Health Organization. Social determinants of health. http://www.who.int/social_determinants/en/. Published 2008.
9. Raphael D, ed. *Social Determinants of Health: Canadian Perspectives.* 2nd ed. Toronto, ON: Canadian Scholars' Press; 2008.
10. McKinlay J, McKinlay SM. Medical measures and the decline of mortality. In: Schwartz HD, ed. *Dominant Issues in Medical Sociology.* New York: Random House; 1987.

11. Institute of Medicine, Committee for the Study of the Future of Public Health, Division of Health Care Services. *The Future of Public Health.* Washington, DC: Institute of Medicine; 2002.

    Institute of Medicine. *The Future of Public Health in the 21st Century.* 2002. Washington, DC: Institute of Medicine; 2002.
12. Taylor H. Introduction to public health practice. http://jhsph.edu/courses/publichealthpractice101/PDF/Session4.pdf. Published 2008.
13. Institute of Medicine. *The US Commitment to Global Health: Recommendations for the Public and Private Sectors.* Washington, DC: Institute of Medicine; 2009.
14. Bill and Melinda Gates Foundation. http://www.gatesfoundation.org/globalhealth.
15. United Nations Department of Economic and Social Affairs, Population Division. World population to 2300. http://www.un.org/esa/populations/longrange2//WorldPop2300final.pdf. Published 2004.
16. World Health Organization. The world health report 2008. http://www.who.int/entity/whr/current//en/. Published 2008.
17. Sen A. *Development as Freedom.* New York: Anchor Books, Random House; 1999.
18. Smith BH, Barnett S, Collado D, et al. Optimizing the use of available resources: problem solving for better health. *World Health Forum.* 1994;15:9–15.
19. Dreyfus Health Foundation. Problem solving for better health handbook. http://www.dhfglobal.org. Published 2009.
20. Hoyt P. An international for approach to Problem Solving Better Health Nursing.™ (PSBHN). *Int Nurs Rev.* 2207;54:100–106.
21. Hoyt P, Fitzgerald J, Smith B, eds. *Global Experience with Problem Solving for Better Health®.* New York: Springer New York; 2009.
22. Freire P. *Pedagogy of the Oppressed.* 30th anniversary ed. New York: Continuum; 2000.
23. StateMaster.com. http:/www.statemaster.com/state/MS-mississippi/. Published 2009.
24. Resnicow K, Page SE. Embracing chaos and complexity: a quantum change for public health. *Am J Pub Health.* 2008;98(8):1382–1389.
25. Scotch M, Parmanto B, Gadd CS, Sharma RK. Exploring the role of GIS during community health assessment problem solving: experiences of public health professionals. *Int J Health Geogr.* 2006;5:39–49.

About the Editor

MADELON L. FINKEL, PhD, is professor of clinical public health and director of the Office of Global Health Education at the Weill Cornell Medical College in New York City. She also is course director in the Department of Public Health, coordinating the epidemiology/biostatistics, evidence-based medicine, and health care systems courses as well as the public health clerkship. Dr. Finkel's interests focus on women's health issues. Research projects include a cervical cancer screening program in rural India, reduction of preterm birth in Brazil, and better management of hypertension in Peru. She has served as consultant to numerous organizations, including law firms, pharmaceutical companies, and health care organizations. She serves on several boards of organizations whose missions are to promote public health. Her book *Understanding the Mammography Controversy: Science, Politics, and Breast Cancer Screening* was published by Praeger (2005). Praeger also published her book *Truth, Lies, and Public Health: How We Are Affected When Science and Politics Collide* (2007).

About the Contributors

Erika Abramson, MD, is a pediatrician and health services researcher at Weill Cornell Medical College in New York City. Her research focus is on the effect of health information technology on medication safety. Her work has examined such questions as whether the transition between different electronic prescribing systems affects medication safety.

Jessica S. Ancker, MPH, PhD, is an informatics researcher at Weill Cornell Medical College in New York City who studies the impact of health information technology on patients, providers, and public health. She is a member of the Health Information Technology Evaluation Consortium (HITEC), which is an academic collaborative designated by the state of New York to perform evaluation research on New York's state-funded health IT initiatives.

Holly G. Atkinson, MD, is assistant professor of medicine and co-director of the Advancing Idealism in Medicine (AIM) Program at Mt. Sinai School of Medicine and adjunct assistant professor of public health at Weill Medical College of Cornell University in New York City. She is chief medical officer for HealthiNation, and board member and past president of Physicians for Human Rights, an organization that shared in the 1997 Nobel Peace Prize. Dr. Atkinson focuses her work on the intersection of health and human rights, especially as it applies to advancing the well-being of women and girls.

Heejung Bang, PhD, is an associate professor, Division of Biostatistics and Epidemiology in the Department of Public Health at Weill Medical College of Cornell University, New York City.

Carla Boutin-Foster, MD, MS, is an associate professor of medicine and associate professor of public health at the Weill Cornell Medical College in New York City. She is the Nanette Laitman Clinical Scholar in Public Health and Community Health as well as the co-director of the Comprehensive Center of Excellence in Disparities Research and Community Engagement at Weill Cornell Medical College and associate director of the Center for Multicultural and Minority Health at Weill Cornell. Dr. Boutin-Foster's research focuses on the psychological and social determinants of health outcomes and on the social epidemiology of health disparities.

ABOUT THE CONTRIBUTORS

Ross C. Brownson, PhD, is professor of epidemiology at Washington University in St. Louis and co-director of the Centers for Disease Control and Prevention—funded Prevention Research Center in St. Louis whose focus is to develop innovative approaches to chronic disease prevention. He is associate editor of the *Annual Review of Public Health*.

Denise Castronovo, MS, is the president of Mapping Sustainability, LLC, a scientific and technical consulting firm for spatial data analysis and a research partner with Tufts Initiative for the Forecasting and Modeling of Infectious Diseases (InForMID). She is interested in the development of novel geospatial methodologies and visualization for infectious disease surveillance, including dynamic mapping and remote sensing analysis.

Ryan Cauley, MD, is a Weill Cornell Medical College graduate. He was elected to the Alpha Omega Alpha Medical Honor Society. He is a first year resident in general surgery at the Brigham and Women's Hospital of Harvard University in Boston, Massachusetts. His areas of research focus on the intersection of surgery and public health and international medicine.

Kenneth K. H. Chui, MS, MPH, PhD, investigates the seasonal patterns of hospitalizations related to various infectious gastrointestinal diseases, and their possible association with extreme weather events. His research interests include applications of time series analyses and geographic information system in nutrition and public health and development of data visualization for efficient communication.

Karen Scott Collins, MD, MPH, is vice president, quality and patient safety at the New York-Presbyterian Hospital in New York City.

Joseph T. Cooke, MD, is an associate professor of clinical medicine and public health at the Weill Cornell Medical Center and chairman of the General Faculty Council. Dr. Cooke is board certified in internal medicine, pulmonary disease, and critical care medicine, and a fellow of the American College of Chest Physicians. He serves as the chief quality and patient safety officer for the New York Presbyterian Hospital Weill Cornell Medical Center. He is the co-chairman of New York Presbyterian Hospital Quality and Patient Safety Committee.

Anthony Dawson, RN, is the vice president for operations, New York-Presbyterian/Milstein Hospital. He supports Milstein's senior vice president and chief operating officer in managing the capital budget and plays a leadership role in implementing the hospital's strategic vision for clinical services.

Inmaculada de Melo-Martín, PhD, MS, is associate professor of public health in the Division of Medical Ethics in the Department of Public Health at the Weill Cornell Medical College in New York City. She holds a doctorate in philosophy and a master's of science degree in molecular biology. Her research interests include bioethics and philosophy of science.

Jonathan E. Fielding, MD, MPH, MA, MBA, is director of the Los Angeles County Department of Public Health and the County Health Office. He is a professor in the Schools of Medicine and Public Health at UCLA, and chairs the U.S. Community Preventive Services Task Force and the Secretary's Advisory Committee on National Health Promotion and Disease Prevention Objectives for 2020.

Madelon L. Finkel, PhD, is professor of clinical public health and director of the Office of Global Health Education at the Weill Cornell Medical College in New York City. Her research focuses on women's health issues and global public health.?

Paul Glare, MD, is chief of pain and palliative care in the Department of Medicine at Memorial Sloan Kettering Cancer Center in New York City. He is trained in internal medicine, palliative medicine, and pain management.

Phillip L. Graham III, MD, MPH, is an assistant professor of pediatric infectious diseases at Columbia University School of Medicine, an adjunct assistant professor of pediatrics at Weill Cornell Medical College, and the pediatric hospital epidemiologist and quality and patient safety officer for women and children's health at New York-Presbyterian Hospital in New York City.

Robert A. Green, MD, MPH, is assistant professor of clinical medicine and associate director of emergency services at New York-Presbyterian/Columbia University Medical Center in New York City. He also is chief patient safety officer of the Columbia University faculty practice organization and the New York-Presbyterian Hospital/Columbia Campus.

Dan Hyman, MD, MMM, a board certified pediatrician, is chief quality officer at New York-Presbyterian Hospital in New York City. He has been the chief medical officer for the Hospital's Ambulatory Care Network and chief children's quality officer for the Morgan Stanley Children's Hospital and the Komansky Center for Children's Health.

Jyotsna S. Jagai, MS, MPH, PhD, is currently pursuing postdoctoral training at the U.S. Environmental Protection Agency. Her area of interest is characterizing the impacts of climate and environment on human health.

Steven Kaplan, MD, a Board Certified Emergency Physician, is currently the Chief Medical Director and Quality and Patient Safety Officer for Ambulatory Care at New York-Presbyterian Hospital in New York City.

Rainu Kaushal, MD, MPH, is an associate professor of public health and pediatrics at the Weill Cornell Medical College and is chief, Division of Quality and Medical Informatics in the Department of Public Health. She is also the director of Health Information Technology Evaluation Consortium (HITEC), an academic collaborative designated by the state of New York to evaluate its health IT initiatives in communities around the state. Her research focuses on evaluating the value and impact of health information technology, particularly interoperable health IT.

Lisa M. Kern, MD, MPH, is an assistant professor of public health in the Division of Quality and Medical Informatics at the Weill Cornell Medical College. She is a health services researcher and internist whose research focuses on measuring the value of health information technology in both clinical and economic terms.

Eliot J. Lazar, MD, MBA, is vice president and chief quality officer at the New York Presbyterian Hospital in New York City. He is a board certified cardiologist.

Rika Maeshiro, MD, MPH, is the director of Public Health and Prevention Projects at the Association of American Medical Colleges (AAMC) where her responsibilities include serving as the deputy principal investigator for AAMC's cooperative agreement with the Centers for Disease Control and Prevention and the principal investigator for the Regional Medicine-Public Health Education Center initiative, an effort to improve population health, public health, and prevention content in medical education.

Christopher M. Maylahn, MPH, is an epidemiologist in the Office of Public Health Practice of the New York State Department of Health. His focus of interest is chronic disease prevention.

Jesse C. McEntee, MA, is a doctoral candidate at Cardiff University's Center for Business Relationships, Accountability, Sustainability, and Society. He is president of McEntee Research and Consulting, a firm focused on the development of public health applications of remote sensing and geographic information system data.

Elena N. Naumova, PhD, is a professor in the Department of Public Health and Community Medicine, Tufts University School of Medicine and director of the Initiative for Forecasting and Modeling Infectious Diseases (InForMID). Her expertise is in the development of analytical tools for time series and longitudinal data analysis for disease surveillance, exposure assessment, and environmental epidemiology.

Vaishali Patel, PhD, MPH, is a health services researcher in the Department of Public Health at the Weill Cornell Medical College in New York City whose current research focuses on a number of different community-based interoperable health information technology initiatives being implemented across New York State, including personal health records, virtual health records, and electronic prescribing applications.

Brian K. Regan, PhD, is director of clinical affairs for the New York-Presbyterian Healthcare System and director of quality and patient safety, external alliances, for New York-Presbyterian Hospital located in New York City. Dr. Regan is a leader for system development and management, including the promulgation and implementation of member performance standards for clinical operations, the facilitation of linkages for patient safety improvements, and administrative and operational efficiencies.

Barry H. Smith, MD, PhD, is clinical professor of surgery and director of The Rogosin Institute at Weill Cornell Medical College in New York City. He also is the director of the Dreyfus Health Foundation, a Division of the Rogosin Institute, where he has worked to further the enhancement of basic and clinical science health care among health professionals in more than 30 countries around the world.

Roma Tickoo, MD, MPH, is an assistant attending in the Palliative Care Service in the Department of Internal Medicine at Memorial Sloan Kettering Cancer Center in New York City. She is trained in internal medicine, geriatric medicine, and pain management.

Paula Trushin is a medical editor and writer who has worked with researchers and physician educators on projects covering a wide range of therapeutic areas, including biostatistics, global health, and medical ethics.

William D. White, PhD, is director of the Sloan Program in Health Administration and professor in the Department of Policy Analysis and Management at Cornell University.

Index

abortion, 13, 197
absolute risk, 164
acadmic medicine, racial and ethnic diversity in. *See* racial and ethnic diversity in acadmic medicine
accreditation, 24, 53, 206, 222–223, 228
Accreditation Council for Graduate Medical Education (ACGME), 227
acute respiratory infection, 4
adolescent substance abuse, 12
Advance Country Strategy and Action Plans, 149
Advanced Cell Technology, 246
Advance Planning and Compassionate Care Act of 2009, 148
adverse event, 10, 21, 46, 47, 48, 50, 150, 171, 180
Advisory Committee on Heritable Disorders and Genetic Diseases in Newborns and Children, 126
affirmative action, 93–94, 101
ageist bias, 12
Agency for Healthcare Research and Quality (AHRQ), 52
AIDS, 6, 113, 118, 166, 195, 259, 268
Alternative Nuclear Transfer (ANT), 246
Alzheimer's disease, 12, 244
American Association of Medical Colleges (AAMC), 23, 94–95, 100, 102, 147, 218–220, 223, 226, 227
American Association of Schools of Public Health, 273, 276
American Board of Internal Medicine, 148
American Cancer Society, 16

American College of Physicians, 148
American Hospital Association (AHA), 147
American Medical Association (AMA), 220, 227; Educational Program in End of Life Care (EPEC), 148
American Public Health Association's (APHA), 219, 227
American Recovery and Reinvestment Act (ARRA), 2009, 80–81
American Society for Photogrammetry and Remote Sensing, 254
American Visceral Leishmaniasis (VL), 257
analytic validity, 125–126
Anderson, Odin, 13, 38, 44, 161
anthrax attacks, 74, 101
Approaching Death, 141, 148
arthritis, 15
Association for Prevention Teaching and Research, 219
Association of Teachers of Preventive Medicine. *See* Association for Prevention Teaching and Research
asthma, 8, 15, 62, 91, 100, 123, 270
Australian palliative care, 143, 144

Baker, Sara Josephine, 14, 205, 268
Bakke v. the University of California-Davis School of Medicine, 94
Bartlett, Roscoe G., 246
baseline risk. *See* control event rate
benefits costs, 67
Berry, Donald, 161
Beveridge, William, 31

Beveridge Report on British Social Security, 31
bias, 164, 179, 180, 183
Bill and Melinda Gates Foundation, 5, 273
Billroth, Theodor, 216
Biomedical informatics, 81
biomedical science, 24, 235, 250
biosurveillance, 74, 77
bioterrorism, 74, 270
Blair government, 31–32
blameless culture, 47
blinding, 171, 182
Boston Collaborative Drug Surveillance Program, 178
breast cancer, 16, 17, 98, 123, 127, 130, 178
Bubble boy disorder. *See* immune deficiency disorder
Bush, George W., 247, 248, 249
Business Roundtable, 53

Calvary Hospital in New York, 144
Campaign for Life Coalition, 246
Canada, healthcare systems in, 29–30, 35
cancer, 6, 16, 17, 18, 22, 62, 74, 98, 100, 114, 123, 127, 139, 141, 142, 143, 144, 145, 149, 150, 152, 161, 163, 172, 177, 180, 195, 198, 242, 245, 261, 268, 278
cancer deaths, global, 139
cancer genes, 245
"CanSupport" initiative, 144
cardiovascular disease, 14, 15, 123, 126
Case against Assisted Suicide: For the Right to End-of-Life Care, The, 141
case management, 56, 57, 64, 66, 67, 69
Castle-DeGette bill, 249
causation, 163, 169, 172, 173
Cedars-Sinai Medical Center, Angeles, 80
Center for Medicare and Medicaid Services (CMS), 44, 51–53, 61; diagnostic-related groups (DRGs), 52
Centers for Disease Control and Prevention (CDC), 3, 19, 75, 78, 127, 226, 227
Center to Advance Palliative Care (CAPC), 139, 147, 150, 154
central tendency. *See* Measures of location

Certification Commission for Health Information Technology (CCHIT), 80
cervical cancer, 18, 180
Chattanooga National Medical College, 92
child mental disorders, 19
Civil Rights Act of 1964, 93–94
Clark, D., 143
clean water technologies, 2
clinical decision support, 21, 74, 75–76, 79, 82
clinical guidelines, 56, 76, 201
clinical quality and patient safety, 43–53; error-reporting systems, 47–48; key players in, 51–53; medical error, 46–47; metrics, defining, 44–45; performance improvement, 47, methodologies, 48–51; quality indicators, 43–44
clinical research, 198; case-control, 168–169; cohort, 168; cross-sectional, 168; experimental, 168–169; observational studies, 168–160; randomized controlled trials (RCTs), 169, 171
clinical significance, 176, 177, 183
clinical utility, 125–126
clinical validity, 125–126
cloning, 245, 247, 248–250; and stem cell research, 239–241
Cochrane, A., 196, 198
Codman, E. A, 44
coinsurance, 21, 40, 55, 58, 60, 62
cold cloud duration (CCD), 256, 258
Commission on Osteopathic College Accreditation, 223
Commission on Social Determinants of Health (CSDH), 271
Committee on the Teaching of Preventive Medicine and Public Health, 218
Commonwealth Fund Minority Health Survey, 97
Community-Based Participatory Research, 100, 200
community-based participatory research, 200
Community Guide, 196, 199, 203
comparative effectiveness research (CER), 17, 165
Competencies for Applied Epidemiologists in Governmental Public Health Agencies, 206

computerized provider order entry (CPOE), 75, 78–80
Conference of Professors of Preventive Medicine. *See* Association for Prevention Teaching and Research
confidence interval, 176–177, 183
confounding, notion of, 163–164
Connecticut Hospice, 145
Conservative Party, 31
consumer cost-sharing, 55, 56, 66
Consumer Directed Health Plans (CDHPs), 21, 57–58, 68, 69; benefits design, 65–68; empowering shopping, 61–62; enrollments, 64; implementation of, 64–68; incentives to use preventive and chronic care services, 62; MCO, 66–67; motivating shopping, 58–61; operation example, 62–64; plan design, 58–64; risk exposure, 66; self-selection, 66–67
Contemporary Issues in Medicine—Medical Informatics and Population health: Report II of the Medical School Objectives Project, 220
continuing medical education (CME), 222
contraception, 13
control event rate, 164, 166, 167, 184
coronary heart disease (CHD), 163, 168, 171
Crick, Francis, 123
"Crossing the Quality Chasm," 48
cryptosporidiosis, 259
cultural assessment, 151–152
cultural competence training, 100
cultural diversity, 22, 92, 94, 97, 102

Dartmouth Atlas of Healthcare, 147
data dredging, 178
data interpretation tools, 174–177; clinical significance, 177–178; confidence intervals, 176–177; location vs. spread, 174–175; statistical significance, 175–176
deductibles, 21, 40, 55, 59, 62, 64, 68
DeGette, Diana, 249
dementia, 12
Deming, W. Edwards, 49
Department of Health and Human Services (DHHS), 247, 248
Department of Veterans Affairs medical centers, 94

Departments of Community Health, India, 272
depression, 19
depressive disorders, 19–20
DeSouza, Louis, 144
Development as Freedom, 275
diabetes, 4, 6, 14, 15, 57, 62, 74, 91, 98, 99, 100, 114, 123, 127, 244, 250, 268, 270, 278, 279
diarrhea, 4, 6, 259
Dickey-Wicker amendment, 247–249
disability, 3, 6, 10, 12, 25, 118, 132, 133, 141, 207
Disability-Adjusted Life Year (DALY), 6–7
disease surveillance systems, 75
disease-vector habitat identification, 261, 262
disinfection, 2
Doll, Richard, 3
Dolly, the sheep, 237
Donabedian, Avedis, 43–44
Draft World Cancer Declaration, 2008, 149
Dreyfus Health Foundation (DHF), 275, 279
Drug Abuse Resistance Education (D.A.R.E.) program, 203

Earth Observation System (EOS), 254, 260, 261, 263
economic evaluation, 199
Education for More Synergistic Practice of Medicine and Public Health (1999), 220
elder abuse, 12
electronic health information exchange, 78
electronic health records (EHRs), 75–78, 79, 80, 81, 82
electronic immunization registries, 75
electronic information systems, 73; billing systems, 73; electronic health records, 73
electronic medical records (EMRs), 45, 75–76
embryonic stem cell research, 24, 235, 239, 240, 247, 248, 249
Employment and Disability Institute, Cornell University, 10
Enders, John, 237

endpoint, 182; clinical endpoint, 173–174; surrogate endpoint, 173–174
environmental degradation, 4, 8
epidemiology and biostatistics in health care reporting, 161–185; absolute risk, 164; additional uses of data, 177–179; assessing risks and benefits, 179–180; association, causation, confounding, and bias, 163–164; causal inference from, 172–173; clinical significance, 177–178; confidence intervals, 176–177; data interpretation tools, 174–177; experimental study designs, 169–173; internal and external validity, 174; location vs. spread, 174–175; measurable endpoints, importance of, 173–174; multiple analyses, 177–178; number needed to treat (NNT), 166; observational study designs, 168–171; odds ratio, 166; relative risk, 164, 166; replication of, 171–172; results, issues affecting, 180–185; risk, 164–173; statistical significance, 175–176; systematic reviews and meta-analyses, 178–179; uncertainty in science, role of, 161–162; words, meaning of, 162–163
epigenetics, 241, 242
e-prescribing, 75–76, 79
Equal Protection Clause, Fourteenth Amendment, 94
error-reporting systems, 47–48
essential drugs concept, 8
Essential Medicines Model List, 8
ethnicity, 4, 22, 40, 41, 92, 93, 95, 97, 152, 175, 178
event rate. See absolute risk
evidence based decision making, 193
evidence-based medicine (EBM), 198
evidence-based public health (EBPH), 23, 191, 192, 197, 205, 206, 207; addressing disparities, 206; analytical tools, 199–200; audiences, 197; challenges, 200–204; characteristics, 193; community-based participatory research, 200; context for evidence, 195; economic evaluation, 199; engaging leadership, 205; evidence, defining, 193–194; and evidence-based medicine, similarities and differences between, 198; expanding the evidence base, 204; funding, 203; future opportunities, 204–206; Health impact assessment (HIA), 199–200; leadership, 202; organizational culture, 201; overcoming barriers to dissemination, 204; politics, 202–203; public expenditures, enhancing accountability, 206; public health surveillance, 198–199; public health workforce, strengthening, 205–206; systematic reviews, 199; tenets of, 192–198; triangulating evidence, 195; user groups, 197; workforce competencies, 203–204
evidence for public health practice, 193–194; types, 194–195
executive Order 10925, 93
executive Order 11246, 93
experimental event rate, 164, 167
exposure, definition of, 163

Failure Modes Effect Analysis (FMEA), 50–51; "Five Whys," 50
Family Research Council, 246
fee-for-service, 21, 33, 35
fibroblast, 241
First World Conference on Medical Education, 219
Flexner, Abraham, 92, 93, 216, 217
Food and Drug Administration (FDA), 9, 10, 173, 243
Food and Drug Amendment Act of 2007, 10
foodborne diseases, 9–10
food safety, 9
France, healthcare systems in, 32–34
Freire, Paulo, 276–277
Frieden, Thomas, 276
"Future of Public Health, The," 272

Gearhart, John, 237
gender-based violence (GBV), 13
gender inequality, 4
genetic counseling, 130
Genetic Information Nondiscrimination Act (GINA), 2008, 125, 132–133
genetic screening, 124–127, 129, 132, 133
genetic testing, 22, 123–127, 128, 129, 130, 131, 132, 133; analytic validity, 125–126; clinical utility, 125–126; clinical validity, 125–126;

confidentiality and privacy of genetic data, 132–133; diagnostic testing, 124; estimation of risks, 130; ethical issues, 125; health disparities, 127–128; informed consent, 128–132; newborn babies, 124; predictive testing, 124; preimplantation genetic diagnosis, 124; prenatal genetic diagnosis, 124; prices, 127; and screening, 124–125; usefulness of, 125–127

Geographic Information Systems (GIS), 253, 257, 261, 262

Germany, healthcare systems in, 34

germ theory of disease, 2, 268

Geron Corporation, 243

Global Access to Pain Relief Initiative, 149

Global Alliance for Vaccines and Immunization, 14

global burden of disease (GBD), 6, 8, 15

Global Earth Observation System of Systems (GEOSS), 254

global health, 5, 8, 18, 113, 270, 273

Global Health program, 273

global nongovernmental organizations (NGOs), 5, 144

global warming, 8

Gould, Stephen Jay, 163

graduate medical education (GME), 222, 227, 228; public health, 227

Grameen enterprises, 8

Gratz v. Bollinger, 94

Great Britain, healthcare systems in, 30–32

Grutter v. Bollinger, 94

Guide to Community Preventive Services, 192, 199

Gupta, Harmala, 144

H1N1 virus, 4, 9, 101, 270

Harvard Medical Practice Study, 46–47

Health and Human Services Appropriations Act, 247

Healthcare Efficiency and Affordability Law for New Yorkers (HEAL NY), 81

health care systems, 3, 15, 20, 39, 40, 145; Canada Health Act of 1984, 35; Canadian system, 29; Department of Health (DH; Great Britain), 32; Emergency Medical Service, Great Britain, 31; Federal Health Insurance Act of 1994, Switzerland, 36; France, 30, 32–34; French National Health Insurance (NHI) scheme, 33; Germany, 30, 34; Great Britain, 30–32; Hospital Insurance and Diagnostic Services Act of 1957 (the HIDS Act; Canada), 35; implications for United States, 36–37; l'*assurance complémentaire* (complementary insurance; France), 33; learning from other countries, 29–30; multipayer systems, 30; Organisation for Economic Co-operation and Development (OECD), 37–38, 39; Otto von Bismarck's Health Insurance Act of 1883, 31; Primary Care Trusts (PCTs; Great Britain), 31; Saskatchewan, 35; *Sécurité Sociale*, 32–33; Standard insurance, Germany, 34; Strategic Health Authorities (SHAs), 31; Switzerland, 35–36, *Tarif de convention* (tariff references), 33; U.S. Statistics, 38–41

health disparities, 10, 97, 98–100, 115, 127–128, 191, 206, 207, 221, 228

health impact assessment (HIA), 199–200

health information technology. *See* Health IT

Health Insurance Portability and Accountability Act (HIPAA), 133, 152

health IT, 21; areas of active research, 81–82; for clinical medicine, 75–76; development and adoption, barriers to, 79–80; financial, 79–80; health information exchange and interoperability, 77–79; human factors, 80; for patients and consumers, 76–77; policy development to promote, 80–81; for public health, 75; social, 80; stand-alone health IT systems, definitions and types, 75–77; technical, 80

Health Level Seven (HL7) messaging standard, 79, 80

health literacy, 77, 81, 98–99, 100

Health Maintenance Organization (HMO), 56, 67

health news reporting, 23; epidemiology and biostatistics in, 161–185

Health of the Public: Academic Challenge program, 225

Health Reimbursement Account (HRA), 59
Health Savings Account (HSA), 59–60
health status, and public health, 112–113
Healthy People Curriculum Task Force's Clinical Prevention and Population Health Curriculum Framework, 222
hepatitis viruses, 19
Herbert, Victor, 278
high-deductible catastrophic insurance plans, 58–59
Hill, A. Bradford, 3, 170, 172
HIV/AIDS, 4, 11, 18, 97, 114, 118, 176, 204, 268, 270, 278, 279
homonymic obstacle, 162
Hopwood v. the University of Texas, 94
hormone replacement therapy (HRT), 171
hospice care. *See* palliative care
Houston-Harris County Immunization Registry, 75
Howard University Medical School located in Washington, D.C, 92–93
Human Genome Project, in 1991, 123
human papillomavirus (HPV), 18
human rights, 6, 13, 22, 109–120; challenges, 118–120; and health, links between, 115–117; Millennium Development Goals (MDGs), 113–115; in public health arena, 117–118; public health and health status, 112–113; and right to health, 110–112
Hwang Woo Suk, 240
hypertension, 15, 123, 268
Hypothesis, 163

immigrant health care, 11
immune deficiency disorder, 237
Improving Palliative Care in Cancer, 150
indemnity insurance, 55
indemnity plans, 21, 55
induced pluripotent stem cells (iPS cells), 237, 238, 239, 241, 245
informed consent, 22, 109, 124, 125, 128–132, 133; competence, 128; disclosure, 128; ethical issues, 129; understanding, 128; voluntariness, 128
initiative du jour, 48
Institute of Medicine (IOM), 10, 20, 22, 46, 48, 51, 53, 95, 97, 141, 146, 148, 150, 191, 205, 221, 227, 228, 272, 273, 278; definition of quality, 43

Internal Revenue Service (IRS) ruling (2002), 59, 62
International Association for Hospice and Palliative Care, 149
International Atomic Energy Agency's Global Cancer Control Alliance, 149
International Children's Palliative Care Network, 149
international human rights law, 140
International Narcotics Control Board, 140, 149
International Observatory on End of Life Care (IOELC), 149
International Union against Cancer (UICC), 149
interoperability, 78–79
"In the Nation's Compelling Interest: Ensuring Diversity in the Health Care Workforce," 95
in vitro fertilization (IVF) clinic, 237, 239, 246, 250

Jaenisch, Rudolf, 246
Janicek, 192–193
Johns Hopkins School of Medicine, 217
Johns Hopkins School of Public Health and Hygiene, 217
Joint Commission, 50, 53
Jordan, E. O, 224
Josiah Macy Jr. Foundation, 220
Jungle, The, 2

Kaiser/Health Research Educational Trust- HERT -Employer Survey, 66–67
Kaiser Family Foundation, 41
Knoxville College Medical Department, 92
Koch, Robert, 2
Kramer, Barry, 161

Land Remote Sensing Policy Act, 1992, 260
Landsat 1, 254
Landsat 7, 260
Landsat Data Continuity Project Mission, 260
Landsat series, 260
land surface temperature (LST), 256, 258
LCME Annual Medical School Survey, 223–224
lean thinking, 49–50

Leapfrog Group, 53
Leonard Medical School (Shaw University), Raleigh, North Carolina, 92
lesbian, gay, bisexual, and transgender (LGBT) health care, 11–12
Liaison Committee on Medical Education (LCME), 100, 102, 222–223, 224
Lister, Joseph, 2
LOINC (Logical Observation Identifiers Names and Codes), 78
long-term care issues, 12
Louisiana Immunization Network for Kids Statewide, 75
lung cancer, 3, 17, 98, 163, 168, 170, 172, 176, 198; non-small-cell lung cancer, 17; smallcell lung cancer, 17

Mackenzie, James, 217
managed care, 21, 56–57, 64, 65, 66–67, 68, 69, 220, 226
Managed Care Organization (MCO), 56–57, 61, 65, 69; CDHP, 66–67
McCain, John, 248
McKeown, Thomas, 219
Medicaid, 29, 37, 39, 40, 44, 51, 52, 61, 74, 99, 150
"Medical Education in the United States and Canada: A Report to the Carnegie Foundation for the Advancement of Teaching," 92–93, 216
medical education in United States, 100–101, 215–229; barriers, 224–225; contemporary medical school curricula, 222–226; contemporary public health challenges, 219–222; graduate medical education, 227; historical background, 215–219; innovations of public health education, 225–226; preventive medicine, specialty of, 227–228
medical error; and patient safety, 46–47
Medical Expenditure Panel Survey (MEPS) 1998, 11
Medical Orders for Life Sustaining Therapy form, 152
Medical Research Institute, New Zealand, 15
Medical School's Mission and the Population's Health, The (1992), 220
Medical School Objectives Project Report, 220

Medical Sciences in the German Universities: A Study in the History of Civilizations, The, 216
Medicare, 29, 37, 39, 40, 44, 51, 52, 53, 59, 61, 141, 145, 146, 150, 228
Medicare Hospice Benefit, 141, 145–146
Medicare Modernization Act of 2003, Title XII, 59
Medicine and Public Health Initiative, 220
Meharry Medical College in Nashville, 92–93
Meissner, Alexander, 246
melanocytic nevus, 18
melanoma, 18
Memorial Sloan Kettering Cancer Center, New York City, 17, 243
Memorial Symptom Assessment Schedule, 151
Mendelian genetics, 129–130
mental disorders, 19
meta-analysis, 150, 178–179, 180, 259
Miasma theory of disease, 2
microbes, 4
"microcredit" initiatives, 8
Millennium Declaration, 6, 113
Millennium Development Goals (MDGs), 6, 8, 113, 114
Millennium Village Projects, 8
misalignment of incentives, 79
"Missing Persons: Minorities in the Professions," 97
Mississippi Delta, 279, 279n2
MMR (measles, mumps, and rubella) vaccine, 162
morphine, 140, 149, 150
mortality, 4, 6, 7, 14, 17, 18, 44, 113, 114, 116, 127, 173, 174, 180, 198, 200, 268, 270; decrease in, 2
multiple analyses, 177–178

National Bone Marrow Donation Center, 239
National Cancer Institute, 145
National Center for Health Statistics, 75
National Center on Palliative Care, 148
National Electronic Disease Surveillance System (NEDSS), 78
National Guideline Clearinghouse, 52
National Health Information Network (NHIN), 78, 81

National Health Service (NHS) hospitals, 31, 32, 142
National Health Service Act 1946, 31
National Hospice Organization Study, 145
National Institute for Clinical Excellence, 32, 143
National Mortality Followback Survey, 148
National Palliative Care, 144
National Quality Forum (NQF), 52, 150, 151
National Service Corps, 148
National Technology and Transfer Act of 1995, 52
Neighborhood Network in Palliative Care (NNPC), 144
New Mexico Blue Cross Blue Shield CDHP plan, 66
New Orleans University Medical College in Louisiana and Tennessee, 92
NIH Guidelines for Research Using Human Pluripotent Stem Cells, 247
number needed to treat (NNT), 166
Nuremberg Codes, 128

Obama, Barack, 7, 248, 249, 276
obesity, 4, 14–15, 16, 74, 113, 123, 207, 244, 270, 279
Occupational Safety and Health Act, 2, 9
odds ratio, 166, 169, 179, 183
Office of Federal Contract Compliance Programs, 93
Open Society Institute's Pain Policy Fellowship, 149
optical character recognition, 75
oral diseases, 12
oral health, 12
Organisation for Economic Co-operation and Development (OECD), 37–38, 39; premium statistical agency, 37
"Organizing for America" group, 276
osteoarthritis (OA), 15–16
out-of-network providers, 56
out-of-plan providers, 56
out-of-pocket payments, 21, 55, 60, 61, 62

Pain and Palliative Care Society (PPS), Calicut, Kerala, 144
Pain and Policy Studies Group, University of Wisconsin, 149
pain management, 98, 140, 142, 144, 149, 150
palliative care, 23, 139, 143, 151, 152, 153; effectiveness, 151; efficiency, 151; equitable care, 152–153; meaning, 141–142; need for, 140–141; origins, 142–144; patient-centered, 151–152; and public health, 146–150; quality effectiveness, 150–153; safety, 150–151; timely care, 152; in United States, 144–146
Parkinson's disease (PD), 243–244
Pasteur, Louis, 2, 268
patient safety, 20, 43, 45, 46, 48, 51, 52, 53, 80
Patient Safety Indicators, 52
Patient Safety Task Force, 52
PatientsLikeMe.com, 77
Peace at Last, 143
Pedagogy of the Oppressed, 276
Peer Review Organizations (PROs), 52
performance improvement in health care, 47; Failure Modes Effect Analysis (FMEA), 50–51; lean thinking, 49–50; Plan, Do, Study Act (PDSA) methodology, 50; risk resiliency, 51; Root Cause Analysis (RCA), 50, 51; Six Sigma, 48–49
Perkins, Tony, 246
personal belief, 97
personal health record (PHR), 76, 78–79, 80; freestanding PHR, 76; tethered PHR, 76
personalized stem cells, 239, 245
Pew Foundation, 225
pharmaceutical industry, 5
pharmaceutical safety, 10
physician-assisted suicide, 141
Plan, Do, Study Act (PDSA) methodology, 50
policy development, 80, 153, 272, 280
polypharmacy, risks of, 12
population-based prevention strategies, 12
population growth, 4, 7
poverty, 4, 5, 6, 8, 13, 113, 114, 206, 207, 271, 275
Powell, Lewis, 94
predictive testing, 124
Preferred Provider Organization (PPO), 56, 62, 64, 66, 67
Pre-implantation Genetic Diagnosis (PGD), 245, 246
preventable diseases, 3, 4

preventive medicine, 24, 218, 219, 222, 223, 224, 225; specialty, 227–228
preventive services, 56, 62, 63, 68, 221
private health insurance, 30, 35, 56, 57
Problem Solving for Better Health® (PSBH) ®, 275–276, 278–279
Proposition 209, 94
Proposition 99, 199, 203
prostate cancer, 16, 17, 98
prostate-specific antigen (PSA) test, 16
"proto-hospices," 142
publication bias, 173, 180–181
public health; definition of, 1, 267; development as field, 267–270; focus, 2; Graduate medical education, (GME), 227; terminology, 224; twenty-first-century challenges, 272–280
Public Health Information Network (PHIN), 78
public health surveillance, 198–199
publicly funded health care financing, 30
publicly managed fund, 30
Pure Food and Drug Act and the Meat Inspection Act, 1906, 2

quality and patient safety (Q&PS), 51
quality assurance, 20, 21, 43, 46, 53
quality health care system; components of, 48
quality indicators, 37, 44, 46, 51, 61
quality metrics, 20, 44–45; Risk or Severity Adjustment methodologies, 45; structural metrics, 44; volume, structure, outcome or process (VSOP), 44

Rabb, Harriet, 247
racial and ethnic diversity in academic medicine, 91; diversity in physician workforce, historical perspectives, 92–95; future challenges, 101–102; healthcare provision, 99–100; health disparities, 97–98; health literacy, 98–99; medical education, 100–101
racial group, 92
rainfall indexes, 258
randomized clinical trial, 3
Reach, Efficacy/Effectiveness, Adoption, Implementation, and Maintenance, 204
Real-time Outbreak and Disease Surveillance (RODS) system, 78
Reason's Swiss cheese model, 46

recall bias, 168
Red Cross, 239
regional health information organizations (RHIOs), 81
regional Medicine-Public Health Education Centers, 226–227
Reinhardt, Uwe, 34
relative risk, 164, 166
remotely sensed imagery, 254
remote sensing (RS) techniques, 24, 253–264; applications, 256; challenges, 260; data, principles of, 254–256; future directions, disease-vector habitat identification, 261; Global Vegetation Moisture Index (GMVI), 257; indexes, 256–260; integration in public health research and practice, 260–261; land surface temperature and diurnal temperature difference, 258; meaning, 254; natural phenomena and aberrations, 261; normalized difference vegetation index (NDVI), 256; public health applications of, 256; rainfall indexes, 258; sea surface temperature, 258; Spectral Vegetation Indexes (SVIs), 257; waterborne infections, novel analytical approaches for, 259–260
replication, 171–172, 200, 204
residency review committees (RRCs), 227
retrospective study designs, 168
right to health, 110–112
risk, 19, 45, 51, 163, 164, 166, 167, 169, 183; absolute risk, 164; absolute risk increase, 164; absolute risk reduction, 164; relative risk, 164, 166
risk management approach, 149
risk ratio. *See* relative risk
risk resiliency, 51
risks and benefits, 126, 129; assessment of, 179–180
Robert Wood Johnson Foundation, 225
Rockefeller Foundation, 215, 217, 225
Root Cause Analysis (RCA), 50, 51
Rose, Wickliffe, 217
Roslin Institute, Scotland, 237
Royal Society of Medicine Foundation, Inc., The, 220

Sacred Heart Hospice, 144
Saha, S, 99

sanitary workers, 217
Saunders, Cecily, 143, 145
school-based prevention programs, 12
scientific uncertainty, 162
screening, 16, 17, 18, 22, 56, 62, 123, 124, 125, 127, 128, 129, 131, 132, 134, 177, 195, 219, 246, 270
sea surface height (SSH), 258
sea surface temperature (SST), 256, 258
Semmelweis, Ignaz, 2
Sen, Amartya, 275
Sentinel System, 10
severe acute respiratory syndrome (SARS), 74, 270, 274
sexually transmitted diseases, 19, 75
Shanti Avedna, 144
Shea, John, 246
Shewhart, Walter, 50
"shopping" for care, 58
shopping for care, 56, 57
Sinclair, Upton, 2
Sisters of Charity, 143
Six Sigma, 43, 48–49, 53; change acceleration process (CAP), 49; Define, Measure, Analyze, Improve, Control (DMAIC), 48; work-out, 49
skin cancer, 18
smallpox, 2–3, 14, 267
Snow, John, 2, 268
social determinants of disease, 3, 115, 118
social medicine. *See* preventive medicine
social networking, 76–77
social solidarity, principle of, 30
Somerville, Margaret, 140
spatial epidemiology, 24, 254, 256, 262
stand-alone health IT systems, 75–77; for clinical medicine, 75–76; for patients and consumers, 76–77; for public health, 75
statistical significance, 175–176, 177, 178, 183, 258; "null hypothesis," 175; "p-value" (probability value), 175; Type I error, or false positive, 175–176, 178; Type II error, or false negative, 175–176
Statutory Health Insurance plan, 34
stem cell lines, 237, 238–239, 240, 241, 242, 245, 248, 249, 250
stem cells, 24, 235–250; challenges, 244–245; Clinton administration, 247–248; and cloning, 239–241; ethical issues, 245–246; history of, 237–238; induced pluripotent, 241–242; meaning, 236–237; "multipotent" cells, 236; Obama administration, 249; pluripotent stem cells, 236, 238, 241; politics of, 247–250; potential of, 242–244; stem cell lines, 238–239
Stevens, Leroy, 237
Strategic Plan for the U.S. Integrated Earth Observation System, 260–261
Study to Understand Prognoses and Preferences for Outcomes and Risks of Treatment (SUPPORT), 141
substance use and abuse, 12, 20
suicide, 19, 20, 141
Sullivan, Louis W., 97
Sullivan Alliance, 97
summary statistics, data, 174; interquartile range, 175; mean, 175; measures of location, 174; measures of spread, 174; median, 175; mode, 175; range, 175; standard deviation, 175
supportive care. *See* palliative care
Switzerland, healthcare systems in, 35–36
systematic review, 150, 178–179, 193, 195, 199, 202, 204, 206; qualitative, 179; quantitative, 179
systems, definition of, 47

Task Force on Workforce Development, 206
tax-advantaged savings accounts, 59, 66
Teaching of Preventive Medicine and Public Health, 225
terminal care, 141, 142, 145
theory, 196
Thompson, James, 237, 258
Tobacco Tax and Health Protection Act, 1988, 203
"To Err Is Human: Building a Safer Health System," 20, 46, 51; definition of error, 46
Training Physicians for Public Health Careers, 221, 228
transitions in care, 78
transparency, 181
triangulation, 195

U.S. Census, 147
U.S. Commitment to Global Health: Recommendations for the Public and Private Sectors, 272

U.S. Conference of Catholic Bishops, 246
U.S. Congressional Budget Office (CBO), 29
U.S. Department of Health and Human Services, 52, 80, 278
U.S. National Cancer Control Network, 142
U.S. Occupational Safety and Health Administration (OSHA), 2, 9
U.S. Preventive Services Task Force, 16
U.S. Statistics, 38–41
umbilical cord blood, 238
"Undergraduate Medical Education for the 21st Century: A Demonstration of Curriculum Innovations to Keep Pace with a Changing Health Care Environment" (UME-21), 226
underrepresented minority (URM), 95, 98, 100
Unequal Treatment: Confronting Racial and Ethnic Disparities, 22, 97
United Nations, 4, 5, 110, 111, 113, 114, 140, 273
United Nations Children's Fund, 5
United Nations Population Fund, 5
United States; healthcare implications for, 36–37; medical education. *See* medical education in United States
United States Medical Licensing Examination (USMLE) program, 224
Universal Declaration of Human Rights, 110, 140
University of West Tennessee College of Physicians and Surgeons in Memphis, 92

UN Millennium Summit, 6
Usual and Customary Rates (UCRs), 62n1
utilization review, 56, 149

validity, 133, 181, 184, 195, 196, 204; analytic validity, 125–126; clinical validity, 125–126; external validity, 174; internal validity, 174; threats, 174
variable, 163
Varmus, Harold, 181, 247
violence, 4, 13, 114, 115, 270
voluntary euthanasia, 141

waterborne diseases, 259, 260
waterborne infections, 260
Watson, James, 123
web-based informational tools, 65
Weill-Cornell Medical College, 235, 243
Welch, William, 217
Welch-Rose report, 217
Who Will Keep the Public Healthy?, 221
Winslow, Charles-Edward A., 1, 112, 267
Women's Health Initiative (WHI), 171
World Bank, 5
World Health Assembly, 149
World Health Organization (WHO), 3, 4, 5, 6, 14, 19, 33, 40, 110, 111, 114, 115, 116, 118, 139, 140, 141, 142, 271, 272, 278; analgesic "ladder" approach, 150; Essential Medicines Program, 8; Model Drugs list, 149
World Medical Association, 128